MODERN AMERICANNESS

Christopher Long

MODERN

AMERICANNESS

The New Graphic Design

in the United States

1890–1940

Christopher Long

KANT

© KANT 2024

© text: Christopher Long

ISBN: 978-80-7437-440-1

For Maria Enge

Contents

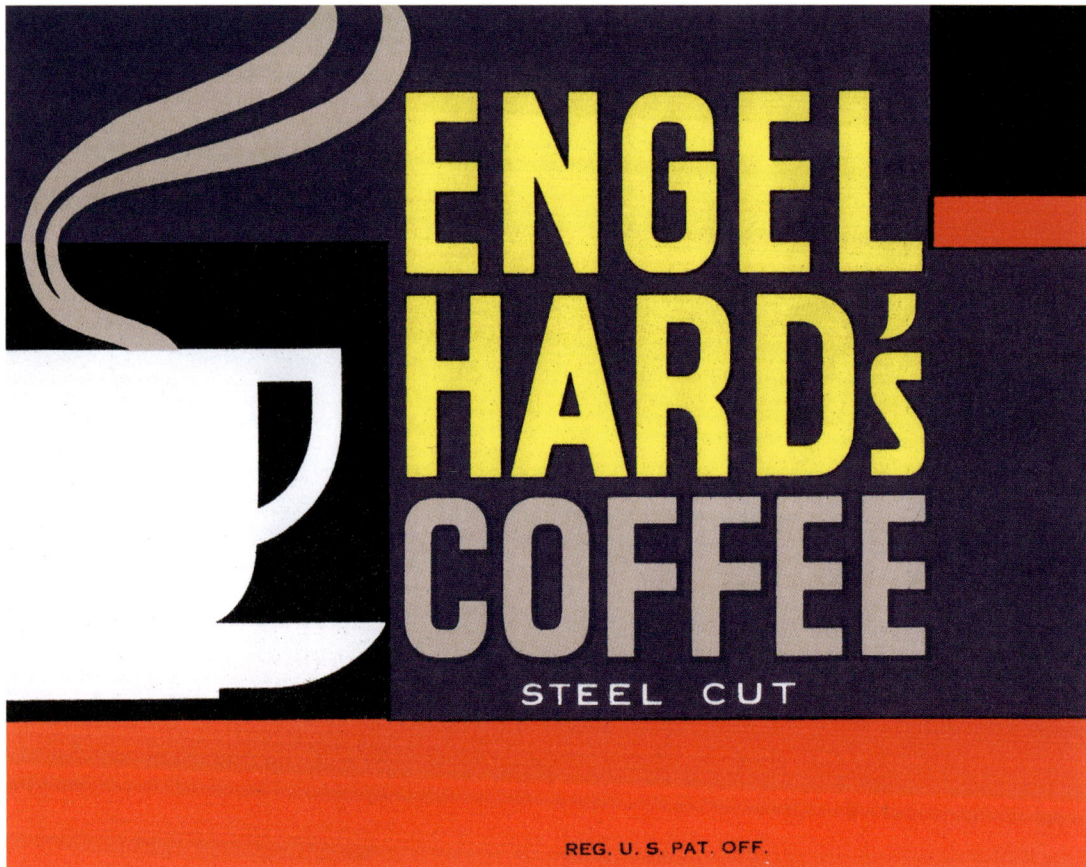

Engelhard's Coffee Steel Cut, ca. 1940. Label, printed for
A. Engelhard & Sons, Co., Louisville, KY. Offset print on paper,
13.8 × 17.6 cm (detail). Collection Christopher Long.

ACKNOWLEDGMENTS

Books are the sum of those who made them. Many hands, many minds were involved in making this one, and I want to acknowledge some of those who had a part in its creation. I was fortunate to collaborate once more with Kati Woock, who edited the text with her wonderfully judicious eye (and ear) for language. I am also grateful to Karel Kerlický, at Kant in Prague, who took this project on and shepherded it through the publication process, and to Jiří Příhoda, who made the gorgeous and fitting book design. It is no mean feat to come up with a concept for a book so replete with great design. I owe a large debt of thanks to Nicolas Allinder and Magdalena Kokešová, who skillfully edited many of the images. And, as always, I want to thank my brilliant wife, Gia Marie Houck, who made many, many improvements to the text.

I want to acknowledge those who aided me with acquiring images for the book, especially Clare Blaine at Wright, Chicago; Maddie and David Sadofski at TFTM, Los Angeles; Amber Blaise, in Los Angeles, and the staff at Poster House, New York.

I am especially grateful to Mark and Maura Resnick, who generously allowed me to reproduce some of the posters and other graphic works from their extraordinary collection. They have assembled a truly far-ranging and representative group of images—nothing less than the full story of American graphic design. I also received an education from Mark, who graciously shared with me many insights from his vast knowledge of American design and made many adroit and useful comments on the text.

The Martin S. Kermacy Centennial Professorship at the School of Architecture, University of Texas at Austin, helped to offset some of the productions costs. Martin was a lovely man, and I am pleased to honor his legacy with another book.

When I began writing this work, during the worldwide COVID-19 pandemic, someone very dear to me passed away. Maria Enge, the mother of my friend of more than fifty years, Martin Enge, died in Graz, Austria, in 2021. Because of the travel restrictions, I couldn't attend her funeral. It is a deep and yearning regret for me that I could only honor her from afar. She was a second mother to me, and she taught me more than I will ever be able to measure about goodness, perseverance, and love. I dedicate this book to her.

PREFACE

While on vacation in Seattle in the late summer of 2017, I wandered into Michael Maslan's Vintage Poster and Photographs shop downtown on University Street. At the time, I was considering writing about the Austrian émigré graphic designer Joseph Binder. I asked Mr. Maslan if he had any of Binder's posters. He had no Binder posters in stock, he told me (he had recently sold one), but he brought out several large folders labeled "Art Deco" and suggested that I look through them. "There might be something in these," he said helpfully. Just then, a young couple came in. It was clear they were not serious shoppers, but Mr. Maslan attended to them with the same courtesy he had accorded me. While he brought out various items for them to see, and they engaged in friendly patter, I went through the folders, inspecting each item carefully. I didn't find any works by Binder, but I was struck by the quality and variety of 1930s American graphic design. Many of the pieces—pamphlets, advertisements, luggage labels, and the like—were, I found, surprisingly accomplished, better than what I had associated with American design of those years. I selected and purchased about twenty items, mostly advertisements and brochures, though I wasn't sure what I'd do with them.

My first idea was to write something akin to Erwin Panofsky's "The Ideological Antecedents of the Rolls-Royce Radiator," an essay I have long admired. Panofsky had first given it as a talk in 1962; he published it the following year in the *Proceedings of the American Philosophical Society*.[1] Despite its ostensibly narrow focus, Panofsky's piece had a grander aim: to grasp the essence of "Englishness" in English design. The whole thing was tongue-in-cheek—Panofsky was unquestionably having fun with

Lester Beall, *Heat Cold*, 1937. Poster, printed for the Rural Electrification Administration, U.S. Department of Agriculture, Washington, D.C. Screenprint on paper, 101.6 × 76.2 cm. Courtesy Poster House, New York.

it—and it was not at all what one might have first expected from the title, "a disquisition on the taste and luxury of the English upper class," as Irving Lavin put it perfectly years later.[2] Panofsky argues that what defines Englishness is a tendency both toward emotionalism (in the form of an Arcadian romanticism) and the rationalism of a purified classicism. The Rolls-Royce radiator, he points out, is in essence a "temple" with a nymph surmounting it—a perfect expression of these two tendencies. I loved that, even it if was a little glib. I wondered if one could say something as pithy and true about American graphic design of the later 1920s and 1930s.

I have specialized in Central European modernism throughout my scholarly career, and I was not particularly well-versed in the literature of modern American graphic design. I did what one does when thinking about plunging into a new area for research: I read through the existing secondary literature. Very quickly, I discovered that there wasn't a great block of scholarship on the topic, at least not before the Second World War. Most of the books and articles I found were focused on the 1950s and beyond, the period in which American graphic design flourished. The coverage before that time was spotty. There were some able studies of the 1890s, the World War I propaganda posters, and the posters associated with the WPA Federal Art Project. And some individual designers, like Will H. Bradley and Lester Beall, had been extensively and well examined. But there were also yawning gaps. The period from about 1900 to 1917, the early post–World War I years, the mid- and later 1920s, and the early 1930s were barely treated—if at all—in any of the accounts I found. And I could find no work that surveyed the whole period in any depth.

I thought I might attempt to fill in these breaks, but I was frankly unsure how I should proceed. Once I had exhausted the existing secondary literature, I turned to reading as much primary source material as I could turn up. Working my way through art and design magazines, such as *The Poster* and *Advertising Arts*, was eye opening. I discovered that there was much more to the story than had been told in the later accounts. Many of the designers working in the United States in the half century before World War II were pursuing ideas and directions of which I—and most other later scholars, it seemed—had only the faintest inkling.

Still, reading through the existing literature only got me so far. I decided to try a different approach. I made a survey of what I could find in various museum holdings and auction catalogues. I found some very accomplished posters but not a comprehensive picture of American design in those years. After trying several other tactics, I discovered a remarkably simple and effective way of gleaning more of the story: I began searching, year by year, through the posters, magazine advertisements, and ephemera for sale on eBay.com. For each year, there were hundreds of items, sometimes thousands. Going through them methodically (and repeatedly, for items regularly sold and new ones appeared), I began to see patterns—distinct trends and developments. Gradually, a narrative began to form in my mind. I was able to pick up on who the significant designers were and how their work evolved over time. I started to see the sources of their ideas—at times coming out of European art and design—but also homegrown ideas about modern life and how it might be visually presented. It became clear what constituted the popular middle. But what I was interested in, what forms the core of the story I tell here, is that which was especially novel, that which was prescient and original. And the best of this work, it turned out, was truly innovative and adept.

As I began intensively researching this book, I chanced upon the story of Earnest Elmo Calkins. I knew nothing about him, but as I probed further, I learned just how important he had been to the rise of modern American advertising art. I saw the possibility of setting him and his ideas up as a sort of lens through which I might show the unfolding of the new graphic design. The more I investigated Calkins's life and career, the more central to the narrative he became.

My aim in this book is to follow the rising tide of modernism in America as it appeared and developed in the wider culture. That tale seemed to be most evident in the domain of advertising, and it is the trail I mostly followed. I did not attempt to cover every important figure or every specific moment. Some readers, I am sure, will fault me for disregarding this or that work, giving short shrift to a specific designer or leaving him or her out altogether. But my goal is not to be encyclopedic: I only want to convey the broad sweep of the new design.

Attentive readers will note that I write little about typography. It is not that I don't deem it important; rather, it is because I believe it is a topic deserving of a book of its own. Here and there, I do address the changes in typography, but only as they relate to the larger story I am seeking to tell.

The same is true of package design. As American companies became ever more sophisticated about how to market their products, they applied the lessons of the new graphic forms to their boxes, bottles, cans, and the like. This, too, remains a fruitful area for research, but it is a story too big to fit into this book.

I am aware that it would be possible to write the history of early modern American graphic design in other ways. I took the approach that I did because it seemed a fitting way to relate what happened. That doesn't mean, however, that other approaches might not be any less revealing or accurate.

Readers will note an essayistic tone in this work. I used this form deliberately in part so as not to lay a claim to thoroughness or completeness, but also to suggest the possibility of multiple interpretations. My hope is that this book will spur further work in the field, for there is still very much to be uncovered, analyzed, and understood.

Salida, Colorado, June 2024

1 Earnest Elmo Calkins

and the Birth
of Modern Advertising Art

Looking back on his long and august career, Earnest Elmo Calkins recalled the moment in 1896 when he discovered art's great power. Calkins, who hailed from the Midwest, was then living and working in New York City (fig. 1). A friend had shared with him an invitation to an art show at the Pratt Institute, in Brooklyn. He went, he later reported, without great expectations, or to be more precise, without "any expectations at all." He was wholly unprepared for what he would see. "It was a very ordinary exhibition, the work of students applying design to imaginary book covers, wallpaper, furniture, just such school work [sic] as one can witness in hundreds of places today," he recalled. The impact of the show on him, though, was like a deep spiritual awakening: "It stirred me as I have seldom been stirred since."[1]

Calkins, who would go on to become one of the founders of modern American advertising, was at the time a junior copywriter at a large advertising agency. But he was ambitious, and, even more, driven to learn. Spurred on by what he had seen that evening, he enrolled in night school at Pratt, determined to absorb all he could about art. He attended drawing classes three evenings a week. He was often exhausted after his day's labors in the office, he remembered, but "too uplifted to mind it."[2]

Calkins found his way to Hugo Froelich, one of the school's best teachers. Froelich was immediately taken with the young man and his palpable enthusiasm. He ignored Calkins's lack of preparation and, as it would soon become all too evident, his utter lack of talent. The winter term the young man spent in life drawing class did nothing to elevate his skills. "I never learned to draw," Calkins confessed. Still, he took away a skill that for his life's work would turn out to be far more valuable: the ability to judge the art, as he put it, "that I foresaw I would be buying in the future."[3]

During his brief and unfulfilled art apprenticeship, Calkins seized upon one other crucial lesson. It would make his career, alter the course of American advertising, and occupy a crucial place in forging modern American imagery. He realized that art could be placed at the center of print advertisements, that it could be utilized to convey powerful messages about products and entice buyers. And it could, he would come to believe, elevate the whole field of selling.

Through his efforts to find a place for art—or, as we would say today, graphic design—on the advertising page, the poster, or the billboard, Calkins remade his profession and help set American graphic design on its own independent course. If America's early graphic artists drew on trends and ideas coming from Europe, over time they would develop their own ideas and methods. For most of the next five decades, until the eve of World War II, American graphic art would mostly miss the cutting-edge abstraction and purification of the best of European design. Yet it would offer other important lessons about consumerism and popular taste. It would come to convey the essence of American life, its modernity, and its distinctiveness.

Calkins was not solely responsible for fostering the look of American graphic design in those years. But its development had everything to do with the turn he helped bring about.

Earnest Elmo Calkins was born in 1868, in Geneseo, Illinois. His father, William Clinton Calkins, was a Dickensian figure—charming, often broke, and given to harebrained schemes. He had arrived in the town, as his son later recalled, "a year or so before, driving a flea-bitten white horse attached to a green . . . wagon, laden with a dozen Eagle Rotary Washing Machines."[4] For the younger Calkins, who would become the consummate ad man, one of the nation's greatest hawkers of wares, his father's instinctive prowess at selling would offer an unavoidable lesson. The elder Calkins had bought the rights to sell the Eagle Rotary Washing Machines. His sales method was effective, if unorthodox. He would go from farm to farm and set up one of his machines. After making his pitch, he would ask the farmer's wife for the dirtiest shirt she had. He would put it into the washer, give the handle a few turns, and then send the woman "after something it would take a few minutes to fetch." While she was away, he would grab the shirt and rub it vigorously. "Thus," Calkins recounted, "he sold eleven machines."[5]

William Calkins stopped his itinerant campaign at nearby Galesburg after selling his last washing machine, the flea-bitten horse, and the wagon. Galesburg, as Calkins vividly portrays in his autobiography, *"And Hearing Not"—Annals of an Adman*, was then "a raw new town, which just thirty years before had been nothing but unbroken prairie."[6] Calkins's father continued eking out a living delivering groceries by day while studying law by night in the office of a friendly lawyer.[7] William Calkins never set foot in a law school, but he managed to pass the bar exam and was elected city attorney.

The small happiness that his newfound prosperity brought the family was shattered when Earnest was still a child. A bout of measles at age six left him partly deaf, though just how much his hearing was affected was not fully recognized until he was ten.

Calkins, nonetheless, made the most of his rural upbringing, augmenting his basic education with important life lessons he collected on his own. Despite his pious Baptist mother's insistence that he never pick up a work of fiction (or anything that was not an expressly religious book), he read voraciously—everything and anything he could lay his hands on.[8] In spite of his increasing deafness, he managed to make his way through high school, and, after graduation, his father found him a job at a local print shop as a "printer's devil"—an apprentice charged with mixing ink, fetching type, and cleaning the presses. The apprentices were often covered with black ink at day's end, hence the name.

Calkins's apprenticeship in design began with his days in the print shop. He learned about the "printer's art": how to compose on the page, which was the true origin of all graphic art. For the previous two hundred years in America, the design of the page, bill, or poster, such as they were, issued from printers. At times, their work could be startlingly beautiful, at others rudimentary, amateurish, or even ugly. Design on the page nonetheless was and remained the printer's domain.[9]

Six months later, his fingers still stained with printer's ink, Calkins entered local Knox College. He barely got by, unable to hear much of what was said or discussed in his classes. He proved proficient at writing, and in his final year he was elected as the editor-in-chief of the college newspaper, the improbably named *Coup d'État*. He failed his final course in geology, but the college's trustees, sympathetic to his plight, overruled the faculty and allowed him to graduate.

Calkins was desperate to leave Galesburg, desperate to find a new and better life. His impulse to experience the world beyond the little prairie town of his youth led him to New York City. He arrived with twenty-eight dollars in his pocket and his union printer's card.

In the summer of 1891, when Calkins stepped off the day boat from Albany, the American economy was already beginning to slow, and the depression that would take hold and last for the next six years was setting in. Jobs were few and becoming ever scarcer. Calkins made the rounds, trudging from one printing house to the next, hoping to land a position. All he found was a succession of temporary situations. He worked briefly for Harper & Brothers, then for Trow Press and *Scribner's Magazine*. For a few days, he was employed "under the gilt dome" of the *New York World*.[10] He managed to secure some writing jobs. Always, though, his deafness, which then had reached a point where he could hear "nothing not specifically directed" to him, was a nearly insurmountable liability.[11]

He eventually landed a longer-term position with a small trade magazine, *The Butcher's Gazette and Sausage Journal*. He quarreled constantly with his boss, an irascible, old-school Jewish butcher named Heinrich Klotz, who used every opportunity to inform Calkins of his shortcomings, real and imagined. Calkins, determined to find a better job, answered an advertisement he saw one day in the newspaper. It turned out that none other than Klotz had placed the ad, and, after receiving Calkins's letter of application, fired him on the spot.[12]

With no income and mounting debts, Calkins decided to return to Galesburg.

1 | Earnest Elmo Calkins, ca. 1890. Special Collections and Archives, Knox College Library, Galesburg, IL.

He went back to his old newspaper, the *Evening Mail*, "writing copy and setting type," which he now thought would be his life's work.[13] One of his side jobs was to prepare advertisements for the local merchants. "In this," he remembered, he was "inspired by the teaching and example of a tiny weekly periodical." That periodical was *Printers' Ink*. It was the first American publication "devoted to the new science, or art, of advertising."[14] Calkins became an inveterate reader of the little journal, devouring every word as soon as it arrived in the office.

One of the newspaper's advertising customers was the owner of the town's hardware store. Calkins learned through an announcement in *Printers' Ink* that Bissell, the national manufacturer of carpet sweepers, was offering a prize for the "best advertisement of a carpet sweeper as a Christmas present" in a local newspaper. Calkins persuaded the hardware store owner to let him submit an ad, which he designed and typeset himself. He won the contest, beating out 1,433 other entries.[15]

Calkins's winning design now looks woefully crude (fig. 2). As was then customary, it was made up almost entirely of text—intended to persuade the skeptical housewife about the merits of the device. The tedium of the copy is relieved only by two sets of repeated images, a woman in silhouette sweeping, set along the left side and top. Still, the printing is crisp and open, the copy is direct, with hardly a wasted word. It was not yet the sophisticated print ad that would make Calkins's career and reputation, but, as the judges must have appreciated, it has about it a breath of freshness.

Armed with the prize money and the recognition from winning a national competition, Calkins decided to leave Galesburg once more. One of his former school classmates told him of a job in Peoria, the nearest larger town, at the local department store. Calkins stayed just long enough to assemble a portfolio of his own advertisements (fig. 3). He sent them off to Charles Austin Bates, who ran one of the leading advertising agencies in New York and, not coincidentally, had been one of the judges for the Bissell prize. Bates responded with an offer of a job.[16]

Calkins was hired on as a writer, to produce texts for advertisements. Bates's firm, the Charles Austin Bates Agency, was one of the first set up expressly to provide original advertising copy and layout for companies and manufacturers. Prior to this time, advertising agencies had functioned mostly as brokers, buying and selling space in newspapers and magazines for their clients. Bates, along with a handful of other agencies, including N. W. Ayer & Son of Philadelphia, Lord & Thomas of Chicago, and J. Walter Thompson of New York, had already taken the initial steps toward forming what would become full-service advertising agencies, developing and executing marketing campaigns.[17] Bates, though, went a step further, creating the Charles Austin Bates Syndicate, to supply ready-made ads to its nearly 4,000 subscribers.[18]

At first, Calkins spent his days churning out prose (and occasionally verse) intended to induce would-be buyers. That soon changed. Bates, who grew increasingly fond of Calkins, made sure that his young charge saw every aspect of the advertising business. Calkins took in each lesson, learning to write crisp, pithy prose, while also seeing how sophisticated advertising campaigns could be conceived and implemented.

2 | Earnest Elmo Calkins, *A Sweeping Statement*, 1895. Newspaper advertisement, originally printed in the *Galesburg Evening Mail*, December 9, 1895, 8, reprinted in Ernest Elmo Calkins, *"And Hearing Not"—Annals of an Adman* (New York: Charles Scribner's Sons, 1946), 149.

It was at this time that Calkins had his artistic epiphany. After viewing the student exhibition at the Pratt School of Design and attending its night art school, he began to envision (despite his dismal performance) what art might do for print advertising, a medium that had been, to this point, largely about words rather than images. "Here," he wrote, "was what advertising needed and lacked, form, visualization, the attractiveness of color and design to strengthen its appeal to the eye!"[19]

The idea was seemingly simple enough. In 1896, however, the path forward was far from clear. Advertising agencies at that time were not set up to produce quality art. The commercial art profession existed, but it was held in low esteem, and most of the artwork the commercial artists produced was mediocre at best. Many of those who worked in the field were talentless hacks; highly trained artists were reluctant to work for advertisers or print media for fear that it would sully their reputations.[20]

Calkins had no illusions about the enormity of the task he faced: "There were two men attached to our organization, typical commercial artists, who drew pictures when required, dull, humdrum, spiritless affairs, hopelessly remote from the joyous, light-hearted sketches turned out by the students at Pratt. Their work was stodgy and labored. I could not convey to such men what I saw so clearly."[21]

With seemingly no other alternatives, Calkins began working after hours, making his own crude layouts. Bates, watching him founder, because Calkins truly had no talent for art, surprised him one day, telling his young protégé that he had "just hired a man who will do the sort of things you like."[22]

The artist was George Ethridge. Ethridge had trained in Germany and France.[23] While in Paris, he had assembled a large collection of French art prints, posters, and designs, which he called "his art education." Calkins found the pictures "useful"— not only because he, too, saw them as instructive, but also because they were not copyrighted in the U.S. and thus could be taken over directly and pieced into advertisements.[24]

Ethridge soon assembled an art department, the first, as Calkins remembered, "attached to an advertising agency, a remarkable advance for the time."[25] A few years later, Ethridge would play an even more important role in promoting quality advertising art. Beginning in 1902, he published a regular monthly column in *Printers' Ink*, with before and after images showing how commercial art might be improved.

The composition of the design staff, however, still did not reflect what Calkins's dream art department would look like. There were no fine artists, only "newspaper artists, cartoonists, and others who had already learned to work in harness."[26] It would take some time before he had the men he needed.

Calkins, ever the idealist, clashed often with Ethridge and Bates, who took a more realistic approach to the problem of how art might be employed in their various advertising campaigns. Yet, despite their differences, over the next nine years, with energy and diligence, the three men would work out the rudiments of modern advertising with fully developed imagery.

It was not only the challenge of incorporating illustrations into advertising copy that faced Calkins and his colleagues. The field of advertising was then undergoing

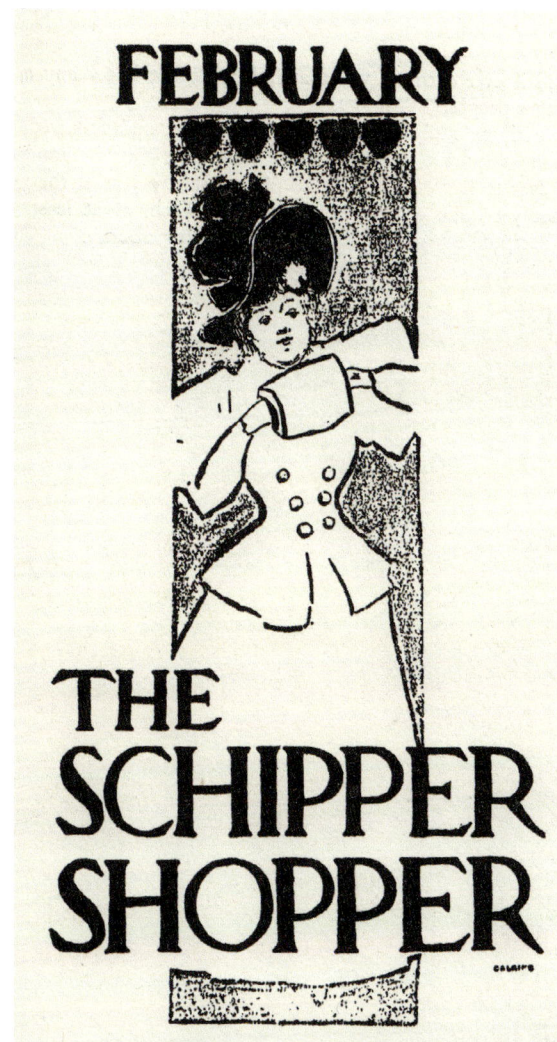

3 | Earnest Elmo Calkins, *The Schipper Shopper: February*, 1893. Newspaper advertisement, reprinted in Ernest Elmo Calkins, *"And Hearing Not"—Annals of an Adman* (New York: Charles Scribner's Sons, 1946), 156.

a wholesale alteration. A revolution in printing technologies was then taking place, and it would change completely and forever the landscape of publishing.

For some three hundred years after Johannes Gutenberg had invented the moveable-type printing press, there had been only small changes to the printing process. The early block presses consisted of a heavy wooden frame with a simple worm screw, turned by a lever that lowered and raised a horizontal plate, or platen. Ink was rubbed into the letters (which were arranged in a tray) with a leather ball attached to a wooden stick. A piece of paper was placed on the type and a thick cloth on top of the paper. The printer turned the screw until the platen was pressed down on the paper, at which point the platen was raised by turning the screw in the other direction.[27] For centuries after Gutenberg's death, in 1468, very little of this changed.

The first significant improvement came in the early nineteenth century. In 1813, George E. Clymer, a printer in Philadelphia, built an iron press in which the motion of the platen was brought about by a lever rather than a screw. The simple action allowed for an entire page to be printed in a single pull. A little more than a decade later, another American printer, Samuel Rust, working in New York, designed his press so that the bed below would slide in and out under the platen when he turned a crank; springs on either side lifted the platen, allowing the paper to be removed and another sheet to be inserted.[28]

Clymer's and Rust's inventions greatly speeded the printing process, but two other technological breakthroughs would change everything, effectively turning printing from an artisanal endeavor into an industrial one. The first was the invention of what became known as the rotary press. Rather than employing flat printing plates, a rotary press relies on cylindrical ones, which turn as the paper is fed through. The spinning plates allow for continuous printing, at very high speeds. The initial patent for the idea was filed in 1790 by an Englishman, William Nicholson, who based his device on earlier French prototypes. Others, in France and England, experimented with related concepts. But the first complete rotary printing press was not perfected until 1846, when an American named Richard March Hoe was able to work out the fine details. Hoe patented his machine the next year, and by 1853, the London *Times* was being printed on a rotary press. Hoe was also responsible for creating his "web perfecting press" in 1871, which used a continuous roll of paper. Such continuous-feed rotary presses became standard for many forms of printing, revolutionizing, especially, newspaper publishing.

The other crucial shift, which happened almost simultaneously, was the invention of the linotype machine. Up to that time, type had to be handset, which meant that a printer (or his assistants) would have to select each letter individually, then combine them into words, sentences, and so forth. Even a highly skilled typesetter could only assemble a few pages per hour. The linotype system, or what is also known as hot metal typesetting, uses a keyboard, like a typewriter, but with ninety separate keys; the operator or typesetter composes matrices, or molds, and each letter or symbol is formed when the corresponding keys are pressed. The assembled line is then cast as a single piece from molten type metal.[29]

The first linotype machine was built in 1876. Its inventor was Ottmar Mergenthaler, a German immigrant then living in Washington, D.C. Mergenthaler was a clockmaker by trade, but he quickly grasped how to combine various existing printing technologies into a practicable device. In 1886, the first commercial linotype machine was installed at the *New-York Tribune*, and within a short time, nearly every large newspaper in the United States was being composed using the new technology.

The result of these two inventions was a precipitous drop in the cost of printing, which, taken together with significantly cheaper, industrially made paper, made the prices for newspapers and books a great deal more affordable than they had ever been.

Still, as late as the early 1880s, the cost of adding illustrations to printed texts was often prohibitive. Traditionally, images had been introduced into printing plates as woodcuts or etchings; this was mostly the case well into the last quarter of the nineteenth century. It was the advent of photography that began to change the situation.

The first of the new processes for making printable images was photoengraving. Its discovery was closely bound up with the two primary problems of early photography, namely, how to fix images permanently and how to reproduce them serially.

The earliest forms of photoengraving were the invention of two pioneers of photography, Nicéphore Niépce in France, and slightly later, Henry Fox Talbot in England. Niépce, who made the first-ever photographic image in 1827, was seeking a way to create photographic images on plates that could then be etched and used to make prints on paper with a traditional printing press. After experimenting for a time, he came up with a primitive method involving a chemical reactive process. His method was not practicable because it effectively destroyed the original engraving. Talbot, who invented the calotype, or paper negative process, began working with various chemical processes to ensure that his paper prints would not fade. He discovered, though, that he could use a related technique to engrave metal plates. A Czech painter, Karel Klíč, built on Talbot's research, developing a process known as photogravure, which allowed for very high-quality reproductions.[30] The Talbot-Klíč process, as it is known today, is particularly suited for art reproductions because it captures multiple variations in tone.

It was Talbot who also came up with the idea of halftone printing, a more economical method for reproducing photographs on the printed page. In 1852, he obtained a patent for a process using "screens or veils" to break up an image into small dots or lines. Others subsequently worked on the technique, some using screens, some not, but the most successful methods all used dots of varying sizes. By the late 1880s, halftone printing had come into standard use, especially for newspapers and inexpensive books.

While halftone printing technology became the dominant process, there were competing technologies, including collotype, a photographic printing process invented by Alphonse Poitevin in 1855 to produce images in a wide variety of tones, without the need for halftone screens, and duotype, which allowed for making prints in two colors using two halftone plates made from the same negative but etched differently.

One of the breakthroughs in color printing, the Ben Day process, worked in a similar way. Named after its inventor, American illustrator and printer Benjamin

Henry Day Jr., who came up with the technique in 1879, the Ben Day process is based on an optical illusion: small colored dots (or other shapes), set close together, widely spaced, or overlapping, are combined to create the impression of a wide array of colors. With the four-color process (using cyan, magenta, yellow, and black, which later became standard for color printing), Ben Day became an inexpensive way to generate shading and secondary colors, such as green, purple, orange, and flesh tones, on cheap paper. Until the 1970s, most comic books were printed this way.

With his background in printing, Calkins was fully aware of the new technologies and their potential for transforming how advertisements could be printed. He was now determined to take advantage of them.

One of the advertising campaigns he worked on with Bates was for the R & G Corset Company. Like many nineteenth-century American companies, R & G relied on itinerant salesmen, or drummers, to visit local retailers and persuade them to carry their products. Bates convinced the firm's skeptical general manager to try a media campaign, buying full-page, back-cover ads in *Ladies' Home Journal*. Calkins, to whom Bates turned over the task of coming up with a suitable set of ads, felt intense pressure to make it work: the back-cover space cost $4,000; just one of the ads was three times his annual salary.[31]

Working with the firm's art department, Calkins developed a series of layouts, each showing a photograph of a young woman wearing only a corset. Accompanying the photograph was a text explaining the merits of the company's product and its features (fig. 4).

One of the innovations Calkins employed is so commonplace today that it requires comment: the presentation of the company's name set in large, bold print. Surprisingly, this practice had not been standard before. Earlier advertisements had come mostly in the form of announcements, and the company name was frequently an afterthought. Calkins set about to highlight the name in a way that we would now understand as branding. He was not the first to do so, but Calkins would come to be one of the leaders of this new form of advertising.

Equally, if not more, striking to those who saw the ad at the time was the portrayal of the woman in her corset: it was not reproduced as a line drawing, as had long been customary, but as a photograph—printed using the halftone process. The vivid depiction lent the image a compelling reality: what viewers saw was an attractive woman wearing a real corset.

Photographic and halftone images of scantily clad women in their underwear had circulated widely in the 1880s and 1890s. They became a part of mass culture, a form of early soft-core pornography. Some advertisers had sought to get around this problem by showing the corset alone, without its wearer and somewhat sketchily drawn. Others showed women more fully dressed or who were matronly, conspicuously wearing a wedding ring, or with angel's wings and placed on a pedestal as if they were classical sculptures.[32] In 1898, a month before the first R & G advertisement appeared in *Ladies' Home Journal*, its editor, Edward Bok, reacting to what he saw as a disturbing trend, penned an editorial announcing that the magazine's advice

4 | Earnest Elmo Calkins, *R & G Corsets*, 1900. Magazine advertisement from *The Cosmopolitan*, n.p. Halftone print on paper, 20.3 × 14.1 cm. Collection Christopher Long (hereafter CL).

and fashion columns would no longer make reference to undergarments, because the topic could be "extremely and unpardonably offensive to refined and sensitive women."[33] Bok rejected one of the early photographs for the Bates company ad campaign as too immodest; he agreed to allow another to appear only after it had been retouched with "copious chest-protecting ruffles."[34]

Calkins's advertisements nonetheless turned out to be hugely successful. The number of dealers carrying the company's brand increased from some 6,000 to 10,000, and sales grew steadily. R & G all but abandoned their previous strategy of employing legions of salesmen.[35]

The ads succeeded because of their compelling realism. They spoke directly to middle-class women. Calkins understood, long before almost any of his contemporaries, that what he was selling was not merely an item of clothing but an image and a lifestyle. Women wanted to emulate those they saw in the ads: they, too, hoped to be up-to-date, beautiful, and desirable. Making the model appear as realistic as possible by employing photography only lent the advertisement greater power of persuasion, because women could readily imagine themselves wearing the same corset. It was their emotional connection that mattered: the pictorial expression of this linkage was the ultimate selling tool, because it was psychologically directed.

Calkins later claimed that the R & G layouts were "almost the first use of photographic designs in advertising."[36] His contribution to the advent of what would eventually become the field of graphic design, however, was greatly more far-reaching. The ads were a first step toward a new poignancy and immediacy, a way of putting images on a page that made them visually arresting and artistically powerful.

2 The Poster

Craze

In the fall of 1891, a few months after Earnest Elmo Calkins first arrived in New York City, one of the transformative events in American art was taking place in the rooms of the Grolier Club, at 29 East Thirty-Second Street. The inaugural public exhibition of modern European art posters barely drew notice at the time. Calkins seems to have missed the event entirely. And even if he had viewed it, he may well not have seized upon its import. It would be some time before he grasped its lessons.

The illustrated artistic poster—*affiche* in France, where it had its beginnings— was then still a very new idea. Its origins went back to the 1830s, to the work of artists Jean-Jacques Grandville and Honoré Daumier, who had employed the poster as a medium for political protest and satire. The posters of the later 1880s and early 1890s were altogether different, however. They were the products of a new and vibrant form of aestheticism, one that promoted radical simplification and the evocation of modern life.

How many people made the trek to Thirty-Second Street to see the Grolier exhibition that fall is quite unknown.[1] The poster had been long regarded as ephemeral, a throwaway with little value. Few Americans then had any sense of what might have been meant by the concept of a "modern" poster. Even in Paris, where the art poster had its beginnings, the notion that a poster might be of aesthetic interest, even a collectible, was still fresh. Only six years before, in 1884, the first exhibition of art posters had taken place in the city. Soon thereafter, a nearly identical exhibit was mounted in Nantes. These shows were hastily and cheaply prepared: photographs of the Nantes exhibition show that the posters were hung with a clothesline and pin

system, extending the full length of each wall, in long rows with posters stacked from floor to ceiling. The installation in the Grolier Club was probably similar.[2]

The New York show included some one hundred posters and book covers. Most were the work of French artists, half of them by Jules Chéret (who alone contributed forty-five posters) and the French Swiss artist Eugène Grasset. Only seven were from American artists.[3]

Chéret had been making art posters for some twenty years. He was the acknowledged master of the new medium. By the time of the Grolier exhibit, he had created more than one thousand posters—exuberant, joyous depictions of the Belle Époque, with figures (chiefly women and girls) who seemed to float in space, defying the laws both of gravity and perspective (fig. 5). A self-taught artist who began as a printer, Chéret made most of his posters as advertisements—many for the Parisian dance halls and theaters. Others soon joined him in this work: the year after the Grolier Club show, Pierre Bonnard and Henri de Toulouse-Lautrec were designing their own posters, drawing from Chéret and the Art Nouveau, which was then coming into vogue. Alphonse Mucha, who would become the unrivaled master of the Parisian Art Nouveau *affiches*, issued his first poster in 1894, a depiction of Sarah Bernhardt in the play *Gismonda*.

The rise of the poster craze across Europe—and soon in the United States—owed its existence not only to changing sensibilities in the art world. It was also the product of new technology—specifically, how such fine art images could be reproduced. The crucial invention—lithography—had come almost a century before.

It had happened as much by chance as intent. In the mid 1790s, a young Prague-born German actor and playwright, Johann Alois Senefelder, living in Munich, had fallen into debt after the death of his father. He hoped to publish several plays he had written to support himself and his family. But he was unable to afford the cost of engraving the plates. He went to a local printing shop to learn the requisite techniques, intending to do the job himself. So equipped with a basic understanding and a small printing press, Senefelder attempted to engrave them on copper plates—the standard process at that time. He quickly found that he simply lacked the needed skill. He tried intaglio and relief printing processes—again, without success. Then, greatly to the debt of posterity, Senefelder's failures bore fruit. One day, he jotted down his laundry list with a grease pencil on a smooth piece of Bavarian limestone. It occurred to him, in a moment of abrupt and especially lucid inspiration, that were he to etch away the rest of the surface, the markings would be left in relief.

Over the next two years, he experimented unrelentingly with the process, gradually bringing his technique into a workable form, refining the necessary chemical treatments and constructing the new press needed for printing with large stones. Senefelder called his invention *Steindruckerei*, or stone printing. But the French name, *lithographie* (or in English, lithography, literally "stone writing," adapted from Greek) became standard. In 1818, Senefelder published an account of his invention and its techniques under the title *Vollständiges Lehrbuch der Steindruckerey*.[4] A year later, an English-language version, *A Complete Course in Lithography*, appeared.[5] It remained in print well into the early twentieth century.

5| Jules Chéret, *Moulin Rouge*, 1890. Poster, printed by Chaix/Atelier Chéret, Paris. Lithograph on paper, 115.6 × 86.4 cm. Private collection.

Lithography became the preferred medium for many artists in the nineteenth century. It allowed them to draw directly onto the surface of the stone using familiar tools. It was quick, easy, and produced expressive and powerful images. Francisco de Goya, Eugène Delacroix, and Théodore Géricault were among the first to exploit its possibilities; caricaturists, like Daumier, were also early and enthusiastic converts.

Senefelder's original method, however, had its limitations, the main one being that it produced only monochromatic images. In his 1818 book, he wrote about his plans to print in multiple colors, but it was only after his death, in 1834, that practicable methods for what became known as chromolithography came into widespread use. Its true inventor remains unknown. Godefroy Engelmann, an artist and printer in the French town of Mulhouse, near the Swiss and German borders, was granted an English patent in July 1837 for his process of chromolithography that produced consistent results, and he was mostly responsible for commercializing the technique. He was not the first, however: others in France and Germany, including makers of playing cards, were already printing in multiple colors before that time, so the credit must be shared.

Chéret, who was among the first to adapt the method for "artistic" purposes, learned the advanced technique of chromolithography in England in the 1850s. By the late 1860s, he was producing his own color posters. Until the late 1880s, Chéret employed only three colors; after that time, he unfailingly used at least four or five.[6]

The Americans who first saw the art posters coming from France in the late 1880s were enthralled not only by the explosions of color, but also by how it was applied. Lithography, especially in the hands of a master like Chéret, yielded large spreads of consistent color, and precise printing allowed for sharp boundaries between the color fields or for very clear-cut overlap. The colors did not run into each other but retained their autonomy in a way that was visually striking—quite different from other forms of printing then in use.

Colored posters were not entirely new in the United States. Advertising posters, woodblock-printed in one or more colors, had been commonplace since the early nineteenth century, and they remained so well into the 1880s, when they began to be replaced by lithographic prints. The early American lithographic firms, like the Strobridge Company, which began making prints in Cincinnati, Ohio, around the time of the Civil War, produced excellent quality prints. American lithographers often employed immigrant printers, usually German, Irish, or English, who had learned their craft in Europe. The problem in the American context, though, was less the technology than the artwork itself. Almost all early American lithographs were the work of commercial artists, who relied on conventional depictions of people, animals, or objects. Ofttimes, the new technique was also applied to political posters, with less than inspiring results.[7] What changed was the scale of these posters. Many early American posters were made for circuses, theaters, or vaudeville acts; over time, they were enlarged, nearly to the scale of small billboards (fig. 6). Yet their artistic quality was often wanting.

It was a small group of New York publishing houses, several literary "little magazines," and a few artists that gave rise to the art poster movement in America. The

6| *Ringling Bros World's Greatest Shows*, ca. 1913. Poster, printed by the Strobridge Lithography Company, Cincinnati, OH, and New York, NY. Lithograph on paper. Prints and Photographs Division, Library of Congress, Washington, D.C.

first posters began appearing in the United States in 1889. That year *The Century Magazine* commissioned English-born artist Louis Rhead, and Harper & Brothers hired Grasset to create holiday poster designs. The following year, *Harper's Bazar* asked Rhead to design its Easter advertisement (fig. 7).

Unlike the sinuous forms Grasset was producing, Rhead's design was closely attuned to the tastes of the Aesthetic movement—more English "Victorian" than Art Nouveau. Nonetheless, the posters of both men proved hugely popular, significantly boosting sales, and for the next four years the two artists continued to fashion holiday posters for *The Century*, *Harper's Bazar*, *Harper's Monthly*, and *St. Nicholas*.

In 1893, Harper & Brothers took the novel step of advertising a regular issue of *Harper's Monthly*. One of the first of these posters, for April, was a small lithograph, only eighteen inches tall and slightly more than a foot wide. It depicted a man dressed in a green overcoat and a deerstalker cap intently reading a magazine in the rain. The only text read: "HARPER'S FOR APRIL" (fig. 8).

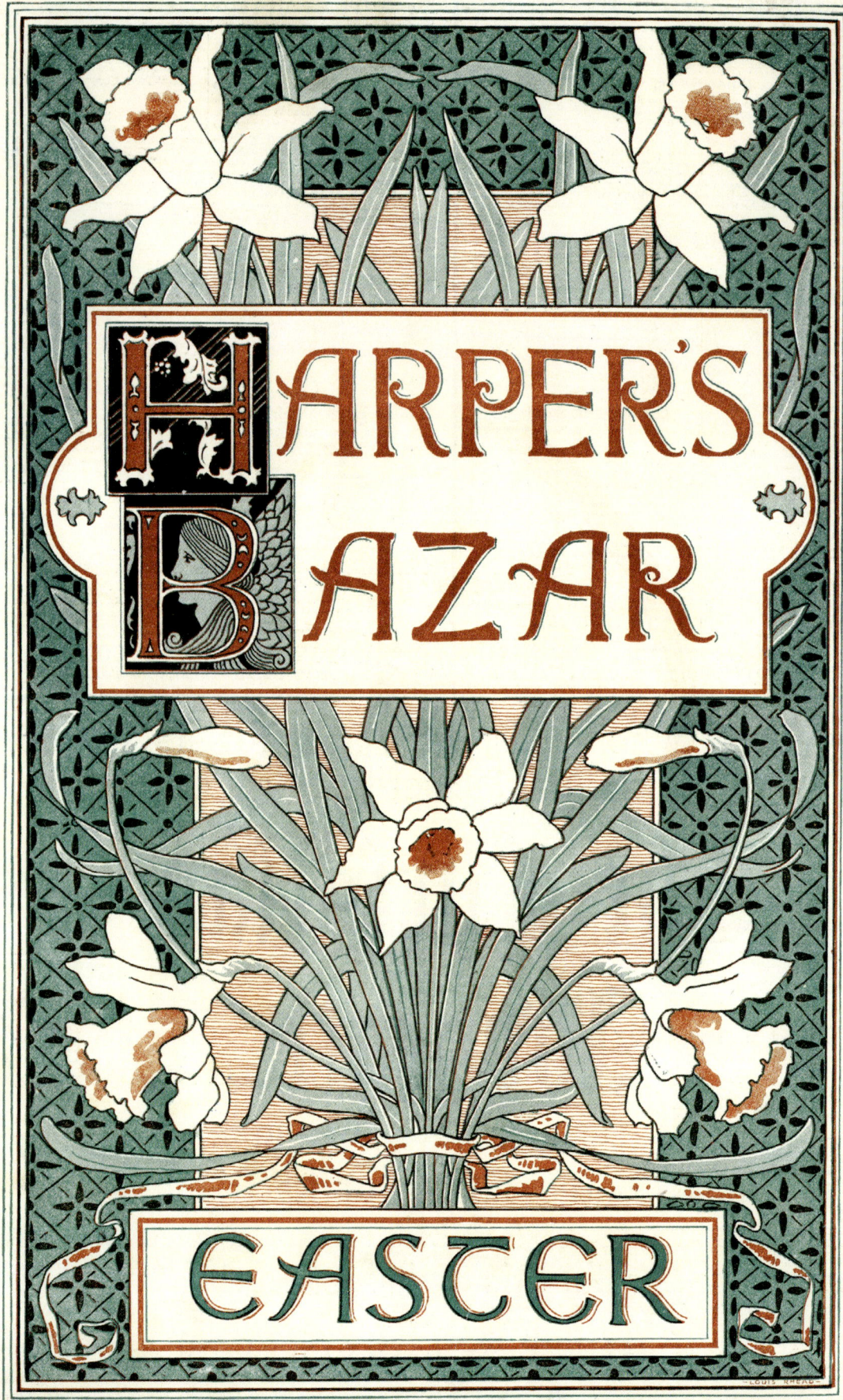

7 | Louis Rhead, *Harper's Bazar: Easter*, 1890. Poster. Lithograph on paper, 41 × 58 cm. Prints and Photographs Division, Library of Congress, Washington, D.C.

8 | Edward Penfield, *Harper's for April*, 1893. Poster. Lithograph on paper, 48 × 33 cm. Prints and Photographs Division, Library of Congress, Washington, D.C.

9 | Edward Penfield, *Harper's June*, 1898. Poster. Lithograph on paper, 23 × 40 cm. Prints and Photographs Division, Library of Congress, Washington, D.C.

The idea, at least as it related to magazines, was without precedent. There was no list of contents. There was no other text at all. And there was nothing about that issue that was in any way special or unusual. It was neither for a holiday nor some other important event. Its appearance suggested merely that the magazine itself was worth the effort for one to go down to the newsstand and purchase it.[8]

The artist who had fashioned this laconic image of daily life was Edward Penfield. Penfield, the son of a flour merchant, had grown up in Brooklyn. He received his elementary education at the local grammar school. But mostly, he studied at home, cared for by his doting mother, who had lost two of her other sons. The young Penfield's uncle was an artist and owner of an engraving studio in Manhattan, supplying "cuts" for some of the city's publishers. Edward decided to follow in his uncle's footsteps and enrolled in school of the Art Students' League. Not long afterward, in 1890, he was discovered by the art director at Harper & Brothers and hired as a staff artist and art editor.[9] He published his first poster for the magazine in March 1893; for the next six years, with only a tiny number of exceptions, he would devise and execute the monthly placards for *Harper's*.[10]

Penfield's posters are notable for their resplendent simplicity. He rarely inserted more than one or two figures, and those figures are almost always shown engaged in everyday activities. He was influenced in this by Toulouse-Lautrec and Théophile Alexandre Steinlen (of cat posters fame), who had advanced the possibilities of two-

dimensional modeling, employing reduced and frank imagery. They specialized, too, in scenes of the everyday (or, in some instances, the not so everyday, as in Toulouse-Lautrec's lurid depictions of Parisian nightlife). Penfield's look was similar but decidedly WASPish: his subjects were well-to-do, white East Coasters, a nod to the magazine's readership. They were invariably well-dressed and animated—there is a decidedly activated quality to most of his scenes—yet there is little complexity to his pictures. Penfield's belief that a "design that needs study is not a poster, no matter how well it is executed," summed up his approach.[11]

Most of Penfield's early posters for *Harper's* portrayed a figure reading or carrying a copy of the magazine. Later, he moved on to images of leisure time or quiet moments of human interaction (figs. 9–11). After 1901, his subjects broadened to portrayals of American life—views, for example, of labor or sport (figs. 12, 13). In all these, Penfield contributed not only the idea that studied reduction could make a poster more visually affective, but also that little scenes of everyday life could be a means to sell something. His posters marked the beginnings of the soft sell, of using subtle persuasion to entice consumers, the concept that would propel much of later advertising.

10| Edward Penfield, *Harper's August*, 1896. Poster. Lithograph on paper, 47.5 × 35 cm. Prints and Photographs Division, Library of Congress, Washington, D.C.

11| Edward Penfield, *Ride a Stearns and be content*, 1896. Poster, printed by J. Ottmann Lith. Co., New York, NY, for the E. C. Stearns Bicycle Agency, Syracuse, NY. Lithograph on paper, 152 × 116 cm. Prints and Photographs Division, Library of Congress, Washington, D.C.

OUTING

THE OUT OF DOOR MAGAZINE
EDITED BY CASPAR WHITNEY

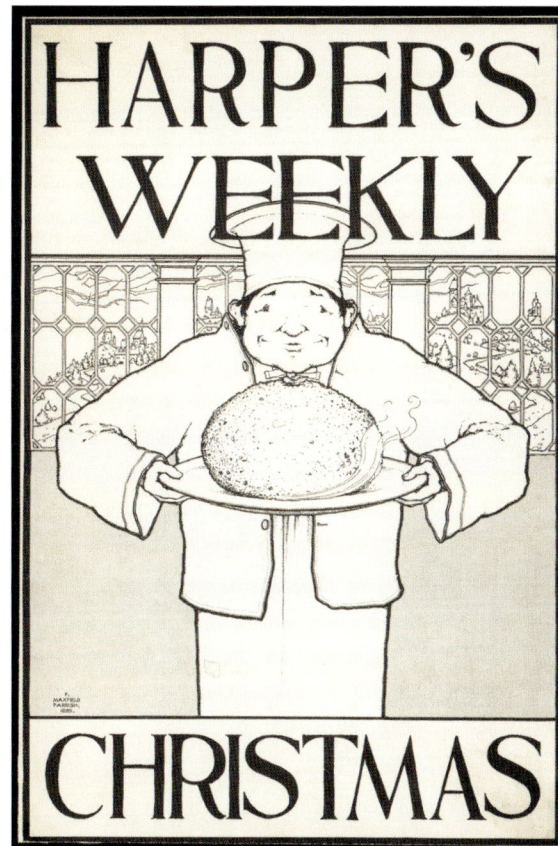

12 | Edward Penfield, *Outing*, 1902. Poster. Lithograph on paper, 52 × 33 cm. Prints and Photographs Division, Library of Congress, Washington, D.C.

---

13 | Edward Penfield, *Cornell*, 1908. Poster, printed by Chas. W. Beck Jr., Philadelphia. Lithograph on paper, 49 × 32 cm. Prints and Photographs Division, Library of Congress, Washington, D.C.

14 | Maxfield Parrish, *Harper's Weekly Christmas*, 1895. Poster. Print on paper, 35 × 24 cm. Prints and Photographs Division, Library of Congress, Washington, D.C.

Maxfield Parrish, another young artist who for a time also made covers and posters for *Harper's*, *The Century*, and *Scribner's*, followed a closely related approach. Parrish was born in Philadelphia of good, upper-class Quaker stock. His father, Stephen Parrish, was a successful landscape painter and etcher. From an early age, the younger Parrish showed a natural talent for art. When the boy was only ten, his father took him to Europe on a tour of the great museums so that they might paint and sketch together. Parrish first tried his hand at architecture, studying at Haverford College, but he soon made the switch to painting, spending three years at the Pennsylvania Academy of the Fine Arts.

In the years after the turn of the century, Parrish became a sought-after book illustrator and muralist, known for his classically inspired fantasies and his vibrant colors. (Parrish blue is named for him.) His graphic work of the mid 1890s, though, is more restrained, following the same tendencies Penfield showed toward a distinct matter-of-factness, flatness, and large blank spaces (figs. 14–16).

Neither Penfield nor Parrish drew directly from French Art Nouveau, at least not in its more fervent and florid guise. They employed ornament sparingly, preferring to foreground the figures in their compositions, setting them against neutral or even empty backgrounds. In truth, both artists were as much, if not more, indebted to Japanese *ukiyo-e* woodcuts than the unalloyed Art Nouveau. Examples of ukiyo-e had begun to circulate in Europe and United States in the 1870s. They had an immediate and powerful influence on some of the early French Impressionists, including Edgar Degas and Édouard Manet, as well as painters like Toulouse-Lautrec. Of the American poster designers, Arthur Wesley Dow was the modernist perhaps most deeply touched, and he was the first to carry the influence of the ukiyo-e into art poster design.

Dow was another New Englander, from an old family in Ipswich, Massachusetts. His father, David Dow, held a collection of jobs—farmer, carpenter, repairman, gravedigger, and undertaker—but the younger Dow had a more patrician upbringing, attending the local grammar school and, afterward, the studio art classes of Boston artist James M. Stone and the Académie Julian in Paris.

Upon returning to the United States, Dow was appointed assistant curator of the Japanese collection at the Museum of Fine Arts, Boston. The museum's department had assembled a significant collection of ukiyo-e, and Dow spent hours scrutinizing the works of Utagawa Hiroshige, Tsukioka Yoshitoshi, and especially Katsushika Hokusai (fig. 17). When he began to receive his own commissions for posters and other commercial work, he incorporated ukiyo-e techniques and themes, combining them with the language of the Art Nouveau. His oft-reproduced poster for *Modern Art* magazine was an updated Japonisme landscape enveloped by Art Nouveau florets (fig. 18).

Other American devotees of the art poster embraced the Art Nouveau even more unequivocally and, in some instances, a great deal more effectively. Rhead began experimenting with Art Nouveau elements around 1895. Over the next half dozen years, his poster style absorbed its sinuous lines and floriferous forms, albeit in a manner than was closer to the British interpretation of the style (figs. 19, 20).

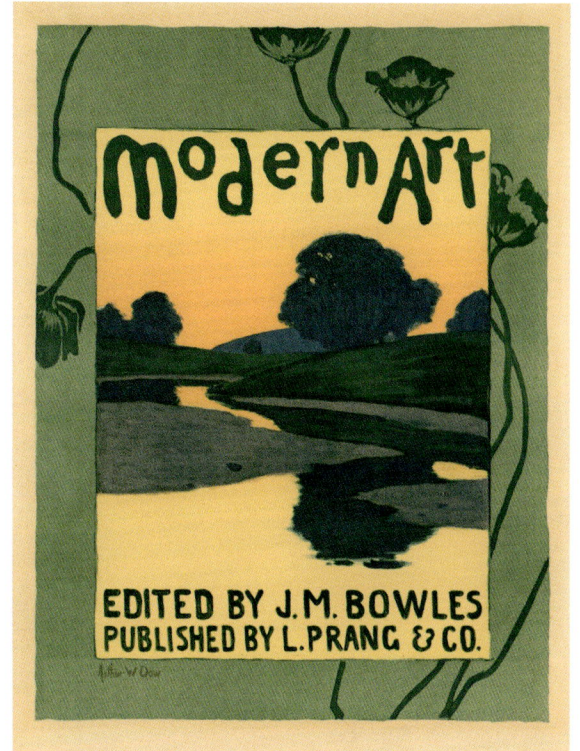

15| Maxfield Parrish, *Harper's Weekly Bicycle Number*, 1896. Lithograph on paper, 41 × 58 cm. Prints and Photographs Division, Library of Congress, Washington, D.C.

16| Maxfield Parrish, *The Century*, 1897. Poster, printed by Thomas & Wylie Lithographic Co., New York, NY, for the Century Company, New York, NY. Lithograph on paper, 50.2 × 33 cm. The Resnick Collection.

───────

17| Katsushika Hokusai, *Kirifuri Waterfall at Kurokami Mountain in Shimotsuke*, from the series *Shokoku taki-me-guri*. Woodblock print, ink, and watercolor on paper, 37.1 × 26.2 cm. Metropolitan Museum of Art, New York. Henry L. Phillips Collection, Bequest of Henry L. Phillips.

18| Arthur Wesley Dow, *Modern Art: Edited by J. M. Bowles*, 1895. Poster, printed by L. Prang & Co., New York. Lithograph on paper, 52 × 38 cm. Prints and Photographs Division, Library of Congress, Washington, D.C.

19| Louis Rhead, *Photochrome Engraving Company,*
New York, 1895. Poster. Lithograph on paper, 35 × 28
cm. Prints and Photographs Division, Library of Congress,
Washington, D.C.

20| Louis Rhead, *The Century Magazine for June,* 1896.
Poster. Lithograph on paper, 57 × 27 cm. Prints and Photographs Division, Library of Congress, Washington, D.C.

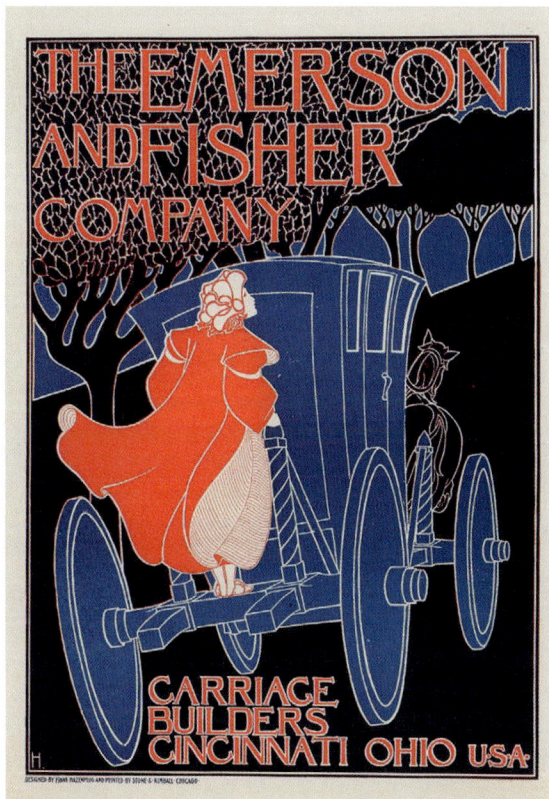

But if Penfield, Parrish, and Rhead were notably successful in the commercial realm, a small number of younger artists, mostly working for the little literary or art magazines, were more radical in their break from conventional depiction. Elisha Brown Bird, Alice Russell Glenny, Frank Hazenplug, Blanche McManus (Mansfeld), Ethel Reed, and Charles Herbert Woodbury—to list only some of the most prominent—went further in investigating how color, form, and the written word might be arranged in two-dimensional space (figs. 21, 22).

New York, Boston, and Chicago were then teeming with young artists looking to express modern life and break with the realism that had long dominated American painting. Most had some formal training in the United States or in Europe. Some drifted back and forth between traditional easel painting and commercial art. A few, like Bird, had previously worked as cartoonists or caricaturists for the newspapers.[12] But nearly all had come to the new art by way of their unorthodox lifestyles and a yearning sense that a new world was in the offing. They were the leading edge of what became America's first modern-age youth revolt.

21 | Florence Lundborg, *The Lark August*, 1895. Poster, printed for William Doxey, San Francisco, CA. Relief print on paper, 41 × 33 cm. Prints and Photographs Division, Library of Congress, Washington, D.C.

22 | Frank Hazenplug, *The Emerson and Fisher Company, Carriage Builders, Cincinnati, OH*, 1896. Poster, printed by Stone & Kimball, Chicago, IL. Lithograph on paper, 50 × 35 cm. The Resnick Collection.

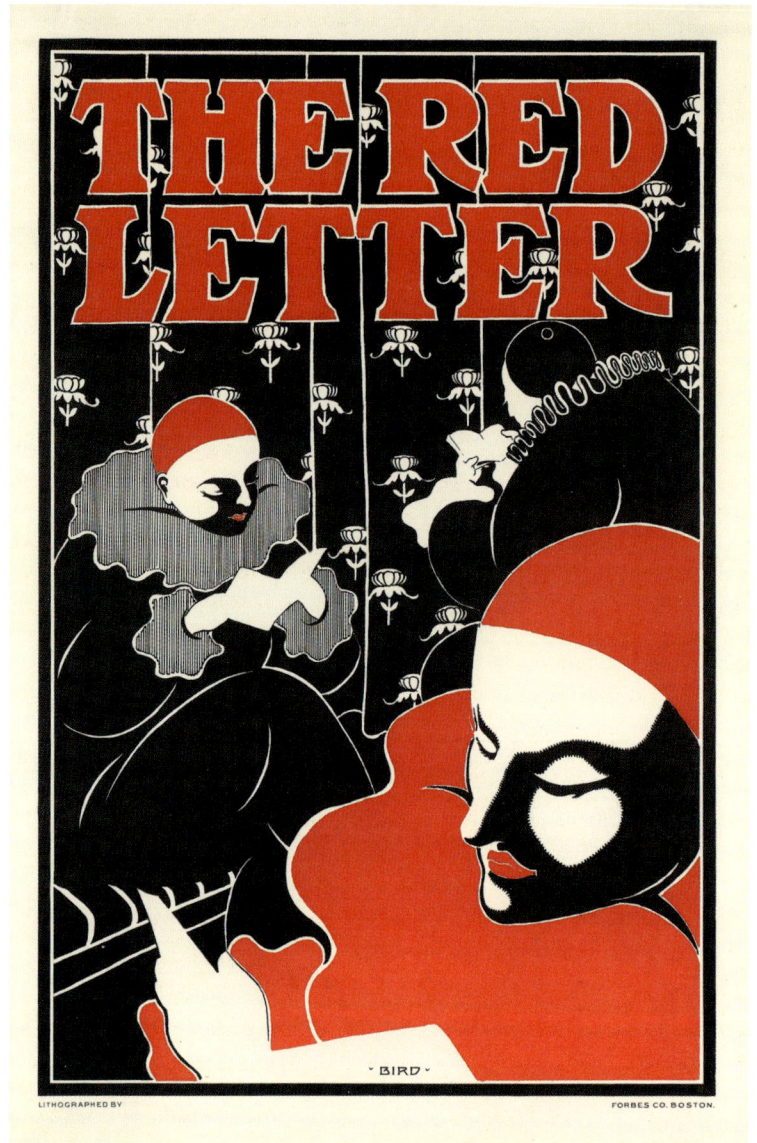

23 | Elisha Brown Bird, *The Poster*, 1896. Poster, printed by Will H. Clemens, New York, NY. Lithograph on paper, 49 × 32 cm. Prints and Photographs Division, Library of Congress, Washington, D.C.

24 | Elisha Brown Bird, *The Red Letter*, 1896. Poster, printed by Forbes Co., Boston, MA. Lithograph on paper, 66 × 45.75 cm. Private collection.

25 | Alice Russell Glenny, *Women's Edition (Buffalo) Courier*, 1895. Poster. Lithograph on paper, 75.8 × 54.6 cm. Prints and Photographs Division, Library of Congress, Washington, D.C.

Bird's 1896 design for the magazine *The Poster*, with its twin muses, "Miss Art" on the left and "Miss Litho" on the right, reprises the sinuous lines of the French and Belgian Art Nouveau, even while referencing a William Morris textile in the background (fig. 23).[13] Bird had his start as an architecture student at the Massachusetts Institute of Technology, where he tuned his drafting skills and turned them to graphic design, working for *The Inland Printer*, *The Chap-Book*, *The Red Letter*, and *The Century*, as well as several book publishers. One of his most compelling works was his poster advertising *The Red Letter*, also printed in 1896 (fig. 24). Depicting three costumed readers—surely of *The Red Letter*!—it is a tour de force of bold colors (red and black, on a white background), intertwining lines and forms, and forceful lettering.

Alice Russell Glenny's 1895 poster advertising the women's edition of the *Buffalo Courier* draws even more unequivocally on the French Art Nouveau, joining it with the sensibilities of the classical revival (fig. 25). Glenny's sweet and frank presentation was an exception for the American poster movement, however. Charles Herbert Woodbury's 1895 poster for the July edition of *The Century* and Charles Warde Traver's 1896 poster for *The Echo*, both hailing Fourth of July festivities, rely on lively figures and vibrant color fields set out in a manner that blends Japanese woodcuts, the Art Nouveau, and the brash graphic idioms of Toulouse-Lautrec and contemporary English artist Aubrey Beardsley (figs. 26, 27). In a similar way, M. E. (Mary Eleanor) Curran adapted a related version of the Art Nouveau to a romanticized setting of a Mexican-inspired festival in *La Fiesta de Los Angeles* (fig. 28).

The field for experimentation, though, was very large, ranging from Marianna Sloan's poster for the *Women's Edition of The Press* (which was strongly indebted to Morris and the other artists of the English Arts and Crafts movement) to Western artist Maynard Dixon's poster for *Overland* magazine and the book *Lo-To-Kah* (figs. 29–31). Dixon's designs, with their insistent lettering, aggressive colors, and large masses, were early indications of what was to come in American graphic art: a forceful, matter-of-factness that conveyed the country's rawness and individualism.

The master of this new stylistic amalgam—a hefty and distinctive form of the Art Nouveau—was Will H. Bradley. Largely self-taught, preternaturally gifted, and imbued with irrepressible energy, Bradley emerged in the mid-1890s as the most far-seeing and original of the American poster artists. Walter Dorwin Teague later remarked that it was Bradley who opened American design to the "sun and air" and made an "indigenous art."[14]

He was born William Henry Bradley in Boston in 1868. While he was still a small child, his family moved to the shoemaking town of Lynn, Massachusetts, where his father drew cartoons for one of the local dailies. After his father's early death, in 1874, Bradley moved with his mother to Ishpeming, Michigan, to be with her sister and sister's husband. At twelve, forced by the family's circumstances to work, Bradley became an apprentice for a weekly newspaper, the *Iron Agitator*, earning three dollars a week.

As it had been for Calkins, the small-town newspaper office became his training ground, school, and laboratory. When the paper's job printer left, Bradley dropped out

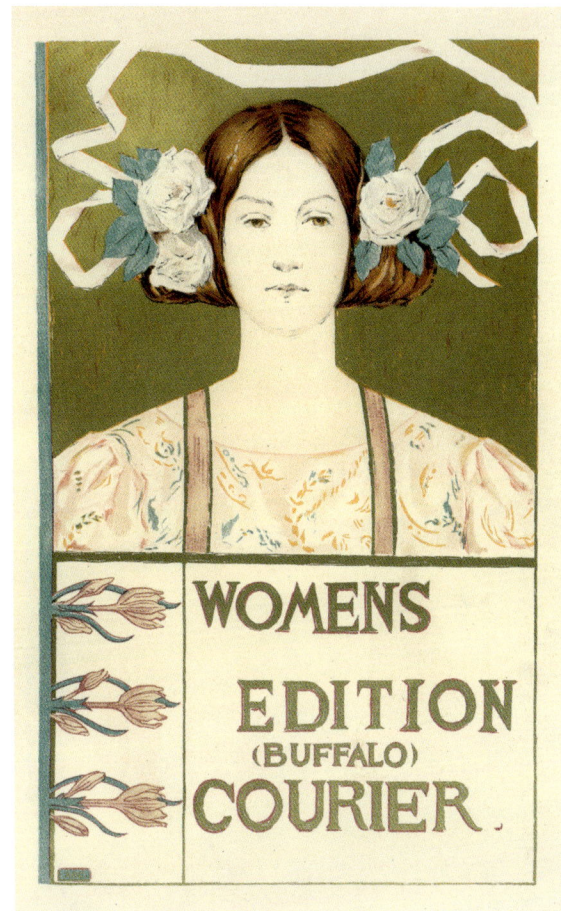

26 | Charles H. Woodbury, *The July Century, New York*, 1895. Poster. Lithograph on paper, 48.3 × 34 cm. Prints and Photographs Division, Library of Congress, Washington, D.C.

27 | Charles Warde Traver, *The Echo*, 1896. Poster. Lithograph on paper, 33 × 24 cm. Private collection.

28 | M. E. (Mary Eleanor) Curran, *La Fiesta de Los Angeles*, 1897. Poster, printed by Los Angeles Lithographic Company, Los Angeles. Lithograph on paper, 68.6 × 48.3 cm. The Resnick Collection.

29 | Marianna Sloan, *Women's Edition: The Press Thanksgiving Eve, Nov. 27th*, 1895. Poster, printed by Philadelphia Press, Philadelphia, PA. Lithograph on paper, 88.2 × 51 cm. Prints and Photographs Division, Library of Congress, Washington, D.C.

30| Maynard Dixon, *Overland January*, 1896. Poster. Lithograph on paper, 39.4 × 25.4 cm. Huntington Library, San Marino, CA. Gift of Jay T. Last.

31| Maynard Dixon, *Lo-To-Kah by Verner Z. Reed*, 1897. Poster. Lithograph on paper, 39.6 × 37.5 cm. The Resnick Collection.

of school and took over the position. He remained in the printing plant for the next four years, learning all he could about printing processes, machines, and typography.

He also began to draw. Along with his responsibilities for printing the newspaper each week, Bradley began making posters for the town's merchants. Despite a lack of formal training, he rendered everything with surprising facility. A visiting landscape painter from Chicago named Frank Bromley admired one of his posters and offered to help him become an artist. Two weeks later, Bradley was on a train bound for the big city.[15]

He first worked on a succession of small art commissions, then for mapmaker Rand McNally. He quit that job to take another position at Knight & Leonard, one of Chicago's leading commercial printers. The work paid well, but Bradley was determined to set up his own freelance art studio, and, by 1893, the year of the Chicago exposition, he had his own office in the Monadnock Building.[16]

One of his many commissions was to design a series of covers for *The Inland Printer*, a leading trade magazine. Another was to design a poster for a Broadway play, *The Masqueraders*, by Henry Arthur Jones. Bradley took the novel step of signing the massive twenty-eight-sheet poster, which earned him notice and an invitation to visit New York, where he saw firsthand the posters of Penfield, Rhead, and some of the Europeans.

Upon his return to Chicago, he moved to Geneva, on the city's outskirts, where he set up a studio in a cottage overlooking the Fox River. There he began to transform the stylistic directions of his day into a personal and powerful idiom. *The Twins*, the May 1894 poster he created for *The Chap-Book*, one of the first of the country's little magazines, is often said to be among the earliest American graphic works to borrow directly from Art Nouveau (fig. 32).[17] Bradley also drew from ukiyo-e and Beardsley. Yet his arrangements were personal and distinctive, mimicking—while also transforming—his influences.

The Twins poster brought Bradley instant fame. New commissions soon came flooding in, by his own recounting "Holiday covers for *Harper's Weekly*, *Harper's Bazaar*, *Harper's Young People*, later renamed *Harper's Roundtable*, page decorations for *Vogue*, a series of full-page designs for Sunday editions of *Chicago Tribune*."[18]

32| Will H. Bradley, *The Chap-Book No. 1 The Twins*, 1894. Poster, printed by Stone & Kimball, Chicago, IL. Zincograph on paper, 51 × 36 cm. Prints and Photographs Division, Library of Congress, Washington, D.C.

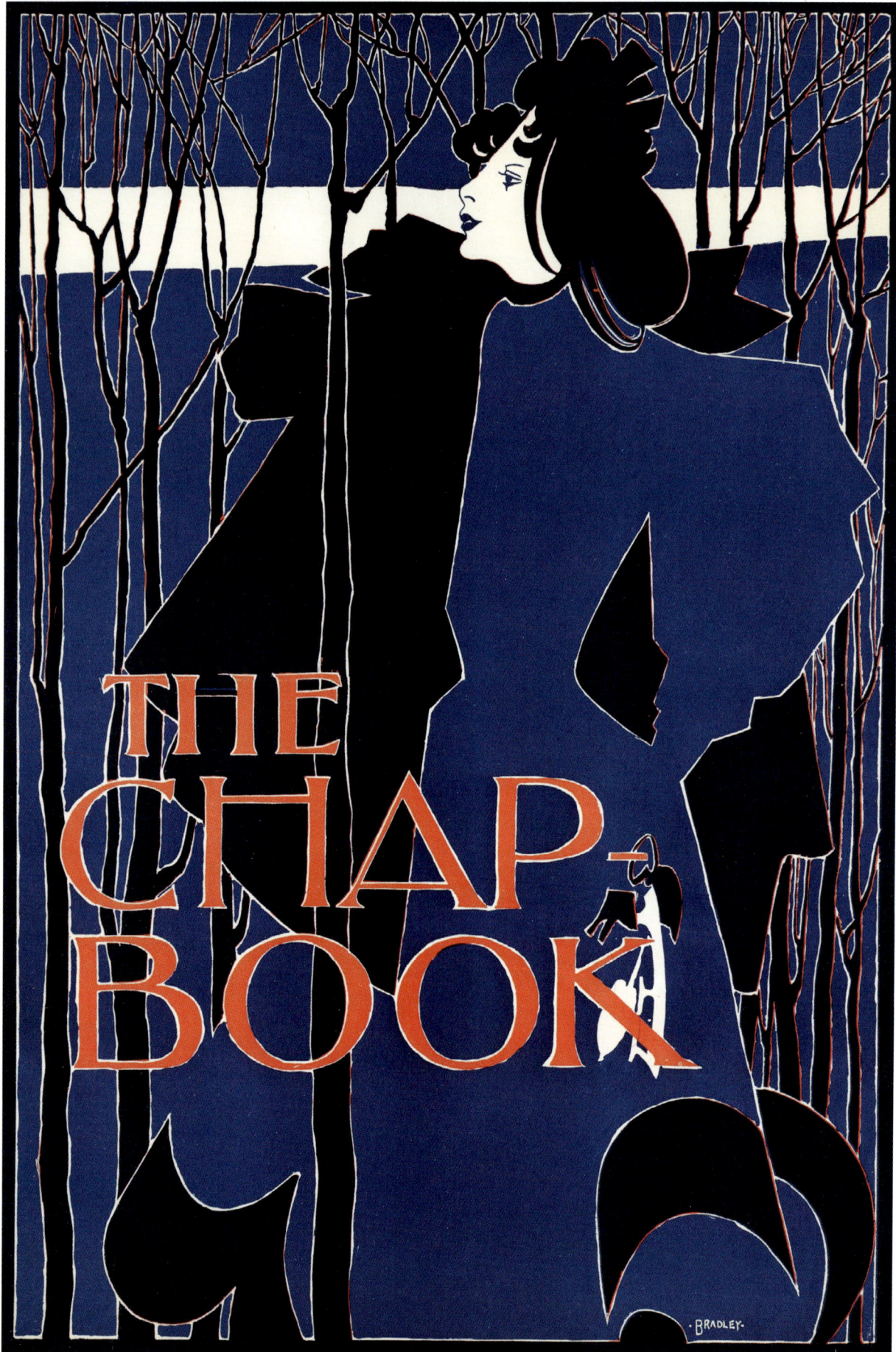

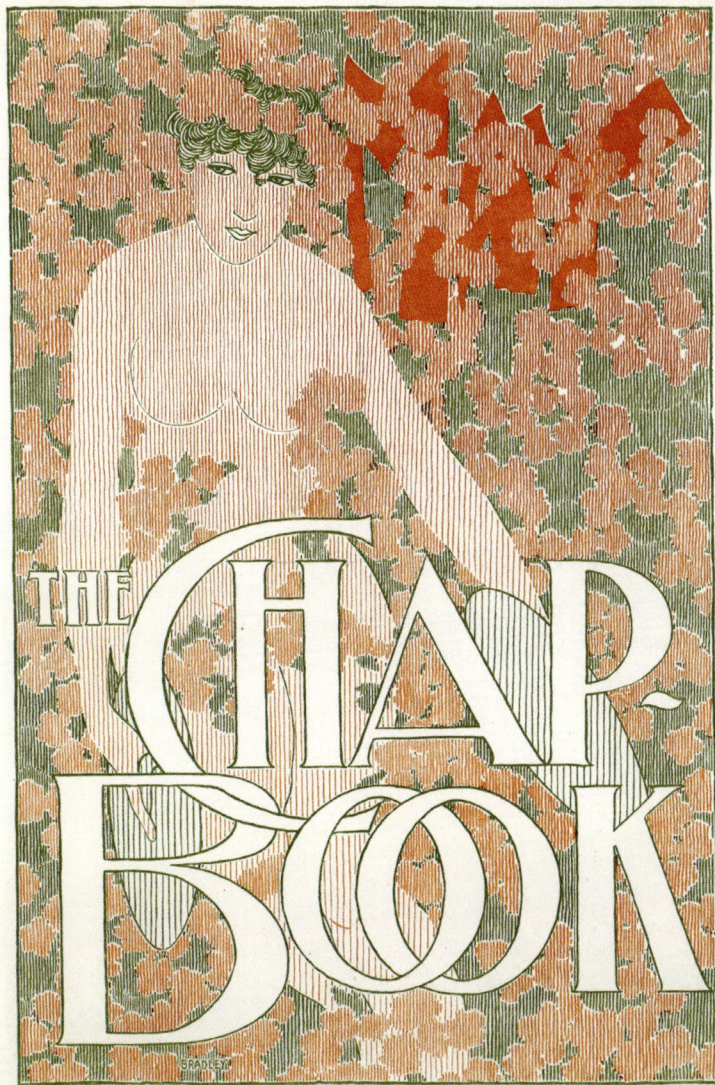

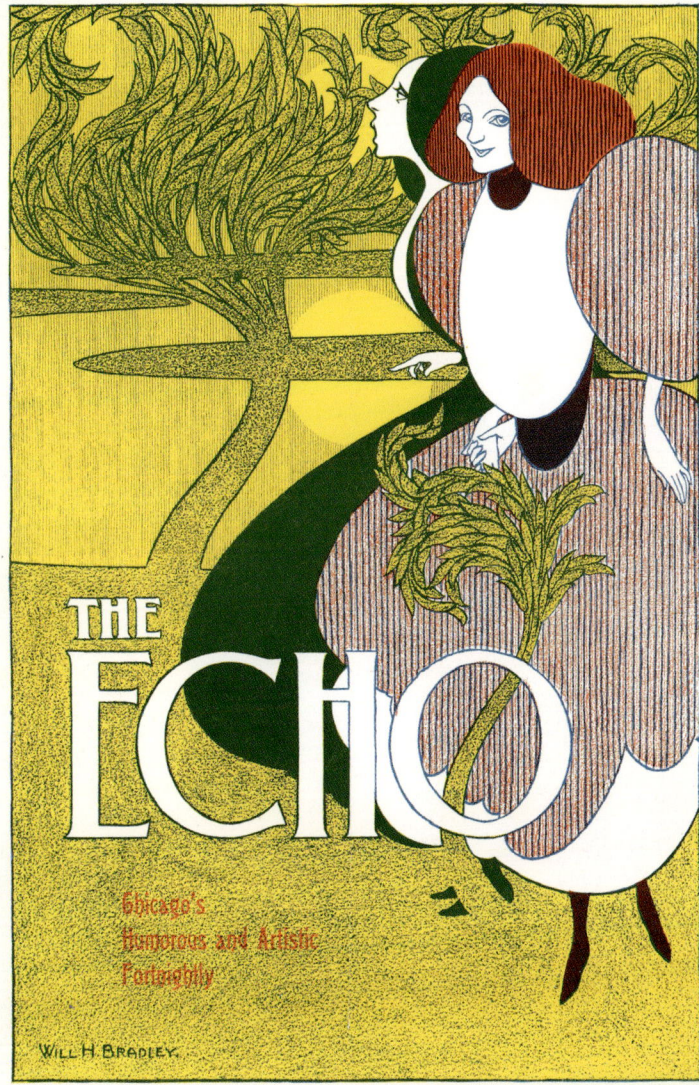

His greatest designs, however, were the posters he made for *The Chap-Book*. After his first effort, Herbert Stuart Stone, the magazine's twenty-three-year-old editor, commissioned Bradley to create six more posters. The second, also printed in 1894, is of a woman in blue, set in a forest of saplings (fig. 33). It uses only three colors: blue, black, and red. But Bradley's adept handling of the forms, all outlined in white, subdivides the surface, creating an impression of complexity and richness, while making the whole scene appear elemental and immediate.

The fourth of Bradley's *Chap-Book* posters, which appeared in May of the following year, has the same effect but uses different pictorial means (fig. 34). He achieves the division of the picture through fragmentation—through the interruption or continuation of closely spaced, parallel vertical lines, which are very cleverly woven into the surface. It is much like a tapestry that has only its warp, with no weft to be seen.

Almost out of the blue, Bradley was suddenly everywhere—on walls, kiosks, billboards, covers, and magazine pages (fig. 35). The imagery he fashioned for each occasion was fresh and vigorous. *The Modern Poster* he made in 1895 for Charles Scribner's Sons

33| Will H. Bradley, *The Chap-Book No. 2*, 1894. Poster, printed by Stone & Kimball, Chicago, IL. Zincograph on paper, 51 × 36 cm. Prints and Photographs Division, Library of Congress, Washington, D.C.

_____

34| Will H. Bradley, *The Chap-Book May No. 4*, 1895. Poster, printed by Stone & Kimball, Chicago, IL. Zincograph on paper, 51 × 36 cm. Prints and Photographs Division, Library of Congress, Washington, D.C.

35| Will H. Bradley, *The Echo*, Chicago, 1895. Poster. Zincograph on paper, 59 × 40.5 cm. Prints and Photographs Division, Library of Congress, Washington, D.C.

36 | Will H. Bradley, *The Modern Poster, No. 32*, 1895. Poster, printed for Charles Scribner's Sons, New York, NY. Letterpress (relief process) on gray paper, 51 × 33 cm. Prints and Photographs Division, Library of Congress, Washington, D.C.

37 | Will H. Bradley, cover of *Bradley: His Book* (Springfield, MA: Wayside Press), 1896. Poster. Lithograph on paper (borders: relief process), 106 × 75 cm. Prints and Photographs Division, Library of Congress, Washington, D.C.

———————

38 | Will H. Bradley, *Narcoti-Cure*, 1895. Poster, printed by Wayside Press, Springfield, MA, for the Narcoti Chemical Company. Zincograph on paper, 50.3 × 35.9 cm. Prints and Photographs Division, Library of Congress, Washington, D.C.

has about it a hint not only of Beardsley but also James McNeill Whistler and a few of the English painters of the previous generation (fig. 36). Always, though, Bradley was able to recast and refine his influences, to lend each work his own special look.

In 1896, he moved to Springfield, Massachusetts. There he founded the Wayside Press and began publishing his own monthly arts periodical, *Bradley: His Book*, which featured his work alongside that of various writers of the day and his fellow artists, including Morris. One of the posters he made advertising the magazine is pure Arts and Crafts, with elements of Morris's aesthetic merged with those of Edward Burne-Jones (fig. 37). But also speckled throughout the pages of these initial issues are examples of advertisements Bradley had made for past and current clients. It was this purely commercial application of his work—far more than his art posters—that would become his true and steady occupation and constitute perhaps his most important contribution to the advent of modern American graphic design.

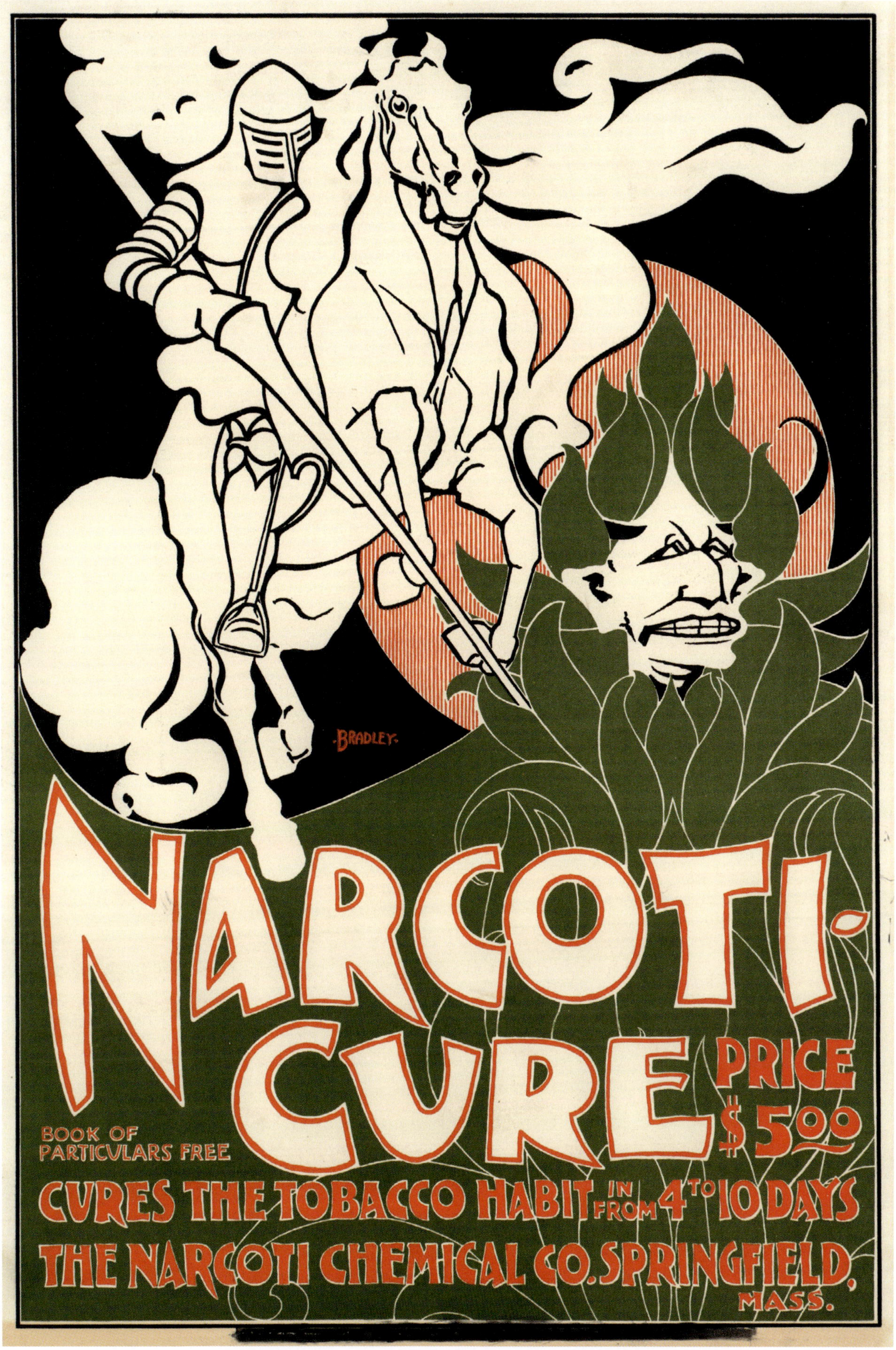
BRADLEY
NARCOTI-
CURE
PRICE
$5.00
BOOK OF
PARTICULARS FREE
CURES THE TOBACCO HABIT IN FROM 4 TO 10 DAYS
THE NARCOTI CHEMICAL CO. SPRINGFIELD,
MASS.

VICTOR BICYCLES

OVERMAN WHEEL CO.
Boston• New York• Detroit• Denver•
San Francisco• Los Angeles• Portland Ore

39 | Will H. Bradley, *Victor Bicycles: Overman Wheel Co.*, 1896. Poster, printed by Forbes Co., Boston, MA. Lithograph on paper. 67.2 × 100.6 cm. Prints and Photographs Division, Library of Congress, Washington, D.C.

40 | *Ault & Wiborg Company Makers of Inks*, ca. 1900. Poster. Lithograph on paper, 27.5 × 20.4 cm (trimmed). CL.

41 | Will H. Bradley, *Ault & Wiborg Company Manufacturers of Photographic & Letter Press Printing Inks*, ca. 1900. Poster. Lithograph on paper, 26.5 × 17.1 cm (trimmed). CL.

Bradley's engagement with the commercial realities of design extended back to the years of his apprenticeship in Michigan. Nearly from the moment he stepped down from the train carriage in Chicago, he was collecting commissions from manufacturers and local entertainment venues. His earliest advertisements in Chicago—for the Michigan Stove Company, for example—were saccharine and traditional. He rapidly found his own path, working out an impressive array of novel pictorial tactics. His 1895 poster *Narcoti-Cure*, for a Springfield, Massachusetts, company selling a supposed remedy for nicotine addiction, was one of his first masterworks (fig. 38). It shows a knight-errant mounted on a white horse vanquishing a vegetal gremlin— addiction personified—enveloped in tobacco leaves. The message is unmistakable; but it is Bradley's brash handling of the images and his lively graphics that tell the story. There is no need for other words or advertising copy.

Bradley's advertisement for Victor Bicycles from the following year functions in much the same way. A woman in the foreground gazes at another woman cycling by (fig. 39). We grasp immediately that she, too, is finding her own joy while riding through an appealing field of flowers. No text is required; the visual imagery conveys all.

This purely pictorial presentation is repeated in Bradley's advertisements for the Ault & Wiborg Company. Founded in Cincinnati, Ohio, Ault & Wiborg was then the leading maker of lithographic inks and supplies. In keeping with their motto *Hic et ubique* (Here and everywhere), the company established sales offices across the globe, in New York, Chicago, San Francisco, Toronto, Buenos Aires, London, Paris, Yokohama, and many other cities. By the turn of the century, it had become the largest printing ink company in the world. Ault & Wiborg hired well-known artists (including, early on, Toulouse-Lautrec) to fashion its advertisements; in the U.S., these ads appeared in *The Inland Printer, The Printer and Bookmaker, The American Bookmaker*, and other trade publications. At first, they were mostly one-color inserts. But by 1892 the company was running ads with up to sixteen colors, many in the swirling language of the Art Nouveau (fig. 40).[19]

Bradley made his first advertisement for Ault & Wiborg in April 1895. Over the next six or seven years, he would produce twenty more designs, with two- and multicolor variants (fig. 41).[20] One of the most singularly beautiful is of a grove of trees set in a luminous green and yellow landscape (fig. 42). The text repeats only the company's name, its principal offices, and notes that it is a producer of printing inks. It is the bold, saturated colors and Bradley's sumptuous scenography that imparts the message. Also quite distinctive is its marked reduction, for embedded in its abstraction and refinement is a premonition of the new simplicity that was to come.

One additional feature stands out: the elegance of its lettering. It is as fundamental to the imagery as are the trees and their idyllic setting. Bradley was among the first of the new American designers to be gripped by type and typefaces. In his later autobiography, he writes of his discovery of Caslon during his first trip to New York, and how it came to "influence all [his] future work in the field of typography.[21] (Caslon is a set of serif typefaces developed by William Caslon in London in the mid-eighteenth century.)

It took time for Bradley to develop a thoroughgoing knowledge of the history of typefaces, and in this, as in so much else, he was self-taught.[22] Bradley's own contributions included several new typefaces. He designed Bradley Type in 1894, cut from his lettering for *The Inland Printer*. He also created Wayside Roman (1900), Missal Initials (1904), and Bewick Roman (1905). He was keenly aware of the impact of his new typefaces, convinced that type and art together were required to make an arresting image.

By the time he had his epiphany about typography, Bradley was editing and printing *Bradley: His Book*. He was also churning out advertisements for a growing list of clients and designing a continuous stream of magazine covers and posters. His pace of work was all-out, and something had to give. It was Bradley. He collapsed of overwork at the age of 28. He recovered, but he was forced to sell the Wayside Press.

After that, he bided his time. He moved to New York, where he earned enough to get by making covers for *Collier's*. Later, he designed an editorial prospectus and crafted architectural designs for the *Ladies' Home Journal*. In 1907, he became *Collier's* art director. He soon grew restless again and reopened his own studio in 1910, renting a space in the newly finished Metropolitan Tower. Within weeks, he was overseeing the art editorship of *Metropolitan, The Century, Success, Pearson's*, and the *National Weekly*.[23]

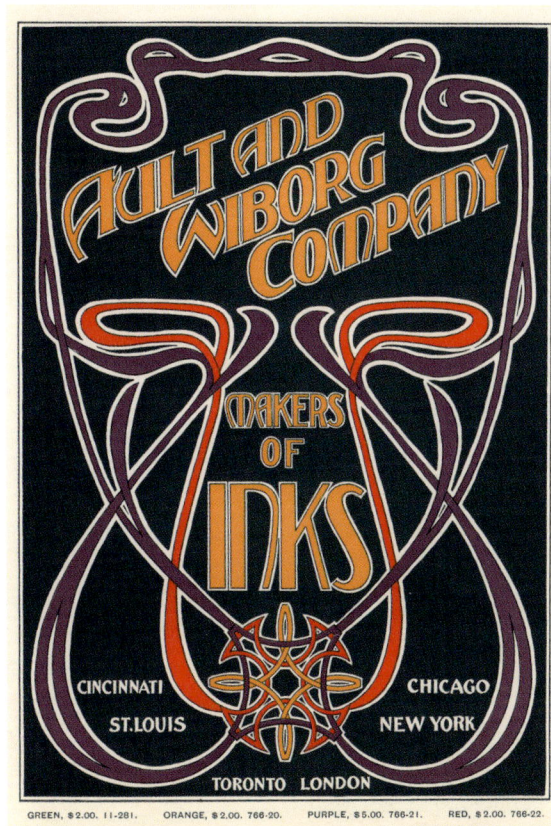

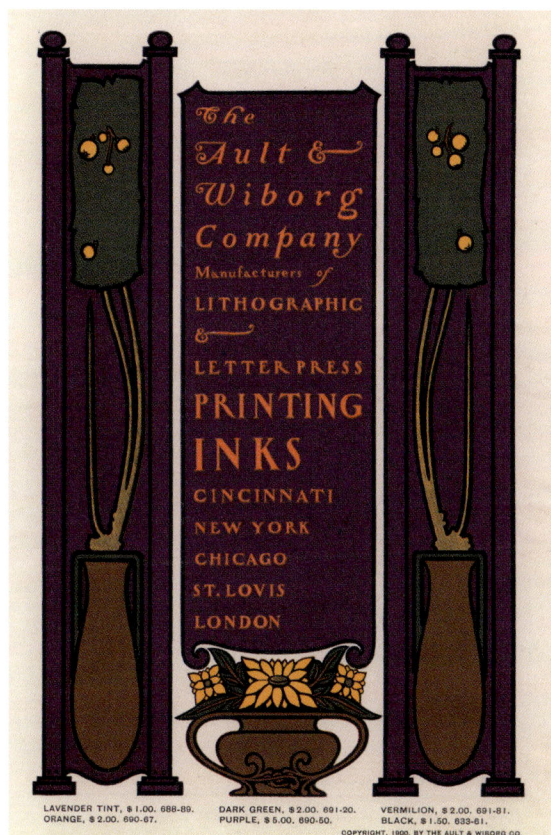

Will Bradley's Art Service
for Advertisers

Over
3000 Designs
Furnished in
Plate Form
Ready for
Printing.

131 East 23rd Street
New York

42 | Will H. Bradley, *Will Bradley's Art Service for Advertisers*, ca. 1912. Advertising leaflet. Letterpress on paper, 15.1 × 8.5 cm. CL.

43 | Will H. Bradley, *Ault & Wiborg Company Manufacturer of Lithographic & Letter Press Printing Inks*, ca. 1900. Poster. Lithograph on paper, 32 × 24 cm. Print Department, Boston Public Library.

It was in this period, prior to 1915, when he began working for William Randolph Hearst, that Bradley made his last signal contribution to the rise of modern American graphic design. He started an "Art Service for Advertisers," offering, as one of his pamphlets promised, "over 3000 Designs Furnished in Plate Ready for Printing" (fig. 43).[24] It was the next logical and practical route toward the full commercialization of art in advertising, the idea that Calkins, too, was pursuing.

Bradley's little pamphlet contains one consequential nugget, one of the best and most direct early summations of the goal of modern graphic design: "The first duty of any advertisement should be to arrest attention. If your ad, because of its art and typography, creates a favorable first impression, it will get by the barriers of the waste basket to the mind of the receiver where your copy can tell the story."[25]

Like most of the artists who had been caught up in the poster craze of the 1890s, Bradley would go on working for many years afterward. For Hearst, he served as art director for several movies; later, he would establish Dramafilms, his own production company. He wrote, produced, and directed his own films, among them *Bitter Fruit* (1920), *Moongold* (1921), and *The Tame Cat* (1921). But Bradley's conversion to advertising art was a vibrant sign of things to come. Many who found their beginnings during the poster craze followed the path into advertising art; others, like Parrish, would find their way back to fine art; and still others, like Penfield, turned to illustration.

For nearly a decade, the lure of the art poster was at the forefront of modern American design. And then, just as quickly as it had arisen, the craze gave out. In 1899, the year after the first of Calkins's R & G ads appeared, an unnamed critic for the *New York Times* summed up all that had been achieved during the eight or nine years when the art poster reigned supreme: "Our walls and fences became things of beauty, and many of our shop windows a delight . . . what the craze and its devotees accomplished, even if unwittingly, [was] the raising of the standards of artistic advertising in all its branches."[26]

The impact of the poster craze, though, extended long afterward, for it had very much to do with the advancements in poster and advertising art that would come over the next several decades. And the poster craze had achieved something else, something even more far-reaching and important. Not only Bradley, with his consummate experiments in color, form, and space, but also many of the other young Americans working in places like New York, Boston, Chicago, and Los Angeles, had shown the possibilities of a distinctive new art, a graphic design language that was decidedly American. The traces of the French Art Nouveau and the English Arts and Crafts were still evident in their work. But no one could mistake their posters for European designs.

3 Supremely

Satisfying

Three years after his breakthrough advertising campaign for R & G Corsets, Earnest Elmo Calkins was laying plans with Ralph Holden, another member of Charles Bates's office staff, to leave the firm and open their own agency. Calkins had grown tired of having to defend his ideas of advertising art to Bates, who thought that the sole purpose of illustrations was to capture viewers' attention "so that they would read the copy."[1] Bates's only requirement for art was to make the advertisements presentable, "to look as well as possible under the conditions."[2] "In telling your story as it should be told," he wrote in *Printers' Ink* in 1899, "you may find that it is impossible to make pretty ads, but to my mind the telling of the story is much more important than the appearance of the ad."[3] Calkins was now convinced of the opposite—that advertising art, despite its commercial obligations, could and should be part of the wider domain of high art. He wanted advertising art to have value, and he saw no contradiction between the practical realities of selling and what such art might aspire to.[4]

In Ralph Holden, Calkins found a kindred spirit, a visionary who believed that advertising could and should be better. Holden was born in Philadelphia in 1871.[5] His father was a printer, but Holden first worked in the office of the freight department of the Baltimore and Ohio Railroad. Determined to seek out a better life, he went to New York in search of a job in publishing. His wife had been contributing fashion drawings to *Ladies' Home Journal*; with no other leads, he tried his luck, making the rounds of the various national magazine offices. The advertising manager at *The Century Magazine* convinced him that he should apply to Bates's firm.

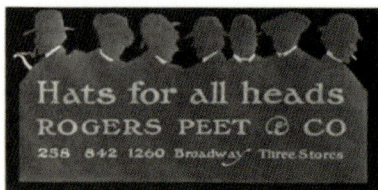

STREET Car Advertising, like all other advertising, should be part of a well-thought-out plan.

We can make the advertising plan, if you wish, or we can simply make the street car cards to go with your plan.

These two designs are a part of a set of twelve, which has been running in the Broadway cars.

The name of our booklet is "The Better Advertising." Shall we send it?

Calkins & Holden

ST. JAMES BUILDING NEW YORK

44 | Advertisement for Calkins & Holden, 1902. From *Profitable Advertising*, July 1902, 98. CL.

45 | Walter Fawcett, *Calkins & Holden: The Better Advertising*, 1902. Reprinted in Ernest Elmo Calkins, *"And Hearing Not"—Annals of an Adman* (New York: Charles Scribner's Sons, 1946), 206.

Holden had two qualities that endeared him to Calkins. He had a pure, stentorian voice, which meant that Calkins, despite his ever-worsening deafness, could readily understand him, even have fluent discussions with him, which the two men did at length. Holden also revealed an intuitive understanding of the advertising business: he agreed with Calkins that advertisements needed to exhibit far greater visual sophistication.

Holden had started working at the agency after Calkins; he, too, soon became disillusioned with Bates. He was critical of Bates's poor managerial skills, but, even more, he resented Bates's stinginess in paying his employees. He began trying to convince Calkins that they could do better on their own.

In 1902, with two thousand dollars the two men managed to borrow (half of it from one of Calkins's banker friends), they launched Calkins & Holden Advertising (fig. 44). They rented an office in the St. James Building, in the Flatiron District. Their assigned telephone number was Columbus 1492. The first ad they produced for their new firm was fittingly titled "Discovered."[6]

From the outset, the two partners agreed to divide the responsibilities. Holden was to meet with prospective clients and oversee the day-to-day running of the business; Calkins would manage the creative side of the firm, framing the advertising campaigns and supervising every aspect of the production of the ads.

Calkins immediately set about assembling a staff for the art department, which he was now convinced should be at the center of the new firm's operation. His first hires were Walter Fawcett, a skilled renderer and caricaturist, and Earl Horter, a young painter and illustrator still attending art school at night.[7]

Fawcett came up with the agency's distinctive logo, which combined the letters *C* and *H*. He designed most of the company's early advertisements, and he was also likely responsible for the Art Nouveau–inflected brochure the company put out in 1904 (figs. 45, 46). Very much more, though, he had a lead part in the firm's first large campaign, for Hornby's Oats Company of Buffalo, New York.

Hornby's had started as a purveyor of horse feed, later branching out to breakfast cereals under the H-O brand. Fawcett and Calkins, looking for a way to attract attention for the new product, devised an ad featuring a whimsical hippopotamus (fig. 47).[8] The animal had nothing to do with the cereal: it was a piece of a children's puzzle contest, the Kinderbeasts, which grew to a set of ten animals "dissected into squares, disks, triangles, and oblongs," as Calkins later recalled. "These were put one in each package, and prizes of watches were offered for sets of ten correctly put to-

gether." Since the hippopotamus was put into only a small number of packages, the odds of winning were sharply reduced. But just as Calkins had calculated, the game served to increase sales and interest.[9]

All the animals depicted in the ads were eye-catching. Fawcett's playful renderings set them apart from most of what was then being inserted into newspapers and magazines. They had true visual power. But Calkins was convinced that the advertisements could and should do more. For another of Hornby's products, a flaked breakfast cereal called Force, he created a fictious character, Sunny Jim, to serve as the brand "personality." Sunny Jim, the ads explained, began as the moody and friendless Jim Dumps. After being introduced to Force, he was transformed into a jolly and beloved fellow.[10] Fawcett fashioned a bespectacled cartoon figure in a waistcoat and top hat to personify the character (fig. 48).[11] The campaign immediately made Force a leading national brand—fulfilling precisely Calkins's view that visuals could make a difference.

Calkins soon had the opportunity to expand on the idea of a representative character in another of the agency's early campaigns, for the Lackawanna Railroad. To power its locomotives, Lackawanna used hard, anthracite coal, which burned

46 | Walter Fawcett [attrib.], cover of *The CH Book*, 1904. Brochure, printed by Barnes Crosby Company, Chicago, IL, for Calkins & Holden Advertising, New York, NY. Lithograph on paper, 15.9 × 11.7 cm. CL.

47 | Walter Fawcett, *H-O*, advertisement, for Hornby's Oats Company, Buffalo, NY, 1902. Reprinted in Ernest Elmo Calkins, *"And Hearing Not"—Annals of an Adman* (New York: Charles Scribner's Sons, 1946), 220.

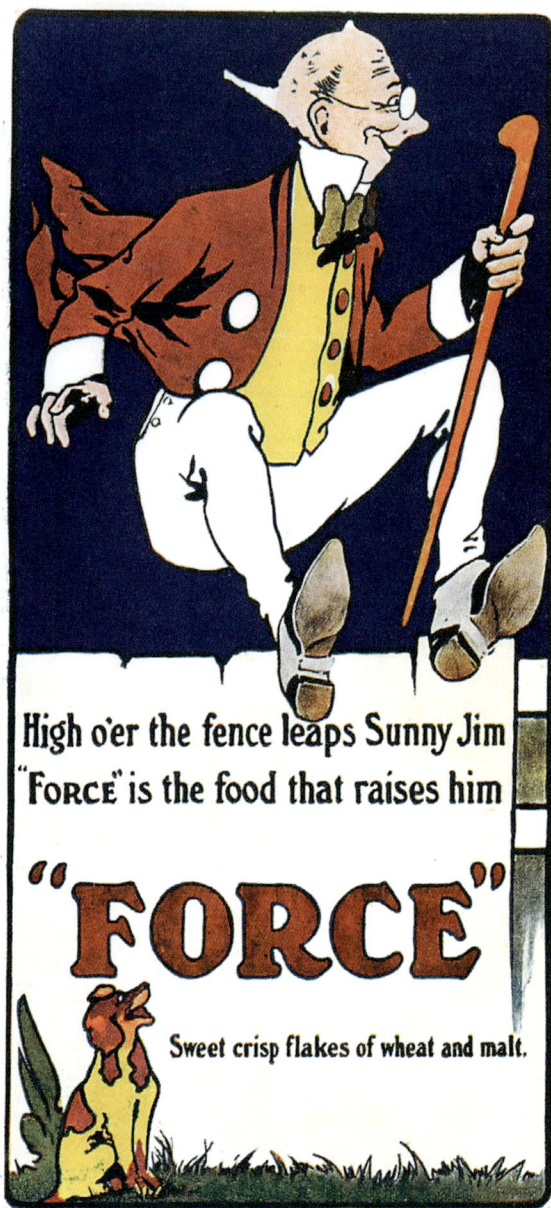

48 | Walter Fawcett, *Force*, 1904. Postcard advertisement for Force Food Company, Buffalo, NY. Lithograph on cardstock, 12.7 × 7.6 cm. CL.

much cleaner and thus produced far less ash than the soft coals employed by the other railroads. The company had successfully based its previous advertisements on cleanliness; Calkins saw no reason to change that. Teaming with the new advertising manager at the railroad (the same man Calkins had previously worked with at Hornby's Oats), he introduced the concept of a young woman, dressed all in white, who traveled on the Lackawanna Railroad expressly *because* of its cleanliness.

Calkins called the character Phoebe Snow. (One observer at the time described her as "that immaculate impossible lass."[12]) With the firm's junior copywriters, he produced a series of short poems—eventually there would be more than sixty—in a "jigging meter" that "was supposed to suggest the song of the rushing train."[13] The first one went:

> Said Phoebe Snow,
> About to go
> Upon a trip to Buffalo:
> "My gown keeps white
> Both day and night
> Upon the Road of Anthracite.

Calkins had artist Harry Stacey Benton devise an image of an attractive young woman. The agency hired Marian Murray Gorsch, a "well-known artist's model, who had posed for a great deal for advertising" to play the part.[14] She was photographed at various venues along the Lackawanna line seated in the train cars, on the platforms, climbing down from the train, and in the cab of the locomotive. These photos were then rendered by Benton and printed on card stock. The identical Phoebe Snow character was repeated in each of the subsequent ads, many in the form of streetcar placards, which were mounted inside the cars, just above the windows on either side (fig. 49). These were regularly changed out with new ones, so that the public could follow Phoebe Snow's continuing adventures.[15]

The campaign ran until 1917, and it was a huge success. The eye-catching depictions and catchy jingles made Phoebe Snow and her travels (she even found romance along the way) highly memorable: even decades later, older people in Buffalo and other cities along the line could recite some of the verses.[16] With this campaign, only their second major one, Calkins & Holden effectively invented the idea of branding using a fictitious character. (At least in the American context; a few others, like the Michelin man in France, had come earlier.) It was a concept that would influence very much of twentieth-century advertising, from the Planter Company's Mr. Peanut to the unfortunate, caricatured Aunt Jemima.

Calkins & Holden was hardly the only American advertising firm to promote the concept of branding. In 1899, N. W. Ayer launched the first multimillion-dollar campaign for the mainstay product of the new National Biscuit Company. Uneeda Biscuit was introduced to the public with the slogan "Lest you forget, we say it yet, Uneeda Biscuit." Even earlier, in the mid-1890s, Claude Hopkins, one of the pioneers of new

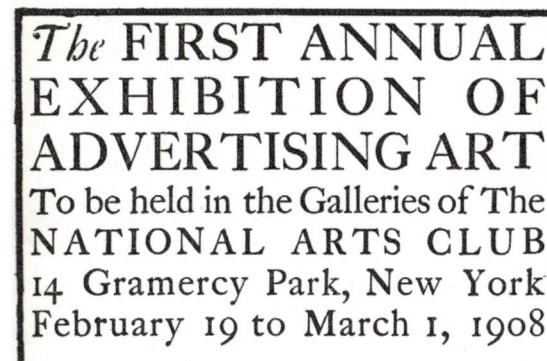

advertising in the Midwest, had put together a three-year-long campaign for Pabst Brewing that featured, among others, a scene from medieval Germany with the slogan "Milwaukee Beer is Famous, Pabst Has Made It So" (fig. 50). (This later morphed into the more familiar slogan, "The Beer that Made Milwaukee Famous.")

The striking images for the Pabst ads were made by the Chicago firm of Binner Engraving. Founded by Oscar Binner, the company was one of the country's largest such firms, with a complete staff of printers and artists. They had made some of the first posters for Ault & Wiborg (before Will H. Bradley began working for them), and Binner's own publicity materials represented its work as "modern advertising," due to their use of the most up-to-date printing techniques.

That was true as well in the stylistic sense: Binner's German medieval layout for Pabst borrowed directly from contemporary English Arts and Crafts graphic design, especially from William Morris's Kelmscott books. The Pabst ads, with their bold, forceful appearance, stood out from the cluttered and badly designed layouts that covered most magazine pages in those years. And they came off well, even when poorly reproduced on newsprint.

To celebrate the progress that had been made in advertising art, Calkins organized an exhibition, in 1908, at the National Arts Club in New York City (fig. 51). His idea for the show, which ran from February 19 to March 1, was "to segregate what was really good, so that it could be seen by itself." It would, he wrote, demonstrate "that not only is the standard of art in advertising high, but that this work bears the names of many men already famous in other lines of work."[17]

The results, as it turned out, were decidedly mixed. Though he was hesitant to say so publicly, Calkins confessed in private that a good number of the submissions were underwhelming. The most accomplished entries were for cover art for magazines and thus not advertising in the strictest sense, while nearly all the ads fell well below the standard he had hoped to set.[18]

49 | Harry Stacey Benton, *Says Phoebe Snow ...*, 1903. Advertising placard for the Lackawanna Railroad. Lithograph on cardstock, 27.9 × 42.2 cm. Private collection.

50 | Herman C. Lammers, *Nerves? Pabst Malt Extract*, 1896. Magazine advertisement, printed by the Binner Engraving Company, Chicago, for the Pabst Brewing Company, Milwaukee, WI. Offset lithograph on paper, 25.4 × 18.8 cm. CL.

51 | *The First Annual Exhibition of Advertising Art*, 1908. Newspaper advertisement, reprinted in Ernest Elmo Calkins, *"And Hearing Not"—Annals of an Adman* (New York: Charles Scribner's Sons, 1946), 171.

52| *Drink Coca-Cola 5¢*, ca. 1899. Poster. Lithograph on paper. Prints and Photographs Division, Library of Congress, Washington, D.C.

———

53| *Hot—Tired—Thirsty? Coca-Cola*, 1910. Magazine advertisement for the Coca-Cola Co., Atlanta, GA, from *Woman's Home Companion*, May 1910, 72. Lithograph on paper, 32.2 × 21.1 cm. CL.

Calkins, however, was unwilling to admit defeat. He organized two more exhibitions at the National Arts Club, in 1909 and 1910. The results, despite Calkins's considerable efforts behind the scenes, were equally dismal: neither attracted much in the way of press coverage, and the few reviews that did appear were mostly negative.[19] Calkins slowly came to realize that the only way to alter the situation was to solicit the country's top illustrators to work with him. He was now more convinced than ever that business held great opportunities for artists—that, in time, the top artists would work for advertisers, and the ads would become a leading forum for the definition and display of great art.

As it would happen, the first breakthrough came not from one of the established advertising agencies, but from a small upstart company working for the Atlanta-based Coca-Cola Company. Coca-Cola was a comparative latecomer to print advertising; it was not until 1904 that its first ads began appearing in national publications.[20] Before that time, the company had relied on posters and in-store giveaways, such as trays and glasses, to establish its presence in the marketplace. (The iconic contoured bottle would not appear until 1915.[21])

The images on the original Coca-Cola posters and trays were predictable: a glass of the beverage in a posh setting or in the hand of a figure—invariably an attractive young woman—accompanied by a terse slogan, most often "Drink Coca-Cola." The company's name was always spelled out in its now familiar cursive script. Beginning in 1895, Coca-Cola tried a new approach. The company hired a young music hall singer and actress named Hilda Clark to be its "face." Clark, shown sporting elaborate dresses and hats, was supposed to project the very picture of wholesomeness and turn-of-the-century chic (fig. 52). Her image, printed with high-quality multicolor lithographic processes on paper and tin, was nearly everywhere, and it would remain so until 1904, the year after she married, and Coca-Cola canceled her contract.

Asa Candler, the company's president, and his nephew, Samuel Candler Dodds, who headed the marketing department, then changed course, hiring the local Atlanta Massengale Advertising Agency to craft a print campaign. Candler and Dodd's decision to switch to print advertising was in large measure a response to the adoption of four-color printing by the major national magazines, which made the advertisements far more visually appealing than the previous black-and-white ones. Many other national companies had either preceded them or followed suit.

What was surprising was their decision to engage the Massengale Agency. Almost all national campaigns in this period were being handled by one of the top five firms: N. W. Ayer & Son, in Philadelphia; J. Walter Thompson, Charles Alan Bates, or Calkins & Holden, in New York; or Lord & Thomas, in Chicago. St. Elmo Massengale was barely twenty years-old when he founded the Massengale Agency, the South's first major ad company; and he was still in his twenties when Candler and Dodd turned to him to run their print campaign.[22] It turned out to be a shrewd decision. Massengale was a true innovator, and he would soon become a force in the advertising industry. (Later, he would be instrumental in the establishment of the

Hot--Tired--Thirsty?

Want to taste a delicious beverage?
Every arrow of any size, kind or color
points to

Coca-Cola

TRADE MARK
REGISTERED

It is cooling, refreshing, thirst-quenching. Touches
the palate with a vim and vigor of deliciousness.
So *whenever*, wherever or however you see
an arrow, think of Coca-Cola.

5c
Everywhere

54 | *Thirst Content, Drink Coca-Cola*, 1911. Magazine advertisement for the Coca-Cola Co., Atlanta, GA. Offset print on paper, 26.3 × 36.9 cm. CL.

American Association of Advertising Agencies, and he worked tirelessly to institute a code of ethics for the field.)

Before he was hired by Candler and Dobbs, Massengale had assembled an extensive library of publications and rate tables. He knew precisely how to secure the best placements in the national publications.[23] With his guidance, the new Coca-Cola advertisements were soon ubiquitous; by 1911, the company's annual advertising budget had soared to more than $1 million. The ads also exhibited a notable degree of refinement, and that had everything to do with Massengale and Dodds.

Dodds had been with Coca-Cola from the outset. At age eighteen, he started with A. G. Candler & Company, then a wholesaler of drugs; a year later, Asa Candler bought the rights to Coca-Cola, transforming the business into a beverage maker and distributor. Dobbs became the company's first traveling salesman, and in a few years, with unstinting energy and an abundant stock of cleverness, he worked his way up to become Vice President and Manager of Sales and Advertising.[24]

Up to the time when Candler and Dodds launched the print campaign, Coca-Cola was still sold exclusively at soda counters and pitched as a drink for the affluent. Dodds wanted to target the country's rapidly expanding middle class. He focused on magazines such as *Collier's*, *The Saturday Evening Post*, and the *Christian Advocate*.[25] To attract attention, he hit on a simple but effective strategy: the advertisements would feature an arrow or arrows pointing to the product. He coined a slogan to go with it: "Whenever you see an arrow, think of Coca-Cola."[26]

One early print ad, from 1910, featured a large red circle with the distinctive script Coca-Cola logo set inside; outside are four arrows pointing insistently toward it, exhorting one to buy the product (fig. 53). It is remarkable not only for its direct messaging but also for its prescience: it had reached a degree of abstraction and distillation that would rarely be seen again for decades.

The Coca-Cola arrow (after this time, there was generally only one) appeared in the company's ads for several more years, looping around the text and images and pointing at a glass with the company's logo (fig. 54). Increasingly, though, Coca-Cola's print advertising turned on the idea of projecting a "lifestyle." In the period from 1912 to 1917, many of its ads featured young, attractive women, seen outdoors leisurely sipping the beverage from one of the company's trademark glasses (figs. 55, 56). What was implied—unmistakably—was that Coca-Cola should be an intrinsic part of any summertime or outdoor idyll, that it was "Refreshing" (a word that appears very often in the copy) and therefore "Supremely Satisfying."

What is especially smart about the designs is the way in which the artist or artists—Coca-Cola in this period never "signed" its ads with a creator's name—appropriated the language made popular by Penfield and others during the poster craze, then reduced it even further. The viewer is left mostly with the figures alone and their evident sense of enjoyment.

The Coca-Cola ads after 1910 also evince a greater flatness than had been the case in the 1890s. The company's earliest print ads still relied to some degree on traditional perspective; within a decade, this had given way to a very modern handling of those depicted and their surroundings. It was a subtle but direct form of messaging

55 | *Supremely Satisfying, Coca-Cola*, 1914. Magazine advertisement for the Coca-Cola Co., Atlanta, GA. Halftone print on paper, 20.4 × 14 cm. CL.

56 | *Athletic? Drink Coca-Cola*, 1914. Magazine advertisement for the Coca-Cola Co., Atlanta, GA, from *Women's World*, May 1914, inside front cover. Halftone print on paper, image: 30.4 × 21.6 cm. CL.

Five wonderful pieces of concentrated goodness wrapped dustproof in a roll

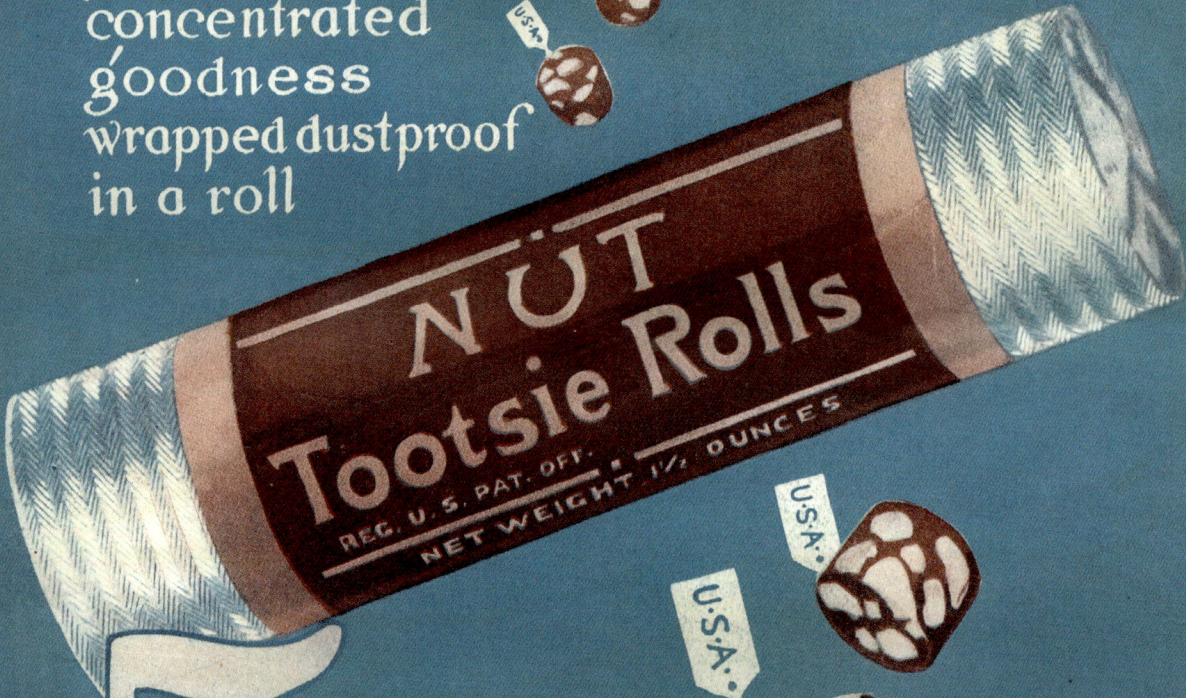

NUT Tootsie Rolls
REG. U. S. PAT. OFF.
NET WEIGHT 1½ OUNCES

5¢

about modernity and cleanliness, a particularly important concept when many foods were adulterated.

Other companies were quick to adopt this form of messaging, including Nut Tootsie Rolls, originally a form of chocolate taffy invented in 1907 by Austrian-born immigrant Leo Hirschfield. Hirschfield named the product after his daughter Clara, nicknamed Tootsie. It was the first individually wrapped candy for sale in the United States.[27] A wonderfully conceived 1914 advertisement conveys this perfectly, showing a "Vacation Special" biplane bombarding the beach with little candies issuing from their "dustproof roll" (fig. 57).

The Nut Tootsie Roll advertisement came perhaps closest to what Calkins was aspiring to when he had set out his first campaigns—advertising art that was eye-catching, whimsical, and lucid in its messaging, but also accomplished and up to date in artistic terms. In the first decade of the century, some of those who had first come to prominence during the art poster craze, including Penfield and Parrish, continued working for the leading magazines. A few even made advertisements, such as Penfield's drawing for Kodak around 1905 (fig. 58). But these connections between the artists and the world of the big advertising agencies were tenuous. Most of the illustrators (the term by this time had come to distinguish them from "fine artists") were reluctant to make the full turn to advertising work because of the taint associated with commercial art. The best illustrators were willing to produce covers for the national magazines (which held a certain prestige), or even illustrate the stories inside, but advertising, other than posters, was still too closely wedded in the minds of most with crass commercialism (fig. 59).[28]

In the early years of the century, a new generation of illustrators came to the fore. Its leaders were Howard Pyle, Charles Dana Gibson, James Montgomery Flagg, and N. C. Wyeth. Pyle was so much in demand and so respected that he had little need to stoop to advertising work. In 1906, *McClure's* offered him $36,000 a year to become the magazine's art director. (Pyle agreed to work half-time for $18,000 but found that he was ill-suited for the job.)

Gibson similarly was far too successful to have to turn to advertising: his idealized Gibson Girls and virtuoso pen-and-ink drawings of the Gilded Age *nouveaux riches* provided him a very comfortable living—without having to toil for the ad agencies. Flagg made many covers for the magazines and countless illustrations for books, but he accepted advertising commissions hesitantly. In 1915, Calkins & Holden commissioned him to create advertising art for Edison Photo and Adler Rochester Overcoats. He accepted, though only on the condition that his name would not be associated with the campaigns.[29] Even N. C. Wyeth, who was younger than the others (he had been a student of Howard Pyle), only rarely took up offers from advertisers. One of the few exceptions came in 1906, shortly after he married and was still finding his way. He made an advertisement for Cream of Wheat (fig. 60).[30]

The imagery was typical Wyeth: a rugged individualist, a cowboy, a standard figure of his early work, delivering Cream of Wheat to a distant ranch. It was "plain spoken" in the way that most of American illustration was. The legend at the bottom tells the full story: "Wherever the Mail Goes Cream of Wheat Goes." At a time when

57 | *Vacation Special*, 1914. Advertisement for Nut Tootsie Rolls, the Sweets Company of the America, Inc., New York. Halftone print on paper, 31.2 × 23.9 cm. CL.

---

58 | Edward Penfield, *A Kodak Christmas*, ca. 1905. Poster for the Eastman Kodak Company, Rochester, NY. Lithograph on paper, 36.2 × 22.8 cm. Private collection.

NO. 2640   APRIL 12, 1906   PRICE 10 CENTS

LESLIE'S WEEKLY

JAMES MONTGOMERY FLAGG

EASTER

Painted by N. C. Wyeth for Cream of Wheat Company.   Copyright, 1907, by Cream of Wheat Company.

WHERE THE MAIL GOES, CREAM OF WHEAT GOES.

59| James Montgomery Flagg, cover of *Leslie's Weekly*, April 12, 1906. Halftone print on paper, 39 × 26.7 cm. CL.

60| N. C. (Newell Convers) Wyeth, *Where The Mail Goes Cream of Wheat Goes*, 1908. Magazine advertisement, from *The Youth's Companion*, August 27, 1908, Ill. Halftone print on paper, 35.5 × 24 cm. CL.

———

61| Power (Michael Augustine) O'Malley, cover of *Harper's Weekly*, January 18, 1913. Halftone print on paper, 36.4 × 24.2 cm. CL

rural postal delivery was at last bringing the promise of a connection to the outside world to even the most isolated homesteads, this statement held real power and appeal.

No doubt advertisers would have wanted more ads from Wyeth or any of the other prominent illustrators, for that matter. But the artists collectively held their distance. For most, even the notion of illustration itself—painting for purely commercial purposes—was problematic. Wyeth, even though his work as an illustrator made him quite well-to-do, later bemoaned his "accursed success in skin-deep pictures and illustrations," and he complained bitterly of having to sell himself to those "who want to buy me piecemeal."[31]

Even those illustrators who were less renowned showed a reluctance to cross what seemed to be the very wide divide from magazine covers to ads. Irish-born Power O'Malley (originally Michael Augustine Power), who in 1913 produced one of *Harper's Weekly*'s most affecting covers—an image of an enormous bird of prey glowering at an oncoming biplane, a remarkable statement of the changing times—showed no interest in advertising and instead spent much of his time and energy on traditional easel painting (fig. 61).

Calkins, observing the scene with his usual acute sense of what was to come, knew instinctively what he had to do. Even before he mounted the inaugural advertising art exhibition, he had decided that he would approach the illustrators himself and persuade them to work with him. The timing was ideal, at least from Calkin's point of view. In August 1907, the Calkins & Holden advertising agency launched its most ambitious campaign to date, a national magazine series for the Pierce-Arrow Motor Car Company. Calkins sought out many of those in the top echelon of illustrators to work on the ads.[32]

Pierce-Arrow, based in Buffalo, New York, was a luxury brand, manufacturing expensive automobiles for the upscale market. Its six-cylinder cars became status symbols for the country's elite, from the toniest East Coast tycoons to Hollywood's new starlets. Calkins set about to craft a set of special advertisements intended to elevate and promote the Pierce-Arrow line.

A few years before, in 1905, one of the company's cars had won the prestigious Glidden Tour, an endurance contest to discover and celebrate the most reliable car on the market. Calkins was determined, though, not to sell the cars based on their engineering quality, but rather as status symbols. He also wanted to change completely how the ads looked. At a time when most automobile advertisements relied on text to describe the technical virtues of their products, Calkins took the opposite approach: the Pierce-Arrow ads would have almost no text, aside from the name of the company and, in a few instances, a brief title. Instead, each layout, created by the crème of national illustrators, would offer a scene in which the cars and their occupants would be shown in specific situations.

One of the early ads, from 1909, was painted by J. C. Leyendecker, soon to become one of the country's most recognized artists. A couple, in elegant evening dress, is emerging from a building—perhaps a theater or an upscale restaurant (fig. 62). Waiting, in the foreground, is the chauffeur, who is seated at the wheel of a Pierce-Arrow

THE PIERCE-ARROW MOTOR CAR COMPANY, BUFFALO, NEW YORK. (Licensed Under Selden Patent)
Members Association Licensed Automobile Manufacturers

62 | J. C. (Joseph Christian) Leyendecker, *The Pierce Arrow*, 1909. Magazine advertisement for Pierce-Arrow Motor Car Company, Buffalo, NY, 1909, from *Life*, August 12, 1909, n.p. Halftone print on paper, image: 25.2 × 20.4 cm. CL.

63 | Edward Penfield, *The Pierce Arrow*, 1910. Magazine advertisement for Pierce-Arrow Motor Car Company, Buffalo, NY. Halftone print on paper, 24.7 × 20.3 cm. CL.

car. The title identifies the car brand, and everything in the picture speaks of wealth, luxury, and quality. It is a statement about those who own Pierce-Arrow Motor Cars; it is also aspirational for those who might someday be able to afford one.

Another of the ads, from 1910, was the work of Penfield. An impeccably dressed woman has just climbed out of her car. As she walks away, she is closing her purse, presumably having just tipped the doorman, who is standing next to the car (fig. 63). Condensed into the briefest of moments, like a snapshot, is the explicit imagery of genteel life.

Louis Fancher's advertisement of 1911 is titled *At the Horse Show* (fig. 64). It, too, bespeaks the domain of America's upper crust. Everyone is in crisply tailored dress, and nothing, not even the tiniest blade of grass, is amiss. Adolph Treidler's ad of 1913 features perhaps the most exclusive setting of all: it is placed before what is very recognizably the White House (fig. 65). A woman carrying her dog walks toward the

viewer; a Pierce-Arrow car is driving past her, having just picked up passengers; others in the background appear to be waiting for the next car.

That none of these advertisements has explanatory text—or even some direct call to buy—underscores the novelty of Calkins's approach. Pictorially, each layout is resolutely modern—modern through reduction and simplification, but also modern because what we see are "up-to-the-minute" people going about their daily business, even if that business is very far from the reality of most Americans. They are, much like Penfield's early posters, examples of the soft sell, of marketing through emotional response. Calkins would have much to do with formulating and propagating the idea, and, even more than Penfield, it was he (and his staff artists at Calkins & Holden) who would work out how to apply it to mass advertising campaigns.

The Pierce-Arrow ads appeared mostly on the back or inside covers of leading weekly or monthly magazines. This not only ensured that the largest number of

64| Louis Fancher, *At the Horse Show*, 1911. Magazine advertisement for Pierce-Arrow Motor Car Company, Buffalo, NY. Halftone print on paper, 27.3 × 22.1 cm (trimmed). CL.

65| Adolph Treidler, *The Pierce Arrow*, 1913. Magazine advertisement for Pierce-Arrow Motor Car Company, Buffalo, NY, from *Life*, September 30, 1909, inside front cover. Halftone print on paper, 25.6 × 20.1 cm. CL.

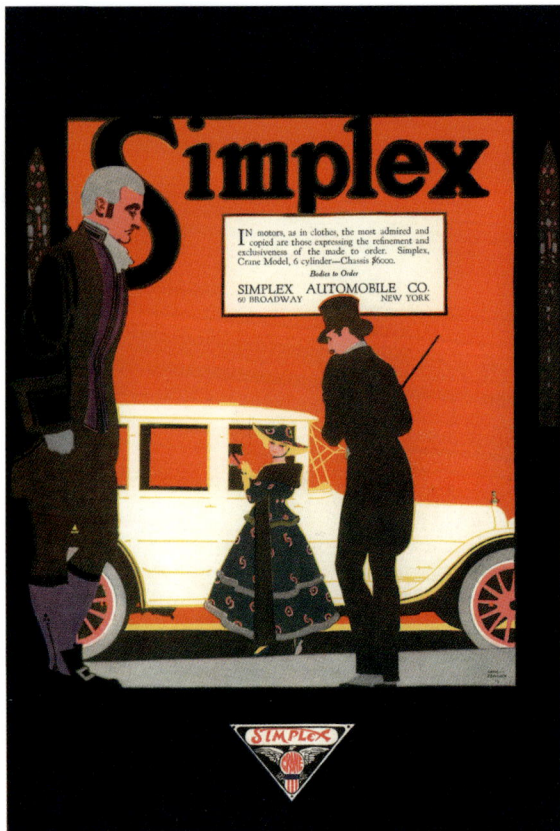

66 | Louis Fancher, *Simplex*, 1916. Magazine advertisement for the Simplex Automobile Company, New York, NY, from *Country Life in America*, December 1916, 83. Halftone print on paper, image: 31.1 × 21 cm. CL.

67 | *Remy*, 1916. Advertisement for Remy Electric Co., Detroit, MI. Halftone print on paper, image: 25.5 × 17.9 cm. CL.

_____

68 | Coles Phillips, *Overland $615: O.K.'d by the Nation*, 1915. Magazine advertisement for the Willys-Overland Company, Toledo, OH. Halftone print on paper, 55.9 × 40.6 cm. CL.

people would see them, but it also meant that they would be printed in the best color and on the best paper. In that way, the ads mimicked the art posters of the 1890s. Calkins had now grasped the lessons of the art poster movement. In an essay from 1900, he claimed that "Any business idea can be presented in that simple, quick-acting, flat form which is called the poster style."[33] This would remain his mantra for the next decade and a half.

Other early car brands followed suit. The Simplex Car Company, based in New York City, and Remy, an electric car company headquartered in Detroit, published similar advertisements, borrowing directly from the Pierce-Arrow look (figs. 66, 67). The Willys-Overland Company in Toledo, Ohio, however, adopted a distinctive approach, hiring Coles Phillips, who was known for his stylish images of women and his reliance on negative space (the emptying out of space around or between subjects in an image), to make paintings of women driving alone (fig. 68). The designs were intended to appeal to young women, who were just beginning to get behind the

A Book
about Colorado
for 6 cents.

A COUNTRY anywhere from 6,000 to 15,000 feet above sea level, where the air is light and dry and easy to breathe—that is why so many persons in ill health go there. A country more delightful than Switzerland in scenic attractions, an ideal place to rest, with a number of golf courses, plenty of the best trout fishing, and with large and small game in abundance. A country filled with really good hotels, boarding-houses and ranch houses, where you can live and enjoy life for very little money.

That is what Colorado is. It is not an expensive place to visit, indeed there are few places where you can get so much for so little, and it only takes two nights on the road to get there from the Atlantic Coast, only one night from Chicago or St. Louis.

Our book on Colorado tells all about the country in an interesting way. It is full of illustrations and maps. It will tell you all about Colorado. The price is six cents in postage stamps. Will you not send to me for a copy and read it carefully to find out whether that is not just the place for you to go next summer to spend your vacation?

P. S. EUSTIS, Passenger Traffic Manager, C. B. @ Q. Ry., CHICAGO

MAZDA

"Not the name of a thing, but the mark of a service"

As the turbines draw from Niagara the energy that sets the motors whirling—so MAZDA Service draws from the flood of new thoughts in lighting, the ideas that help the lamp-makers make better lamps.

— The Meaning of MAZDA —

MAZDA is the trademark of a world-wide service to certain lamp manufacturers. Its purpose is to collect and select scientific and practical information concerning progress and developments in the art of incandescent lamp manufacturing and to distribute this information to the companies entitled to receive this Service. MAZDA Service is centered in the Research Laboratories of the General Electric Company at Schenectady, New York. The mark MAZDA can appear only on lamps which meet the standards of MAZDA Service. It is thus an assurance of quality. This trademark is the property of the General Electric Company.

RESEARCH LABORATORIES OF THE GENERAL ELECTRIC COMPANY

wheel, to evoke a broad impression of leisure, independence, and modernity. In that sense, they are closely related to Bradley's young woman on a bicycle, who was seeking her own form of liberation.

Calkins & Holden's Pierce-Arrow advertisements—and those of their imitators—were visually predicated on scenes in which the product, the automobile, was present, but not exactly placed at the center of the scene. The title, the name of the car, always in bold print, made it clear what was being sold; but the eyes of most people, looking at the pages would not necessarily first land on the automobile itself. The great majority, if not nearly all, of nineteenth-century American advertising layouts had functioned in the opposite way, foregrounding the objects (or sometimes services) to be sold, with an accompanying explanatory text. In the decade before the outbreak of World War I, one of the main innovations in advertising art—and hence, what would soon become fully "graphic design"—was a refinement of this idea. In essence, it was a refocusing on the object for sale (or at times, the text alone) in a way that was meant to catch the eye—and the mind.

The first stage of this development is evident in an advertising layout for the Burlington Railroad from 1903 (fig. 69). It features a large white circle on a black background, with boldface text at its center promoting a booklet about Colorado, one of the states the railroad served. It was related to the travel posters of the era, enticing people to travel via train or ship to some far-off destination. Yet rather than an alluring view of the place, it was an offering of a more in-depth, printed advertising booklet. It employed very plain language and typography: "A Book about Colorado for 6 cents," in a manner that was so direct that it is difficult *not* to read it.

This strategy of visual "capture" was the guiding idea behind another very advanced advertisement of the period, for the General Electric Company's Mazda light bulbs (fig. 70). Here, a bit of simple geometry—a large square—frames the main body of the text. The viewer's eyes are instead drawn to the lightbulb itself—flattened and reduced—and the main heading, the name of the product, set in bold type.

The notion of using a highly pared-down rendering of the object for sale first made its appearance in Germany, in the form of the *Sachplakat* (literally, object poster). The idea came from Lucian Bernhard around 1904. Ludwig Hohlwein and others, borrowing from the simplified Jugendstil language that had been developed in Munich starting in the early 1890s (and which, in turn, had been stimulated by the French and Belgian Art Nouveau), soon followed Bernhard's lead. The consummate example is Bernhard's 1908 poster for the Stiller shoe company: it shows only a shoe, and the name Stiller in blue, all set on a yellow background. It would be some time before most American designers would widely adopt this idea, in great measure because the leading advertising firms were still wedded to "copy" and would be for decades. In the years prior to the American entry into World War I, however, a small number of them would at least make a push in the direction of a new simplicity.

For the Washburn-Crosby Company, the makers of Gold Medal Flour, an unknown designer fashioned an advertisement that has many of the components of the Sachplakat: a foregrounded object, isolated and depicted very simply, with limited

A WOMAN'S ANSWER

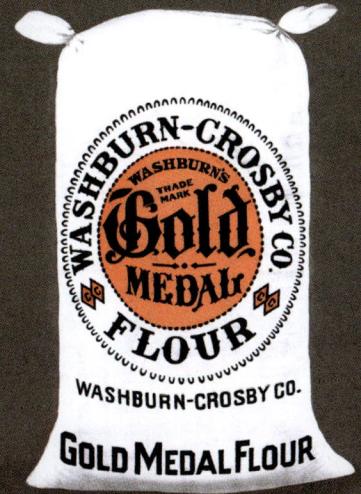

Every Day–The Grocers Say

photo quality very low resolution

Eventually

WASHBURN-CROSBY'S

GOLD MEDAL FLOUR

Why Not Now?

69| *A Book about Colorado for 6 cents*, 1903. Magazine advertisement for the Burlington Railroad, Chicago, IL, from *The World's Work*, March 1903, n.p. Letterpress on paper, 20. 8 × 14 cm. CL.

70| *Mazda "Not the name of a thing, but the mark of a service,"* 1916. Magazine advertisement for the General Electric Company, Schenectady, NY, from National Geographic Magazine, November 1916, n.p. Halftone print on paper, 25.5 × 16.7 cm. CL.

71| *A Woman's Answer Every Day–The Grocers Say*, 1910. Magazine advertisement for Washburn-Crosby Co., Minneapolis, MN. Halftone print on paper, 32.2 × 25.3 cm. CL.

72| *Eventually Why Now Now?*, ca. 1915. Advertising card for Washburn-Crosby's Gold Medal Flour. Offset lithograph on cardstock, 15.9 × 9 cm. CL.

text (fig. 71). It still featured more text than the Germans were inserting, and it was still reliant on what was swiftly becoming the outmoded practice of using rhyme. Nonetheless, the Gold Medal design represented a considerable leap forward from standard American advertising forms. A few years later, Washburn-Crosby took this idea even further, shrinking the bag of flour down to its label, and condensing the copy to a one-word slogan—"Eventually"—which is followed, in much smaller type, by the question: "Why Not Now?" (fig. 72). The near abstraction of the landscape scene at the bottom and the application of just three colors—black, grey, and yellow—was surprisingly close to what the Germans were doing.

A similar—and strikingly reduced—ad came from the Wrigley's Chewing Gum Company in Chicago (fig. 73). It depicted a single package of gum, set at an angle, against a black background, with two short texts, one set above, one below: "Fine For Breath" and "Fine For Teeth." It was an extraordinary and powerful piece, one that was fully consistent with the Sachplakat concept.

The Gold Medal and Wrigley's advertisements were the exception, however. More common in the United States in this period was the "amplification" of an object set in a conventional scene, such as the oranges in a postcard (and a matching poster) for the Orange Day festival in Santa Barbara, California (fig. 74). But there are also examples from this period of the further compression of the visual language of the earlier art poster movement. A 1915 newspaper advertisement for Mogul Cigarettes, made by German immigrant Hans Flato, represents this trend (fig. 75). Through silhouetting and the substitution of a linear background, the scene—a well-dressed man and woman seated on a bench at the beach—retains the frank messaging that had been central for the posters of the 1890s. Yet it does so in a manner that is inherently close to modernist "subtraction."

73 | *Fine for Breath. Fine for Teeth. Wrigley's Spearmint,* 1910. Magazine advertisement for Wm. Wrigley & Co., Chicago, IL. Halftone print on paper, 32.1 × 25.3 cm. CL.

74 | *Eat California Oranges,* 1915. Advertising card, printed by Star Engraving Co., Houston, for California Orange Day, 1915. Halftone print on cardstock, 13.8 × 9.1 cm. CL.

75 | Hans Flato, *Mogul Egyptian Cigarettes Just Like Being in Cairo,* 1915. Newspaper advertisement for S. Anargyros Corporation, New York, NY. Halftone on newsprint, 15.5 × 21 cm. CL.

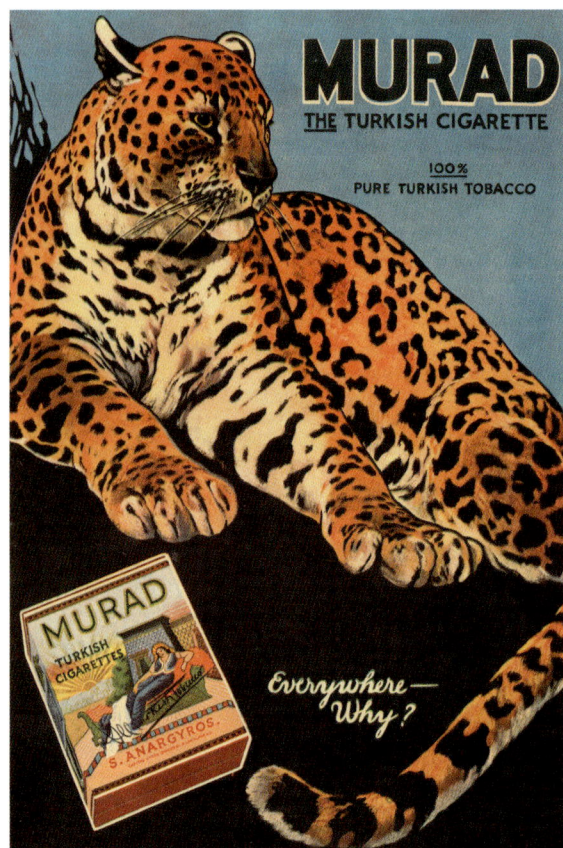

76| *Murad the Turkish Cigarette*, 1914. Advertisement for S. Anargyros Corporation, New York, NY. Halftone on paper, image: 30.4 × 20.7 cm. CL.

77| J. C. (Joseph Christian) Leyendecker, *The Century: Midsummer Holiday Number, August,* 1896. Poster. Lithograph on paper, sheet: 54.1 × 40.4 cm, image: 38.2 × 35.5 cm. Private collection.

78| J. C. (Joseph Christian) Leyendecker, *November Number: The Inland Printer, November, Now Ready,* 1896. Poster. Lithograph on paper, 31 × 27 cm. Private collection.

Other advertisements from the eve of the war achieved a related look through color blocking, the isolation of products or figures, and assertive typefaces. An advertisement for Murad Turkish Cigarettes—the same company that sold Mogul—turned on exoticism, an image of a leopard, which dominates the scene (fig. 76).[34] But it is the pictorial command the uncredited artist achieves here, realized through bold, colorful printing and insistent texts, that makes it particularly affective.

What connected these sundry approaches was their reliance on art (increasingly, of course, modern art), which is to say on the purely visual, as the primary form of communication. This was the far-reaching revolution that Calkins had promoted and sought to foster. His efforts, though, had put him in opposition to most of his contemporaries in advertising. Hopkins, for example, continued to maintain that fancy advertising images were elitist. He insisted that they ran counter to the tastes and interests of ordinary people and thus were destined to fail. "Fine art work [*sic*], like fine language," he later wrote, "merely makes buyers wary."[35]

Calkins countered that art in advertising could bring a degree of sophistication into the homes of those who had no ready access to high culture; in that way, it could "build taste" and serve as a democratizing force.[36] Still, Calkins, despite his enthusiasm for the idea of popularization, was also careful about promoting an art that would limit the size of his audience. His target—the Pierce-Arrow ads aside—remained the broad American middle class.[37] Around 1907, shortly before the first Pierce-Arrow advertisements appeared, Calkins & Holden was at work on an advertising idea that would push advertising art even further into the mainstream.

The campaign, which turned out to be protracted—extending all the way through the early 1920s—was for Cluett, Peabody & Company of Troy, New York, makers of Arrow Collars. Even more than the designs for Pierce-Arrow, the Arrow Collars ads presented an enduring set of images. But instead of a group of artists, they relied on the talents of a single illustrator: J. C. Leyendecker.

Joseph Christian Leyendecker was one of the first stars of American advertising art. He was born in 1874, in Montabaur, Germany, a drowsy little town in the Rhineland near Koblenz. In 1882, not long after he had turned eight, his family moved to Chicago. His father, a brewer by trade, took up a position at the very successful McAvoy Brewing Company, where his wife's uncle was the president.[38] Even as a young child, Leyendecker started drawing and painting obsessively. Soon after the family settled into their apartment in Hyde Park, Leyendecker remembered, he "was already covering schoolbooks with rudely colored examples of my work. At home, I kept myself busy with more pretentious paintings, which, for want of canvas, were done on oilcloth of the common kitchen variety. Whatever their faults, these pictures lacked nothing in size. They were all dutifully presented to long-suffering friends and relatives."[39]

At age eleven, Leyendecker designed a label for the McAvoy Brewing Company. Another of his mother's uncles, who was by this time running the company, turned it down. But a few years later, the same uncle asked his nephew to create labels and advertising. One of the surviving drawings offers a glimpse at his advancing skills. It is a busy affair: a shirtless worker grasping a scythe in one hand is drinking a beer; seated before him is a well-dressed woman with two nymphlike children, one of them presenting a bottle of the brew to his mother. The image is infused with more theatricality than was common, even in those years. For a young boy without training, however, it is a work of unabashed graphic dexterity. It also portended what would become Leyendecker's very pronounced facility for composing complex scenes with multiple figures.[40]

By age fifteen, Leyendecker had resolved to become an artist: "I felt I'd reached the saturation point in the oilcloth field, so I decided to find a job." He bundled up three of his large oil-cloth canvases and made his way to a local engraving firm, J. Manz & Company. "The boss inspected a stag at bay, a chariot race and a Biblical subject, with amusement, but he did tell me to report for work." Leyendecker was first hired as an unpaid errand boy; before long, however, he was put to work on one of the firm's most important projects, the *Royal Scroll*, a Bible study folio in two volumes.[41] Leyendecker produced sixty of the illustrations. It was his first commercial commission.[42]

Despite his early success, Leyendecker was determined to improve his skills. He enrolled in the School of the Art Institute of Chicago, and three evenings each week he studied drawing and anatomy with Dutch-born master draftsman John Vanderpoel. He also continued to work at J. Manz & Company, where in the meantime he had been promoted to staff illustrator.[43]

It was in this period, in the spring of 1896, that Leyendecker had his true coming out. He took part in a competition to design a cover for *The Century*'s August holiday issue. He won first prize with a "vision" of a young woman in a field of giant poppies and other flowers (fig. 77). The second prize went to another unknown artist, Maxfield Parrish.[44]

With money he managed to save from his job with Manz, Leyendecker embarked on a yearlong study trip to Paris accompanied by his younger brother Francis Xavier (who would also make his name as an illustrator). The two brothers enrolled at the Académie Julian, taking lessons with famed portraitist Jean-Joseph Benjamin-Constant and historicist painters Jules Joseph Lefebvre and Jean-Paul Laurens. Both brothers also attended the Académie Colarossi, which like the Académie Julian offered excellent technical training.

Leyendecker dutifully made the rounds of the Parisian museums and galleries, meeting, among others, Alphonse Mucha. He studied the posters of Chéret and the lithographs and paintings of Toulouse-Lautrec, and he took in what he could of the work of the Impressionists. In April 1897, he had his first exhibition at the Salon du Champs de Mars.

On the recommendation of Will H. Bradley, Leyendecker received a commission for a dozen posters and covers for *The Inland Printer* (fig. 78). The Leyendecker brothers returned to Chicago later that year and rented a studio in the Stock Exchange Building. Joe Leyendecker, as he was familiarly known, started painting covers for *Collier's*; he also made the first of the 322 covers for *The Saturday Evening Post* he would produce over the next forty-four years.

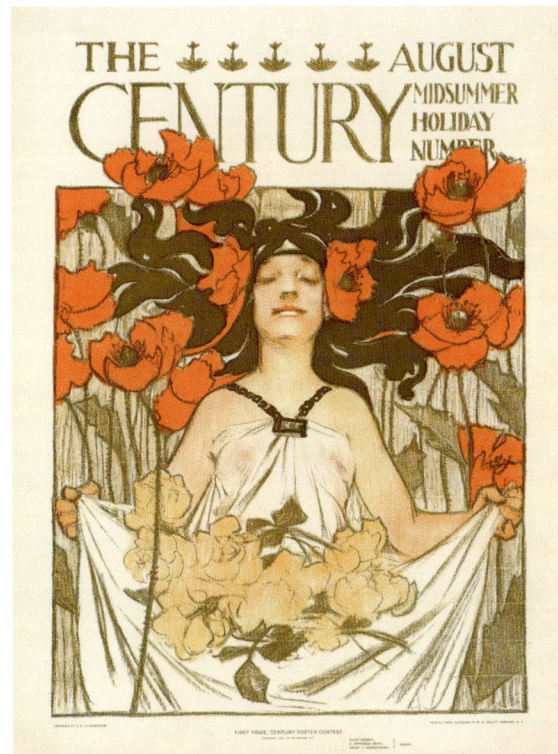

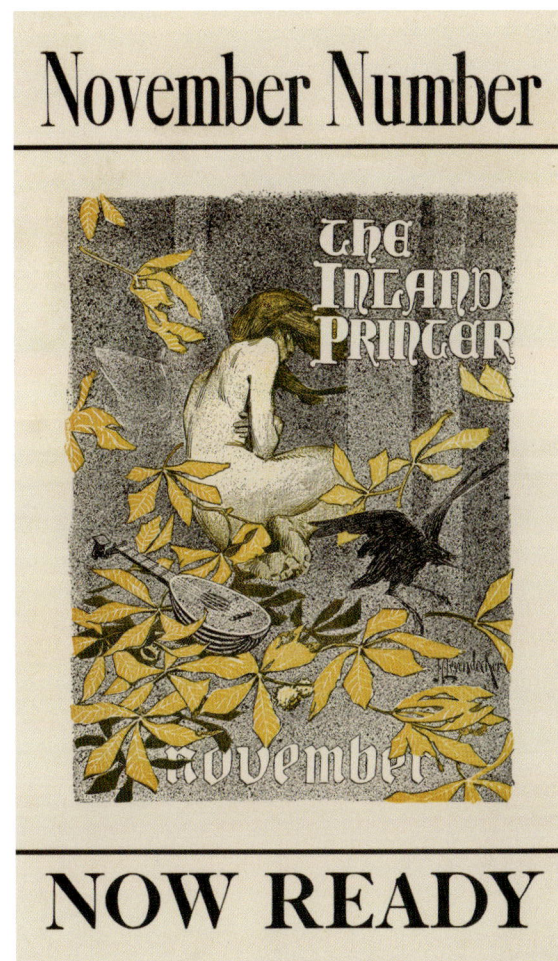

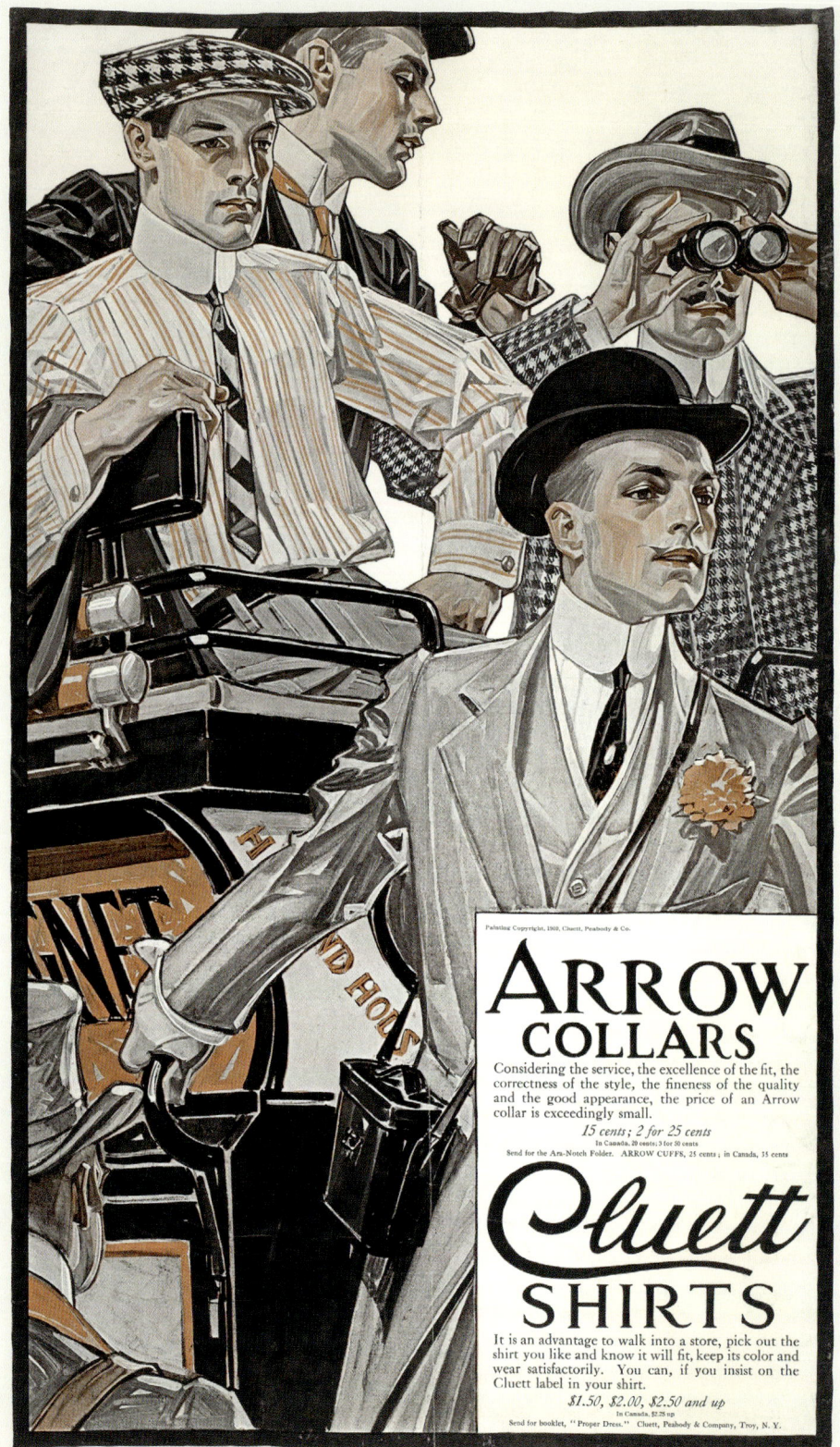

79| J. C. (Joseph Christian) Leyendecker, *Arrow Collars: Cluett Shirts*, 1910. Advertisement for Cluett, Peabody & Co., Troy, NY, from *The Saturday Evening Post*, October 8, 1910, 34–35. Halftone print on paper, 37 × 59 cm. CL.

80| J. C. (Joseph Christian) Leyendecker, *Arrow Collars and Cluett Shirts* ("At the Races"), 1911. Advertisement for Cluett, Peabody & Co., Troy, NY, from *The Saturday Evening Post*, September 30, 1911. Halftone print on paper, 37 × 59 cm. CL.

ARROW COLLARS AND CLUETT SHIRTS
are favored by men who are familiar with the trend of fashion, and
who, in their dress, impart an impression of distinguished individuality.

There is an ARROW COLLAR for every
taste, every face and every occasion. 15c each 2 for 25c

Enough of the shirt appears to show that
it is a color-fast perfectly fitting CLUETT. $1.50 and up

Send for PROPER DRESS and EVENING ATTIRE, two good books on fashion, by an authority.

CLUETT, PEABODY & COMPANY, Makers, 457 River Street, Troy, N. Y.

But the brothers' stay in Chicago was brief. In 1900, along with their sister Mary, they moved to New York City, where it was easier to secure commissions from national publishers. Leyendecker continued his magazine work, and both brothers started lucrative, long-term relationships with apparel manufacturers, including Interwoven Socks, Hartmarx, and B. Kuppenheimer & Co.[45]

Calkins probably first encountered Leyendecker around 1905 at the Players Club in Gramercy Park, one of the principal haunts of the publishing world, or nearby, at the National Arts Club. He knew immediately that Leyendecker was the artist to help realize his dream of a new advertising art.

Leyendecker was already hugely successful. A popular magazine reported in 1908 that "Leyendecker was booked 12 months in advance and charged the vast sum of $350 for one commercial illustration—what an ordinary worker then might earn in a year.[46] He was particularly celebrated for his magazine covers.[47] Not long after his move to New York, he had hit on his signature look, the formula he would employ for the rest of his career, which extended well into the 1940s. His new painting style retained elements of the academic technique he mastered in Paris, but it relied on a looser, broad-brushed application of paint, which Leyendecker put on thinly and quickly. The result is an intriguing admixture of formality and casualness. The figures come off almost as hyperreal because they appear somehow too handsome and too composed. This was notably the case for Leyendecker's male models. They were invariably clean-cut, square-jawed, and athletic, with more than a dose of a patrician mien. His favorite model was his longtime partner and lover, Charles Beach, a young man from Ontario, Canada, whom his brother had first hired as a model. Beach appears over and over in Leyendecker's illustrations, especially those for Arrow. But many other astonishingly handsome young men are also depicted in his work, a veritable gallery of the buff and the beautiful.

It is unclear whether Calkins took notice of the homoerotic quality of Leyendecker's work—a feature all too evident today. He seems to have focused instead on the power of the images to convey the ideal American male, which he and the client must have thought would make for the ideal sales vehicle. He also saw plainly, and appreciated, the brilliance of Leyendecker's painting; it was, in his mind, *real* art.

Many of Leyendecker's early ads for Arrow collars and Cluett shirts are group scenes, men (and an occasional woman) engaged in some leisure activity—in the theater, on an outing, or at the races (fig. 79). The figures are invariably unnaturally handsome, hyper-WASPy, and categorically upper crust. His 1911 advertisement *At the Races* underscores this by naming each of the characters: Glenroy, Tenby (the only woman), Dorset, Arcanum, and Margate—names so Anglo-Saxon and so privileged that they nearly come off as parody (fig. 80). The snobbishness virtually drips from the paper.

The ads, as Calkins and the managers of Cluett, Peabody & Company knew from the outset, were aspirational. They were an invitation to white-collar workers across the nation (working-class people, after all, had little need for such clothing) to rise to the same level of sophistication. Even the lowliest bank clerk could hope someday to be like Glenroy or Margate. The campaign was predicated both on escapism (since such a rapid social rise was possible but not very realistic) and driving ambition—a perfect draw in those years when industrialization and modernization were creating at least some opportunities for upward mobility.[48]

The distillation of these ideas was the Arrow Collar Man, who came to define the fashionable American male during the early decades of the twentieth century. It is uncertain who came up with the concept. It may have been Leyendecker who had brought it to Charles M. Connolly, the advertising director for Cluett, Peabody & Company. Calkins and Connolly, at any rate, immediately recognized its force as a tool for branding. The subsequent advertising campaigns they spearheaded made use of repeated images of an extremely handsome man (very often Charles Beach), portrayed with only his head, collar, and tie visible (fig. 81). The purposeful focus on the man and collar offered a flawless image of the product and of its associated meanings.[49]

With the Pierce-Arrow and Cluett, Peabody & Company advertising campaigns, Calkins had proved that art-based advertising could be a forceful instrument for selling. He had found the means to elevate the aesthetic standards of American advertising. Illustration remained a mainstay in American print ads for the next three decades. Art—popular art, that is, which is effectively all that this form of commercial illustration was—placed into ads, would slow the progress of modern graphic

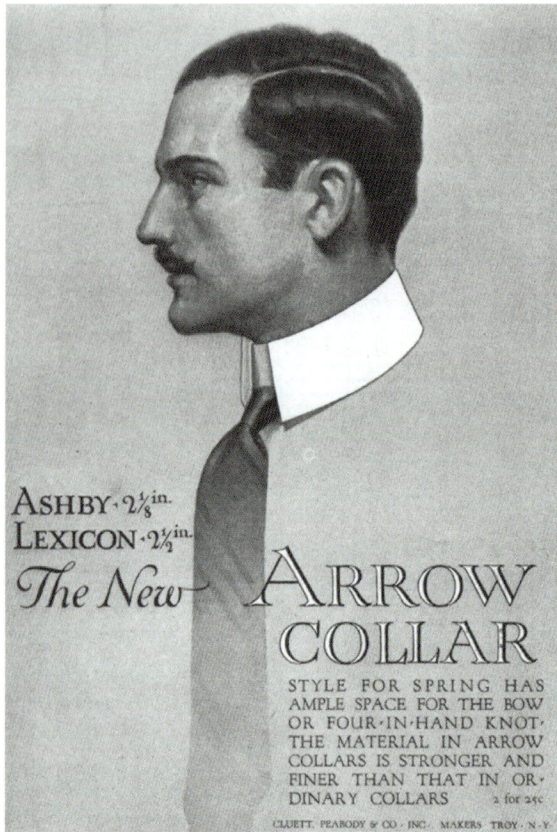

81 | J. C. (Joseph Christian) Leyendecker, *The New Arrow Collar Shirt*, 1914. Magazine advertisement for Cluett, Peabody & Co., Troy, NY. Halftone print on paper, 20.4 × 14.1 cm. CL.

design in America. For all the skill Leyendecker (or Norman Rockwell, his true successor) possessed, their paintings never quite became high art in the minds of most at the time—contrary to Calkins's hopes. Illustration was popular, and it helped to sell a great many things. But it was not the same as "design on a page"—full two-dimensional composition. Commercial illustration as it was in the early years of the last century could and never would be that. But even before the outbreak of World War I in Europe, another revolution, one in many respects more sweeping, was already making it appearance in American design.

4 Stopping

the Rushing Eye

The half dozen years before the United States' entry into World War I were good to Calkins & Holden. By then, the firm had become a national leader in the advertising field, and new clients and major accounts continued to pour in, including Thomas Edison and the Edison Company. Calkins took special satisfaction in working with a fellow deaf man, though he soon discovered—as nearly everyone did—that Edison could be difficult, demanding, and impulsive.[1]

Calkins was still finding it challenging to produce "artistic designs." There were, he noted, "so few artists available who could supply the atmosphere desired."[2] Nonetheless, he remained steadfast in his faith in advertising art. He was now wholly and unswervingly persuaded that the beauty of advertising art would triumph, that art would overcome the basest tendencies of commerce.[3]

He was no longer alone in his quest. New advertising firms, founded and operated by younger men then just entering the field, were establishing robust art departments. And the older, traditional firms, fearing rising competition, were rapidly transforming, moving away from the model of agencies that merely bought and sold space in newspapers and magazines. They, too, were devising advertising campaigns and "designing" the ads.

Calkins was certain that the day was coming when commercial art would rival that of the old masters. "Industrial art," he wrote, "is as natural and logical an expression of this age as was religious art of the fifteenth century. In the middle ages [sic], the church was the powerful influence, the one that dominated men's minds

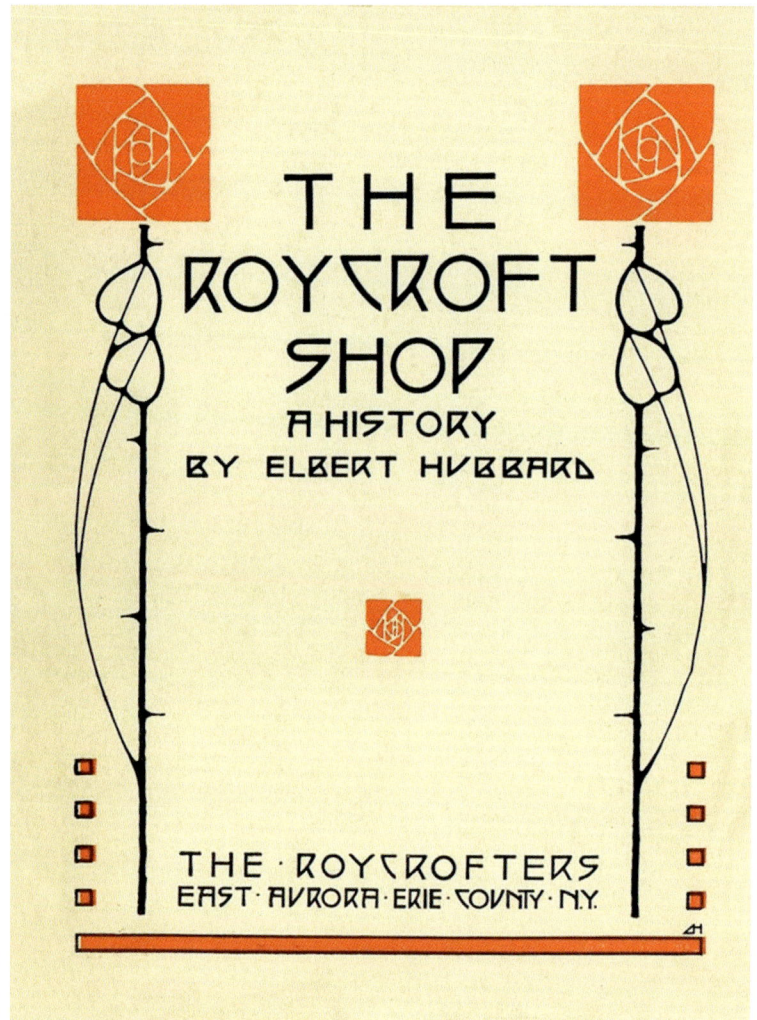

82 | Dard Hunter, title page for *Justinian and Theodora: A Drama Being a Chapter of History and One Gleam of Light During the Dark Ages* by Elbert Hubbard and Alice Hubbard (East Aurora, NY: The Roycrofters), 1906. No. 2 of 106 copies. Printed on Japan vellum, 20.5 × 15.2 × 2 cm. Private collection.

83 | Dard Hunter, *The Roycroft Shop*, by Elbert Hubbard (East Aurora, NY: The Roycrofters), 1909, 8vo. CL.

―――――

84 | Dard Hunter, *Little Journeys to the Homes of Great Business Men: Philip Armour*, by Elbert Hubbard (East Aurora, NY: The Roycrofters), 1909, 8vo. CL.

85 | Ethel M'Clellan Plummer, design for the June 1914 cover of *Vanity Fair*. India ink, gouache, and watercolor over pencil on paper, 44.2 × 30.4 cm. Prints and Photographs Division, Library of Congress, Washington, D.C.

and conditioned their thinking. It naturally drew art to its propaganda, as it drew wealth, politics and literature."[4]

What Calkins didn't see, what he could not even hazily discern because it was in no way part of the everyday flurry of business in New York, was that an entirely new form of graphic art was already beginning to appear. It was taking place outside the popular American newspapers and magazines, and far beyond the world of big advertising.

One of the makers of this novel design direction was Dard Hunter. Hunter was born and raised in Steubenville, Ohio, where his father published a local newspaper and ran a printshop. After attending Ohio State University in Columbus, Hunter went to work for Elbert Hubbard, the visionary (and wonderfully eccentric) founder of Roycroft, the company and colony he established in East Aurora, New York, to produce Arts and Crafts furnishings, books, and other articles. Hubbard, who had his first success as a traveling salesman for the Larkin Soap Company (the same Larkin Company that hired Frank Lloyd Wright to design its headquarters in Buffalo), was part huckster, part missionary for the cause of reform. When he wasn't selling visitors on his ideas or the many products that were central to Roycroft's bottom line, he was publishing

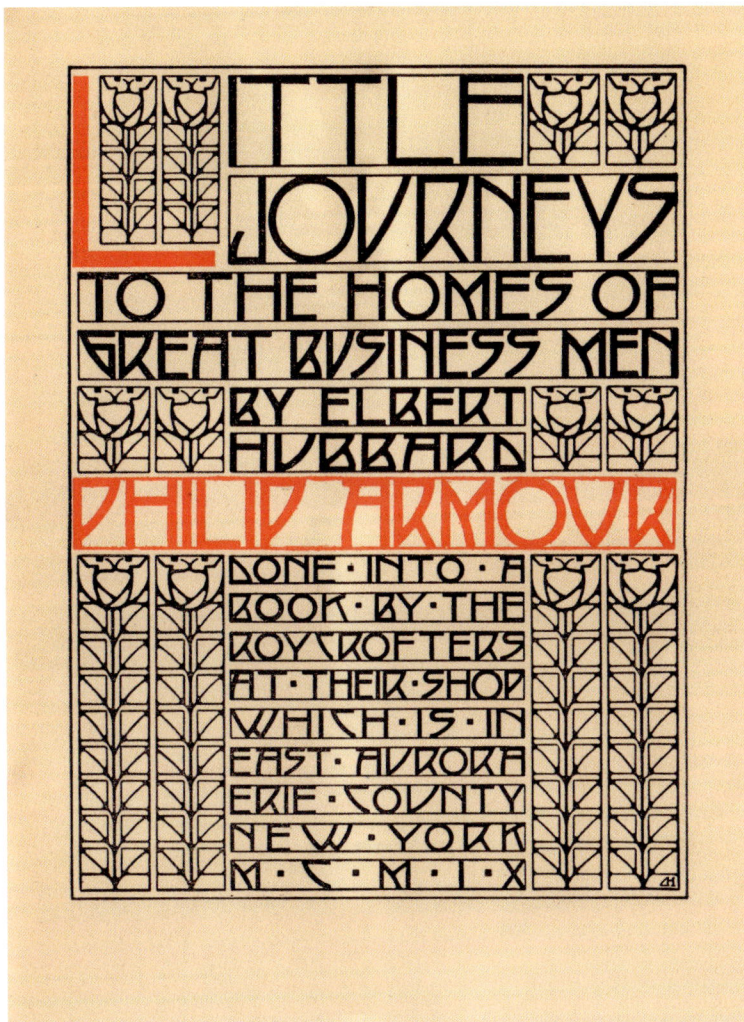

a series of books and pamphlets (often co-authored with his wife, Alice) filled with his idiosyncratic views on social reform and business practices.

The sheer number of these works gave Hunter the chance to experiment with an array of typefaces, layouts, and book decorations. Hunter's early work at Roycroft blended what was then current in British and American Arts and Crafts design with his own distinctive mannerisms. Before long, however, he became interested in the work of Josef Hoffmann and the Viennese modernists. When Hunter married Edith Cornell, a pianist at Roycroft, in 1908, they spent part of their honeymoon in Vienna. Hunter returned the next year to take courses at the Graphische Lehr- und Versuchs-anstalt, a school emphasizing the newest trends in Jugendstil graphic art. He quickly picked up a working knowledge of Viennese techniques, which he applied to Hubbard's books, pamphlets, and sales brochures (figs. 82–84).

Hunter's Viennese-inflected Arts and Crafts idiom soon achieved a certain notoriety; even so, it still was rare in America. In the early 1910s, the French and Belgian version of Art Nouveau, with its swirling forms and considered abridgement, was far more common, appearing in magazines, pattern books, newspapers, and even modest ads for local fairs (figs. 85–88).

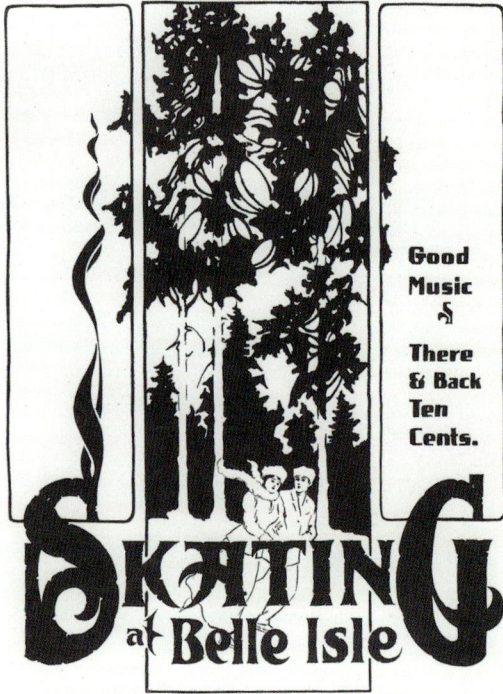

Good
Music
s
There
& Back
Ten
Cents.

Skating
at Belle Isle

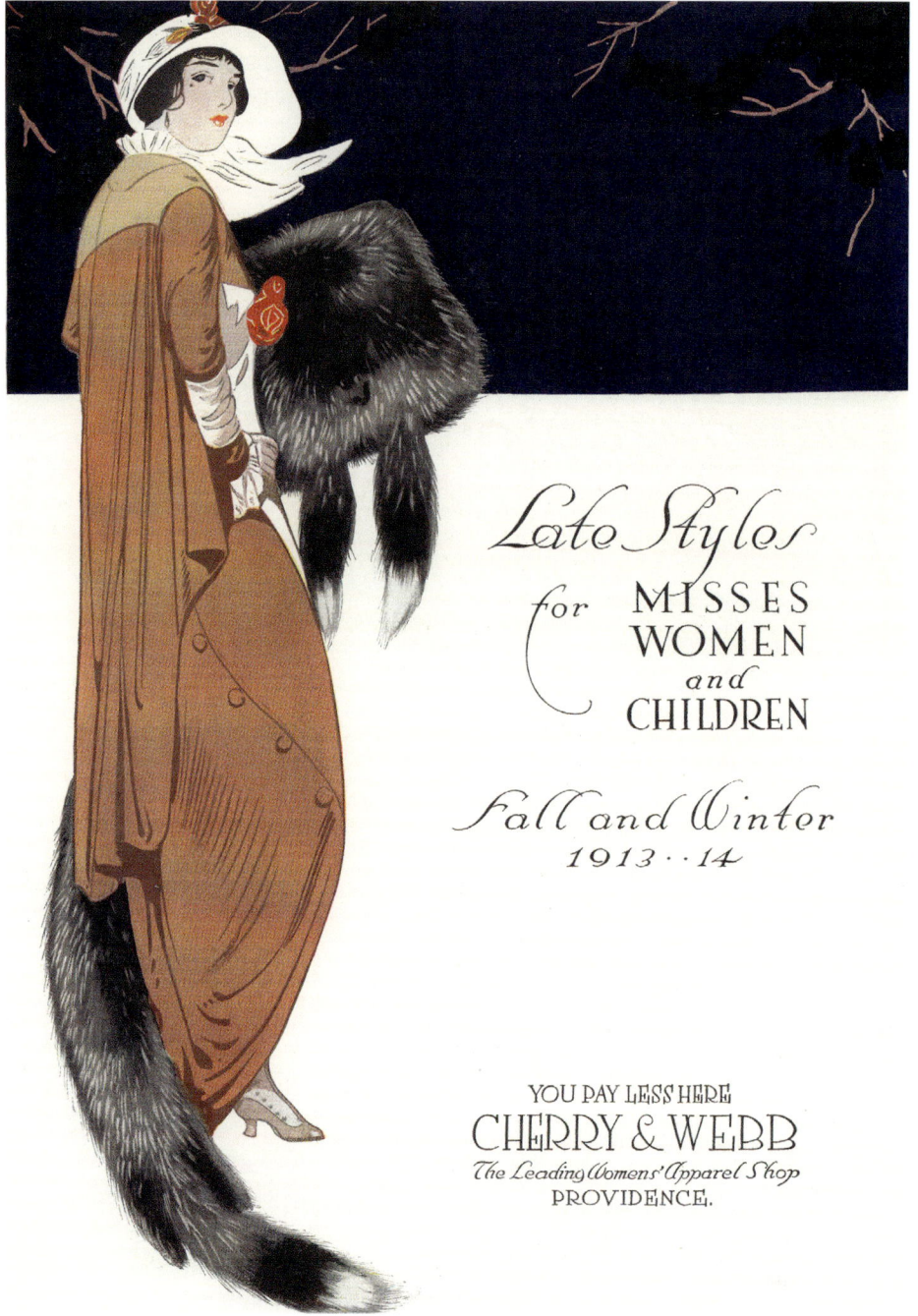

Late Styles
for MISSES
WOMEN
and
CHILDREN

Fall and Winter
1913··14

YOU PAY LESS HERE
CHERRY & WEBB
The Leading Womens' Apparel Shop
PROVIDENCE.

86 | Chas. J. Strong and L. S. Strong, *Skating at Belle Isle*, 1910. Pattern design from *Strong's Book of Designs* (Chicago: Frederick J. Drake, & Company, 1917), n.p. Offset print on paper, image: 21.5 × 16.4 cm. CL.

87 | *Late Styles for Misses Women and Children*, 1913. Magazine advertisement for Cherry and Webb, Providence, RI. Lithograph on paper, 26.2 × 18.6 cm. CL.

88 | *California Raisin Day, April 30: Eat Raisin Bread*, 1910. Postcard, printed by Fresno Souvenir Post Card Publishing Company. Offset lithograph on cardstock, 8.8 × 14.1 cm. CL.

There was also a small subset of designs that brought together the Art Nouveau with a stylistic amalgam of pronounced linearity and the geometrization (in the parlance of the time, conventionalization) of natural forms. This form-language was quintessentially American, associated most closely with Frank Lloyd Wright and his followers. It shows up often in publications linked to Prairie Style design in the decade or so before the United States entered World War I.

One of the chief makers of this form-language was Alfonso Iannelli. Iannelli was born in Italy and moved to the United States as a child.[5] Around 1912, while living in Los Angeles, he was hired by the Orpheum Theatre to design posters and lobby show cards for traveling vaudeville acts. One of these hand-painted cards promoted the comedy act of Adair and Adair (fig. 89). It has an acrobat hanging upside down from a bar; on the lower right side are two cut-outs, where changing photographs of the Adair brothers and performance dates could be posted. What is immediately striking in Iannelli's design—beyond the lyrical and geometricized depiction of the acrobat—are the areas where the words are concealed by the figure. Because we can't readily see all the letters, we are made to pause—in reality, we are "forced" to look, to work out the words. Iannelli also displays a remarkable and prescient sense of how to arrange the words on the surface in a way that appears almost random—or, at least, casual in a modern way. Each of the more than one hundred posters he produced for the Orpheum speaks in this language of a relaxed immediacy and vibrancy (fig. 90). His friends urged him to publish them, but he resisted because he didn't want to become known merely as a poster artist.[6]

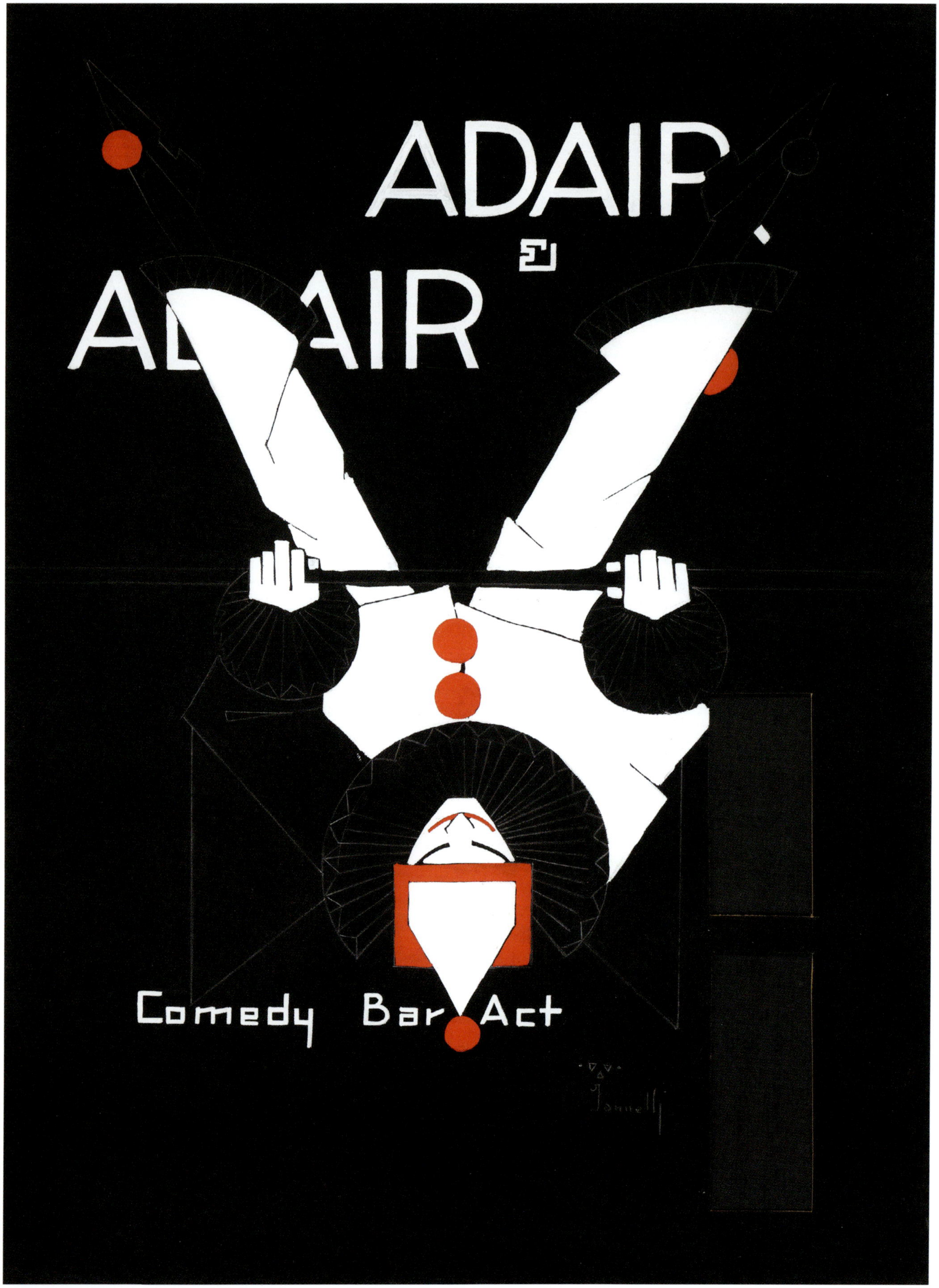
ADAIR & ADAIR
Comedy Bar Act

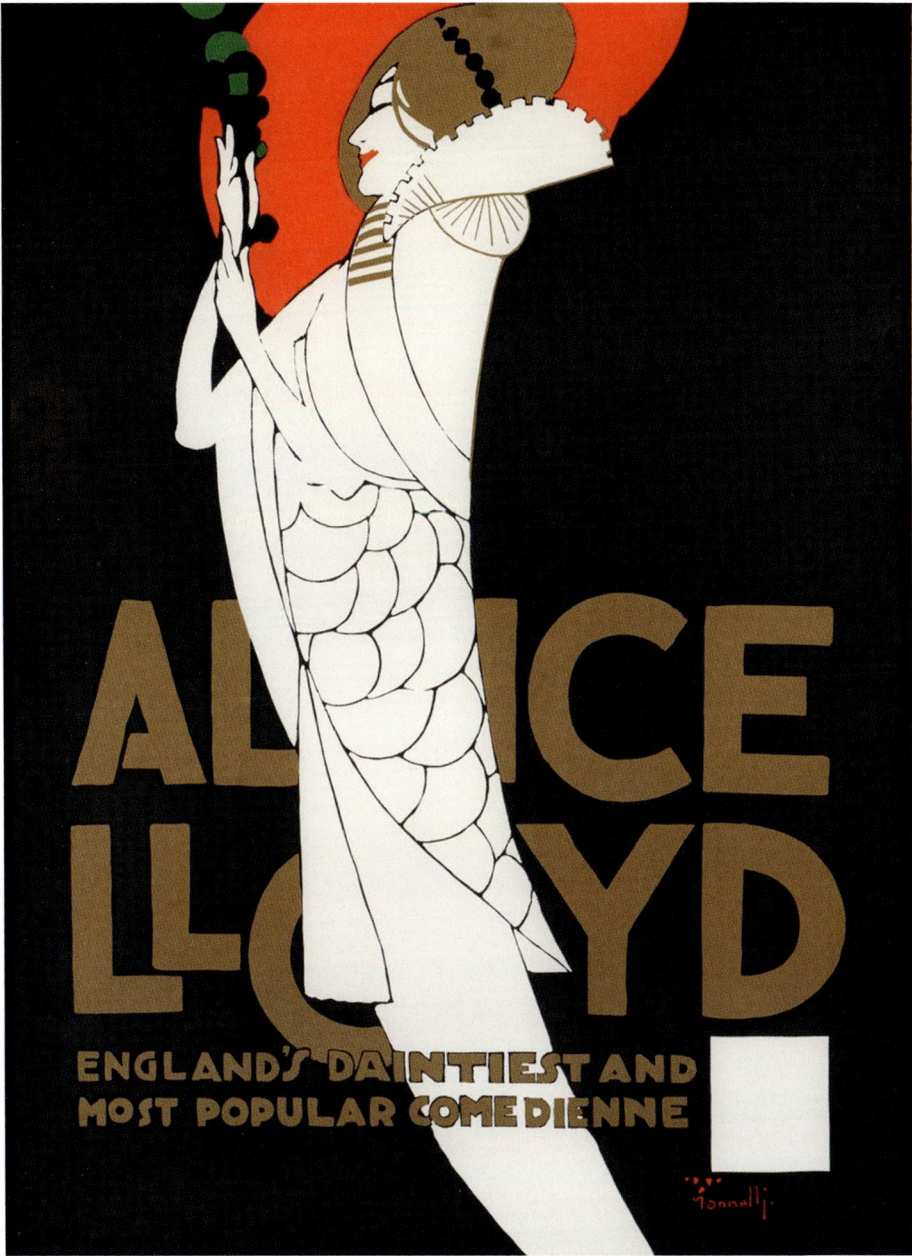

89| Alfonso Iannelli, *Adair & Adair Comedy Bar Act*, ca. 1914. Original art for the Orpheum Theatre, Los Angeles. Tempera and colored pencil on artist's board, 102 × 76 cm. Signed on the lower right "Iannelli." The Resnick Collection. Photo: Courtesy Wright, Chicago.

90| Alfonso Iannelli, Alice Lloyd, ca. 1914. Poster, printed for the Prpheum Theatre, Los Angeles. Lithograph on paper, 100 × 75 cm. Private collection. Photo: Courtesy Wright, Chicago.

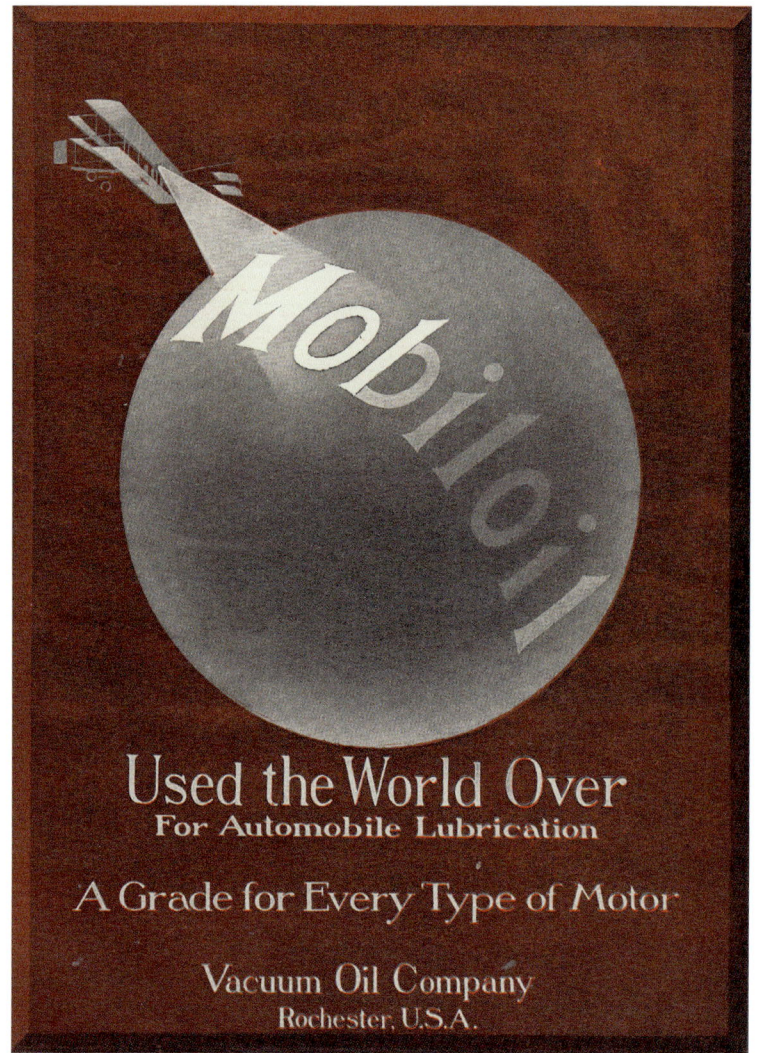

A different—and arresting—version of the Art Nouveau appeared in a series of advertisements for Mobil Oil Company around 1910. Designed by an unknown artist, they rely on the softened, almost nebulous forms of the early Art Nouveau, but they are greatly more simplified, so that the main features stand out even more (fig. 91). One of these ads is especially forward-looking: a view of the planet Earth with a biplane shining a light spelling out "Mobiloil" on the surface (fig. 92).

Yet the change in those years that would have perhaps the widest impact and set American design on a new path came from a very different branch of advertising: the billboard, or, as it was becoming known, outdoor advertising.

American billboards of the late nineteenth century had been rudimentary in design. Most featured only a slogan, a company name, or a plea to buy—occasionally paired with an image of a product (fig. 93). They relied on standard fonts, and their arrangements were neither especially imaginative nor appealing. In large cities—and even in many smaller ones—billboards covered great swaths of the urban landscape, sometimes enveloping entire buildings (fig. 94). Yet there was little in their presentation to attract special notice. The American cityscape of those years was often a scene of

91 | *Mobiloil Perfect Lubrication*, 1910. Magazine advertisement for Vacuum Oil Company, Rochester, NY. Halftone print on paper, image: 25.1 × 18.4 cm. CL.

92 | *Mobiloil Used the World Over*, 1911. Magazine advertisement for Vacuum Oil Company, Rochester, NY. Halftone print on paper, image: 19.5 × 14.2 cm. CL.

93| Billboards in San Francisco, late 1890s. Outdoor Advertising Association of America Archives, John W. Hartman Center for Sales Advertising and Marketing History, Duke University Libraries.

94| Billboards in New York City, ca. 1913. Outdoor Advertising Association of America Archives, John W. Hartman Center for Sales Advertising and Marketing History, Duke University Libraries.

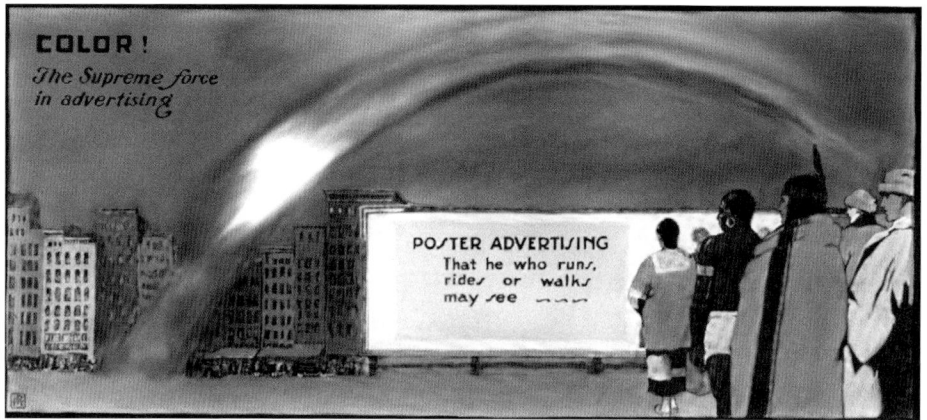

visual cacophony, a situation that certainly diminished the effectiveness of individual billboards. The important changes that would transform outdoor advertising came from two farseeing firms, one on the West Coast, the other in New York.

In 1901, Walter Foster and George William Kleiser founded Foster & Kleiser Outdoor Advertising in Portland and Seattle. Foster had been a bicycle racer in San Francisco. For a time, he also sold outdoor advertising for a man named Thomas H. B. Varney in Oakland. Through this work, he met George Kleiser, a San Francisco dentist. Within the space of a few weeks, they decided to launch their own outdoor advertising business.

They incorporated the firm in 1902; in less than a decade, they became the nation's most innovative billboard company. In 1912, Foster & Kleiser, now headquartered in San Francisco, put up the first twenty-four-sheet poster structure in the United States. The same year, they began the conversion of their horse-drawn wagon fleet to trucks.[7] A few years after that, they acquired a large, existing plant in San Francisco, and by 1916, they were offering an illuminated outdoor advertising service on Market Street.

In the design of their billboards, Foster & Kleiser first followed the lead of the other large outdoor advertising firms. Soon, though, the company introduced two very significant alterations. For one, they started to simplify their ads. In place of long descriptions or verse, they employed only a few words—mostly the name of the product or maker and something else (a short phrase or a single adjective) to render it distinctive. They relied on pictorial imagery, and the images they chose were much pared-down—easy to recognize and without unnecessary detail. One of the consequences of this strategy was that these new billboards were readable from a speeding motor car. It was a brilliant move: as car ownership increased precipitously in those years, the company became a leader in the burgeoning field of highway advertising.

But Foster & Kleiser also did something else, something truly original that would transform the very nature of the business. They began hiring artists. Not hack commercial artists, but men and women with skill and ambition. And they hired them from the ranks of the nation's emerging young modernists. They brought them together in a large, well-equipped studio, and they granted them an extraordinary

95| Harold von Schmidt, *Do It Electrically! The Modern Aladdin*, 1916. Poster, reprinted in *The Poster*, October 1916, 52.

96| Frances Robinson, *Color! The Supreme force in advertising*, 1916. Poster, reprinted in *The Poster*, September 1916, 45.

———

97| International Art Service, *Mo-Jo Pure White Chewing Gum*, ca. 1913. Box cover. From *Printing Art*, February 1915, 485.

degree of freedom to do their work. At a time when many of the major advertising agencies on the East Coast were treating those in their art departments little differently than the clerks in their mail rooms, Foster & Kleiser was pioneering a new and modern work environment.

The art director of the new San Francisco office was twenty-three-year-old Harold von Schmidt. Born nearby in Alameda, Schmidt had studied at the School of the California Guild of Arts and Crafts. After working as a cowhand and construction worker, he joined Foster & Kleiser, and by 1916 he had risen to national prominence, winning a competition to design a billboard promoting the use of electricity.[8]

The Modern Aladdin shows a young boy summoning a present-day genie, who is pressing a light switch (fig. 95). The characters come off as cartoonish, but the genius of Schmidt's rendering rests with its wonderfully lucid messaging. Electricity in that time was still magical; it was also accessible. The absolute directness of the figures and the little skit they are putting on was new for American advertising art, and, as it turned out, a highly effective way to reach the public.

Almost at the same moment, one of Schmidt's colleagues at the San Francisco Foster & Kleiser office made what is perhaps an even more potent expression of modernity, a billboard promoting advertising itself (fig. 96). It was the work of Margaret Frances Robinson (who went by her middle name in her early years). The design won a second prize in a national competition put on by the Poster Advertising Association.[9] Frances Robinson, who later became known for her paintings of the French Quarter in New Orleans, here also relies on a city view. Over it is a blurred rainbow, and we see a group of quite varied people—city folk, Native Americans, African Americans, and Asian Americans—all looking at a billboard. The inscription reads "Poster Advertising. That he who runs, rides or walks may see." In the upper left corner is a second message: "Color! The Supreme force in advertising." It is brilliant in its presentation, not only because the scene and story are perfectly meshed, but also because Robinson introduces a visual language that is both unpretentious and luminous.

Among those designing billboards at the company's San Francisco headquarters by 1917 were Western muralist Maynard Dixon, French-born painter Maurice Del Mue, and Roi Partridge, a Seattle printmaker and artist who was married to the photographer Imogen Cunningham. They were joined by Kem Weber, a German-born designer and architect who had been visiting San Francisco when World War I broke out in Europe and became marooned there. They would come to form a tight circle of friends that also included the young photographer Dorothea Lange, who would later marry Dixon.

Compared with the usual complement of staff artists at most of the mass publishing houses, they were superbly well-trained: Dixon had studied—albeit briefly—with Arthur Mathews at the California School of Design; Del Mue learned painting at the San Francisco Art Association and the Paris École des Beaux-Arts; Partridge had attended the National Academy of Design in New York, learned new methods of etching in Munich, and then took up printmaking in Paris under the mentorship of Bertha Jaques; Weber had studied in Berlin with Bruno Paul, one of the leading progressive designers in Germany. They brought to their work at Foster & Kleiser

not only consummate skills but also a knowledge of the latest currents in modern art and design.

Their impact on Foster & Kleiser's look was profound and immediate. Suddenly, with little run up and even less fanfare, Foster & Kleiser's billboards were at the very leading-edge of the new design in America.

Foster & Kleiser was not the only company pursuing the latest means of visual representation. For a time, around 1915, Foster & Kleiser had a formidable rival in New York in the International Art Service.

Its founder was a twenty-six-year-old recent German immigrant named Arthur F. Wiener. The son of a Berlin business writer, Wiener had trained in graphic arts and subsequently worked for various Berlin commercial art studios, along with some of the city's major newspapers. He had all the right connections: he knew the leading Berlin graphic artists, lithographers, and printers. Those contacts would prove crucial in his efforts to bring a new design conception to America.

Wiener arrived in New York in 1908 intending only to see the newest American design before returning to Germany. But inspired by the vitality of the city, he made the decision to stay. In 1911, with the backing of three friends, he opened his own design studio.[10] Wiener touted his connections with the Berlin advertising and lithography firm Hollerbaum & Schmidt, which had been one of the leaders in Germany of the new reductive Sachplakat style. Hollerbaum & Schmidt had given Lucian Bernhard, the unrivaled master of the Sachplakat, his start, and it was Bernhard's distinctive style—and that of Julius Klinger, Ludwig Hohlwein, and a few others from its impressive stable of the German modernists—that Wiener now sought to sell to American clients.[11]

The IAS, as Wiener's company soon became known, also presented a new business model. Not only did Wiener supply his clients with the company's individual modern poster and billboard designs, but he also offered them a great deal more, "total design" that included a unified look for advertisements, letterheads, business cards, packaging, signage, and labels (fig. 97).[12]

At the end of 1912, Wiener moved his firm to a building on West Forty-Second Street, across from Bryant Park. The new office tower, which served as the headquarters of the Aeolian Company (a manufacturer of pianos and other musical instruments), also housed the studios of many of the city's foremost architects and artists.[13]

The IAS's chief designer was a young artist named Willy G. Sesser. Born Wilhelm Georg Sesser in Vienna in 1886, he had studied art and graphic design at the progressive Debschitz-Schule and the Munich Academy of Fine Arts before emigrating to the United States in October 1911. Almost immediately, he began working for Wiener.[14]

The IAS at first experienced tough sledding, as Wiener wrote at the time:

None of us knew what kind of reception would be given our ideas and their execution by the American advertiser. We found out soon enough, however. Strangers in strange surroundings, the first disappointment came very quickly.

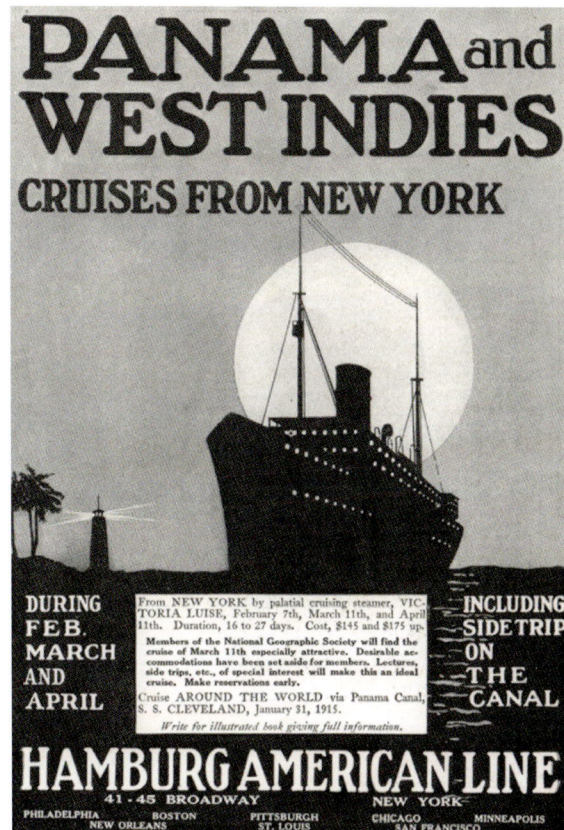

98| Willy G. Sesser, *To Egypt—North German Lloyd*, 1913. Poster, printed by Munro & Hartford Company, New York, NY, for North German Lloyd Steamship Company, Hamburg, Germany. Lithograph on paper, 88.9 × 63.5 cm. Hoover Institution Library and Archives, Stanford University.

99| International Art Service, *Panama and West Indies Cruises from New York, Hamburg American Line*, 1914. Magazine advertisement. From *National Geographic*, January 1914, n.p. CL.

HUPMOBILE
"Car of the American Family"

1915

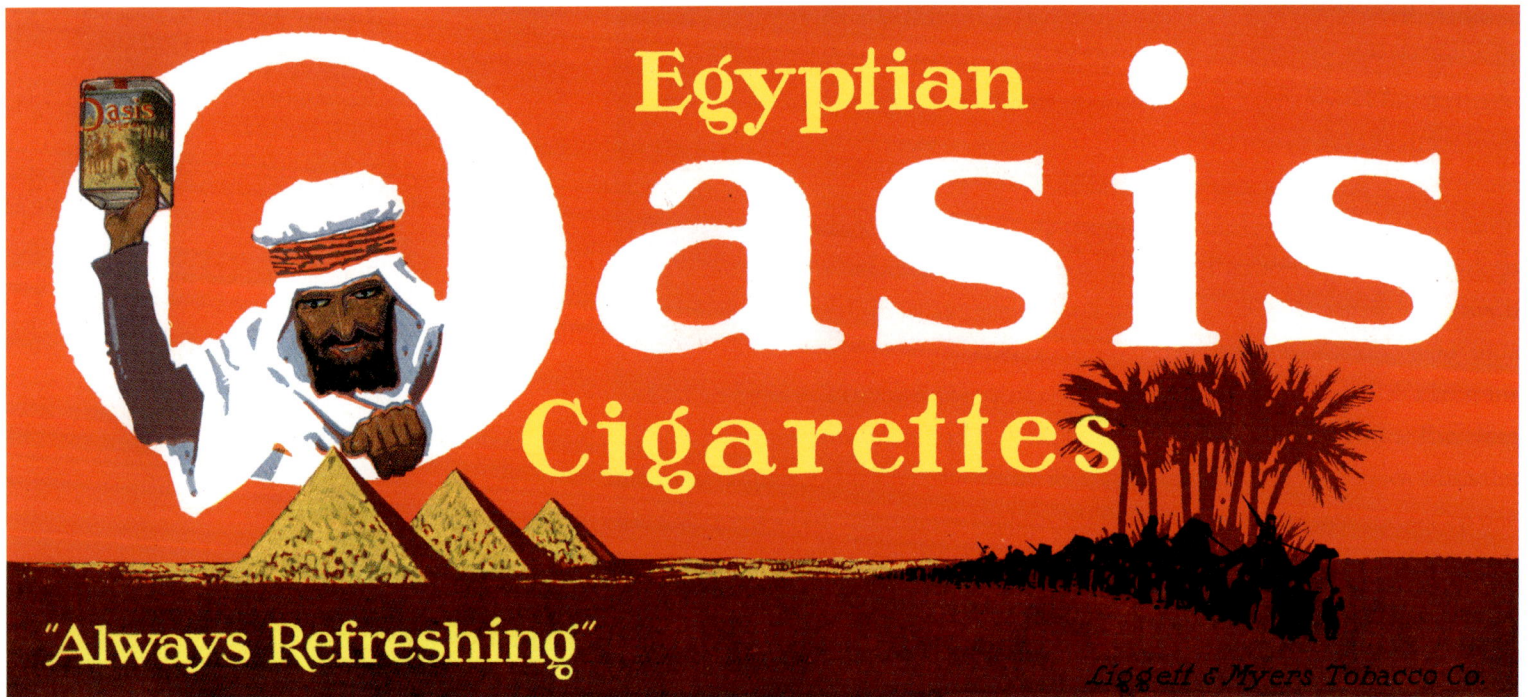

Egyptian
Oasis
Cigarettes

"Always Refreshing"

Liggett & Myers Tobacco Co.

Accustomed as we were to working with broad-minded lithographers proud to produce pieces of art and willing to make sacrifices in order to promote such work, we naturally counted on the enthusiastic support of those men in America. But we soon had to learn that quantity meant more to them than quality; that the American lithographer prefers large machines which produce a lot of work at low prices than to eliminate competition by producing better work, work expressive of individuality, and surrounding himself with artists whose aim it is to produce nothing—not even the humblest little box without giving it some suggestion of personality, and so to add to the everyday needs a touch of art.[15]

The first breakthrough for Wiener and his company accordingly came not from an American client but a familiar German firm: the Hamburg-based shipping giant North German Lloyd, which commissioned the IAS to produce a series of travel posters. One of these stands out. It was a poster advertising tours to Egypt. With only a few words—"To Egypt" and "North German Lloyd" (along with the name and address of their New York agents)—Sesser conveys the intended message (fig. 98). Two different fonts, serif and sans serif, establish a hierarchy: first where and then by what means. Like all good travel posters, it visually states the case for why one should go: an azure-blue sky, an almost ghostly image of the Sphinx that fades toward the bottom into swirling sands, over which a well-to-do couple with their child in tow make their way with the aid of native guides. Today, one must look past the taint of cultural imperialism to see its qualities. But set across the poster's surface is a fetching play of imagery, color, and form. It is a graphic tour de force and quite unlike anything else then on the American scene.

By 1913, the house style of the IAS had become a language of flattened forms and bold colors, set into "blocks" that were often limned in black (fig. 99). The look was bold and dramatic, or, at times, exuberant and playful—though always with a focus on the product being sold and the name of the maker. None of the IAS designs were Sachplakate in the purest sense because they always projected scenes—little narratives or activated vignettes—rather than simply depicting an object for sale. An IAS billboard for the Hupp Motor Car Company, for example, shows a group on a fun outing in the countryside; the company's poster for Fatima cigarettes spoke to the Egyptian origin of that company's tobacco (figs. 100, 101).

Wiener spent very much time and effort not only promoting the IAS but also the cause of the new graphic design. He contributed articles to *The Poster*, including the first profile of Lucian Bernhard in English.[16] And with John Cotton Dana, the progressive director of the Newark Public Library (the predecessor of the Newark Museum), he arranged for the touring 1912 *German Applied Arts* exhibition, mounted by the Deutsches Museum für Kunst in Handel und Gewerbe (German Museum of Art in Trade and Commerce), to come to the United States.[17] In late 1913, Dana then organized *German Advertising Art*, a show of posters exclusively from the Berlin collector Hans Sachs, editor and publisher of *Das Plakat* (The poster), the leading German publication of the poster movement.[18]

100| International Art Service, *Hupmobile "Car of the American Family,"* 1915. Billboard design for the Hupp Motor Car Company. From Herbert E. Martini, *Applied Art: A Collection of Designs Showing the Tendencies of American Industrial Art*, vol. 1 (New York: F. K. Ferenz, 1919), plate 23 (bottom). CL.

101| International Art Service, *Egyptian Oasis Cigarettes "Always Refreshing,"* 1915. Billboard design for Fatima Cigarettes. From Herbert E. Martini, *Applied Art: A Collection of Designs Showing the Tendencies of American Industrial Art*, vol. 1 (New York: F. K. Ferenz, 1919), plate 23 (top). CL.

CITY PLANNING EXHIBITION

NEW YORK PUBLIC LIBRARY
NOV. 24, TO DEC. 7, 1913

"The Greatest, Most Beautiful and Most Important in History"

February 20 to December 4

PANAMA PACIFIC
INTERNATIONAL
· EXPOSITION ·
SAN FRANCISCO · 1915

These exhibitions and repeated showings by the IAS at their offices on West Forty-Second Street influenced some American-born designers, who began borrowing the tactics of pictorial flattening, bold color fields, and minimalist depiction of objects (figs. 102, 103). Suddenly, there was an outpouring of powerful new graphic works. An anonymous magazine reporter got it all exactly right: it was an art, he or she wrote, that "stops the rushing eye."[19]

Sesser continued to be the leader of this new form of graphic art, but he was not the only innovative artist working for the IAS. Wiener employed other recent arrivals from Germany and Austria, among them Winold Reiss, Paul. T. Frankl, and Jacob Asanger.

All three would quickly go their separate ways—driven forth, it should be said, by Wiener's imperious and demanding personality. Reiss established his own design practice and art school in New York; Frankl opened an interior design practice on Lower Park Avenue; and Asanger, after working for various employers in New York, would move out to the West Coast, where he would eventually head Foster & Kleiser's Los Angeles office.

Frankl was never purely a graphic designer. Nonetheless, he used what he had learned during his brief stint at the IAS to prepare a series of ads for his new gallery—bold exercises in stark black and white that drew from the Jugendstil and the contemporary Biedermeier revival (fig. 104). Asanger, too, would for many years reproduce elements of the IAS style in his designs for Foster & Kleiser.

It was Reiss, though, who had the most immediate impact on the field of graphic design. Born in Karlsruhe, Germany, in 1886, he was the son of Fritz Winold Reiss, a prominent illustrator and painter. When Winold was still a young child, the family moved to Freiburg and, later, to the nearby small town of Kirchzarten, deep in the Black Forest. Reiss received his first drawing and painting lessons from his father; he was already supremely skilled in both media by the time he went to Munich to study art. There Reiss enrolled in the Kunstgewerbeschule, the school of applied art. He studied for a time with Julius Diez, who was a prominent member of the Munich Secession. Afterward, he enrolled the Munich Academy, completing his studies with Franz von Stuck, one of foremost painters of the city's vibrant modernist scene.

During his time in Munich, Reiss likely met Asanger and another young German artist, Carl Link. All three ended up in New York, where Reiss quickly found a job at the IAS. He quit a few months later, complaining of "overwork." He opened a decorative arts and furnishings shop, the Crafts and Art Studio, with Asanger and another man.[20] They had little success selling their Jugendstil-inspired furnishings and objects, and Reiss instead started an art school on Lower Fifth Avenue.

Greatly more consequential for the new graphic design, though, was his cofounding, with a publisher named Oscar Wentz, of the Society of Modern Art. The Society put on a few small exhibitions, but it is now more noted for its little magazine, *Modern Art Collector. M.A.C.*, as it became universally known, featured examples of the new art, in bold and brilliant colors. In the inaugural September 1915 issue, Reiss, who was its art director, spelled out its mission: "Our object in bringing out these pages at this time in America is to enable this country to keep in touch with

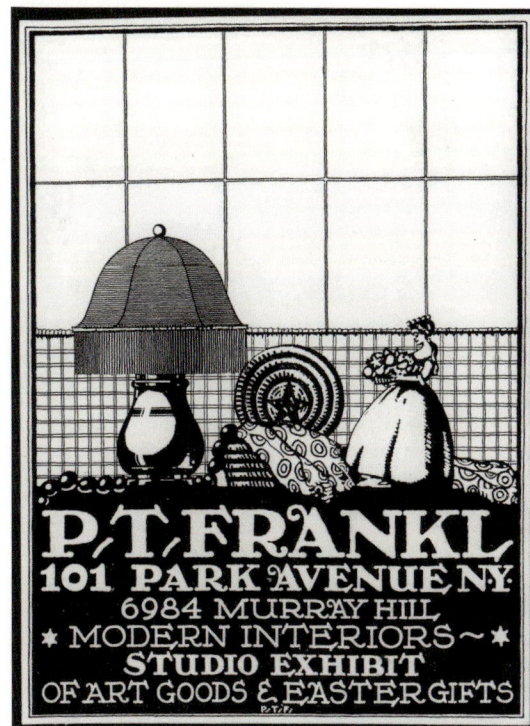

102 | *City Planning Exhibition, New York Public Library Nov. 24, to Dec. 7*, 1913. Poster. Lithograph on paper. The Miriam and Ira D. Wallach Division of Art, Prints and Photographs: Art & Architecture Collection, The New York Public Library.

103 | *Panama Pacific International Exposition San Francisco 1915*, 1914. Poster. The Resnick Collection.

104 | Paul T. Frankl, *Paul T. Frankl 101 Park Avenue, N.Y.*, 1915. Advertisement. Print on paper, 15 × 10.2 cm. CL.

INTERIOR DECORATION

THE BUSY LADY BAKING CO. INC

M. A. C. SUPPLEMENT   T   OCTOBER 1915

USED BY THE BUSY LADY BAKING CO. INC. NEW YORK

CHRISTMAS GOODS

THE BUSY LADY BAKING CO. INC.

BISCUITS

THE BUSY LADY BAKING CO. INC. NEW YORK

MACAROONS

THE BUSY LADY BAKING CO. INC. NEW YORK

105 | Winold Reiss, *Busy Lady Bakery*, 1915. Front and back covers of supplement to *Modern Art Collector*, October 1915. Offset lithograph, 30.8 × 23.4 cm. CL.

———————

106 | Winold Reiss, *Don't Stand Around Moulting*, 1915. Poster from the Photo Engravers Convention, Chicago, printed for the Photo Engravers Board of Trade, New York, NY. Lithograph on paper, 54 × 46 cm. Prints and Photographs Division, Library of Congress, Washington, D.C.

modern artistic European tendencies at a date when travelling to Europe is freighted with difficulties [he is referring to the war then raging in Europe], and thereby encourage the development of the Modern Movement in this country."[21] Recognizing the reluctance of American artists to become involved in "practical" design, Reiss defended commercial art: "there isn't a good artist in Germany who wouldn't design a poster. The new movement gave that work a new basis. No good artist is ashamed to do something because it is used as a commercial aid."[22]

Reiss enlisted the help of several of the other young Central European émigrés living in New York, including Asanger, Link, and Hungarian Ilonka Karasz, all of whom produced covers and other illustrations for the magazine. Many of the images had a distinctly commercial cast. This was especially true for Reiss's designs for the Busy Lady Baking Company, which appeared in the magazine's second issue.[23] The drawings Reiss made were fully consistent with the formal language of the later Munich Jugendstil (fig. 105). Except for the English titles, the bakery interiors and associated images could have been in any larger city in Germany or Austria.

The poster Reiss produced for the Photo Engravers Convention in Chicago, in 1915, was equally almost a direct import (fig. 106). Everything here—the color scheme, the anthropomorphized birds, the color blocking, and the simple squares—had already

Don't stand around moulting: but go to the Photo Engravers' Convention at Chicago, June 17th, 18th, 19th, or next year you won't even have tail feathers left.

PHOTO ENGRAVERS' BOARD OF TRADE OF NEW YORK CITY.

become standard in Munich, Berlin, and Vienna. Only the English-language caption identifies it as an American product. But Reiss was also then experimenting with a different look, one that was more reduced and purified. His small poster for the Walton Studio, a "sign" for the business depicted as if it were a present suspended by a white ribbon, was a play on perspective and form (fig. 107). Everything is manifestly flat; there is no true three-dimensionality, except as the viewer might imagine it. The "gift" rests against the rear "wall" (made up of vertically arranged gray and white rectangles in a checkerboard pattern); and the ribbon is placed over the wall. Yet we see the scene in two ways: a tableau that is entirely flat, merely an illusion of reality, and as a fully three-dimensional construct. The limited color palette—black, white, grey, and gold—only reinforces the contrast between austerity and complexity.

following double page:

107 | Winold Reiss, *Specimens of Modern Advertising Posters Designed by Walton Studio, New York*, 1915. Sample advertisement in supplement to *Modern Art Collector*, October 1915. Lithograph on paper, 26.3 × 18.5 cm. CL.

108 | Winold Reiss, *Photo-Engraving as a Modern Art Artistic Ben Day Work*, ca. 1916. Lithograph on paper, 30 × 23.2 cm. CL.

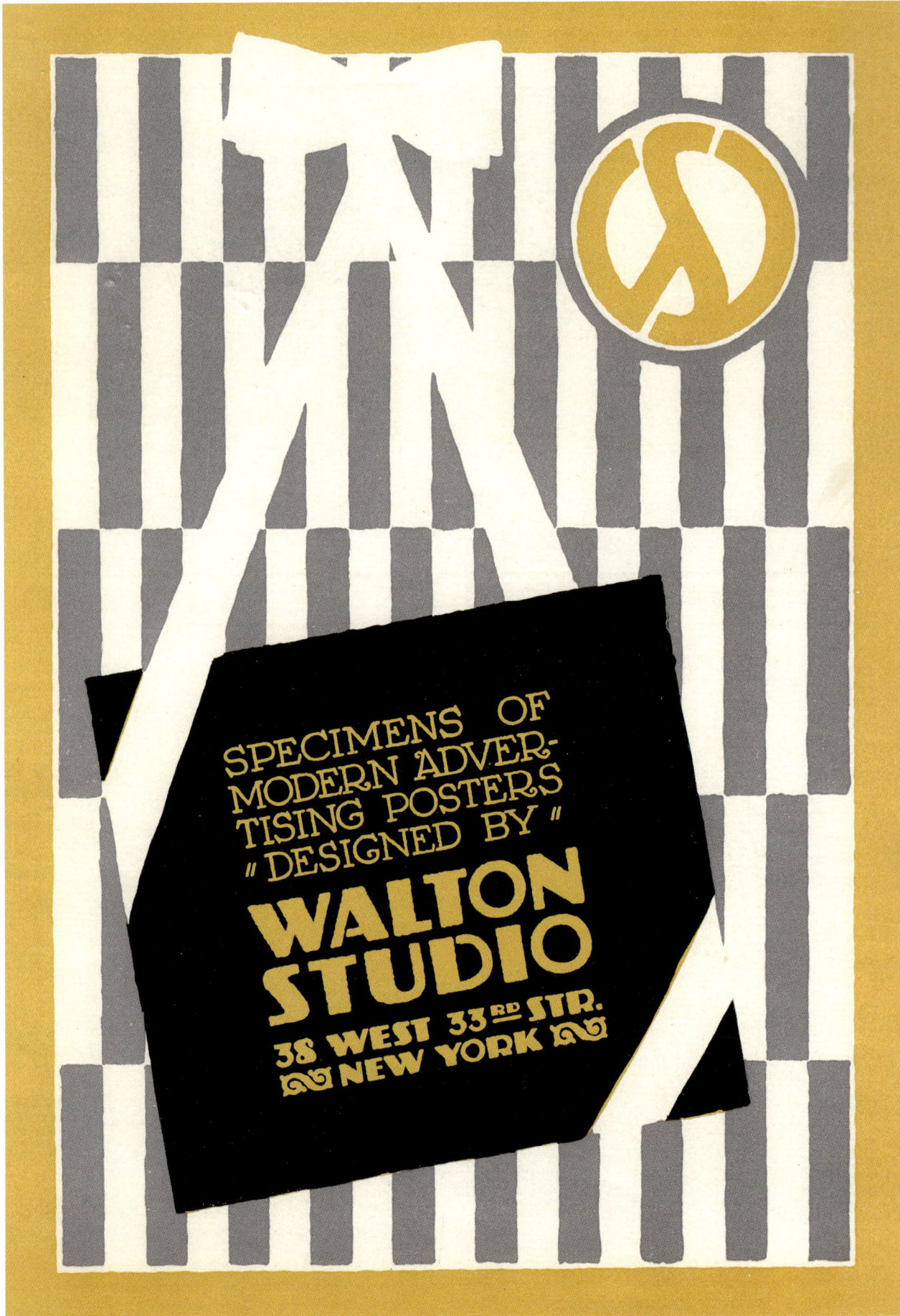

109 | Winold Reiss, *Charity Bazar for the Widows and Orphans of German, Austrian, Hungarian and Their Allied Soldiers*, 1916. Poster, printed by Hegeman, New York. Lithograph on paper, 104 × 71 cm. Prints and Photographs Division, Library of Congress, Washington, D.C.

110 | Hans Flato, *Genuine Palm Beach*, 1915. Sample magazine advertisement for Goodall Worsted Company, Sanford, ME. Offset print on paper, 11.2 × 17.7 cm. CL.

111 | Hans Flato, *The National Summer Suit Palm Beach*, 1917. Magazine advertisement for the Goodall Worsted Company, Sanford, ME, from *The Saturday Evening Post*, June 30, 1917), 54–55. Halftone print on paper, 30.9 × 47.6 cm. CL.

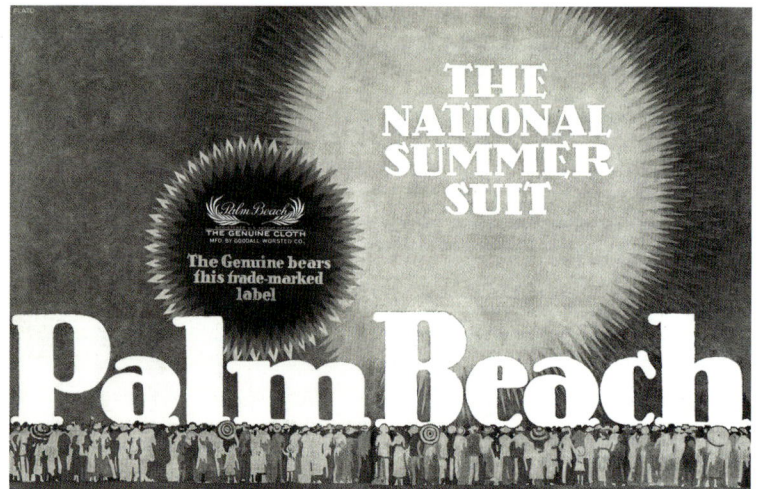

Reiss was exploring another, similar idea at the time: isolating objects or figures and suspending them in space. An advertisement he made for Powers Reproduction Corporation shows an artist as his easel (it is manifestly a self-portrait, right down to the mustache); behind him is a field of vibrant red (fig. 108). The figure's blue painting smock continues beyond the red rectangle, merging with the background of the poster. His palette, too, extends outward. The smock reads as entirely flat, whereas the palette lies over the red square. It is a spatial conundrum that obliges us to ponder for a moment.

In this ad, one can see that Reiss was also attentive to type and its use. He inserted his own typefaces—often hand drawn—at times juxtaposing more than one. In some of his other designs, as in the slightly later poster he made for a "Charity Bazar" [*sic*] to raise money for the widows and orphans of German, Austrian, and Hungarian soldiers, the lettering makes up much of the composition (fig. 109). It is what the eye first fixes upon. Reiss again gives us a sense of perspectival tension: the "castle" overlies the streaming flags of the Central Powers, yet they merge into a border of abstracted American flags that seem to lie atop the castle. We know it cannot be both ways. The discrepancy becomes a mental game—or at the very least, it holds one's attention for a moment, which is certainly what Reiss was seeking to achieve.

Quite aside from these visual games, what Reiss is doing was part of the revolution that would ultimately spawn modern graphic art: he is composing on a manifestly flat surface, with forms and texts that are *almost* liberated from traditional ideas about composition, perspective, and ordering. Each element—whether text, pure form, or something that is figural and represented—has its own autonomy. It exists on the page freely, without being connected to any conventional form of reality. It is thus wholly self-sufficient.

It would take another two decades for graphic designers in America to embrace this idea fully. Designers in Europe, especially in Germany, the Netherlands and Czechoslovakia, would get there much sooner. Still, there were a few artists in the United States in the middle 1910s who were working toward this same of idea of "graphic liberation." One of the strategies that Reiss hinted at, the possibility of setting out the space of an advertisement in such a way that it becomes an exercise in making a block or a void, is brilliantly carried off in a work by Hans Flato.

Born in Germany in 1887, a year after Reiss, Flato, too, had studied art in Munich. He arrived in New York in 1910 and very quickly opened his own design studio. Far more than Reiss (or any of the other Germans and Austrians in New York, for that matter), he understood how text itself could be manipulated to foster visual and spatial interest. His 1915 ad for Palm Beach, the brand name for the Goodall Worsted Company, relies on "competing" checkerboard-like zones of words and white space, enticing one to read but also to pause (fig. 110). Even when Flato, in a subsequent ad for Palm Beach, employed a more standard layout, he placed imagery and text in a related way, making large fields of open space, while cleverly introducing shading and multiple figures to contrive a scene (fig. 111).

There is no evidence that Calkins had any idea of the radical experiments that were then taking place in New York and on the West Coast. Most of these efforts, it should be said, were hidden away, largely in the avant-garde "pocket" of Greenwich Village, with its little art and political magazines, like *The Masses* (fig. 112). Even when Flato's ads appeared in *The Saturday Evening Post*, which Calkins almost certainly saw, they seem to have made little or no impression on him—likely because it wasn't the sort of art that he was championing. He, like most Americans at the time, favored the usual "illustration" ads, and he had little or no interest other directions.

And yet, some American artists were taking notice. Fred G. Cooper, who had begun working professionally in New York in 1904 (for New York Edison, among other major companies), experimented with a simplified, less commercial style that was close to what the German and Austrian émigrés were producing (figs. 113–115). A series of newspaper advertisements for Lowney's Chocolates in 1915 also reveal the Central Europeans' imprint (fig. 116). It is unknown who made these ads, since they are all unsigned—it may well even have been one of the German or Austrian émigrés, perhaps Flato—but, regardless, it is evident that the new design was having an impact.

112| Ilonka Karasz, cover of *The Masses*, December 1915. Offset lithograph on paper. Prints and Photographs Division, Library of Congress, Washington, D.C.

113 | Fred G. Cooper, *Posters*, ca. 1910. Poster, printed by the Marchbanks Press, New York, NY. Lithograph on paper, 40.6 × 27.9 cm. The Resnick Collection.

114 | Fred G. Cooper, *At the 5ᵗʰ Ave. Spirit Land*, ca. 1912. Poster. Lithograph on paper. Private collection.

A few other designs, by American-born designers, reveal how far the new style had penetrated. Carter Housh, a young Midwesterner, who had moved to New York and was making covers for *McCall's Magazine*, created one of the most arresting images of those years. It is a "mock ad" for a fictitious firm, the Renfrew Manufacturing Company (fig. 117). It shows a woman and a small girl, presumably her daughter, standing in a stiff wind, their clothes and hair being blown sharply to the left. The little girl's hat is flying off in the wind. They stand in front of a black ground, the girl in front of her mother. Once more, the perspective doesn't quite work; it is unclear what exactly in the scene—the woman's scarf, the windblown hat—is in the foreground and what lies further back. The scene seems distinctively American, but all the essential ingredients that Reiss and the others had brought with them from Central Europe are present: color blocking, perspectival distortion, the new lettering, and, most of all, an elemental simplicity.

Housh came by all this directly: he was close to the circle around Reiss, Karasz, and the *M.A.C.*, where this image appeared. He doubtless picked up the rudiments from them. There were others, however, who seem to have acquired these influences secondhand. One of the most interesting sets of magazine advertisements in the mid-1910s came from another Midwesterner, Roy Frederick Heinrich.

Heinrich, who signed his work with his initials, RFH, studied at the Connecticut Art Students League with Charles Noel Flagg and Robert Bolling Brandegee. He worked initially as an artist for the *Elmira Telegram* in New York State. Around 1910, he moved to Detroit, where he began illustrating automobile advertisements for Hudson, Packard, Ford, Chevrolet, Buick, Dodge, Chrysler, Cadillac, and other companies.

Heinrich's most compelling ads, however, were for the Zenith Carburetor Company. Heinrich changed "Zenith," the apex of the sun in the sky or a high point more generally, into a god—and what looks like a Norse one at that—who symbolizes the power and quality of the company's carburetor. One of these ads, from 1916, is heavily reliant on copy (as were most American advertisements of the day). Still, it possesses a remarkable power and freshness (fig. 118). "Zenith" is depicted in a triumphal pose, holding the carburetor aloft, surrounded by a victory wreath. The color combination—red, orange, and black—was most unusual for the time. Even more notable, though, is the presentation of the Zenith and the "machine," which are limned in black, outlining distinct and forceful color fields.

Another of Heinrich's ads pushed this mode of visual presentation even further (fig. 119). It presents the Zenith figure seated in a car, racing forward, his face frozen in patent determination. Much of what is apparent in these designs seems to be lifted directly from the Jugendstil—even if the imagery and typefaces appear American.

Where Heinrich was getting his ideas is uncertain. He may well have been looking at what the IAS, Reiss, or the other émigrés were doing. But it is conceivable that he was picking it all up directly from German or Austrian publications. Many of these journals, among them *Jugend*, *Simplicissimus*, and *Ver Sacrum*, circulated in the United States in those years, and American publications and ephemera from the four or five years prior to the U.S. entry into World War I are replete with examples of such direct borrowings. Two poster stamps, one from Baker Hambaugh Engravers, in Chicago, the other from the Kitson and Newman Artists and Photo Engravers studio, in Springfield, Massachusetts, display explicit appropriations from the Austrian Jugendstil (fig. 120). In an age when there were virtually no copyright protections for designs in the United States (the first laws covering the copying of designs, other than trademarks, would not come until more than a decade later), American commercial artists often "borrowed" European designs with impunity. The problem became so pervasive (this was also true in Europe) that *Das Plakat* put out two special issues during the war years highlighting the practice. The magazine included numerous examples of original designs that had been pirated by others, who often changed very little, if anything at all.[24]

A few American designers who had already established their own styles picked up features of the Jugendstil, subtly incorporating them. Will Carqueville's 1916 cover for *The Poster* magazine is an essay on purification (fig. 121). It is an evocation of the

115| Fred G. Cooper, *The Electrical Exposition and Motor Show of 1914*. Advertising brochure for the New York Edison Company, New York, NY. Offset lithograph on paper, image: 9.6 × 7.2 cm. CL.

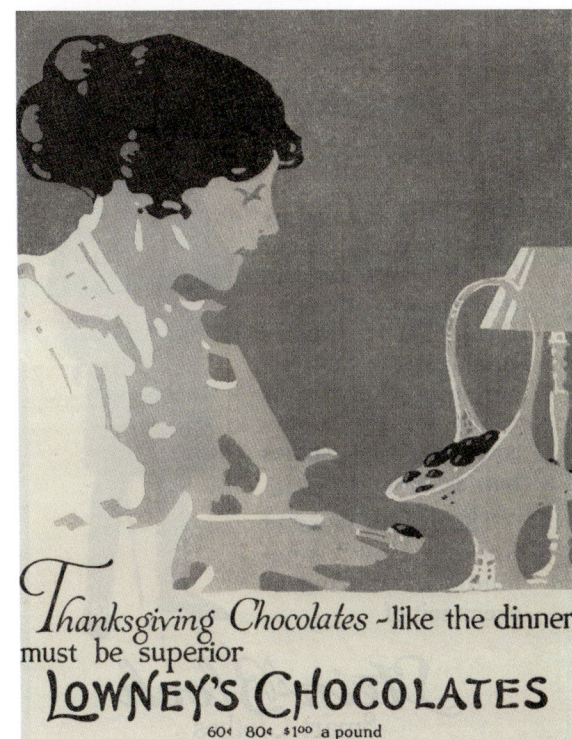

116| *Thanksgiving Chocolates—like the dinner must be superior, Lowney's Chocolates*, 1915. Newspaper advertisement. 15.4 × 11.7 cm. CL.

117 | Carter Housh, *Renfrew Manufacturing Co.*, ca. 1916. Sample advertisement. Offset lithograph, 30.8 × 23.4 cm. CL.

—————

118 | Roy Frederic Heinrich, *Zenith Results*, 1916. Magazine advertisement for the Zenith Carburetor Co., Detroit, MI. Offset lithograph on paper, 25.1 × 16.9 cm. CL.

119 | Roy Frederic Heinrich, *Zenith Power Plus*, 1916. Advertisement for the Zenith Carburetor Co., Detroit, MI. Offset lithograph on paper, image: 14 × 18.5 cm. CL.

120 | Advertising stamps: *Baker Hambaugh Engravers Chicago*, 1915. Lithograph on paper, 5.2 × 5.9 cm / *Kitson & Newman Artists and Photo Engravers*, ca. 1917. Lithograph on paper, image: 6.4 × 4.2 cm. CL.

The Poster
Dec.'16

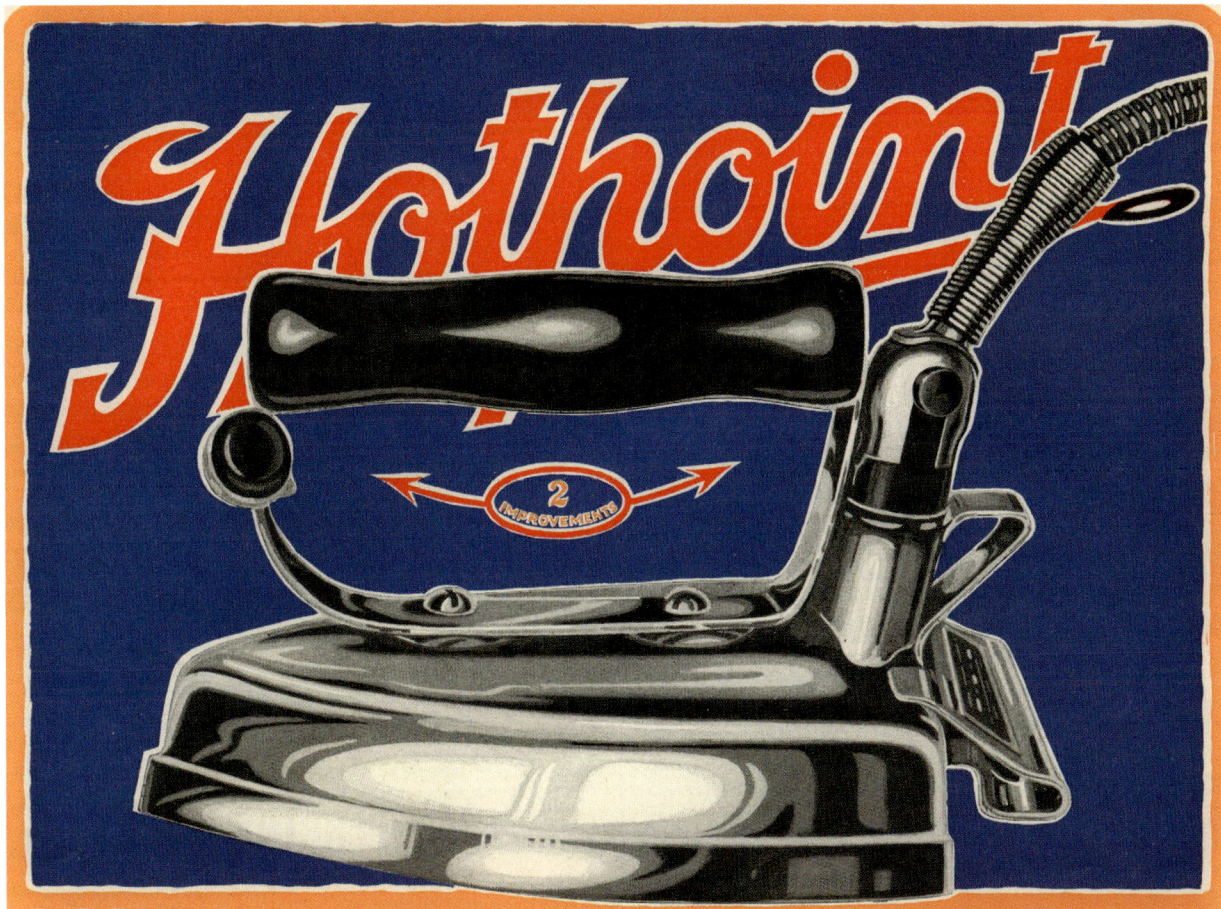

tale of the Christmas star, displaying only the heavenly firmament—nothing else. Coles Phillips's 1917 ad for Holeproof Hosiery is an admixture of his previous "floating" forms with the color-blocking and outlining inherent in the Central Europe Sachplakat (fig. 122). In a related way, the unknown artist who created an advertisement for Hotpoint Irons in 1917 adroitly adapted the Sachplakat emphasis on product and the name of its producer (fig. 123). Yet it comes off as fully American and not a "borrowing" in large measure because of its cursive script, which was related closely to the logos for the Ford Motor Company and Coca-Cola.

The new visual language that had arisen in Central Europe would soon find its way into the mainstream of American life in an even more energized and forceful form. It became one of the mainstays of the propaganda posters that began appearing after America's entry into World War I.

121 | Will Carqueville, cover of *The Poster*, December 1916. Private collection.

122 | Coles Phillips, *Holeproof Hosiery*, 1916. Magazine advertisement, designed for the International Art Service, from *The Saturday Evening Post*, September 16, 1916, 2. Halftone print on paper, 18.5 × 24 cm (detail). CL.

123 | *Hotpoint*, 1917. Magazine advertisement, for Hotpoint Electric Heating Company, Ontario, CA, from *The Ladies' Home Journal*, May 1917, 86. Halftone print on paper, 17.9 × 23.4 cm (detail). CL.

5 Over

Here!

The country's sudden shift to a wartime footing in April 1917 altered the shape and direction of American advertising. Very quickly—a sign of how industrially advanced and fully integrated the economy had become—the U.S. government and American business set about pursuing the war. The various governmental departments, both federal and local, charged with bolstering popular support for the war, immediately began commissioning posters, pamphlets, billboards, and other forms of advertising.

Most of the posters—the best of what came out of this effort—fell into one of three categories. Some were inducements to enlist, others were pleas for Americans to buy war bonds, and still others were meant to urge Americans to support the war effort at home, for example, through conserving food and other vital resources. A small number of posters—true propaganda instruments—were meant to arouse the passions of the public, to "define" the enemy (usually something akin to the "frightful Hun"), and to boost resolve.

The most prolific and important of the wartime poster artists were almost all men (few women received these commissions) who had been prominent in the advertising field before the war. Many, in fact, were well-known, even to the public.

Coles Phillips delivered one of the finest early posters, a plea to save electricity (and, by extension, coal) for the war effort (fig. 124). His design belongs to the annals of the late Jugendstil in America. It has a suspended and illuminated lightbulb surrounded by a halo of patterning (which could have been either Austrian or German), which Phillips conceivably took from an exhibition or magazine. The text—the message—is direct and concise, as is the typeface. The poster is very nearly a Sachplakat

COLES   PHILLIPS

LIGHT CONSUMES COAL
SAVE LIGHT   SAVE COAL

UNITED STATES FUEL ADMINISTRATION

124| Coles Phillips, *Light Consumes Coal Save Light Save Coal*, 1917. Poster, printed by Edwards & Deutsch Litho. Co., Chicago, IL, for United States Fuel Administration, Washington, D.C. Lithograph on paper, 70.8 × 51.9 cm. The Resnick Collection.

———————

125| Louis Fancher, *Over There! Skilled Workers*, 1917. Poster, printed for Aviation Section, U. S. Army Signal Corps, Ketterlinus, Philadelphia. Lithograph on paper. Library of Congress, Prints and Photographs Division, Washington, D.C.

in the best sense, and what makes it even more clever is the beaded cord, which one would engage to turn out the light. It is splendidly present in the composition, hanging across the front of the bulb and extending nearly to the bottom of the poster. Phillips makes abundantly apparent what the viewer is meant to do: pull the cord and shut off the power.

The clarity of the message is no accident: Phillips was one of the most skilled commercial artists of the day. He knew how to sell things—or ideas. That was true as well of Louis Fancher and Adolph Treidler, both of whom had worked with Calkins on the Pierce-Arrow ad campaign. Fancher's poster *Over There!* (the title was a play on the popular war song of the day) for the U. S. Army Signal Corps, like many of the war posters, applied the visual language of the Jugendstil to great effect (fig. 125). There is the usual color blocking, the flattened and layered perspective, silhou-

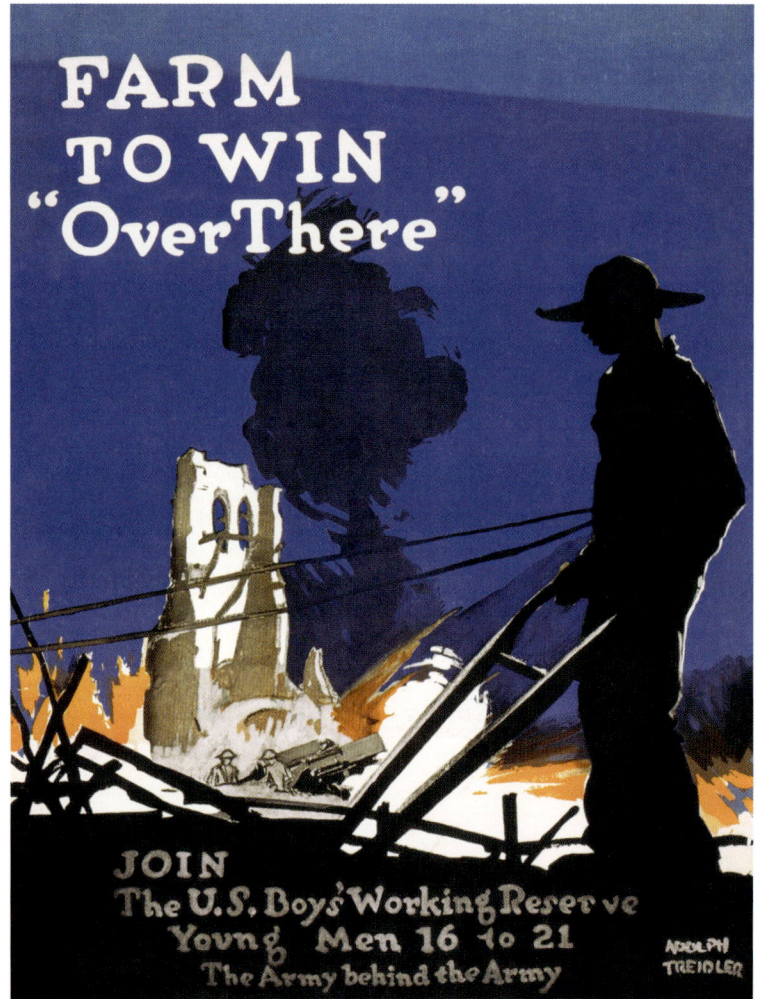

126 | Louis Fancher, *U.S. Official War Pictures*, 1917. Poster, printed by The Hegeman Print, New York, NY. Lithograph on paper, 100 × 71 cm. Library of Congress, Prints and Photographs Division, Washington, D.C.

127 | Adolph Treidler, *Farm to Win "Over There" Join the U.S. Boys' Working Reserve Young Men 16 to 21 The Army Behind the Army*, 1917. Poster, printed by the U.S. Government Printing Office, Washington, D.C. Lithograph on paper, 100 × 72 cm. Library of Congress, Prints and Photographs Division, Washington, D.C.

etting, the replication of elements, and readable text. Yet it is not a "German poster." Quite aside from the English-language legends and the Doughboy at the center, Fancher's way of putting text on the paper—and quite a lot of it—was much closer to American advertising. He was using some of the visual patois of Central Europe, while speaking plainly in English to an American audience in a familiar format.

Another of Fancher's posters, for the official U. S. War Pictures Department, was less conventional (fig. 126). Not only is it greatly more pared down—one sees only a single soldier filming combat with a camera—but much of the surface is black. It is as if we are peering through a thicket to glimpse the scene. All around the soldier, we see the battle: the other soldiers running forward, an airplane above, the explosions of artillery that illuminate the landscape and sky in vibrant orange, yellow, and green. Fancher was always one of the most adept of the prewar artists at creating a concise visual story. In this poster, though, everything is magnified; it is all happening hurriedly, intensely, and terrifyingly.

Treidler, too, knew how to relate a visual narrative with minimal means. In one of his most accomplished war posters, he does so with a stark and gripping juxtapo-

The Girl on the Land
Serves the Nation's Need
apply Y.W.C.A.
Land Service Committe

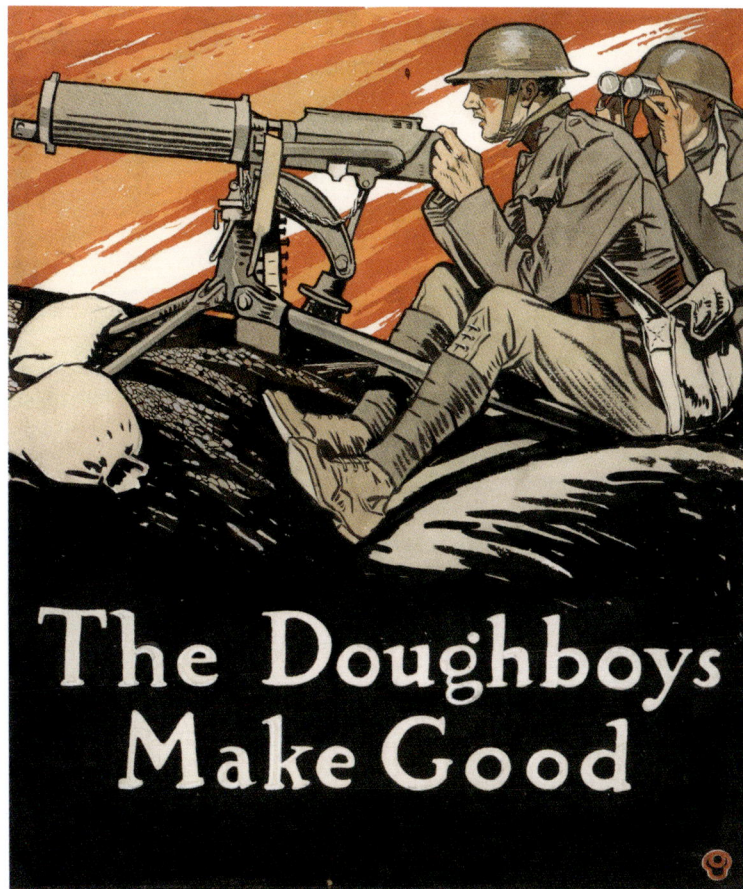

The Doughboys
Make Good

sition (fig. 127). In the foreground, we see a boy plowing a field. He seems placid, calmly going about his task. Behind him is a picture of horrific destruction: a burning village and ruined church, men firing a howitzer, smoke billowing up, and the sky aflame. The poster is a call for boys to join a "farming reserve," to ensure that there will be sufficient food to sustain the war effort. Treidler presents the viewer with a reminder that these two worlds are colliding, that the peaceful farming scene can play a key part in the war. It is a nearly perfect representation, requiring little text to impart the message.

Edward Penfield, who was by that time one of the deans of the modern poster, also contributed his talents to the war effort. One of his poster designs called on young women to work on farms, replacing the men who had gone off to war (fig. 128). It shows four young women carrying tools and leading a team of horses. The women are typical Penfield characters—young, attractive, and unmistakably from "better" families, which was not the target audience for the poster. But American commercial artists had learned that what was aspirational could also be convincing, and the working-class girls the program was seeking to attract could see themselves transformed through the experience. We also see evidence of the changing landscape of graphic design in America. Penfield's drawing style in 1918 was barely altered from his posters from thirty years before, but his color sense and lettering nonetheless owe something to the influence of the Sachplakat.

128| Edward Penfield, *The Girl on the Land Serves the Nation's Need Apply Y.W.C.A. Land Service Committee,* 1918. Poster, printed by The United States Printing & Lithograph Co., New York. Lithograph on paper, 63 × 76 cm. Library of Congress, Prints and Photographs Division, Washington, D.C.

129| Edward Penfield, *The Doughboys Make Good,* 1918. Maquette for a poster. Watercolor, India ink, and opaque white over graphite underdrawing on paper, 35.8 × 44.7 cm. Library of Congress, Prints and Photographs, Division Washington, D.C.

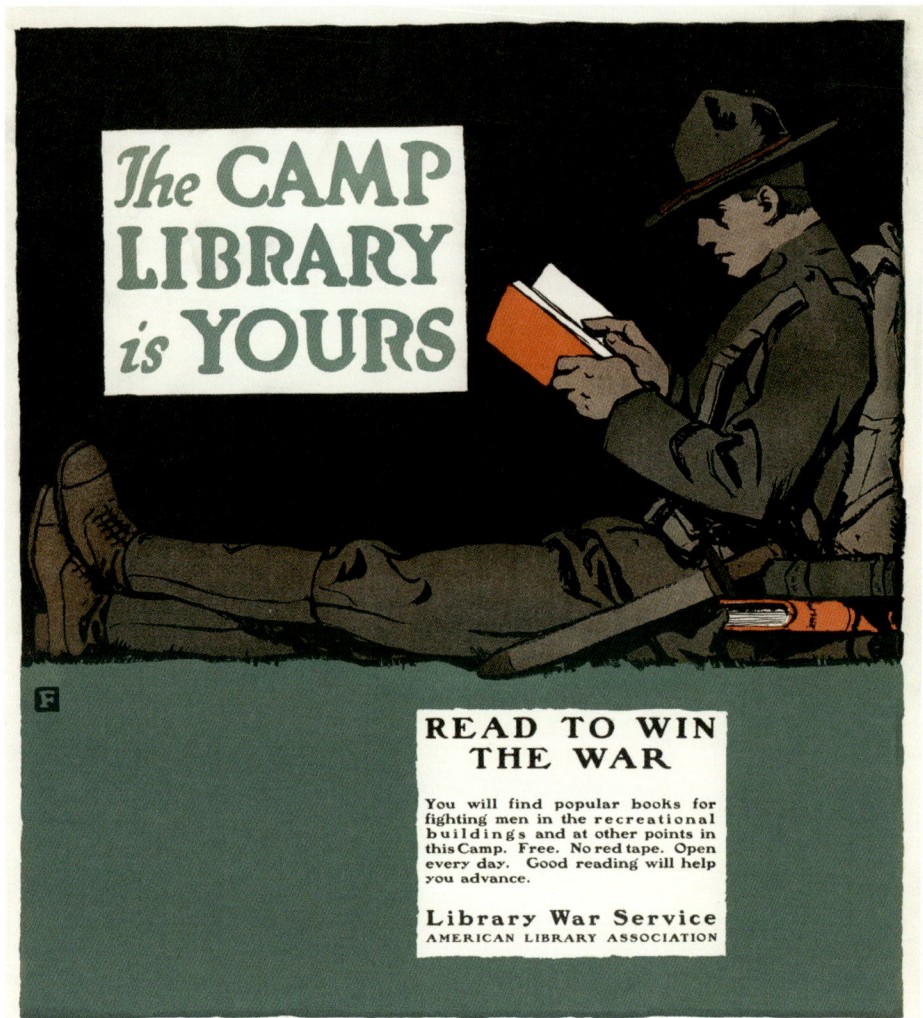

Another of Penfield's wartime designs, *The Doughboys Make Good*, from 1918, was intended to glorify the efforts of the American soldiers already in the field in France (fig. 129). It is a maquette for a *Collier's* magazine cover. By August of that year, when the cover appeared, U.S. forces had already distinguished themselves in the field, halting the German summer offensive. Penfield's cover shows two soldiers in action, one firing a machine gun, the other spotting for him with binoculars. This depiction is vintage Penfield; it is not entirely dissimilar from some of his turn-of-the-century football scenes. He gives us the gravity of the situation not with the figures or their facial expressions, which seem oddly placid or detached, but with a flaming sky that forms the backdrop for the action.

Two other posters, both by C. B. (Charles Buckles) Falls, exhibit very different visual strategies. Falls's poster for the American Library Association was meant to promote reading (fig. 130). (Officials at the War Department were alarmed by the low literacy rates they found among the recruits, even the native-born American soldiers.) For a "war poster," it is a remarkably peaceful scene: a soldier sitting and leaning on his backpack, reading a book. Much like Penfield's work, it is an admixture of the influences coming out of the poster movement and the more recent German and Austrian *Plakatstil*.

130| C. B. (Charles Buckles) Falls, *The Camp Library Is Yours Read to Win the War*, 1917. Poster, printed for the American Library Association, Washington, D.C. Lithograph on paper, 83 × 70 cm. Library of Congress, Prints and Photographs Division, Washington, D.C.

———————

131| Ernest Hamlin Baker, *A Speedy Termination of the War*, ca. 1917. Poster. Lithograph on paper, 47.6 × 31.5 cm. Private collection.

A SPEEDY TERMINATION OF THE WAR

This depends more than anything else on the support the United States gives the Allies. Our country cannot do justice to the job, unless railroad men get busy and do their part.... Are you awake to your responsibility?

THE NATION IS COUNTING ON YOU

ERNEST·HAMLIN·BAKER

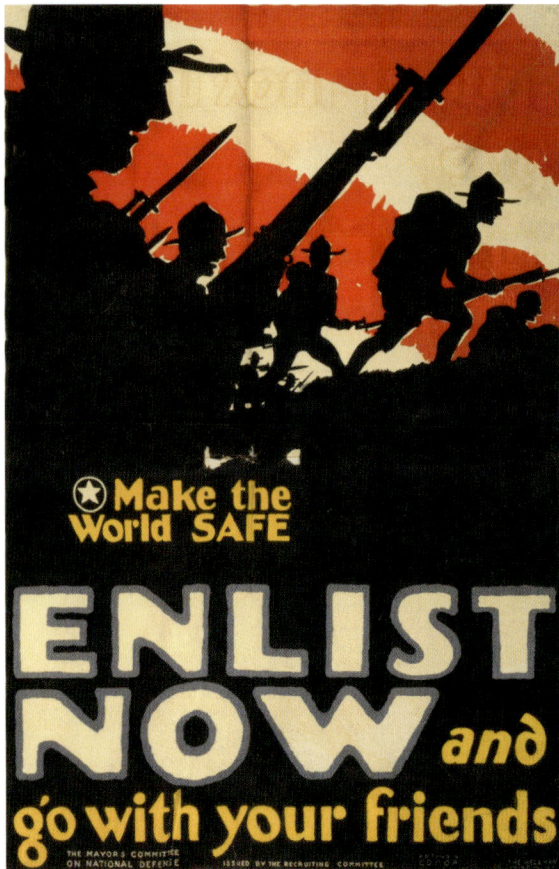

132 | Arthur N. Edrop, *Make the World Safe—Enlist Now and Go With Your Friends*, 1917. Poster, printed by The Hegeman Print, New York. Lithograph on paper, 100 × 68 cm. Library of Congress, Prints and Photographs Division, Washington, D.C.

133 | Ellsworth Young, *Remember Belgium Buy Bonds Fourth Liberty Loan*, 1918. Poster, printed by United States Printing & Lithography Co., New York. Lithograph on paper, 77.4 × 50.9 cm. Library of Congress, Prints and Photographs, Division Washington, D.C.

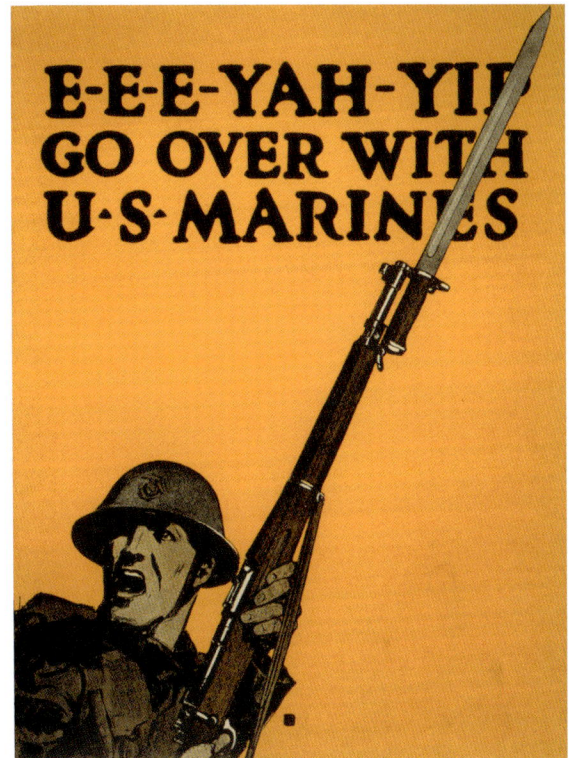

Ernest Hamlin Baker's *A Speedy Termination of the War* is an almost poetic presentation of the instruments necessary to carry out the war, all set out serially and in a strikingly linear fashion—with the sort of repetition that had become a centerpiece of Viennese design (fig. 131). Another innovative poster is *Make the World Safe—Enlist Now and Go With Your Friends*, by Arthur N. Edrop (fig. 132). It relies on considerable foreshortening (the soldiers "going over the top" are pulled up very close to the viewer) and magnification through silhouetting. We see only the plain figures, with virtually no detail. Edrop, though, is careful to give us their rifles and bayonets at the ready. And, to intensify the scene and convey a patriotic message, everything we see is happening set against the red and white stripes of an American flag, positioned in such a way that it can also be read as the flashes of distant artillery. American pre-war advertising had often featured one or more of these visual techniques, but never so fully in tandem and never to such dramatic effect.

134| John E. Sheridan, *Victorious War Strength Bethlehem Motor Trucks Dependable Delivery*, 1919. Magazine advertisement. Halftone print on paper, 34.8 × 25.9 cm. CL.

135| C. B. (Charles Buckles) Falls, *E-e-e-yah-yip Go over with U.S. Marines*, 1917. Poster. Lithograph on paper, 71 × 54 cm. Library of Congress, Prints and Photographs, Division Washington, D.C.

JOIN ME
THE FIRST TO FIGHT
ON LAND AND SEA
U·S·MARINES

136| C. B. (Charles Buckles) Falls, *Join Me*, 1917. Poster for the U. S. Marine Corps. Screen print with halftone color on paper, 28 × 55 cm. Library of Congress, Prints and Photographs Division, Washington, D.C.

This employment of almost but not quite minimal means is the underlying theme of another of the most memorable of the war posters, *Remember Belgium*, by Ellsworth Young (fig. 133). Ostensibly, it is a plea for the public to buy war bonds, but the moral is all too apparent. A German soldier—instantly identifiable because of his spiked helmet—is dragging away a screaming girl. It is perhaps the most lurid of all the American propaganda posters: the evil Germans who purportedly rape, pillage, and murder. It is a literal representation of "the rape of Belgium." Lost in this, though, are the brilliant—and quite prescient—structures of Young's visual narrative. Most of the poster is taken up with a green backdrop, which is speckled and blotched here and there to suggest the full battlefield. There are a few telling details: the destroyed village and the mustache of the soldier (which makes him appear even more menacing). And there's the fact that we don't see where the man and girl's hands are joined: just enough is given to us to imagine the rest of the scene. Just enough—not more. It is classic "illustration," but in American graphic design of this era it hardly got any better.

There are other posters that achieve similar results by focusing on an individual figure. John E. Sheridan's *Victorious War*, an advertisement for Bethlehem Trucks, which was made just after the war's end, is as much about the man as the machine (fig. 134). The truck sits in the background; before it, we see a soldier, his tunic removed, holding a large, gleaming artillery shell. His presentation and posture are homoerotic, but the overriding imagery speaks about something else. We do not see his face—we aren't meant to—for the poster is about the muscles and human "fiber" that won the war. That the truck had a role in all this is also stated, but it is secondary. Even the bold text is not what we see first. It is the man.

Three of C. B. Falls's designs are telling examples of this emphasis on the individual. Two are recruiting posters for the Marines. One has a man in the lower left corner, holding his gun up and looking back, calling for others to follow him into combat (fig. 135). The text, in bold black set over a yellow field, sits behind the bayonet, which conceals some of the letters. But every element in this composition demands attention: the soldier, the gun, the bayonet, the text—even the black square that Falls used as a signature.

Falls's other Marine poster is more commanding, if less energetic (fig. 136). It depicts the head of a soldier and his hat, collar, and gun. He is staring straight at us; his intense gaze and square jaw are meant to be the essence of Marine toughness. The gun, set at an angle, divides the poster; to the left, the man, to the right, the text, with the words "Join Me" in bold. The face, which at first seems so completely presented, is mostly zones of shadow and light. It is defined only where it needs to be so that we can read it as a face. We take for granted that it is a figural depiction; much more, though, it is an exercise in diminishment: the Marine's features are the least form necessary. It is the all too obvious drama that draws us in.

This is true, too, for what is perhaps the most captivating of Falls's war posters, a call for amateur wireless operators to join the Navy (fig. 137). With its splendid dynamism and almost comic book–like presentation, it seems some two decades too early. A signalman is at its center, holding a banner aloft. Behind him is a lightning bolt—or, more appropriately, a radio wave, though it doesn't look like one—cutting through a starry black sky. The colors are unusual for that time, especially in combination—a blue and a blue-green with orange lettering, set against black and white. The posture of the signalman is pure action, giving the scene an extraordinary sense of energy. He is not quite looking directly at us, but his whole manner is confrontational.

The apotheosis of this aesthetic of visage and stare is James Montgomery Flagg's *I Want You* poster (fig. 138). It is now so familiar, so ubiquitous that its strangeness is lost to us. An older man (Flagg in what is a rather peculiar self-portrait), wearing what looks like a clown suit, is glaring directly at us, his finger pointing in a manner that is "selective" and accusatory. The full gesture is less a beckoning to service than a command to do so.

Flagg, who was one of the most popular and successful illustrators of the day, is drawing on an archetypal American symbol, Uncle Sam, which first rose to popularity in newspapers and magazines in the mid-nineteenth century. The poster is also manifestly a reimagining of British designer Alfred Leete's earlier recruitment poster showing Lord Kitchener in a nearly identical pose. Flagg introduced his now-iconic version on the July 6, 1916, cover of *Leslie's Illustrated Weekly Newspaper*, as a plea for war preparedness. The following year, after the war started, he also tried out an image of a Marine for a poster (fig. 139). It, too, was successful—it is a good and effective presentation—but Flagg must have realized that it lacked the power and immediacy of his Uncle Sam, which became one of the best loved images of the

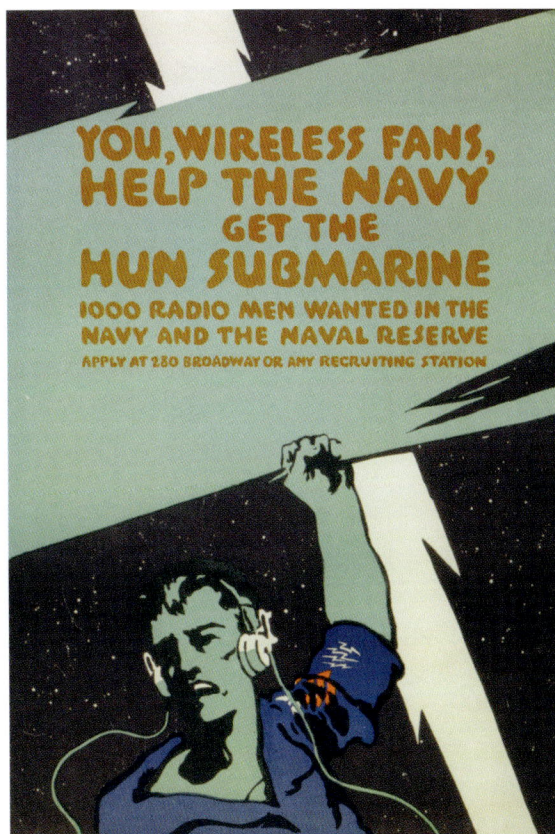

137 | C. B. (Charles Buckles) Falls, *You, Wireless Fans, Help the Navy get the Hun Submarine 1000 Radio Men Wanted in the Navy and the Naval Reserve*, ca. 1917. Poster. Lithograph on paper, 111.9 x 71.1 cm. Library of Congress, Prints and Photographs, Division Washington, D.C.

war—and long after that. Flagg's Uncle Sam, indeed, was so fully embraced that he repeated it often, in various forms. Many of the other artists of those years also referenced it in their posters or advertisements. The next year, the young Norman Rockwell, soon to achieve great public fame with his *Saturday Evening Post* covers, made a magazine advertisement for Del Monte acclaiming the company's efforts to contribute "to the National Food Basket" (fig. 140).

The difference between what Rockwell and Flagg were doing cuts to the heart of what would constitute the new graphic art. Both artists are relying on caricature. Their figures are notably well-drawn and have real presence. Flagg is already gesturing toward something else, however: namely, the separation between the mere pictorial and the liberation of symbol and words that allow them to float more freely on the surface of the page or poster. The words below seem to be set just in front of the gesturing old man; and they, too, have their independence. The whole poster is a form of shorthand—just what is needed to seize the eye and make the point. Rockwell comes close to this, but Flagg, even if he was not fully cognizant of it, is giving us an

138 | James Montgomery Flagg, *I Want You for U.S. Army*, 1917. Poster. Lithograph on paper, 102.3 × 75.5 cm. Library of Congress, Prints and Photographs Division, Washington, D.C.

139 | James Montgomery Flagg, *First in the fight Always faithful Be a U.S. Marine!*, 1918. Poster, printed for the U.S. Marine Corps. Photolithograph on paper. The Resnick Collection.

140 | Norman Rockwell, *A California Contribution to the National Market Basket*, 1918. Magazine advertisement for Del Monte, California Fruit Canners Association, Oakland, CA. From *The Saturday Evening Post*, January 26, 1918, 87. Halftone print on paper, image: 31 × 23.6 cm. CL.

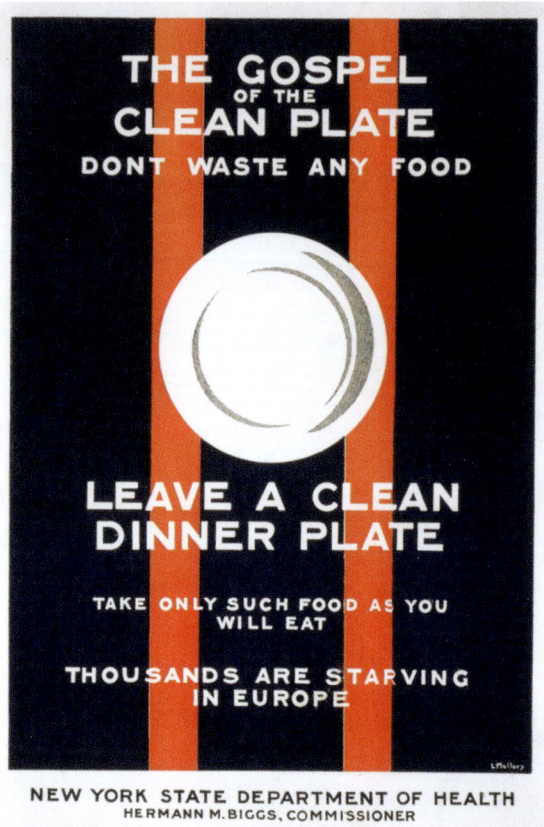

THE GOSPEL
OF THE
CLEAN PLATE
DON'T WASTE ANY FOOD

LEAVE A CLEAN
DINNER PLATE

TAKE ONLY SUCH FOOD AS YOU
WILL EAT

THOUSANDS ARE STARVING
IN EUROPE

NEW YORK STATE DEPARTMENT OF HEALTH
HERMANN M. BIGGS, COMMISSIONER

RED CROSS
JOIN

SINCLAIR'S
MAGAZINE
OCTOBER 1917

Triumphs of Petroleum

141 | L. Mallory, *The Gospel of the Clean Plate Don't Waste Any Food*, 1917. Poster, printed for the New York State Department of Health. Lithograph on paper, 35.5 × 25 cm. Library of Congress, Prints and Photographs Division, Washington, D.C.

142 | *Join*, ca. 1917. Poster, printed for the American Red Cross. Lithograph on paper, 56.2 × 35.6 cm. Museum of Fine Arts, Boston. Gift of John T. Spaulding.

143 | Carl Link, cover of *Sinclair's Magazine*, October 1917. Color lithograph on paper, 26.5 × 16.9 cm. CL.

---

144 | Carl Link, *The hot scourge of the city Why suffer from the lash when you can enjoy–*, ca. 1917. Brochure, printed by the Society for Modern Art for Bossert Bungalows, Brooklyn, NY. Offset lithograph on paper, 25.7 × 20.4 cm. CL.

early glance into the future when everything will become a game of elements set freely into two-dimensional space.

A few of the other war posters came close to this. The *Gospel of the Clean Plate*, the work of an artist who signed him or herself L. Mallory, is stripped to a bare minimum (fig. 141). We see only an empty plate resting on two parallel vertical red lines. Beyond that, there is only text. And "mere" text, or very close to it, is what defines another very good poster. It is a red cross with the word "Join" (fig. 142). Using the most basic means, a few words to remind people of something or call them to action, is a perfect way to make propaganda. The tactic was in a sense a refinement of the nineteenth-century handbill. But it is the mode of refinement that stands out. The plate and the cross are not incidental: they are part of the message, but they are distillations, meant to signify something, as directly and unambiguously as possible. In each case, they are placed fastidiously on the surface, positioned to catch and hold the eye, while enhancing the overall look of the poster. The red cross is the best of these, for it functions almost like a word. It is effectively one of the two "words" of the message.

What makes the American posters of World War I so important to the story of the rise of American design is that they were the results—perhaps better, the accumulations—of all that had happened over the previous three decades: the lessons of the poster craze, the growing understanding of how *visual* or artistic advertising could work, and the incorporation of the new visual language forms coming from Art Nouveau and the later Jugendstil. Without the dictates of commercial advertising, which remained heavily reliant on copy, they came very close to being a full-fledged revolution in graphic design. When the war ended, however, so did much of this progress; the commercial constraints that previously limited artists surfaced once more.

Yet there was also a give-and-take relationship between the most progressive wing of advertising and the war posters.[1] Some of the lessons the artists had learned in promoting government messaging came back to the big advertising agencies—or, at least, to those firms and artists working on the fringes.

There are examples of graphic design made during the war or just after the armistice for commercial clients that are certainly related to the wartime propaganda exercises. A magazine cover Carl Link designed for oil giant Sinclair can be read as a war poster (fig. 143). Link's brochure for a New York City program to ameliorate urban heat islands is in the same vein, though it is greatly more animated (fig. 144).

One firm that emerged toward the end of the war would assume a leading part in carrying the newest advances into the postwar era. Advertising Artists, Inc., for several years—until about 1925—would produce some of the most cutting-edge American advertisements. It was not exactly a new firm; rather, it was a follow-on to the company that had already had an outsized impact on American design: the International Art Service. Advertising Artists, Inc., began operating in early 1918 out of the same office in the Aeolian Building previously occupied by the IAS. Harry A. Weissberger, who had been the IAS's secretary-treasurer, and Willy Sesser, who had been its chief designer, were its founders.

Weissberger was born in 1879 in Prague where his father was serving as U.S. consul general. He studied for a time in Vienna and began working for the IAS a few years before the U.S. entry into the war.[2] At first, he had a limited role; but, before long, he assumed the part of office manager, overseeing the day-to-day running of the firm.

The IAS was a casualty of the American entry into the war. The firm was, in the eyes its clients and customers (and everyone else, for that matter), associated closely with Germany and modern German design—an enormous liability.[3] The coup de grâce came when Wiener became part of a scandal having to do with his support

145| Advertising Artists, Inc., *Buy Bull Dog Garden Hose*, ca. 1918. Advertisement, for Boston Hose and Rubber Co., Cambridge, MA., from Herbert E. Martini, *Applied Art: A Collection of Designs Showing the Tendencies of American Industrial Art*, vol. 1 (New York, F. K. Ferenz, 1919), plate 17. Lithograph on paper, sheet: 35 × 27.4 cm; image: 22 × 15.5 cm. CL.

146| *Buy Bull Dog Garden Hose*, ca. 1916. Magazine advertisement, for Boston Woven Hose and Rubber Company, Cambridge, MA. Halftone print on paper, 20.2 × 14.1 cm. CL.

147 | Advertising Artists, Inc., *Pulmosan Sandblast Helmet*, ca. 1918. Advertisement for the Multi Metal Separating Screen Company, New York, from Herbert E. Martini, *Applied Art: A Collection of Designs Showing the Tendencies of American Industrial Art*, vol. 1 (New York, F. K. Ferenz, 1919), plate 26. Lithograph on paper, sheet: 27.4 × 35 cm; image: 21.9 × 29.8 cm. CL.

———————

148 | Advertising Artists, Inc., *Let Alexander feed the power to your plant*, ca. 1917. Advertisement for Alexander Brothers, Philadelphia. From Herbert E. Martini, *Applied Art: A Collection of Designs Showing the Tendencies of American Industrial Art*, vol. 1 (New York, F. K. Ferenz, 1919), plate 3. Lithograph on paper, sheet: 35 × 27.4 cm; image: 29.2 × 21.4 cm. CL.

of the American Truth Society, an anti-British and pro-neutrality organization fronted by Jeremiah A. O'Leary, the editor of *Bull* magazine.[4] Wiener was charged with raising funds for the American Truth Society, a violation of the Espionage Act. He was arrested and sent to Ellis Island as a "dangerous" enemy alien.[5] His very public arrest, coupled with the fact that anti-German sentiment had become so virulent, made it impossible for the firm to continue to do business. With Wiener gone, the IAS ceased operating. The new company sent out notices specifically mentioning that all its officers were "American."[6]

By the first months of 1918—possibly earlier—Advertising Artists, Inc., was making posters and magazine ads. One of the carryovers from the IAS was an advertisement for Bulldog, a company that manufactured rubber garden hoses (fig. 145). The rudiments of the design—sharp outlining, flattened perspective, and bold text and depictions—were emblematic of the work of both firms. Sesser, or whoever else might have designed the ad, understood well how to create a compelling graphic statement.

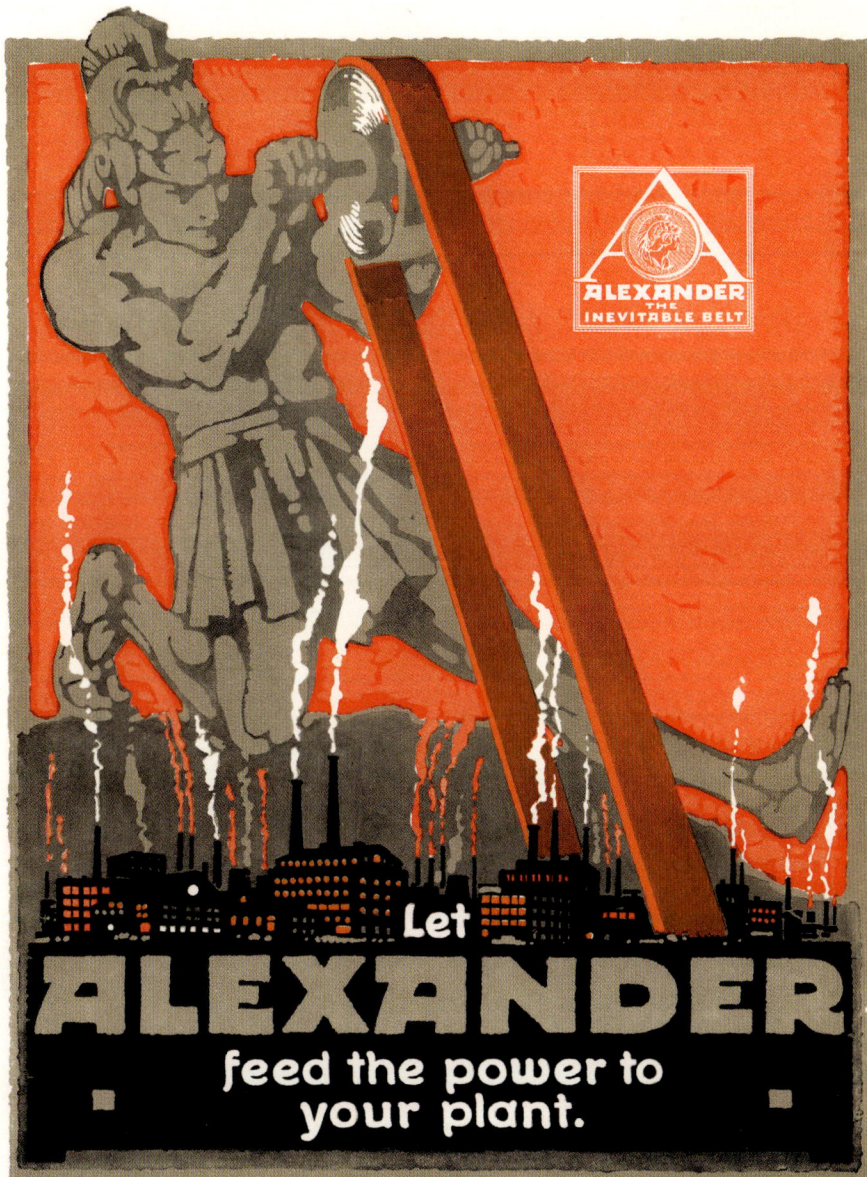

For at least a year or two, Bulldog had been placing a very similar advertisement in magazines, made for them by another, unnamed agency (fig. 146). The comparison is revealing. The original Bulldog design was superior to most American magazine ads of those years, communicating quite effectively the nature of the product and why one should buy it. But the Advertising Artists version is simply better: it is vibrant, appealing, and attention-grabbing—unavoidable even.

Two other ads by Advertising Artists from around 1918, one for the Pulmosan sandblasting helmet, the other for Alexander industrial belts, are equally arresting (figs. 147, 148). They sport the same brilliant colors and bold lines and typefaces but are greatly more animated, snippets of industrial activity that look more like scenes from a film.

Alexander had previously employed another artist, William Gray Purcell, to design its advertising, letterhead, and other corporate papers. Purcell was then working mostly as an architect in Chicago, building houses in the Prairie Style with his partner George

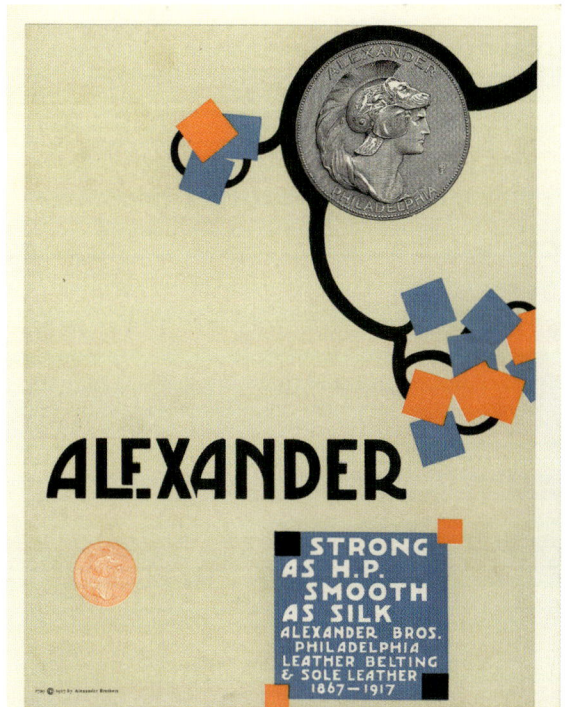

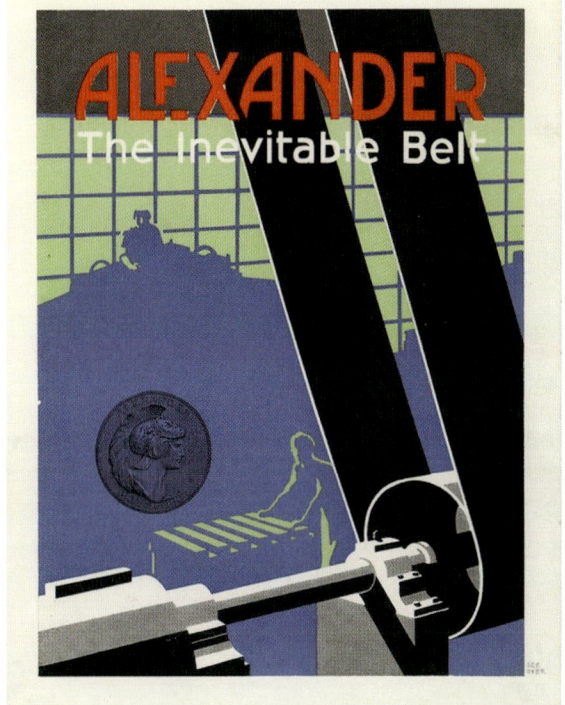

149| William Gray Purcell, *Alexander Strong as H.P. Smooth as Silk*, 1917. Poster for Alexander Brothers, Philadelphia. Lithograph on paper. William Gray Purcell Papers, Northwest Architectural Archives, University of Minnesota Libraries.

150| William Gray Purcell, *Alexander The Inevitable Belt*, ca. 1917. Poster for Alexander Brothers, Philadelphia. Lithograph on paper. William Gray Purcell Papers, Northwest Architectural Archives, University of Minnesota Libraries.

151 | Advertising Artists, Inc., *Distant Control eliminates Train Stops*, ca. 1918. Advertisement, from Herbert E. Martini, *Applied Art: A Collection of Designs Showing the Tendencies of American Industrial Art*, vol. 1 (New York, F. K. Ferenz, 1919), plate 12. Lithograph on paper, sheet: 35 × 27.4 cm; image: 29 × 20.2 cm. CL.

152 | Advertising Artists, Inc., cover of *Solving Advertising Art Problems*, 1919. CL.

153 | Advertising Artists, Inc., page from *Solving Advertising Art Problems*, 1919, 84. CL.

Elmslie. Graphic design for Elmslie was decidedly a side occupation, but he had a keen sense of the new, and he turned out several remarkable posters for Alexander.

One of these, from 1917, is a consummate example of Jugendstil-inspired abstraction, a mostly blank field, with a geometricized trailing vine, speckled with square florets, wrapping around an ancient coin depicting Alexander the Great (fig. 149). The lettering and text box on the lower right are as cutting edge as anything typographical being made in the United States in those year. More forward-looking still was a second poster Purcell fashioned the same year, a factory scene nearly precisionist in its presentation (fig. 150). In the foreground are a belt and engine; behind them, in the shadows, we see a silhouetted man working, the Alexander coin, and the barest hints of the factory's interior. Even compared with the level of diminishment and abstraction in some of the best war propaganda posters, this is a startlingly novel mode of depiction.

Alexander then hired Advertising Artists to take over their ad campaigns. The poster Advertising Artists made for the company, probably in early 1918, is not as simplified, but it is greatly more activated; the Alexander figure is intensely engaged in his efforts to control the spinning belt. He looks almost as if he has stepped out of history to demonstrate the resilience of the product.

Several of the Advertising Artists posters and magazine ads were reprinted in a portfolio: *Applied Art: A Collection of Designs Showing the Tendencies of American Industrial Art*. It was published in 1919, the first of a promised series of deluxe sets of plates showing the best in American graphic work. (It was to be the only one.[7]) The editor was Herbert E. Martini, an American artist and art materials supplier with German roots who was closely connected with the art scene in Greenwich Village. He teamed with printer F. K. Ferenz, a Viennese émigré who published artwork and advertisements in some of the Village's little magazines. Both men had connections with the *M.A.C.* and with Winold Reiss. Martini sometimes placed advertisements for his firm, Martini Tempera Colors, in the *M.A.C.*; and one color he offered, "Sesser Green," was named after Willy Sesser.[8] The large portfolio included fifty plates, many in color. From all outward signs, Martini and Ferenz published it to promote modern commercial art and illustration and their own businesses.[9]

Most of the plates in the *Applied Art* portfolio—which included works by Martini, Ferenz, Ernest Hamlin Baker, and others—reflected the cutting edge of American graphics. But one of the plates, by Advertising Artists, pushed well past that boundary. It was an announcement of a new technology, distant train control, which allowed operators to signal train engineers to halt or proceed (fig. 151). It is so forthright that its novelty is nearly lost to us now. We see only the signal tower, a brief text, and little else aside from a restrained depiction of a village and train tracks, set at the bottom. There is nothing else on the page, nothing to detract from the idea, nothing to "miss." It is its very ordinariness that draws the eye. We look precisely because there is so little to see.

In 1919, Weissberger, who was the animating force behind the Advertising Artists' rise, published a small, 124-page book (fig. 152). Most of it is taken up with examples of billboards, car cards, magazine advertisements, window displays, and

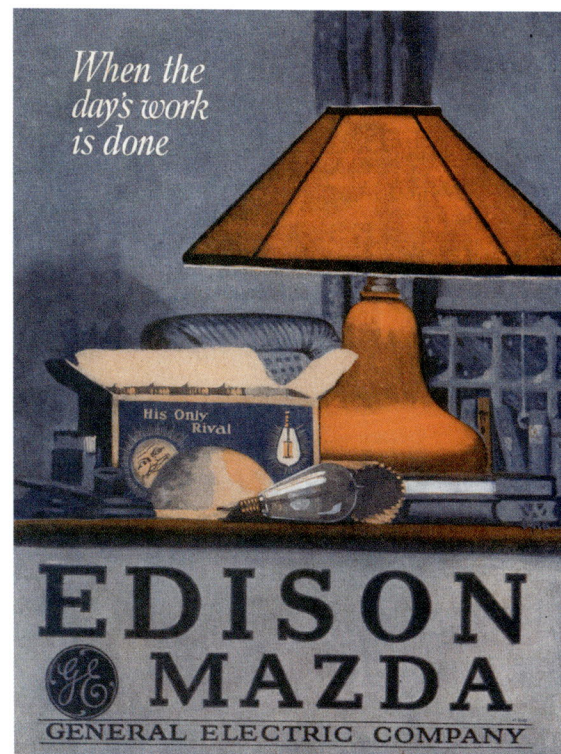

154| Advertising Artists, Inc., *Edison Mazda When the Day's Work Is Done*, 1919. Magazine advertisement for the General Electric Company, Schenectady, NY, from *The Saturday Evening Post*, January 18, 1919, 73. Halftone print on paper, image: 31.1 × 23.8. CL.

155 | Advertising Artists, Inc., "*Making the world sweeter,*"1920. Magazine advertisement, for the Sweets Company of the America, Inc., New York, NY, from *The Saturday Evening Post*, January 3, 1920, 124. Halftone print on paper, image: 31.2 × 24.1 cm. CL.

156 | Advertising Artists, Inc., Nut Tootsie Rolls, "*Making the world sweeter,*" ca. 1920. Magazine advertisement for The Sweets Company of the America, Inc., New York, NY. Halftone print on paper, image: 31.2 × 23.9 cm. CL.

packaging, all described as having been produced by the company. Some of the ads, however, are older, the work of the IAS, though there is no mention of the earlier firm. Each image is accompanied by a short text explaining the idea (or ideas) behind the design. What stands out is how aware—and sophisticated—Weissberger is about how the ads functioned, and what means were necessary for them to do so.[10] For a car card for Sloan's Liniment, for instance, the caption explains: "The figure is purposely subdued and treated in silhouette form so as not to detract from the action desired to be illustrated." For two newspaper ads for White Rock Mineral Water, the caption reads: "Two of a series of one column—50 line [*sic*] newspaper advertisements reduced. Simplicity of treatment; white space used advantageously" (fig. 153).

In the book's introduction, Weissberger, who wrote the text, makes clear the firm's guiding principles: "Artwork in advertising has but one duty: *to sell something.*

It may be employed for immediate sales, or its object may be to create prestige for the advertiser."[11] To this, he adds a not-so-subtle response to those corporate heads who were resistant to embrace the new graphic style: "Artwork must sell the public—not please the advertiser. Many a brilliant selling idea has been shelved because it did not strike the fancy of the advertiser."[12] Weissberger concedes, though, that in American advertising, copy was still king—that any design had to "be worthy of, and an efficient aid to, the copy which it accompanies or supplements."[13]

The ads the company made over the next few years were fully in accord with these precepts. One, for Edison's Mazda lightbulbs, featured a softly glowing table lamp—the perfect expression of the product—and the slogan: "When the day's work is done," promoting the idea of nighttime leisure (fig. 154). More eye-catching was the series of ads the firm made for Nut Tootsie Rolls with the slogan "Making the world sweeter." To underline the point, they presented images of an anthropomorphized Earth. In one instance, we see the moon chasing after a roll of the candies, in another the moon is shown with one candy stuck to its "head" in what appears to be a sendup of French film pioneer George Melies's 1902 short, *A Trip to the Moon*, which depicts a rocket ship hitting the moon's "eye" (figs. 155, 156).

For at least two or three years after the war, the look that Advertising Artists, Inc., had made popular was adopted by some other artists. A few extracted only the color ideas, which was the case in an ad for Indian Head Cloth by Charles Herbert Woodbury; others, such as Ernest Hamlin Baker's ad for Victor Traps, were closely related to the language Advertising Artists had pioneered (figs. 157, 158).

American tastes were soon to change. For much of the next decade, the mainstream of American advertising would be driven by a persistent conservatism and economic necessity. There would, however, be a few brighter moments—and some bold experiments.

157| Charles Herbert Woodbury, *Instead of Linen— Indian Head Cloth*, 1918. Advertisement for Amory, Browne & Co., Boston, MA. Halftone print on paper, 36.9 × 24 cm. CL.

158| Ernest Hamlin Baker, *Victor Traps Sure to Go–Sure to Hold*, 1919. Advertisement, from Herbert E. Martini, *Applied Art: A Collection of Designs Showing the Tendencies of American Industrial Art*, vol. 1 (New York, F. K. Ferenz, 1919), plate 29. Lithograph on paper, sheet: 27.4 × 35 cm; image: 22.5 × 16 cm. CL.

6 A Renewed

Vision

After loudly promoting the cause of art in advertising for more than two decades, Earnest Elmo Calkins did something that, although neither he nor anyone else quite realized it at the time, would greatly slow the appearance of modern graphic design in the United States. It seemed at first to be the opposite, a logical and progressive move, one that was widely and enthusiastically applauded in the advertising industry and by the commercial artists who toiled therein. In early 1920, he and Louis Pedlar, another executive at Calkins & Holden, cofounded the Art Directors Club of New York.

The new association was a follow-on to the exhibitions of advertising artists Calkins had organized before the war. He continued to proclaim to anyone who would listen that advertising was first and foremost about image-making. "Art," as he put it, "is the most real and practical weapon in the whole armory of advertising." The new Art Directors Club, Calkins insisted, would "dignify the field of business art in the eyes of artists" and communicate the message that "artistic excellence is vitally necessary to successful advertising."[1]

In March 1921, the new group mounted its first juried exhibition in the rooms of the National Arts Club, at 119 East Nineteenth Street. Calkins expressly chose the location because he believed that the association with such a respected organization would lend weight to what he hoped would be a pivotal moment in American art.

Admission was free, and people from all walks of life were encouraged to attend. But the posters and newspaper ads that appeared that late winter disclosed a deeper truth. Their tagline, "Every American business man [sic] should see this Exhibition,"

FIRE

The Outlaw

FIRE will thrive so long as it has property to feed on. America's staggering losses will continue so long as carelessness prevails.

Insurance replaces what is destroyed, but the menace remains. That is why you should insure with the HARTFORD FIRE INSURANCE COMPANY, which promptly repays you for property destroyed and also gives you, at no extra cost, a fire prevention service that removes the menace of fire so far as it is humanly possible to do so.

Hartford Fire Insurance Co.
Hartford Conn.

The Hartford Fire Insurance Company and The Hartford Accident & Indemnity Co. write practically every form of insurance except life. Any agent or broker can get a Hartford policy for you.

159 | René Clarke, *Fire The Outlaw*, 1920. Magazine advertisement, for Hartford Fire Insurance Co., Hartford, CT, in *The Saturday Evening Post*, May 1, 1920, 157. Offset print on paper, 32 × 24.5 cm (trimmed). CL.

made clear the show's true objective: it was intended to sell the nation's corporate leaders on the idea that advertising art was good for their bottom line.[2]

In hindsight, that first Art Directors exhibition revealed something else: that much of the progress that had been made during the war had been lost. Many of the best known and established American commercial artists took part in the show, including C. B. Falls, Earl Horter, J. C. Leyendecker, Edward Penfield, Maxfield Parrish, and Norman Rockwell; they, in turn, represented all the major national advertising agencies. The results, however, fell well below the best works of the previous five or six years. A great deal of what went up on the walls could be rightly classed as workaday illustration—and much of it on the conservative side at that. Only a tiny number of designs showed the impress of the recent European art movements.

The awards, announced at a gala dinner on March 2, reflected the tastes of Calkins and the club's other leading figures—the tastes of men well into middle age, with worn-out ideas of art and its purposes, men who were interested mostly in selling things. The first prize, for painting and drawing, went to W. E. Hoitland for a pedestrian image of a dancing "Carmen." Fred R. Cruger won the black-and-white illustration prize for a less-than-adventurous depiction of an American artillery unit in action on the Western Front. There were a few bright spots, including an elegant ad for Pierce-Arrow, made by Adolph Treidler, and a series of posters, created by René Clarke, for Wesson Oil. But they were few and quite far between.

The best of the works on display was a maquette from Clarke (which became a magazine ad) for the Hartford Fire Insurance Company (fig. 159). It features a handsomely rendered flaming wolf—fire itself—set against a bold black background. The wolf's front right paw extends outside the black box, appearing as if the animal is moving toward the viewer, bringing its menace. The word "Fire," above on the left, and "The Outlaw," in the lower right-hand corner, luridly set out the message.

In a short article in *Printers' Ink Monthly* published immediately after the exhibition closed, Calkins declared his satisfaction with the event and the work shown, lauding "the beauty from an art point of view of a great many of the designs" and "their story-telling power."[3] But that was the problem. The Art Directors annual exhibitions over the next decade and a half, at least until the mid-1930s, sanctioned advertising art that was salable and popular, but which did little to advance the cause of graphic design itself.

That precise formulation, *graphic design*, as we now use it, was not coined until the following year. It was first put into print in a newspaper article written by William Addison Dwiggins. Dwiggins, whose reputation was mostly founded on his work as a typographer, wrote simply but prophetically, that "advertising design... is the only form of graphic design that gets home to everybody."[4] Dwiggins also underscored another important point: that adverting design was only one form of the larger enterprise of "graphic design."[5] He lays out a "moral code" for advertising artists, one that, in essence, called for a wholly new approach to graphic art:

Cultivate simplicity. Have simple styles of letters and simple arrangements.

In the matter of layout, forget art at the start and use horse-sense.

Have pictures consistent with the printing process. Printers' ink and paper are a convention for light and shade and color. Stay inside the convention.

Be niggardly with decorations, borders and such accessories. Do not pile up ornament like flowers at a funeral. Scheme the white spaces—paper is indeed a "part of the picture." Manipulate the spaces of blank paper around and among the printed surfaces to make a pleasing pattern of areas.

Get acquainted with the shapes of the type letters themselves. They are the unit out of which the structure is made—unassembled brick and beams. Pick good ones and stick to them.[6]

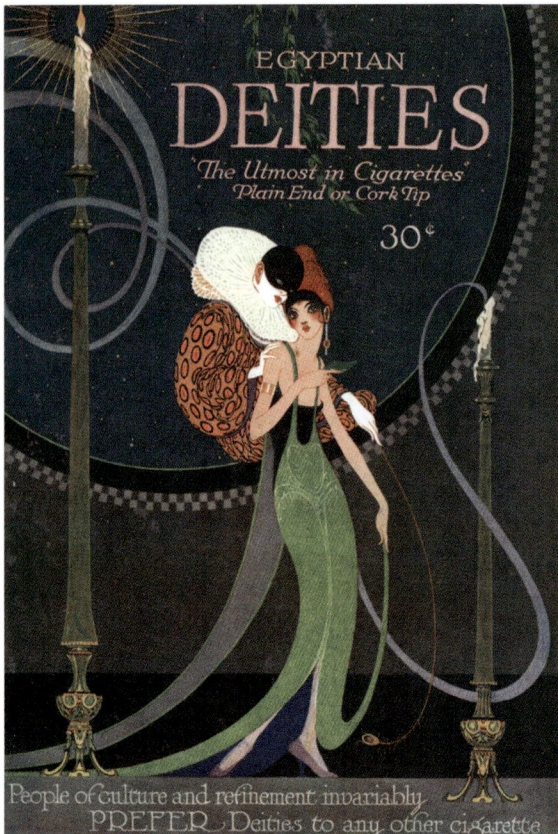

Dwiggins was working with publisher Alfred A. Knopf as a book designer; there are hints of this in his "code." Yet he understood a central issue concerning *imagery* that was not yet standard practice for the Art Directors. It comes out in two things he writes, namely, that the art (and here he is clearly thinking of illustration in the traditional sense) should be secondary to the overall idea; and, even more fundamental, that graphic design is, to paraphrase him slightly, about scheming the white space. He is saying in essence that graphic art is at its heart conceptual, that it is fundamentally a matter of two-dimensional composition—long before these ideas became gospel in American advertising.

Beyond the world of the Art Directors Club and the big agencies on Madison Avenue (which was just then turning into a stand-in expression for the American advertising industry), the search for a new aesthetic went on. In those first few years after the war, there was a parade of new design ideas, most of them inspired by the recent turns in European art. Art Deco, in its nascent French form, was already appearing— even in mainstream advertising (fig. 160). And Winold Reiss and a few others were working in the mode of German Expressionism (fig. 161). The most prescient designs, though, were in a different language altogether, and they appeared in places far removed from the world of American big business and advertising. It was in the little cultural and political magazines coming from "outsider" places, like Greenwich Village (which had already been main source for new ideas) and Harlem, that a wholly new form of American graphic design was being conceived.

The covers and advertisements of these publications became fields for every sort of experimentation. Their makers faced none of the restrictions that limited the commercial artists working for the big advertisers or magazines. Some of their designs— especially portraits—amounted to little more than caricature. Yet what was compelling and important was the willingness of these artists to mix and match styles freely—everything from what remained of the Art Nouveau to the new classicized Art Deco, Expressionism, Futurism, Cubism, and more—and to do so without hesitation or restriction (figs. 162, 163). The resulting amalgam was often distinctive and uniquely American—and very different from what was being made in Europe at the time.

This activity was not limited to New York. There were pockets of avant-gardism in other U.S. cities, including Detroit, Philadelphia, Cleveland, San Francisco, and Los Angeles. Some of those who were part of this world were frustrated commercial artists, looking for a form of release outside their jobs. Many were engaged—culturally, artistically, socially, or politically—with the cause of reform.

One of the most energetic of these groups was the Kokoon Arts Club, in Cleveland. It was a raucous, freewheeling consortium of artists, founded in 1911 by Carl Moellman, William Sommer, and Elmer Brubeck to promote the cause of modernism. The club put out tribute books for its annual fundraising balls filled with splendidly animated renderings, many of them advertisements (fig. 164).[7] For years, Kokoon's artists also announced these balls with brilliantly colorful and fanciful posters (fig. 165).

Other innovative design of the 1920s came from a wholly different place: the political left. The artists and designers associated with the sundry socialist and communist groups in the big cities had a limited scope of messages: they "spoke" about the ills of capitalism and the power of the working class—nearly ad nauseum, it should be said. But they did so in a forceful and lucid way, and they fashioned indelible images, many borrowing from the latest currents of art. Especially important for the future was the pronounced informality of their posters, pamphlets, and handbills, which sometimes used hand-lettering (rather than standard print typefaces).

On Hugo Gellert's 1924 poster *Vote Communist*, made for the American Communist Party, we see a brawny worker, entirely in red, holding up a hammer and sickle (fig. 166). His feet are spanning the landscape, city and factory to the left, farm and countryside to the right. The placement of the worker and the lettering at first seem to be no different from what would see in commercial advertising. Yet if one examines the image more closely, it is evident that everything simply rests on the page, freely and independently. Though still mostly conventional, it a premonition of the more "liberated" graphic design Dwiggins was trumpeting.

160| Fred Packer, *Egyptian Deities The Utmost in Cigarettes Plain End or Cork Tip*, 1919. Magazine advertisement, from *Country Life*, December 1919, 88. Halftone print on paper, sheet: 35 × 31.1 cm. CL.

161| Winold Reiss, *Crillon, 15 East 48th Street, New York City*, 1919. Advertisement. Offset lithograph. 28.6 × 21.3 cm. CL.

162| Frank Walts, cover of *The Crisis*, May 1920. Offset lithograph on paper, 24.8 × 17.1 cm. Private collection.

163| M. S. [?], cover of *The Quill*, September 1920. Offset lithograph on paper, 17.2 × 14.1 cm. Private collection.

164 | Edwin G. Sommer, *The Green Cab Co.*, advertisement, 1924. The Resnick Collection.

165 | James Harley Minter, *Bal Papillion*, 1931. Poster, printed by the Crane Howard Litho. Co., Cleveland, OH, for the Kokoon Arts Club, Cleveland, OH. Photolithograph on paper, 50.2 × 35.6 cm. The Resnick Collection.

166 | Hugo Gellert, *Vote Communist*, 1924. Poster, printed for the Communist Workers Party, New York, NY. Lithograph on paper, 55.9 × 34.3 cm. The Resnick Collection.

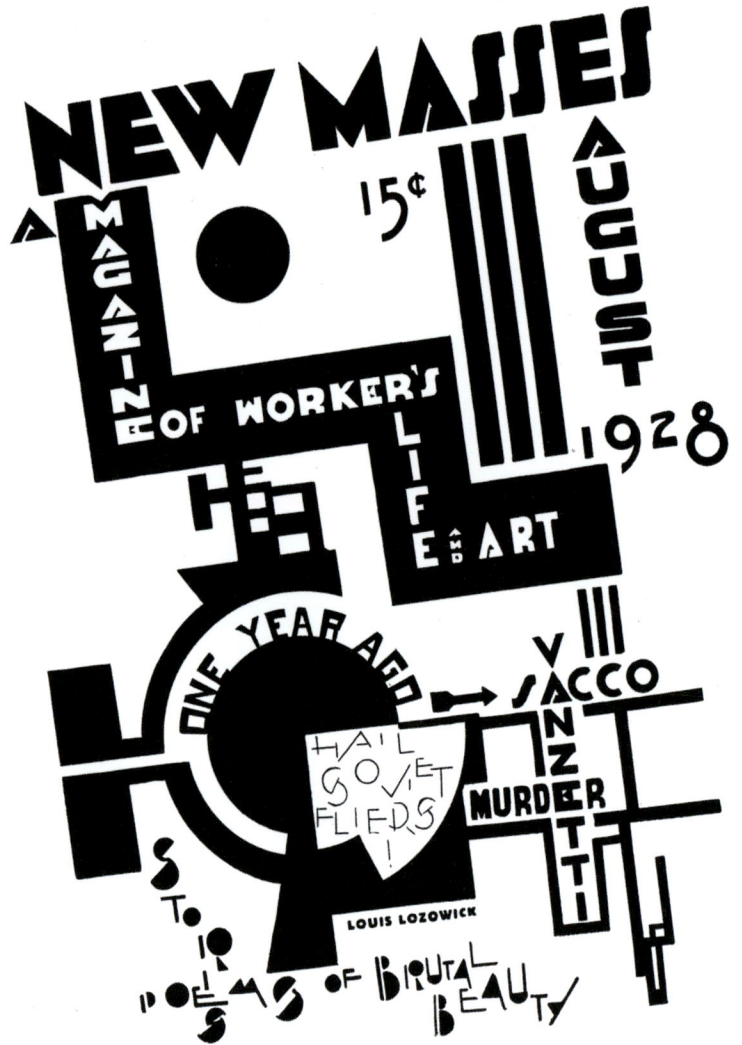

167 | Louis Lozowick, cover of *The New Masses*, October 1926. Lithograph on paper, 27.9 × 21.9 cm. Private collection.

168 | Louis Lozowick, cover of *The New Masses*, August 1928. Halftone print on paper, 27.9 × 21.9 cm. Private collection.

As the 1920s wore on, what was also becoming ever more visible in the graphic designs of the American left was a mounting allegiance to the newest art currents. Louis Lozowick was the American forerunner of this turn to modernism and perhaps the most innovative of the American graphic artists of those years.

He was born in 1892 in a small village in Kyiv Oblast in present-day Ukraine. He first attended the Kyiv Art School before moving to the United States, where he continued his studies at the National Academy of Design and Ohio State University. For nearly five years, from 1919 to 1924, Lozowick traveled through Europe, spending time in Paris, Moscow, and Berlin. After returning to New York, he joined the editorial board of *The New Masses*. Lozowick, by then, was well versed in the newest artistic developments in Europe, including Cubism, Constructivism, and the Dutch De Stijl, and he adapted their form-languages, applying them to the many covers he made for the magazine. His October 1926 cover design shows a fractured urban scene, sliced and flattened to the point where it has almost become pattern (fig. 167). More radical and evocative still was his August 1928 cover, which shows the influence of El Lissitzky and Piet Mondrian, among others (fig. 168). These works stood a galaxy apart from anything in the mainstream American media of those years.

And yet, even in the commercial orbit of the 1920s, one could find progressive design. If not as radical, the best of these were, in their own ways, as sophisticated—it not more so—than what was in the little magazines. This was true especially in their display of individual objects (or, sometimes, objects in groups) and how they communicated messages.

A Goodrich Silvertown Cord Tires magazine advertisement from 1919, for instance, could readily be called a Sachplakat (fig. 169). The whole left-hand side is given over to an image of a single tire cutting though a sort of liquid rainbow. The text—the copy—on the right was then standard for American mainstream advertising. It is not, though, what one mostly perceives. It is the tire, pure and unconnected, floating in its own space, that lures the eye. That it is separated from the text was an important advance. It would still be many years before the major American advertising agencies were willing to dispense with copy entirely; but the idea that the object could stand on its own—and sell itself—was already a significant step.

A Texaco ad from a few years later represents another breakthrough: the idea that an object (or objects: here, a lineup of test tubes) can represent a concept (fig. 170). The company isn't selling test tubes; it is promoting the notion that its fuels

169 | *Silvertown Cord Tires "Best in the Long Run,"* ca. 1919. Magazine advertisement for the B. F. Goodrich Rubber Company, Akron, OH. Halftone print on paper, two sheets, each 35.3 × 24.4 cm. CL.

170 | *Every test tube tells a story Texaco Motor Oil*, 1925. Magazine advertisement for the Texas Company, Houston, TX, from *The Saturday Evening Post*, August 22, 1925, 72–73. Halftone print on paper, 2 sheets, each 33.1 × 26.1 cm (cropped). CL.

are "science-based" and, thus, better than those of the competition. The slogan, "Every test tube tells a story," is literally true, for it is the science story that is at the heart of the ad. The rendering technique used by the unknown artist (possibly working for Advertising Artists, Inc., given its stylistic language) is not new; it goes back to the mid-1910s and the influence of the new German poster style. In the background, one sees a landscape, a "production narrative," leading from the oil field to the modern city. It is the perspectival effect, though, that is most interesting: the test tubes are pulled forward, even though they read almost as flat; and their scale is altered: they are much bigger than anything else we see.

Another magazine advertisement from around the same time, for Fry gasoline pumps, works in both ways, which is to say as a form of Sachplakat and as a type of oblique messaging (fig. 171). A single gas pump stands alone, taking up much of the page. (There is a facing page, with text, but it is almost inconsequential.) What the ad conveys is not merely the idea that one should buy (or use) such a pump, but why: that it is accurate, that the amount of gas pumped is visible and therefore reliable. The ad achieves this, even without the text; most of what is being "said" comes through the image alone.

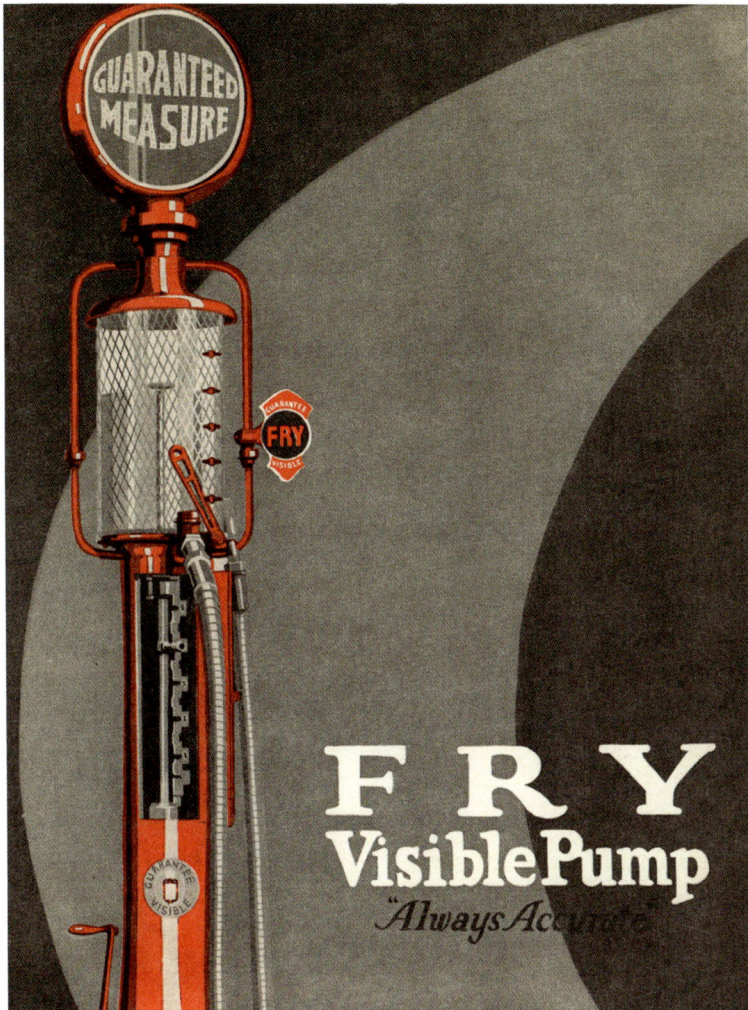

René Clarke, who continued to work for Calkins & Holden, created a related advertisement. It shows the product—Wesson Oil—drizzling slowly into a pan (fig. 172). The stream flows through the words "Pure Delicious Vegetable Fat," but it is the image itself that is meant to convince the consumer. Clarke made it beautiful, setting the scene on a sumptuous blue background, with a shiny silver pan below. The genius though, is in the can: that Clarke turned it upside down obliges us to look, to pause and read the label, to see the name of the product. It is a very astute form of branding—exactly the marketing strategy that Calkins & Holden were now promoting.

All these ads are modern in another way. They are not only modern in terms of how they depict the objects, but also because the objects themselves—a tire, test tubes, a gas pump, a can of cooking oil—are explicitly artifacts of modern life. What made so many of the commercial artworks of this era stand out as American is that they offer testimony to the realities of a country that had already been profoundly reshaped by industrialization and mass marketing.

The degree to which this was a fixed experience is demonstrated in another series of magazine advertisements of the mid-1920s, for the Campbell Soup Company. Campbell's had by this time introduced its classic can and label.[8] Whoever designed

171 | *Fry Visible Pump "Always Accurate,"* 1924. Magazine advertisement for Guarantee Liquid Measure Company, Rochester, PA, from *The Saturday Evening Post,* March 1, 1924, 126. Halftone print on paper, 34.6 × 25.7 cm. CL.

172 | René Clarke, *Wesson Oil,* 1926. Advertisement for Wesson Oil Company, Savannah, GA. Halftone print on paper, 26.8 × 18.3 cm (trimmed). CL.

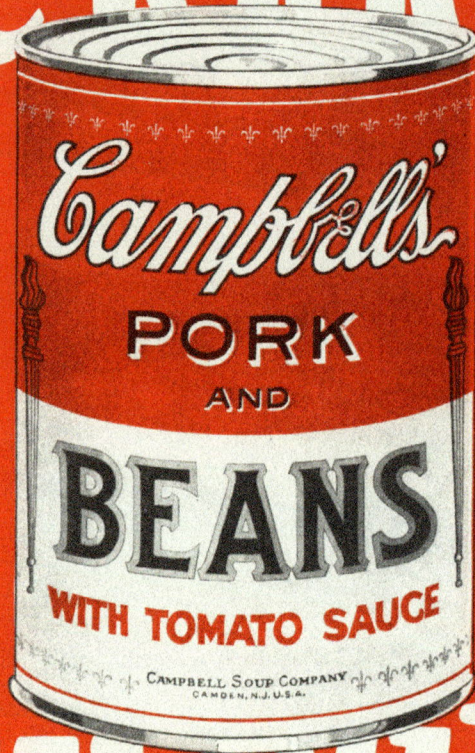

The food for your outing

Campbell's PORK AND BEANS WITH TOMATO SAUCE

CAMPBELL SOUP COMPANY
CAMDEN, N.J. U.S.A.

Everybody will be taking Campbell's Beans along.

For the holidays at the seashore and mountains, for the meals in the open, for the picnics and the big hikes.

They are such delicious food, such substantial food.

And they're mighty convenient food!

Be sure to be liberally supplied and be sure the beans are Campbell's!

12 cents a can, except in Rocky Mountain States and in Canada

Slow~cooked   **Digestible**

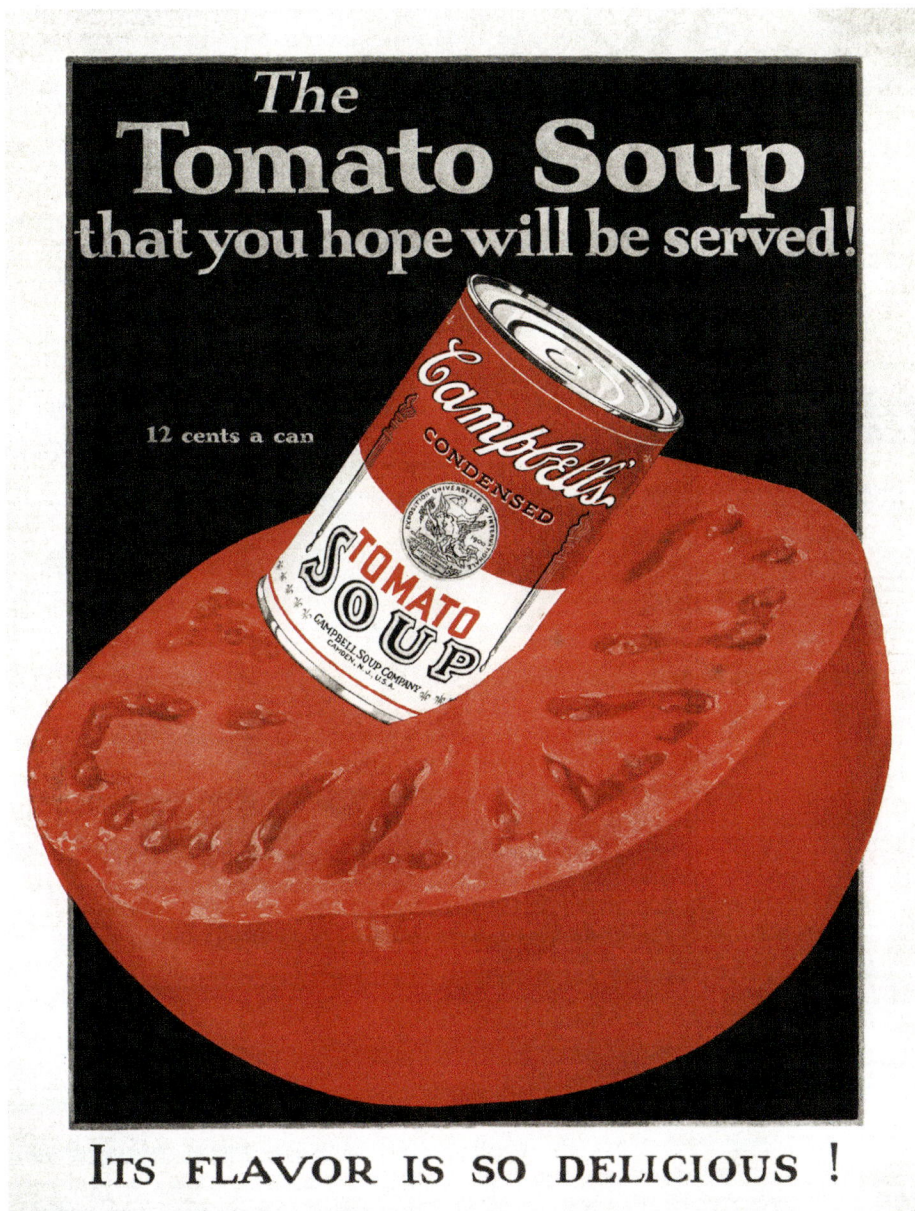

Figure: *The Tomato Soup that you hope will be served!* advertisement. The slogan reads "The Tomato Soup that you hope will be served!" with "12 cents a can" and "ITS FLAVOR IS SO DELICIOUS!"

their ads (they are unsigned, though again it may have been one of artists associated with Advertising Artists)—understood the power of that image; the ads the company ran in national magazines in the mid-1920s all feature the can (with varied labels) and simple slogans (fig. 173). There is also copy, but it is greatly reduced in size and length. What leaps out instead is the iconic can and the large lettering of the slogan itself. Many of the ads also rely on bright crimson backgrounds, which make the other elements stand out even more. In some of these designs, bits of the texts are covered by the cans. But there is something else notable about them: many cast the product in a manner meant to make it unforgettable.

This tactic is remarkably and indelibly on display in an ad from 1925 (fig. 174). It shows a can of Campbell's tomato soup resting at an angle, embedded in a giant and luscious half-tomato. The slogan reads: "The Tomato Soup that you hope will be served!" Most of the message, however, is visual. If it is this tomato that we see in

173 | *The Food for your outing*, 1924. Magazine advertisement for the Campbell Soup Company, Camden, NJ, from *The Saturday Evening Post*, May 31, 1924, 29. Halftone print on paper, 34.6 × 25.7 cm. CL.

174 | *The Tomato Soup that you hope will be served!*, 1925. Magazine advertisement for the Campbell Soup Company, Camden, NJ, from *The Saturday Evening Post*, August 22, 1925, 25. Halftone print on paper, 32.5 × 25.7 cm. CL.

175| John Held, cover of *Vanity Fair*, June 1920. Half-tone print on paper, 32.3 × 24.8 cm. Private collection.

176| *Eversharp Put it on paper*, 1926. Magazine advertisement for Wald Company, Chicago, IL, in *The Saturday Evening Post*, February 27, 1926, 110. Offset print on paper, 33.2 × 25.7 cm. CL.

the soup, how can it not be delicious? It is plain and direct storytelling. It is also graphically adroit: the tomato and can rest on a black background, which makes the tomato even more noticeable, even more appealing. And the silvered text recedes somewhat into the background. It is secondary; the tomato and can are primary.

The impact of these magazine tomato cans is undeniable—a fact that Andy Warhol (who remembered seeing these ads in his childhood) would later demonstrate. Yet it is not only the presence and appeal of the cans themselves that was innovative: it is that they essentially hover in space, unencumbered by what surrounds them. There are other examples of commercial design in this period that display a related spatial emancipation. A cover for *Vanity Fair*, drawn by John Held Jr., has four men golfing, teeing off to a green set at the opposite corner from where they are standing (fig. 175). In between is a conspicuous void, a large field of blue, which makes up much of the cover. Like most of Held's works, it is caricature, and the joke is that the men are teeing off to a fictitious nineteenth hole.[9] But quite aside from the playfulness is the stark presentation of emptiness. The void takes up the center; everything else is pushed to the edges, their odd placement making the scene more arresting.

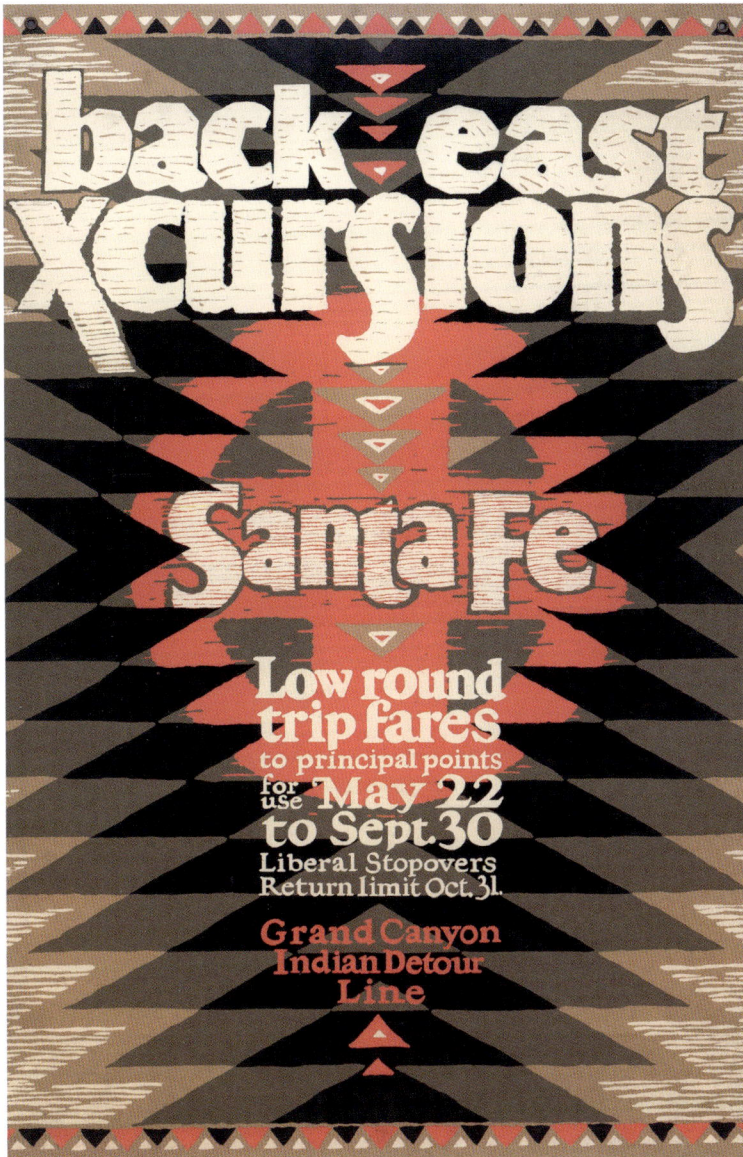

A similar approach plays out in a 1926 magazine advertisement for Eversharp pens (fig. 176). Set near the center is a pen and a text in smallish print. Most of the surface, however, is white space: it is "sky." Flying through it are two rows of biplanes that meet at the lower left corner. The presentation creates a conundrum of sorts: is the pen floating in the sky? Or are the airplanes attached to the paper? And then there is the very different scale of the elements: the planes are tiny in comparison with the pen. Moreover, the text is flat, put directly on the page; the airplanes we see in perspective; and the pen seems to occupy some place in between.

Less daring, but no less progressive, is a series of advertisements for the Santa Fe Railway Company. Many of these designs came from Sam Hyde Harris, who created some of the most enduring posters of the period.

Born in a small village in Middlesex, England, in 1889, Harris moved with his family to Los Angeles in 1903, where he eventually enrolled in classes at the Art Students League of Los Angeles and the Cannon Art School. He became celebrated for

177| Sam Hyde Harris, *Back East Xcursions*, *Santa Fe*, 1924. Poster, printed for Atchison, Topeka, & Santa Fe Railway System, Chicago, IL. Silkscreen on board, 91.4 × 61 cm. The Resnick Collection.

178| *California Limited*, 1921. Magazine advertisement, for Atchison, Topeka, & Santa Fe Railway System, Chicago, IL. Offset print on paper, image: 22 × 14.6 cm. CL.

179| *Xcursions Santa Fe Far West Vacations*, 1927. Magazine advertisement, for Atchison, Topeka, & Santa Fe Railway System, Chicago, IL. Offset print on paper, image: 25 × 16.8 cm. CL.

180| Hernando G. Villa, *The Chief. . . is still chief*, 1931. Poster, printed by Newman-Monroe Co., Chicago, IL, for Atchison, Topeka, & Santa Fe Railway System, Chicago, IL. Lithograph on paper, 105.4 × 71.1 cm. The Resnick Collection.

his Impressionist paintings of the California landscape; but throughout his career he also worked as a commercial artist, producing everything from store windows and signs to posters for national advertising campaigns.

One of Harris's most affective Santa Fe posters, issued in 1924, features a Navajo weaving with bold and intricate patterning (fig. 177). The overall scheme—the form lettering and their spacing—were likely the work of another, unnamed designer, who evidently produced many, if not all, of the company's magazine advertisements (figs. 178, 179). Nonetheless, Harris's paintings, including a memorable one he later made of the Grand Canyon, became an indelible part of the Santa Fe Railroad's identity; later, they also influenced more than a few WPA posters. That was true as well of another influential Santa Fe poster: Hernando G. Villa's *The Chief* of 1931 (fig. 180). Villa, based in Los Angeles, specialized in depictions of Native Americans, the California missions, and Mexican vaqueros; they became the imagery for some of the Santa Fe's popular posters of the 1930s.[10]

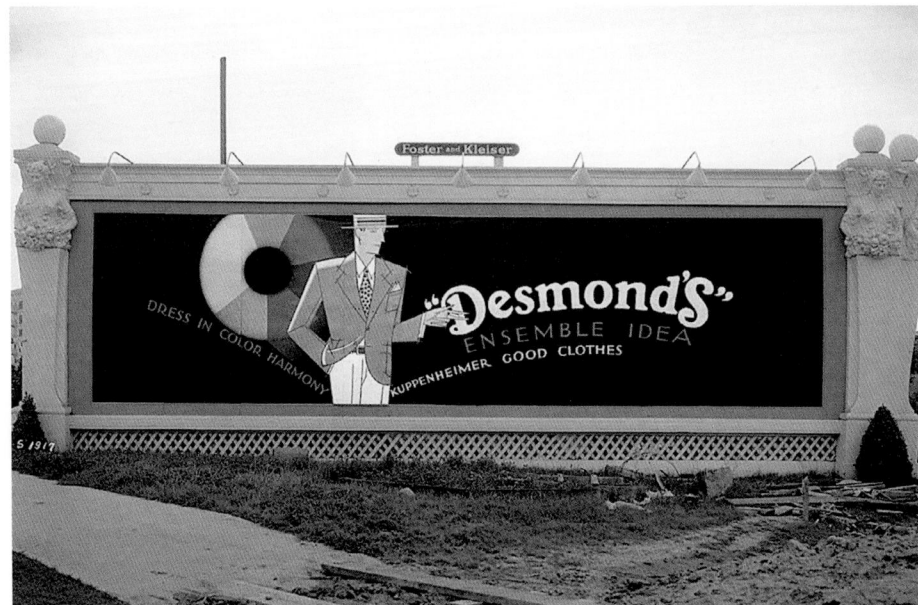

181 | Jacob Asanger, *Straws by Stetson, Silverwoods, Sixth and Broadway*, ca. 1925. Billboard in Los Angeles for Foster & Kleiser. Clear Channel Outdoor, San Antonio, TX.

182 | Jacob Asanger, *gifts from Hollywood*, ca. 1926. Billboard in Los Angeles for Foster & Kleiser. Clear Channel Outdoor, San Antonio, TX.

183 | Jacob Asanger, *"Desmond's" Ensemble Idea*, ca. 1927. Billboard in Los Angeles for Foster & Kleiser. Clear Channel Outdoor, San Antonio, TX.

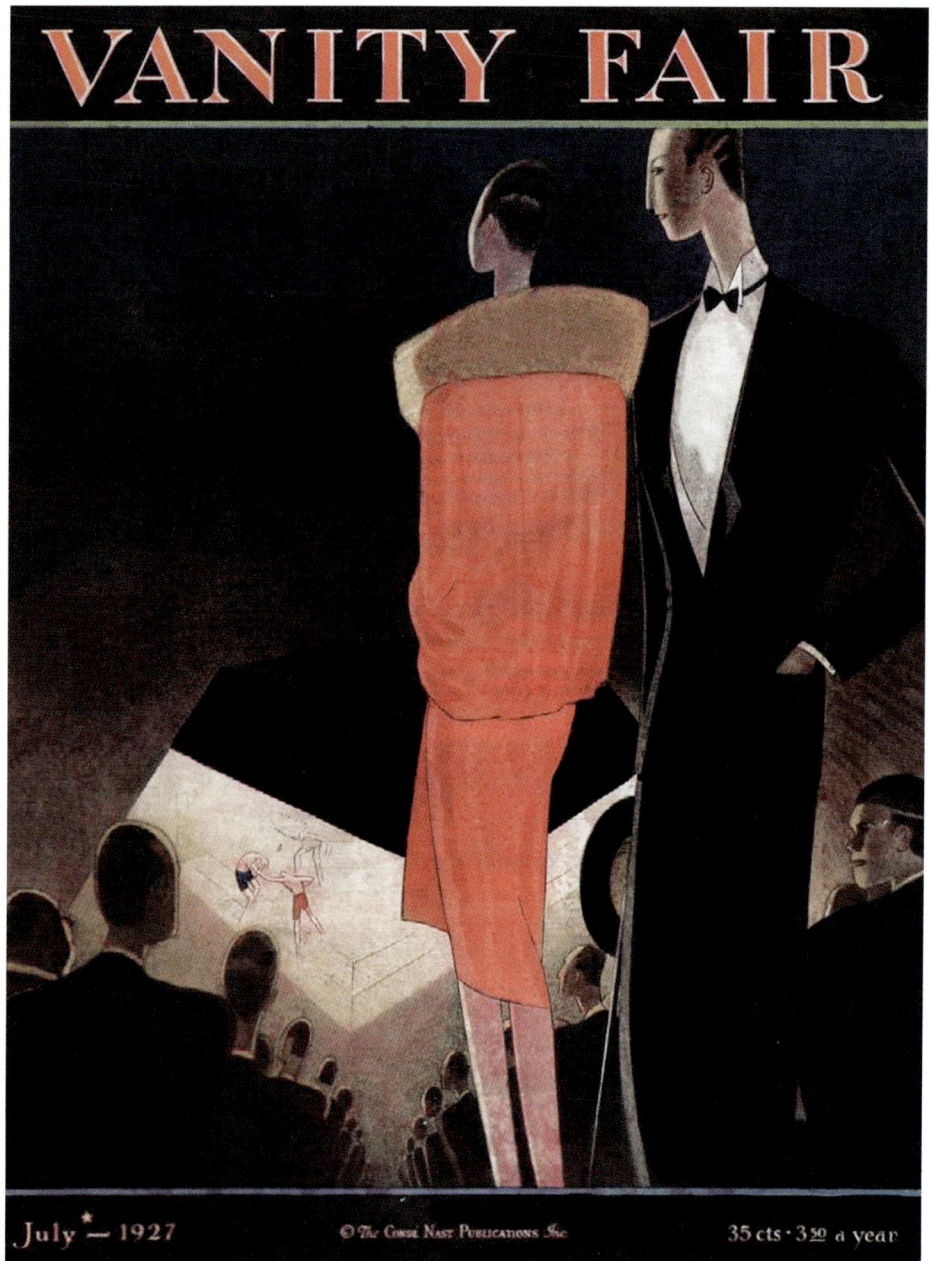

VANITY FAIR

July — 1927   © The Condé Nast Publications Inc.   35 cts · 3.50 a year

The Santa Fe magazine ads rely on iconic imagery—traditional Navajo designs, imposing chiefs, and the like. They also reflect the willingness of some progressive American designers of the period to dispense with conventional symmetries and syntax of elements. The texts and other elements in many of the ads are pushed to one side or the other, the lettering is often of very different sizes.

This form of graphic "liberation" also stands out in some West Coast billboards of the middle years of the decade. Many were created by Jacob Asanger, who by this time had moved to Los Angeles and was heading up the Foster & Kleiser studio there.[11] Asanger's personal idiom relied on the placement of ordinary objects—frequently geometricized—in large spatial fields with minimal texts. His billboard for Silverwoods, a men's clothier in downtown Los Angeles, is a model of messaging with minimal means (fig. 181). We see only some straw hats and the announcement that they come from Stetson, the well-known hatmaker. Another of Asanger's billboards, displaying Christmas gifts, looks back at the geometricized forms he had encountered in his student years in Munich before the war (fig. 182). A slightly later design, for local clothier Desmond's, is more in the spirit of fashion illustration, but it still has Asanger's characteristic nod to austerity (fig. 183).

Yet for American graphic art, the most compelling shift in this time was neither spatial nor was it entirely about visual "narrative." It was stylistic. The great event of 1925, the *Exposition Internationale des Arts Décoratifs et Industriels Modernes*, was held in Paris that spring, summer, and fall. Legions of Americans made the trek to Paris, and many (though certainly not all) came home enthused about the new "modernistic" mode. The result was an almost immediate redirection of American sensibilities.

Earnest Elmo Calkins, who went to Paris to see the exhibition, reported to his staff in New York: "It is extremely 'new art' and some of it too bizarre, but it achieves a certain exciting harmony, and in detail is entertaining to a degree. [Everything is] arranged with an eye to display, a vast piece of consummate window dressing."[12] By the time Calkins returned to the office, he realized that a reorientation was necessary—this new, modern art was unavoidable.

He was hardly alone. The willingness on the part of many Americans to accept the new design was partly the result of longstanding Francophilia; it also came from of a mounting belief in the possibilities of a modernized classicism (which at its heart was what the Paris expo's displays were presenting). It was novel yet still somehow traditional; it mollified conservatives and excited those searching for the next thing. "Spearheaded by Calkins and Holden," as Steven Heller memorably describes, "commonplace objects—toasters, refrigerators, coffee tins—were presented against new patterns and at skewed angles; contemporary industrial wares were shown in surrealistic and futuristic settings accented by contemporary typefaces with names like Cubist Bold, Vulcan, Broadway, Novel Gothic and more."[13]

In the United States, the new aesthetic came in two distinct variants. One issued directly from fashion, the other from the language of architecture and applied arts. In the case of the first, it was the fashion magazines—*Vogue* and *Vanity Fair*, above all—that brought the ideas of the new style into two-dimensional design.

Argentine-born William (originally Guillermo) Bolin was at the center of this new trend in fashion. Bolin studied for a time in Paris before moving to New York, where he made many of the elegant covers for the two magazines. His July 1927 *Vanity Fair* cover has all the requisite elements of Parisian flair: a handsome and ultra-chic couple, decidedly au courant typefaces, and a pronounced contrast of light and shadow (fig. 184).

Many of the covers for American *Vogue* and *Vanity Fair* in this period were also the work of French-born illustrator Georges Lepape or Ukrainian immigrant Vladimir Bobritsky (later Bobri). Both employed the then standard blending of sinuous Art Nouveau lines, elegant and attenuated figures, and a vague orientalism.

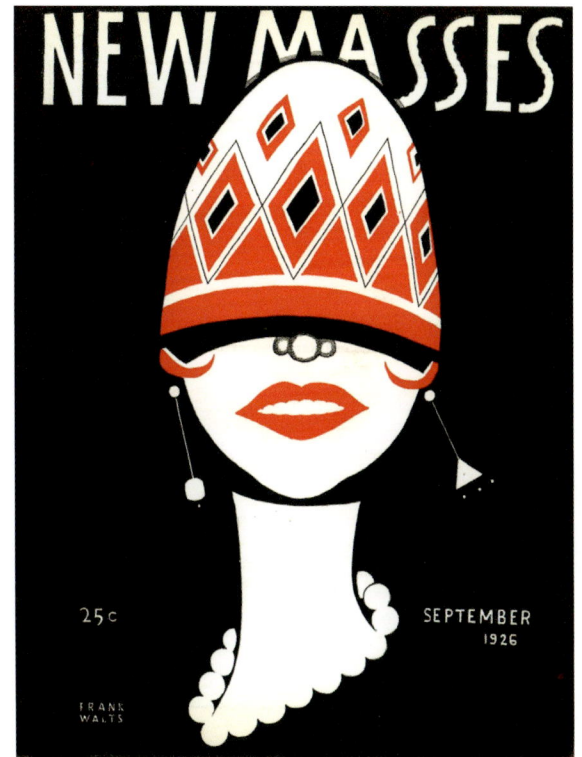

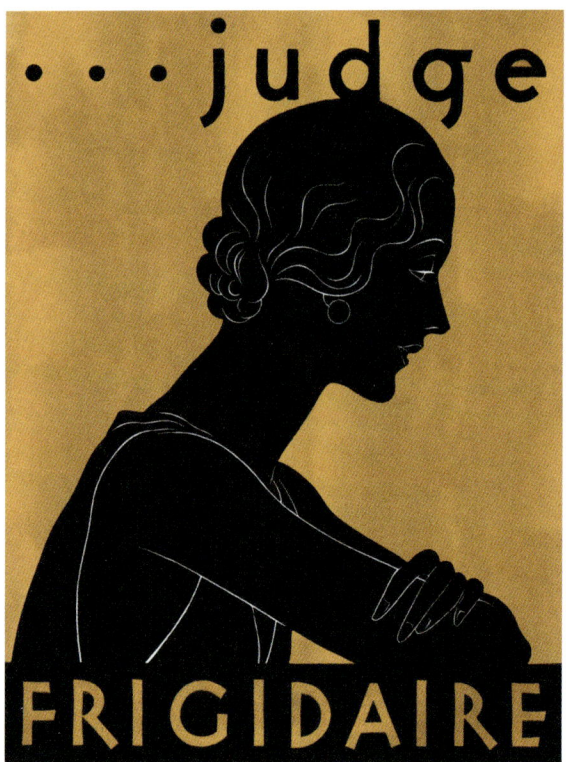

187 | *Universal Electric Ranges*, c. 1928. Brochure cover, printed for Landers, Frary & Clark, New Britain, CT. Offset lithograph on paper, 16.5 × 14.8 cm. CL.

188 | *...judge Frigidaire*, 1931. Magazine advertisement for Frigidaire Co., Fort Wayne, IN. Offset print on paper, 30.7 × 23.8 cm (trimmed). CL.

The studied elegance of Bolin, Lepape, and Bobritsky stood apart from the work of most of the American artists, who tended to produce illustrations that were closer to caricature. Frank Walts, the quintessential Greenwich village designer, came up with one of the best covers of the period, a flapper with brilliant red lipstick and an oversized hat (fig. 185). And a slightly later cover, designed by Agnes Worrell for *Hi-Hat*, the short-lived culture magazine of the Hollywood arts community, offered an array of modernistic visual ingredients, though in a way that was more severe, more linear and pointed than those of the European-trained designers (fig. 186). Worrell, long a fixture of the West Coast scene, also published in *Vogue*, *Harper's Bazaar*, and other trendy magazines. Her loose and disaggregated drawing style became her trademark.

Vogue and the other Condé Nast publications—*Vanity Fair* and more improbably *House & Garden*—remained the source of avant-garde fashion experimentation through the 1920s. They became even more experimental after M. F. Agha became Condé Nast's art director.

Agha, born Mehemed Fehmy Agha, in 1896, was the son of Turkish parents then living in Russia. He first studied at the polytechnic in Kyiv; later, after earning a degree in Oriental languages in Paris, he rose to prominence working for *Vogue* in Paris and Berlin. In 1929, Condé Nast himself persuaded Agha to take over the art direction of the American edition of *Vogue*. Agha gradually also assumed the art direction of the company's other magazines. He introduced sans serif typefaces and persuaded leading artists and writers, including Carl van Vechten and Edward Steichen, to contribute their work. His emphasis on what one might call stylish legibility became the guiding look of the company's publications. Agha, though, was under no illusions about the challenge of weaning Americans away from traditional imagery and layout. "The painful process of training the public eye for the new vision," he wrote in 1932, "has to be completed first by modern architecture, decoration, and typography—only then can advertising afford to use the new visual language."[14]

But most of the prominent ad agencies (and, for that matter, others outside of the world of Madison Avenue) responded to the new design language coming out of Paris in a different way. Some drew from the new modernized classicism, emphasizing stair-stepped or zigzag forms, strong color contrasts, and purified geometries, which became the standard expression for new, cutting-edge architecture and interior design, as well as advertising and packaging (fig. 187). Others appropriated the look of Parisian fashion but in a sparer manner, a form of elimination, focusing on a single figure or scene. A Frigidaire advertisement from 1931 is a splendid example of this studied "removal": it has only a woman, in silhouette, set against a gold background, with the word "judge" (fig. 188). Only on the next page does the copy reveal its full purpose.

The leading modernist designers in New York, however, quickly moved past the language of the Art Deco, opting instead for a cleaner and simpler style based on pure geometries and new typefaces. An ad for the Paul T. Frankl's New York gallery, was modern in that other way: it is about reduction and clarity, the possibility of using minimal means—forms and words—to deliver its message (fig. 189). Even

1 9 2 9

FURNITURE CREATIONS

of paul t. frankl

beginning april 5th the
1 9 2 9
furniture creations of
paul t. frankl
will be shown at the
frankl galleries.
style leadership is gained
not by copying and re-
peating but through new
c r e a t i v e   w o r k.
you will find our new
furniture   models
m o d e r n
in design and style and
in their perfect execution.
conservative only in price.

FRANKL GALLERIES
4   EAST   48   STREET   NEW   YORK

American **U**nion of **D**ecorative **A**rtists and **C**raftsmen

LUCIAN BERNHARD
16 WEST 49th STREET
NEW YORK CITY
TEL., BRYANT 8288
INTERIOR
DESIGN ●

DONALD DESKEY
145 WEST 57th STREET
NEW YORK CITY
CONSULTANT
DESIGNER ●

ALICE DONALDSON
313 WEST 20th STREET
TEL., CHELSEA 1325
DESIGNS — DECORATIONS
IN GOLD AND SILVER ●

PAUL T. FRANKL
6 EAST 48th STREET
NEW YORK CITY
VOLUNTEER 0520
DESIGNER ●

AUDAC stands convinced that contemporary life demands an
appropriate setting and that it is the work of the artist of all
ages to mould the external world to suit the life of his time.

AUDAC realizes that the cultural contribution of an era is as
clearly reflected in the decorative as in the other arts.

AUDAC was founded to give these convictions organized aid
and voice.

AUDAC stands for
The advancement of the new tendencies in the dec-
orative, industrial and applied arts.
The elevation of standards in contemporary design.
The development of STYLE rather than styles.

WOLFGANG AND POLA
HOFFMANN
655 FIFTH AVENUE
WICKERSHAM 3659
INTERIOR ARCHITECTS
AND DESIGNERS ●

ELLEN M. KERN
136 LIBERTY ST., N. Y. C.
TEL., HITCHCOCK 7669
CONSULTING DECORA-
TIVE DESIGNING ●

FREDERICK KIESLER

ARCHITECT ●

PETER LARSEN
27 WEST 8th ST., N. Y. C.
STUYVESANT 8937
DESIGNER OF
WROUGHT IRON ●

ROBERT L. LEONARD
40 WEST 67th STREET
TEL. TRAFALGAR 8980
ADVERTISING ART
DESIGNING ●

WINOLD REISS
108 WEST 16th STREET
TEL., CHELSEA 1450
INTERIOR ARCHITECTURE
AND DECORATIONS ●

more prophetic was an advertisement for AUDAC, the American Union of Decorative Artists and Craftsmen, which was the leading modernist collective at the
time (fig. 190). It is unsigned but is almost certainly the work of graphic designer
Robert L. Leonard, who was closely involved with the group. Like Frankl's ad, it, too,
relies only on a few bits of geometry and the careful placement of text. The new sans-
serif typeface makes a statement, but it is the arrangement of the words that drives
the composition.

Some of the best American designs of the late 1920s and early 1930s blended
these two directions. A billboard for upscale clothier Van Raatle, designed by Alexey
Brodovitch, exhibits how classical restraint and a modern poetic sensibility could
be fused together (fig. 191). Brodovitch, a Russian émigré who had spent time in
Paris before moving to the United States in 1930, would later become the influential
art director of *Harper's Bazaar*; here, he presents an image both of refinement and
reduction.[15]

189| Paul T. Frankl, *1929 Furniture Creations of paul t.
Frankl*, 1929. Magazine advertisement. CL.

190| Robert L. Leonard [attrib.], *American Union of Dec-
orative Artists and Craftsmen*, 1930. Magazine advertisement, from *Creative Art 6* (April 1930), supplement, 76.
CL.

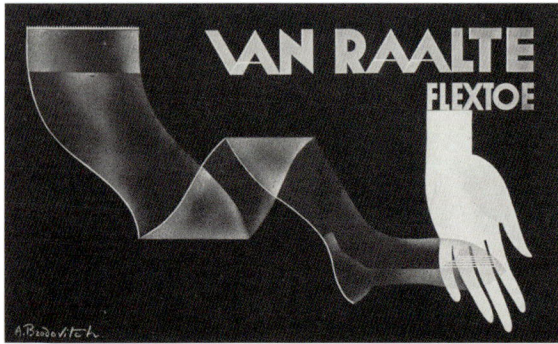

Brodovitch's billboard could have readily appeared in France or elsewhere in Europe in this period. More American in spirit—because of its content *and* form-language—was the work of Otis Shepard and his wife, Dorothy. Otis Shephard had begun working for Foster & Kleiser in the San Francisco office in 1917. By 1928, he was head of the art department, and he hired the young Dorothy Van Gorder as a staff artist. They married the following year and spent their honeymoon in Europe, where they met Austrian poster designer Joseph Binder, whose smooth and under-stated airbrush technique they both adopted. Shepard used it to convincing effect in a 1933 "practice" beer ad (fig. 192). Even before that, the couple had collaborated on an ad campaign for Chesterfield cigarettes, producing one of the signature bill-boards of the era, a stylish young "flapper" set into a black and red geometrized frame (fig. 193). The couple decided around that time to move to New York and set up a freelance practice. Dorothy, who was an excellent designer in her own right, pro-duced ads for several clients. One of the standouts is her billboard for Underwood Typewriters (fig. 194). With its distinctive precisionist language, it is among the mas-terworks of the era.

The Shepherds, if leaders in the field, were not the only Americans pursuing new ideas. One ingenious strategy was a form of fracturing—splitting a set of im-ages, like the pseudo-film sequence in an ad for Harold Lloyd's first "talkie" *Welcome Danger* (1929) (fig. 195). The notion of setting out multiple images at once worked as an effective preview of the film itself; it had the added advantage of making the whole page more fluid and dynamic. It reads like a film (a string of "cells"), and a wonderfully animated one at that. In a related way, an unknown designer relied on a simple visual trick for a luggage label for the short-lived New York Airways in 1928 (fig. 196). Here, a diagonal bifurcates the field, flipping what is either black or white in the image. Another new tactic was repetition, especially of lines or shapes— for example, in an advertisement by Winold Reiss for the Hotel St. George in Brook-lyn (fig. 197). Designers at the time also achieved a similar effect with perspectival distortion, an idea that appears on a luggage label for the Barbizon Hotel in New York (fig. 198).

Among the most popular representations of the realities of the machine age— so much so that they even made their way onto a label for an apple crate—were sym-bols of force—gears, cogs, radio waves, lightning bolts, and the like—which became an almost ubiquitous way of conveying the new (fig. 199). Yet perhaps more essentially American in those years was a rhythmic dynamism—a visual language of form and movement that was closely wedded to jazz.

Many of the best examples can be found in movie posters or sheet music from Tin Pan Alley. Some are about pure line and movement, often depicting figures danc-ing ecstatically. A brilliant example of this is the sheet music cover for "Underneath the Harlem Moon" in 1932 (fig. 200). Its creator was Sidney Leff, who produced hun-dreds of covers in those years.

Many of the most accomplished works associated with this jazz-age aesthetic came out of the Harlem Renaissance, the flowering of African American arts and cul-ture in Upper Manhattan. One of the signature designs was Winold Reiss's cover for

191 | Alexey Brodovitch, *Van Raatle Flextoe*, 1931. De-sign for a billboard, from Art Directors Club, *Tenth Annual of Advertising Art* (New York: Book Service Company, 1931), 18. CL.

192 | Otis Shepard, *here's how Platz*, 1933. Sample ad-vertisement, from *Advertising Arts*, May 1933, after page 17. Halftone print on paper, 17.2 × 21.7 cm. CL.

193 | Otis and Dorothy Shepard, *Chesterfield After all— It's TASTE*, 1930. Design for a billboard. Private collection.

194 | Dorothy Shepard, *Underwood Typewriters*, 1931. Design for a billboard. Private collection.

After all –
it's TASTE

Chesterfield

UNDERWOOD TYPEWRITERS

Now HEAR Harold Lloyd in his first talking picture!

You'd think he couldn't possibly be any funnier, but you'll *hear* he is when you see him in "Welcome Danger," Harold Lloyd's first sound and dialog picture. *Twice* the laughs than ever before! ❧ You'll be all eyes and ears when you see it—it has laughs, thrills, romance, youth, gayety, everything! And what a treat for the children—more fun than a three-ringed circus! ❧ Don't miss seeing and hearing Harold Lloyd in "Welcome Danger." You'll laugh at every minute of it, and it will give you something to talk about for weeks after!

HAROLD LLOYD
IN
"WELCOME DANGER"

Produced by the Harold Lloyd Corporation. A Paramount Sound and Dialog Release—one of Paramount's super entertainments of the New Show World. Also presented silent for theatres not yet equipped for sound. *"If it's a Paramount Picture it's the best show in town!"*

TUNE IN!
Paramount-Publix Radio Hour, with your favorite stars of stage and screen on the air, every Saturday night, 10 to 11 P. M. Eastern Standard Time, over the Columbia Broadcasting System.

Paramount Pictures
PARAMOUNT FAMOUS LASKY CORPORATION   ADOLPH ZUKOR, PRES., PARAMOUNT BLDG., N. Y.

THE INTERIORS OF THE FOLLOWING ROOMS AT
HOTEL ST. GEORGE BROOKLYN
WERE CONCEIVED AND DESIGNED BY
WINOLD REISS

GRAND BALL ROOM
INCLUDING THE LIGHT EFFECT FOR WHICH ENGINEERING DETAILS WERE SUBSEQUENTLY DEVELOPED BY MR. MANFRED MESMER AND HIS STAFF
GRAND FOYER TO BALL ROOM
BALL ROOM VESTIBULE AND CLOAK ROOM
GRAND SALON AND FOYER
SUITE OF FIVE BANQUET ROOMS AND FOYER
SUITE OF FOUR PRIVATE DINING ROOMS AND CLARK GALLERY
THE CHINESE AND TOWER ROOMS AND FOYERS
THE ROOF DINING ROOM 25TH FLOOR
THE EGYPTIAN ROOF AND COLONNADES
THE CAFETERIA AND COFFEE SHOPS
THE POOL LOBBY AND LUNCH ROOM
ALL LADIES AND MENS RETIRING ROOMS

WINOLD REISS STUDIOS
108 WEST 16TH STREET NEW YORK
SPECIALIZING IN HOTEL RESTAURANT AND CLUB INTERIORS

NEW YORK AIRWAYS INC

NEW YORK AIRWAYS INC.

NEW YORK   ATLANTIC CITY
BALTIMORE   WASHINGTON

B P
BARBIZON-PLAZA
CENTRAL PARK SOUTH   NEW YORK CITY
NAME

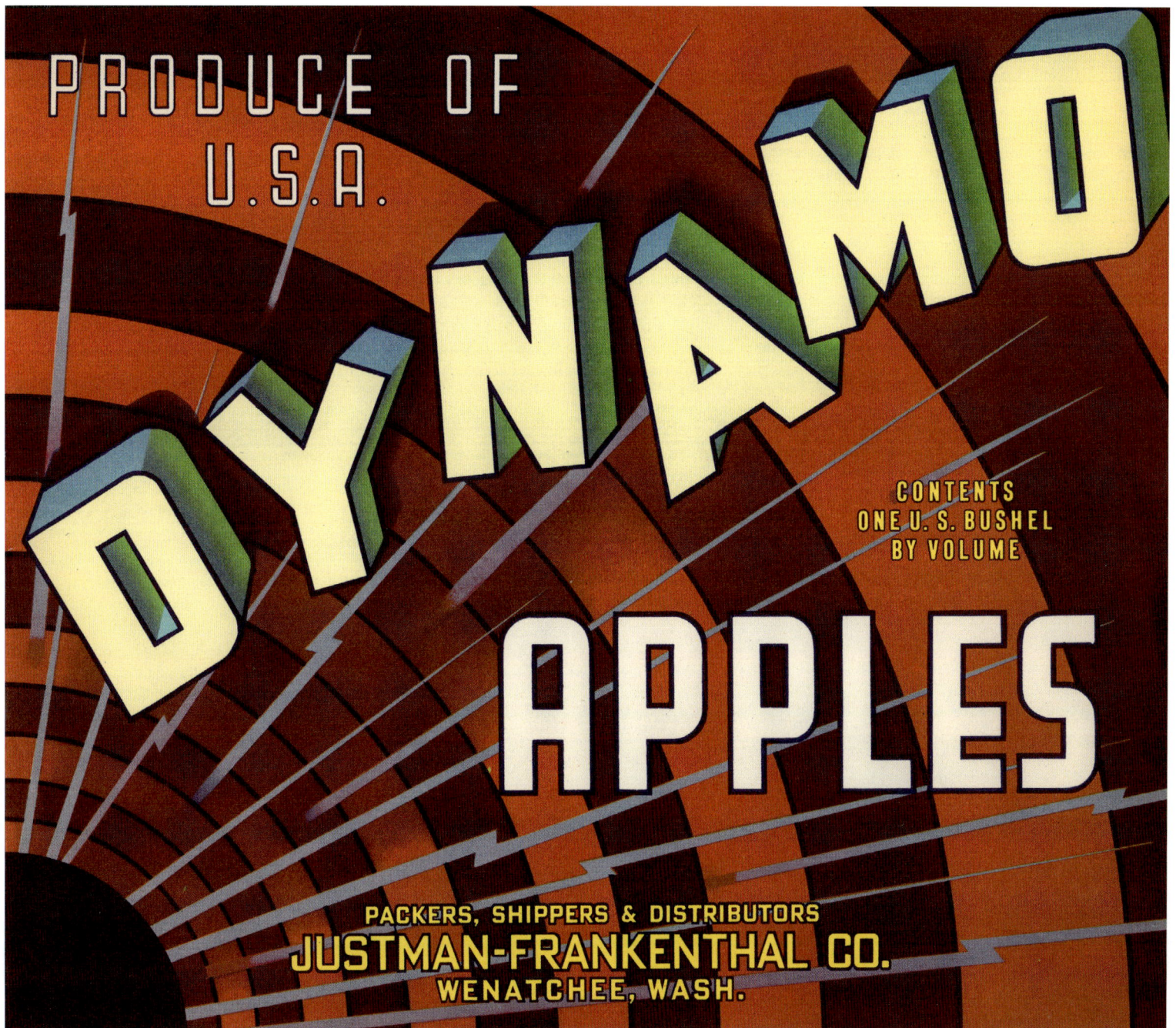

195| *Harold Lloyd in Welcome Danger*, 1929. Magazine advertisement for Paramount Pictures, New York, NY, in *The Saturday Evening Post*, October 19, 1929, 56. Halftone print on paper, 33 × 25.5 cm. CL.

196| *New York Airways, Inc.*, ca. 1928. Luggage label, printed for New York Airways, Inc., New York, NY. Offset print on paper, 9.7 × 7.2 cm. CL.

197| Winold Reiss, *Hotel St. George*, 1929. Advertisement. Offset lithograph on paper, 29.5 × 21.6 cm. Prints and Photographs Division, Library of Congress, Washington, D.C.

198| *B P Barbizon-Plaza Central Park South New York City*, ca. 1930. Luggage label. Offset print on paper, height: 10 cm. CL

199| *Dynamo Apples Produce of U.S.A*, ca. 1935. Label, printed for Justman-Frankenthal Co., Wenatchee, WA. Halftone print on paper, 22.8 × 26.1 cm. CL.

200 | Sydney Leff, "Underneath the Harlem Moon," 1932. Cover for sheet music, published by De Sylva, Brown and Henderson, Inc., New York, NY. Halftone print on paper, 30.7 × 23.2 cm. CL.

Opportunity: A Journal of Negro Life. It was based on African masks, a popular theme for modernist artists going back at least to Picasso's 1907 *Les Demoiselles d'Avignon* (fig. 201).

But the most captivating and original designs of the Harlem Renaissance came from Aaron Douglas. It was the African American Douglas, much more than any of his white contemporaries, who forged the graphic language of interwar Harlem. Born in Topeka, Kansas, in 1899, Douglas graduated from the University of Nebraska with a degree in fine arts in 1922. He moved to Harlem in the mid-1920s and quickly made his mark with his powerful geometric forms and figures (fig. 202). His many magazine and book covers, with references to African masks, sculptures, and evocations of African dance, formed a distinctive synthesis, merging European modernism and African heritage (fig. 203). Douglas's work was widely influential; the language of a Black liberation he and others had invented was picked up by commercial white artists like Albert Wilfred Barbelle, another prolific sheet music designer (fig. 204).

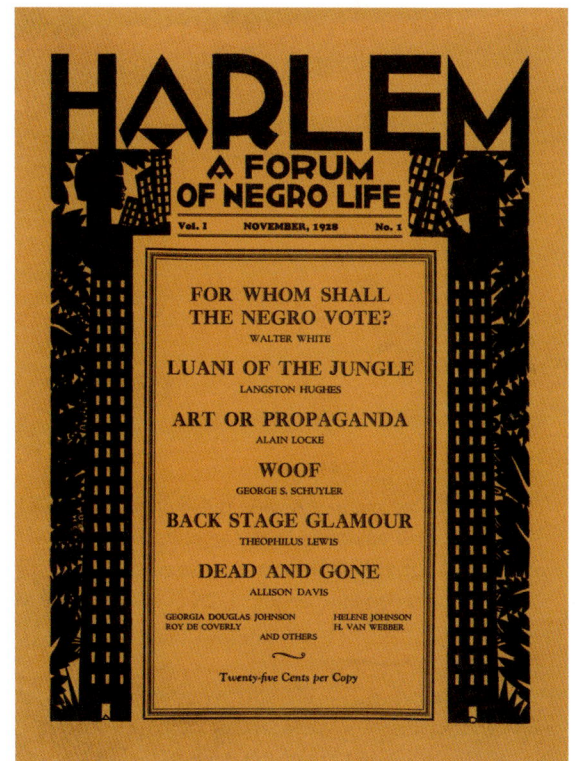

201 | Winold Reiss, cover of *Opportunity: A Journal of Negro Life*, January 1925. Schomburg Center for Research in Black Culture, Jean Blackwell Hutson Research and Reference Division, The New York Public Library, New York, NY.

202 | Aaron Douglas, cover of *The Crisis*, May 1927. Schomburg Center for Research in Black Culture, Jean Blackwell Hutson Research and Reference Division, The New York Public Library, New York, NY.

203 | Aaron Douglas, cover of *Harlem: A Forum of Negro Life*, November 1928. Schomburg Center for Research in Black Culture, Jean Blackwell Hutson Research and Reference Division, The New York Public Library, New York, NY.

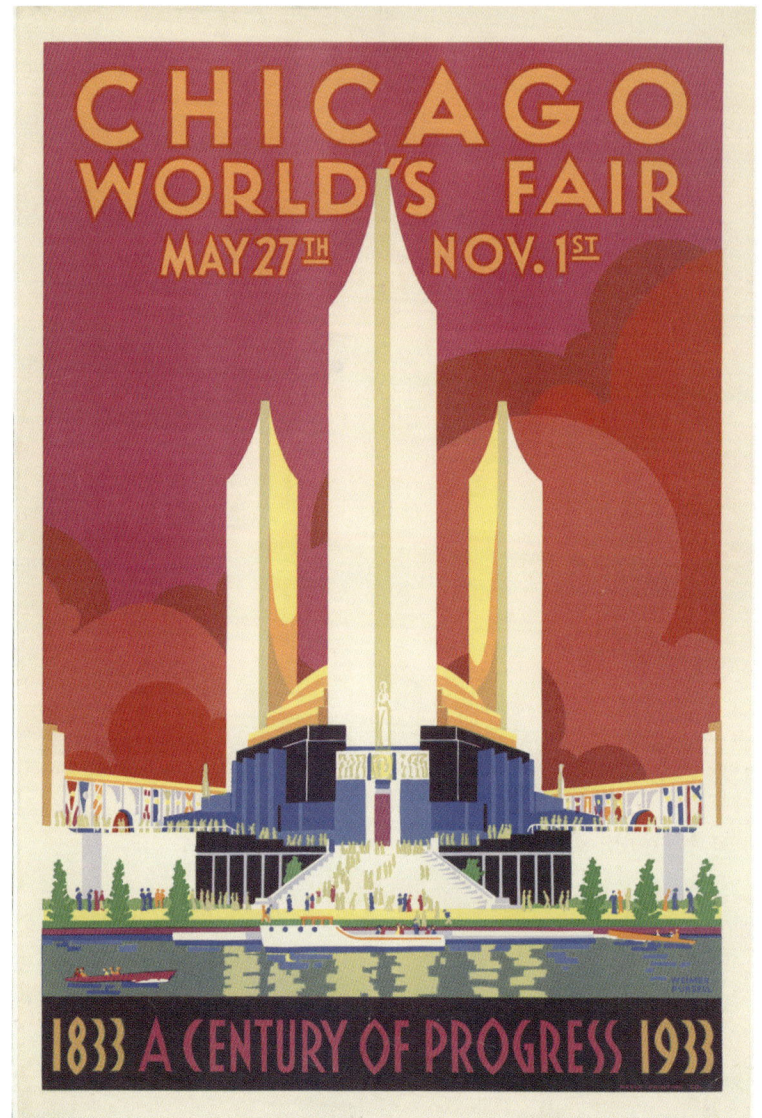

204 | Albert Wilfried Barbelle, "Lew Leslie's Rhapsody in Black," ca. 1931. Cover for sheet music, printed for Shapiro, Bernstein & Co., New York, NY. 30.6 × 23.2 cm. CL.

205 | Weimer Pursell, *Chicago World's Fair*, 1933. Poster, printed by Neely Printing Co., Chicago, IL, for *A Century of Progress Exposition*, Chicago, IL. Lithograph on paper, 105.4 × 69.5 cm. The Resnick Collection.

206 | Joseph B. Birren [attrib.], *Go! Chicago World's Brightest Spot A Century of Progress*, 1933. Poster. Printed by The Cuneo Press, Inc., Chicago, IL for *A Century of Progress Exposition*. The Resnick Collection.

These concepts—the syncopated rhythms of jazz, bold contrasts, and an affinity for jutting and angular geometries also carried over to other areas of mainstream commercial art. In some examples, such as Weimer Pursell's excellent poster for the 1933 Chicago World's Fair, the influence comes out mainly in its brilliant color scheme (fig. 205). The restless feeling of movement and form, however, is expressed fully in *Go!*, another poster advertising the fair (fig. 206). It is unsigned but was very likely the work of Joseph B. Birren, who made other, related designs for the fair.[16]

The hallmark of American design in the later 1920s and 1930s, though, was less about specific strategies than it was about formal variety. The language of Art Deco persisted well into the 1940s—and beyond. There were still faint echoes of it in popular advertising in the 1950s and 1960s. But by the early 1930s, a new and even more energized expression had made its appearance.

go!

A CENTURY OF PROGRESS

CHICAGO
WORLD'S BRIGHTEST SPOT

THE CUNEO PRESS, INC., CHICAGO, ILL.

7 The Dynamic

Image

In 1921, an Austrian-born engineer named Edmund Rumpler unveiled his new *Tropfenwagen*—literally "drop car," after its teardrop shape—at the Berlin Auto Show. Rumpler was Germany's first airplane manufacturer, and during the First World War, his company, Rumpler-Werke AG, built warplanes for the German military. What he had learned along the way about aircraft aeronautics, designing, and fabricating, he applied to what is now regarded as the first streamlined automobile.

Rumpler's little car looked like an ungainly boat on wheels, and it was a commercial flop. Only about one hundred of the odd-duckling autos were made, and only two now survive. But streamlining, though it was slow to find acceptance, would come to have a profound and persistent influence on design—especially American design. By the early 1930s, the idea of smoothing and rounding hard edges, of making even sedentary objects appear as if they were (or could be) in motion, became an indispensable feature of the visual language of America, projecting speed, dynamism, and, above all, modernity.[1]

The first industrial designers—Norman Bel Geddes, Raymond Loewy, and Walter Dorwin Teague, among others—took the lead in adopting and adapting the new streamlining in the United States.[2] In 1934, Loewy celebrated this advance in a chart depicting the evolution of the automobile (fig. 207). Only a few years before, he had designed the first streamlined locomotives for the Pennsylvania Railroad. He also devised a new graphic identity for the company, including its brochures and onboard dining menus (fig. 208).

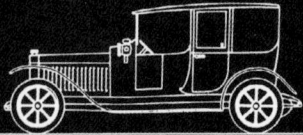

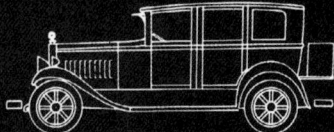
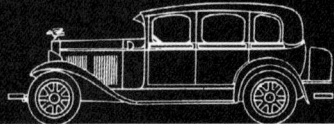
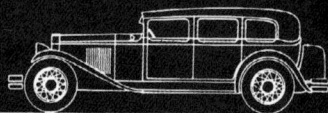

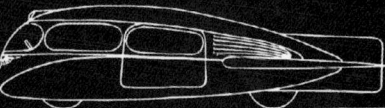
Yet most commercial graphic artists were slow to take up the idea—in part because they lacked a ready visual language for depicting motion. The first responses to this problem—from the early years of the century—now seem risible: automobile advertisements at times showed cars with wings, a less than subtle, and rather technologically challenged, means to indicate that they were being propelled forward (fig. 209). The matter was simpler for ships. One could paint the prow of a ship slicing through the waves, as one unnamed artist did around 1928 on the cover of a brochure advertising the Great White Fleet's summer cruises, a fleet of "banana boats" operated by the United Fruit Company (fig. 210). Here, at least, one gets the sense that the ship is steaming at high speed.

In 1929, Wesley Neff, a Canadian-born freelance illustrator then living in Detroit, devised one set of answers to the problem of projecting speed in graphic form. For an advertisement for Bohnalite pistons, Neff introduced bold figural imagery, clever perspectival elongation, and "speed lines" (essentially, an indication of air movement) to generate a look of dynamism (fig. 211). Neff's lively portrayal of a sporty couple hurtling down the road in their convertible stands in distinct contrast to a Hupmobile ad of the same year, which was all about a staid stylishness (fig. 212). The couple and their car, set in the elegant Place de la Concorde, in Paris, appear as if they part of a fixed display, almost motionless in their perfection.

Other designers also worked out how to make speed readily perceptible—beyond the simple imposition of "speed lines" (fig. 213). Otis Shepard's 1929 advertisement for Plymouth offers an especially adroit solution (fig. 214). It depicts a car that is "de-formed," as if rapid motion itself were reshaping it. Even more compelling is a series of ads made by Walter Dorwin Teague for the Marmon Motor Company. Teague not only introduced extended and dramatic speed lines to call attention to the idea that Marmon's automobiles were very fast; he also distorted the car's bodies, partly dissolving and warping them (fig. 215). In one exceptional ad, he went even further, showing the car climbing steeply, as if it were an airplane taking off (fig. 216).

The next step in this projection of speed is evident in the work of John Vassos. Vassos, a Greek-born immigrant living in New York, had garnered acclaim as an illustrator before he became a noted industrial designer (especially for RCA). In the late 1920s and early 1930s, he illustrated a series of books, with texts written by his wife, Ruth. *Contempo*, which appeared in 1929, and *Ultimo*, which came out the following year, are replete with images of streamlined buildings and places. Vassos's most admired book is his 1931 classic *Phobia*, a dystopian work consisting of twenty-four plates expressing an unease with modernity. One of the plates, "Dromophobia," or the fear of crossing streets, is a forceful essay on motion itself. In its portrayal of two cars, one smaller, one quite enormous, careening down the street and sending the pedestrians running for their lives, is an evocation of speed in its purest—and most menacing—form (fig. 217).

What is not developed in Vassos's remarkable image is the styling of the cars themselves. The surroundings are streamlined; the cars are not. And that was also true for a magazine advertisement Vassos created for the Packard Motor Car Company in

M E N U

ENNSYLVANIA RAILROAD

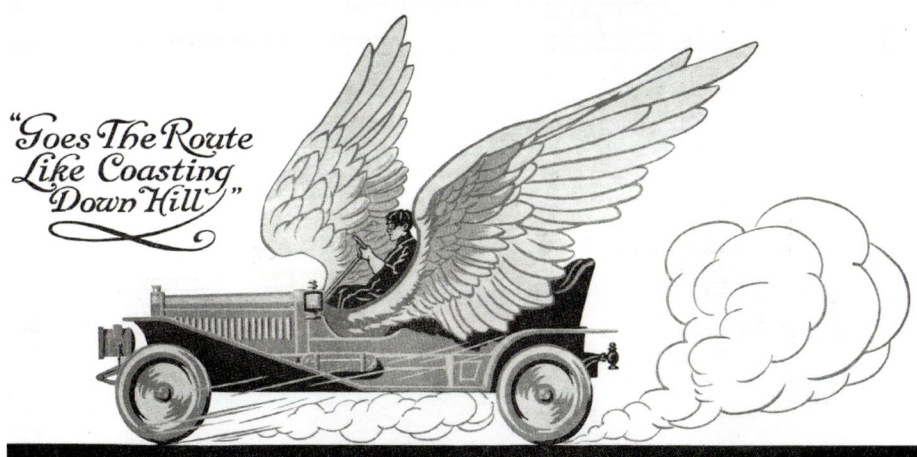

"Goes The Route Like Coasting Down Hill"

Here is a Strong Statement

The Winton Six is **the best purchase** on the market.

We make that statement absolutely without qualification. We fully realize the obligation upon us, as a reputable house, to limit our statements to provable truth. We realize that, since we have had a *longer* experience in manufacturing gasoline cars than has any other American company, the public will not excuse on our part any bombastic statement that might be excusable if made by an inexperienced house.

Therefore, when we say the Winton Six is absolutely the best purchase on the market, we expect you to make no allowances whatever. We are prepared to prove what we say.

We want you to know about the self-starting, sweet-running, six-cylinder

WINTON SIX

207 | Raymond Loewy, *The Evolution of the Motor Car*, 1934. From *Advertising Arts*, March 1934, after page 36. Offset print on paper, each sheet 29.2 × 21.2 cm. CL.

208 | Raymond Loewy, [attrib.], *Menu Pennsylvania Railroad*, 1931. Masthead for printed menu, used onboard the Pennsylvania Railroad. Offset print on paper, 4.4 × 16.3 cm (detail). CL.

209 | *Winton Six*, 1909. Magazine advertisement for The Winton Motor Carriage Co., Cleveland, OH. Halftone print on paper, 34.7 × 26.7 cm. CL.

SNAP!

Snap! You gently give her the gas and out
she shoots—a block ahead of the others!

Never before have you enjoyed such glori-
ous restful motoring.

The secret lies in the piston. If your
car comes equipped with Nelson Bohnalite Pistons, you enjoy revolutionized
modern driving.

By using Nelson Bohnalite Pistons,
reciprocating parts can be light-
ened—acceleration increased—
bearing loads lessened—expansion and contraction controlled.

Today the leading auto-
mobiles in all price classes
come equipped with this
advanced piston.

Choose one of these and
you experience a new
snap in performance.

BOHN ALUMINUM & BRASS
CORPORATION
DETROIT, MICHIGAN
New York   Chicago   Philadelphia
Cleveland   Pittsburgh

NELSON
BOHNALITE
PISTONS

Special
alloy steel
Bohbohns
—the origi-
nal Invar Steel
Struts—are cast
in, to control
expansion and
maintain satisfac-
tory clearances
under all engine
operating conditions

GREAT WHITE FLEET
Summer Cruises
from New York and New Orleans

TO THE Caribbean
AND West Indies
CUBA · JAMAICA · PANAMA
COSTA RICA · COLOMBIA
GUATEMALA · HONDURAS
UNITED FRUIT COM·PANY
STEAMSHIP SERVICE

CREATORS OF THE MODE

AFTERNOON TAILLEUR BY PREMET...CAR BY HUPMOBILE

The Place de la Concorde, Paris

To the style-conscious woman, the New HUPMOBILE Century car flashes its message of smartness and modernity as swiftly and surely as does the latest gown by the Paris Grande Couture. But to the man who knows HUPMOBILE, there is more than beauty in these New Century cars. In their mechanical trustworthiness he sees them as the same old, game old HUPMOBILES. As rugged as they are regal. As responsive as they are smart. As elegant in their road-manners as they are in their looks. Her car for its dash; his car for its deeds! It is this harmony of approval from both sides of the family that has given these New HUPMOBILE Century cars a sales impetus almost startling, even in the fast-moving motor car industry. The New Century Six, $1345 to $1645; the New Century Eight, $1825 to $2625. All prices f. o. b. factory. Equipment, other than standard, extra.

THE NEW HUPMOBILE CENTURY SIX & EIGHT

"CAPITAL TO THE LAKES"

CLEVELAND
AKRON
PITTSBURGH
WASHINGTON

PENNSYLVANIA AIRLINES INC.

FAST SMOOTH

PLYMOUTH can do smoothly more than 60 miles an hour by stop watch because the Plymouth engine develops 48 horsepower . . . because it is the famous Silver Dome high-compression type for which Chrysler Motors engineering is famous . . . with rubber engine mountings, mirror-finished cylinders, full-pressure lubrication and many other important features. Driving fast in a Plymouth is a real pleasure.

PLYMOUTH

CHRYSLER MOTORS PRODUCT

$535

AND UP, F. O. B. FACTORY

Roadster $535; Coupe $565; Sedan, 2-Door $565; Sport Roadster $610; Sedan (4-Door, 3-Window) $625; Coupe (with rumble seat) $625; Sport Phaeton $625; Convertible Coupe $695. F. O. B. Factory.

SOLD AND SERVICED BY 10,000 DE SOTO, DODGE BROTHERS AND CHRYSLER DEALERS

210| *Great White Fleet Summer Cruises*, ca. 1928. Brochure, printed for the United Fruit Company, Boston, MA. Offset print on paper, 22.8 × 10.3 cm. CL.

211| Wesley Neff, *Snap! Bohnalite Nelson Pistons*, 1929. Magazine advertisement for Bohn Aluminum & Brass Corporation, Detroit, MI, from *The Saturday Evening Post*, March 2, 1929, 58. Halftone print on paper, image: 32 × 23.9 cm. CL.

212| *Creators of the Mode The New Hupmobile Century Six & Eight*, 1929. Magazine advertisement for the Hupp Motor Company, Detroit, MI, from *Good Housekeeping*, April 1929, n.p. Halftone print on paper, 29.8 × 21.4 cm. CL.

213| *Pennsylvania Airlines, Inc., "Capital to the Lakes,"* ca. 1930. Luggage label. Offset print on paper, 9.3 × 12.2 cm. CL.

214| Otis Shepard, *Fast Smooth Plymouth*, 1929. Magazine advertisement, for the Chrysler Motors Company, Highland Park, MI. Halftone print on paper, 30.4 × 11.7 cm. CL.

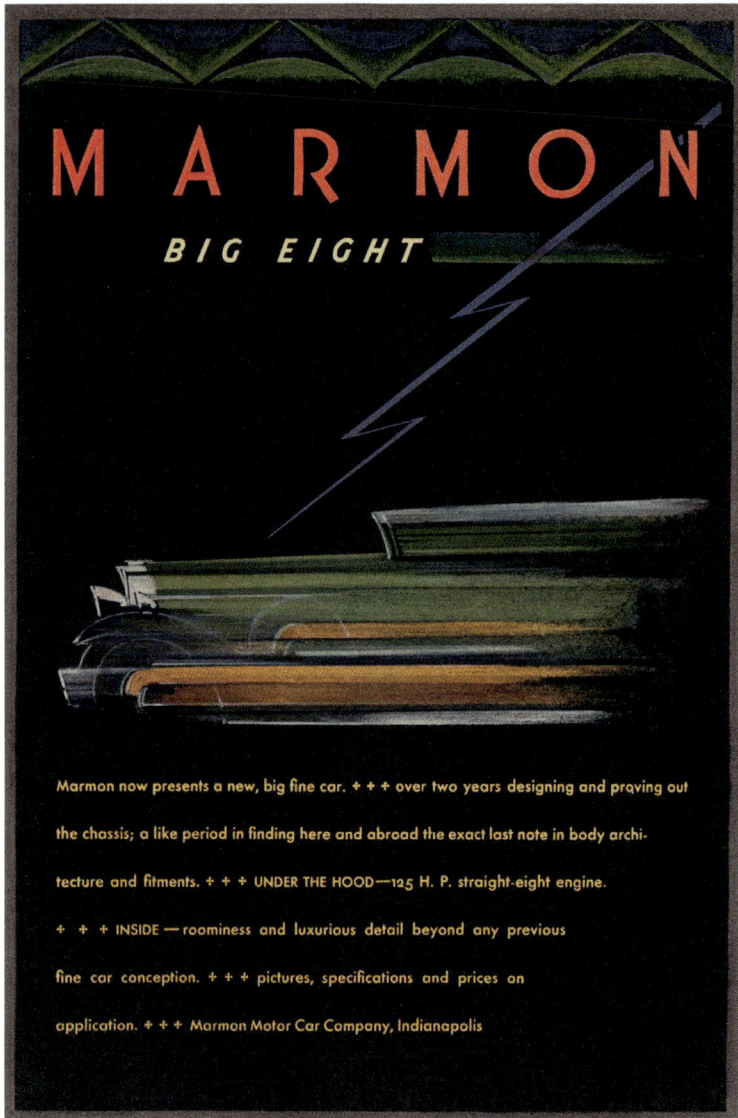

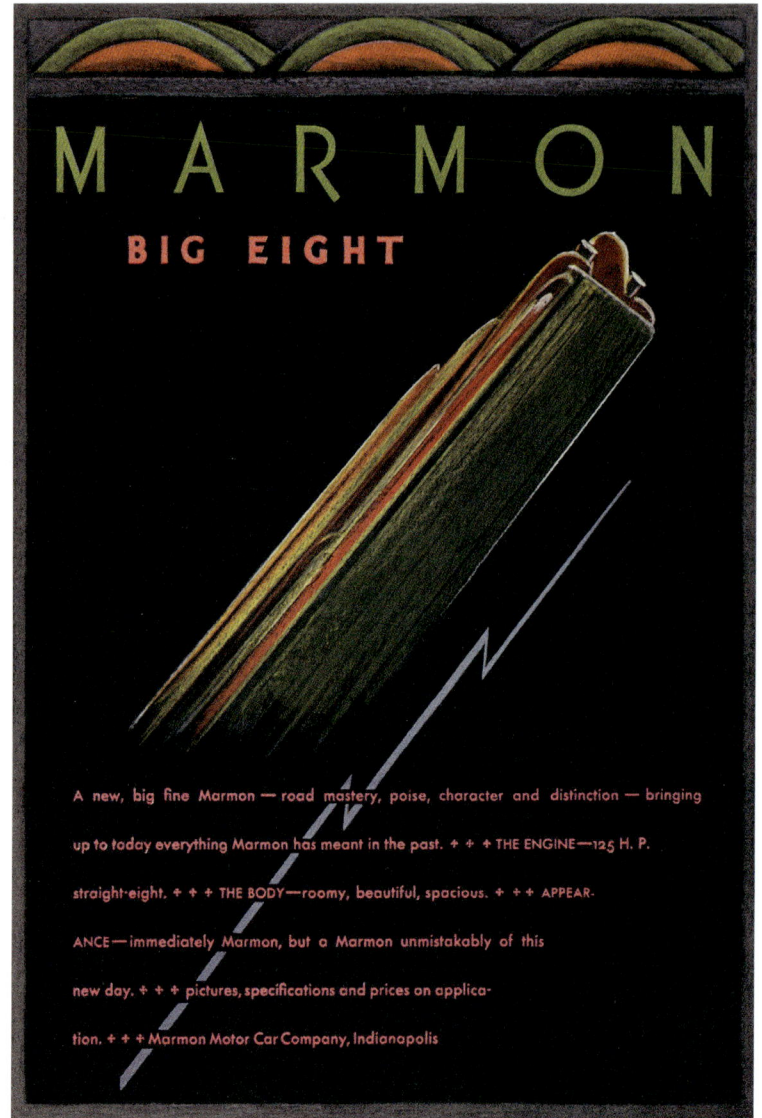

215| Walter Dorwin Teague, *Marmon Big Eight*, 1930. Magazine advertisement for Marmon Motor Company, Indianapolis, IN, from *Vanity Fair*, January 1930, n.p. Halftone print on paper, 28.8 × 21.2 cm (trimmed). CL.

216| Walter Dorwin Teague, *Marmon Big Eight*, 1930. Advertisement, printed for the Marmon Motor Company, Indianapolis, IN. Halftone print on paper, image: 25.9 × 17.8 cm. CL.

1932 (fig. 218). A Packard deluxe model, shown at the bottom of the page, sits at the end of a winding road leading up and through a futuristic metropolis. The bridge and other structures are sporting the new streamlined language, yet the car itself has not been reimagined. It stands in notable contrast to its surroundings. Vassos, though, knew very well how to contrive a scene of pure streamlining. In a magazine layout from a few years before, an ad for the Cammeyer shoe company, he employed a consistent and elegant image: an impossibly thin and attenuated couple dancing through a swirling celestial setting (fig. 219). In the clearing of the "clouds" are two ghostly representations of a woman's shoes, as if the whole vision were a fever dream.

By the 1932, the language of streamlining was becoming almost omnipresent, apart, it should be stated again, from the machines themselves. In an advertisement for Medusa Portland Cement Company, the work of an unknown designer, we even see it applied to an abstracted human figure, his hands dripping concrete to form a "constructed" landscape (fig. 220). Another 1932 ad, for a ball bearing company, takes a different approach: it combines a car with an enormous machined and glis-

ARISTOCRAT
OF THE
METROPOLIS

THE Packard Stationary Coupe is much favored by professional men. This new Aristocrat of the Metropolis—available both on the Packard Eight and Eight De Luxe Chassis—embodies distinction and luxury sincerely appreciated by men whose pursuits call them constantly about the city. Men and women whose activities are business or social also find it a most convenient personal car, both in town and country. A comfortable rumble seat permits extra passengers—large and accessible compartments accommodate belongings. ¶ May we demonstrate the aristocratic Packard Stationary Coupe? May we show you how its *Ride Control* provides a degree of riding comfort that exists in no other make of motor vehicle?

ASK THE MAN WHO OWNS ONE

PACKARD

PACKARD MOTOR CAR COMPANY OF NEW YORK

Eleventh Avenue at 54th Street   Broadway at 61st Street   Broadway at Sherman Avenue
BRONX: 696 East Fordham Road   BROOKLYN: Atlantic at Classon Avenue

PARK AVENUE PACKARD, Inc.   WEST END PACKARD CO., Inc.
6 East 57th Street   Broadway at 106th Street

Cammeyer

SALON de LUXE FIFTH AVENUE at FIFTY THIRD NEW YORK

217| John Vassos, "Dromophobia," 1931. Plate from *Phobia* (New York: Covici Friede Publishers, 1931). Halftone print on paper, 30.4 × 22.5 cm. CL.

218| John Vassos, *Packard, Aristocrat of the Metropolis*, 1932. Sample magazine advertisement, printed for the Packard Motor Car Company, Detroit, MI. Halftone print on paper, 25.3 × 17.4 cm. CL.

219| John Vassos, *Cammeyer Salon de Luxe Fifth Avenue at Fifty Third New York*, 1927. Sample magazine advertisement, printed for A. J. Cammeyer, New York, NY. Halftone print on paper, 25.3 × 17.4 cm. CL.

WHITE PORTLAND CEMENT

IS INDISPENSABLE TO THE CONSTRUCTION INDUSTRY

STUCCO
TERRAZZO
CAST STONE
MORTAR
SWIMMING POOLS

MEDUSA
WHITE PORTLAND CEMENT
PLAIN AND WATERPROOFED

● The architectural preference for concrete does not rest solely upon its manifest stability and workability. It is also founded on artistic considerations. White or colored concrete, in many forms, is now being used in almost every type of building because it produces results that are as attractive as they are permanent. ● Medusa White Portland Cement, plain and waterproofed, produces concrete of the same great strength and durability as regular Gray Portland Cement. It can be tinted as desired, for clear, uniform, permanent color effects. ● Medusa White is the *original* White Portland Cement. For 25 years it has been the outstanding White Cement, used all over the world for better results and better appearance. A few of the hundreds of uses for this White Portland Cement are shown at the left.

MEDUSA PORTLAND CEMENT COMPANY, 1002 Engineers Bldg., Cleveland, Ohio

· 13 ·

New Departure Ball Bearings

Engineers could not have attained the new ease of driving control in the 1932 cars without the aid of additional New Departure Ball Bearings. They do more for motorists today than just reduce friction and prolong car life. New Departures give smooth movement and make shaft alignment permanent, upon which the success of many new refinements depend.
THE NEW DEPARTURE MFG. COMPANY, BRISTOL, CONN.

NOTHING ROLLS LIKE A BALL

220| *White Portland Cement*, 1932. Magazine advertisement for Medusa Portland Cement Company, Cleveland, OH, from *Fortune Magazine*, April 1932, 13. Halftone print on paper, 35.7 × 27.8 cm. CL.

221| *New Departure Ball Bearings*, 1932. Magazine advertisement for the New Departure Mfg. Company, Bristol, CT. Halftone print on paper, 35.7 × 28.4 cm. CL.

222| *Chrysler Royal Imperial Airflow*, ca. 1936. Brochure, printed for the Chrysler Motors Company, Highland Park, MI. Lithograph on paper, 20.3 × 24.2 cm. CL.

223| Peter Helck, *1936 Pontiac Built to Last 100,000 Miles*, 1936. Magazine advertisement for Pontiac Motor Company, Pontiac, MI. Halftone print on paper, 17 × 18 cm (trimmed). CL.

224| Joseph B. Birren, *A Century of Progress Chicago*, 1933. Brochure, printed by Gunthorp-Warren Printing Company, for *A Century of Progress Exposition.*, Chicago, IL. Offset print on paper, 15.7 × 7.7 cm. CL.

tening bearing (fig. 221). This early example of photomontage—a technique that would become ever more important for the new graphic design as the decade went on—was all about how new mechanisms themselves were transforming the look of modernity. (Two years later, a lone ball bearing would grace the cover of the Museum of Modern Art's epochal 1934 *Machine Art* exhibition.[3])

For American commercial art, the decisive moment came in 1934 with the appearance of the Chrysler Airflow, the first full-size production car in the United States to employ streamlining. Chrysler also marketed a companion model under the DeSoto brand, the DeSoto Airflow. Both cars became hugely popular—even beloved—by the public.

The advent of the Airflow spawned a series of ads and brochures in the new style (fig. 222). The competing automobile companies quickly launched their own streamlined models, and with them, a cascade of ads, signs, and printed ephemera. Often, the new cars were shown flying, or even in outer space, as in a Pontiac magazine ad, by Peter Helck, which displayed the company's new model circling the earth (fig. 223).

The language of streamlining was not only applied to cars. Refrigerators, stoves, washing machines, scales, and other "durable goods" were soon transformed through streamlining. The smoothed, sweeping contours also became a form of graphic shorthand for newness itself—applied to an array of posters, handouts, and other printed

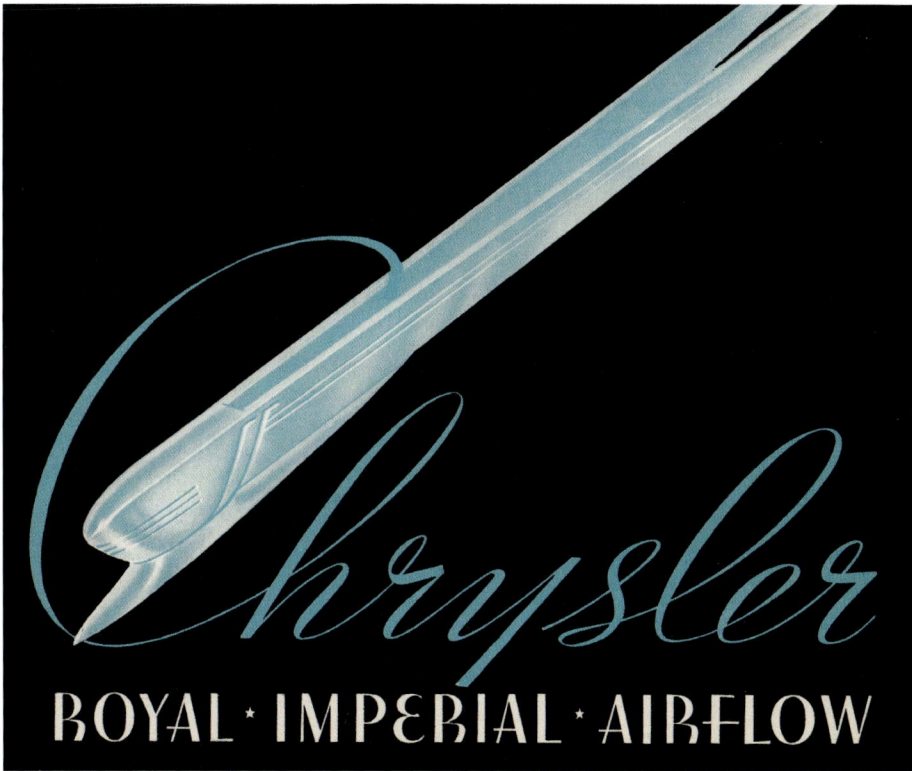

works. Chicago-based Joseph B. Birren's many variant designs announcing the city's 1933 World's Fair offer an early and consummate example of this new idiom (fig. 224). Each features Saturn with swirling rings—as if we ourselves could see the planet hurtling through the sky.

This poetics of swift movement became a means to sell almost anything. Loewy famously streamlined a fully stationary pencil sharpener, producing a product that was silly and beautiful in equal measure. When Futura, a new sans-serif typeface created by German designer Paul Renner, was released in the United States around 1930, it too was marketed with the imagery of movement, a fact that is all the more confounding because Futura's strong geometric shapes were in fact quite static in appearance (fig. 225).

The moving trains of the Futura ad, however, were prophetic. Many of the best "dynamic" graphic designs of the mid-1930s were associated with trains or airplanes—modes of transportation for which streamlining and its aeronautical advantages carried the most sense. The major railroad companies developed their signature streamlined trains—"The Mercury," "The 20th Century Limited," and the "Daylight," among them—to drum up business, and they advertised each service relentlessly with posters, magazine ads, and brochures, each conveying the distinctive look of that company's train (figs. 226–229).

The Century...The Broadway...The Overland...The Golden State...Four of the dozens of superb trains operated daily over American Railroads. ● To express these four and their many sisters, in type as powerful, as clean cut, as distinguished as the trains themselves, has hitherto been rather a problem. ● With **FUTURA BOLD**, however, conveying the same energetic, abstract and logical qualities, this problem fades to the vanishing point. ● Never was there a type face better suited to present the message of not only the railroads but also the entire heavy industries, than this...

FUTURA
the type of today
and tomorrow

THE BAUER TYPE FOUNDRY, INC., NEW YORK
At Two-Thirty-Five East Forty-Fifth Street

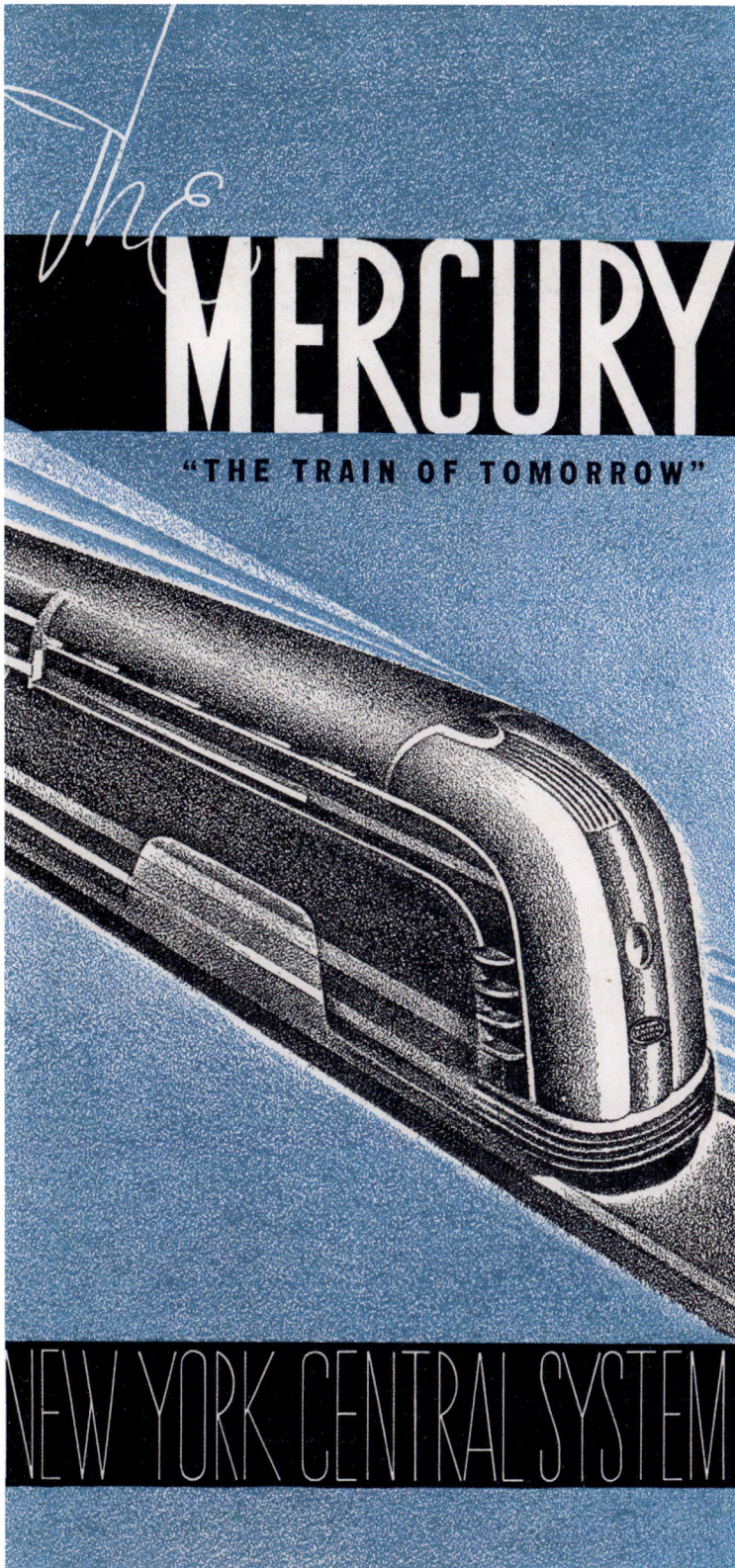

The Mercury
"THE TRAIN OF TOMORROW"

NEW YORK CENTRAL SYSTEM

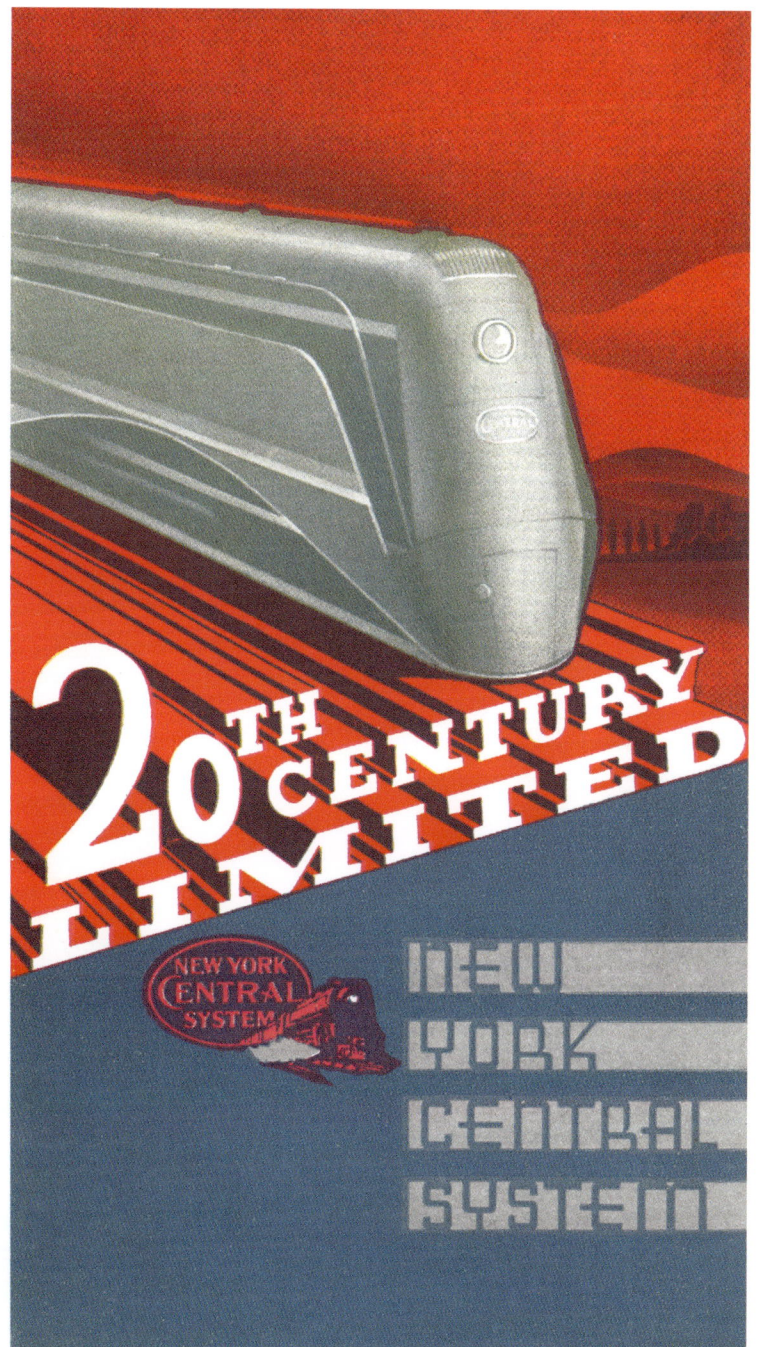

20TH CENTURY LIMITED

NEW YORK
CENTRAL
SYSTEM

NEW YORK CENTRAL SYSTEM

225 | *Futura, the type of today and tomorrow*, ca. 1930. Advertisement from Frank H. Young, *Modern Advertising Art* (New York: Covici, Friede, Inc., 1930), 121. Offset print on paper, 26.2 × 18.8 cm. CL.

226 | *The Mercury "The Train of Tomorrow,"* 1936. Brochure, printed for New York Central Railroad System, New York, NY. Halftone print on paper, 21.3 × 10.1 cm. CL.

227 | *20th Century Limited New York Central System*, 1937. Brochure, printed by Bodley Printers, Inc., New York, NY, for New York Central Railroad System, New York, NY. Halftone print on paper, 18.2 × 10.3 cm. CL.

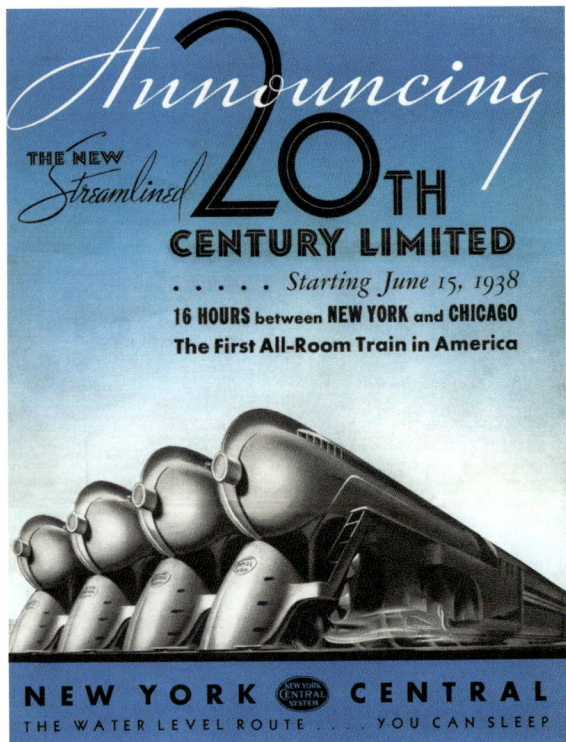

228 | *Announcing the New Streamlined 20th Century Limited*, 1938. Brochure, printed for the New York Central System, New York, NY. Halftone print on paper, 27.7 × 21.2 cm. CL.

229 | Sam Hyde Harris, *Southern Pacific's New Daylight Los Angeles–San Francisco*, 1937. Poster, printed for Southern Pacific Railroad, San Francisco, CA. Lithograph on paper, image: 57.1 × 39.7 cm. The Resnick Collection.

230 | Fred Ludekens, *American Airlines Inc.*, 1936. Timetable, printed by Calvert-Hatch Co., Cleveland, OH, for American Airlines, Chicago, IL. Halftone print on paper, 23.1 × 10.2 cm. CL.

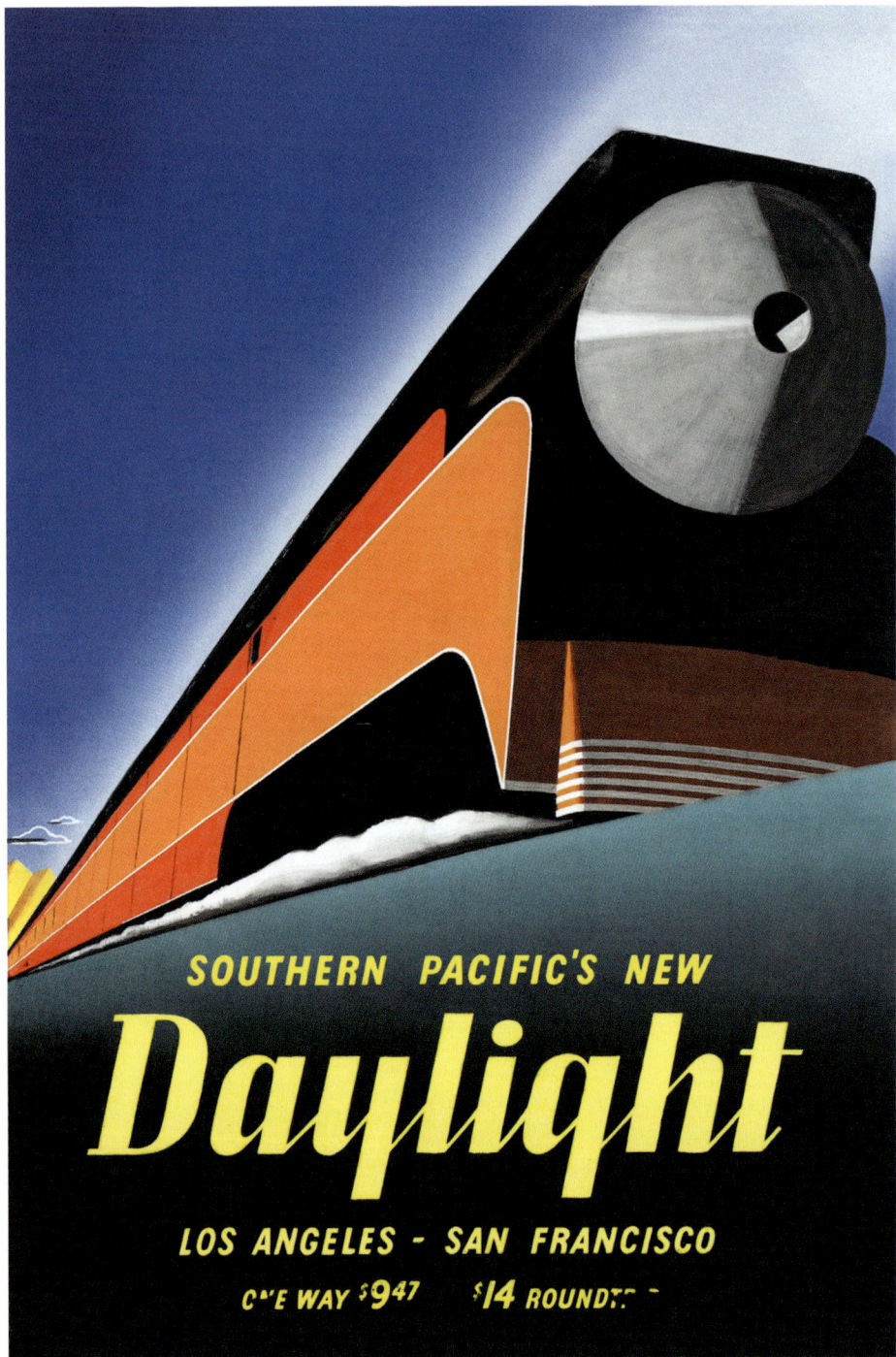

AMERICAN
AIRLINES
INC.

SELECTED
CALIFORNIA
PEARS

MINIMUM NET WEIGHT 46 POUNDS
PACKED & SHIPPED BY
DAY & YOUNG
SANTA CLARA, CALIF.

STREAMLINE

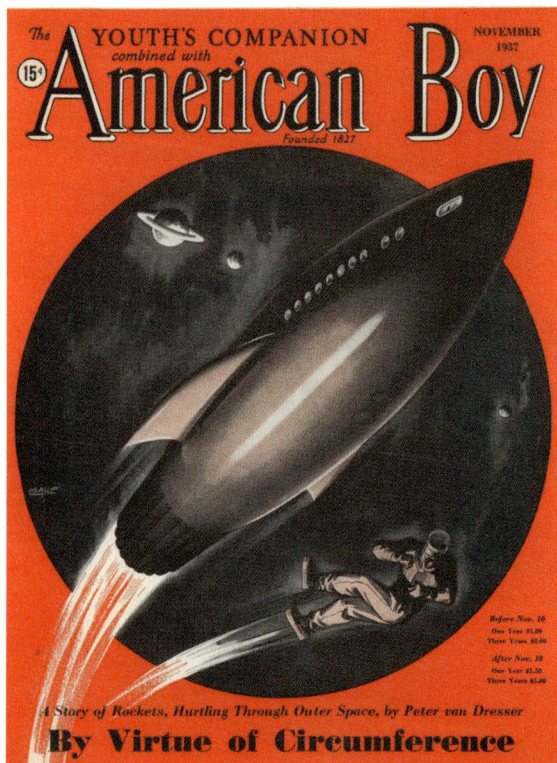

The YOUTH'S COMPANION
combined with
American Boy
15¢
NOVEMBER
1937
Founded 1827

A Story of Rockets, Hurtling Through Outer Space, by Peter van Dresser

By Virtue of Circumference

The new airline companies were not far behind. By 1936, new streamlined airplane models were in service, and the airlines were keen to promote their look and advantages. And it wasn't only the look of the gleaming metal aircraft skins they sought to plant in potential customers' minds; they were eager to exhibit their up-to-date attitude through graphics. A 1936 American Airlines timetable by the California-born designer Fred Ludekens is an early masterwork of modernist restraint (fig. 230).

The phenomenon of streamlining and projecting speed was so pervasive that even an ordinary fruit company embraced it, rebranding their product as "Streamline Pears." The company's crate label is a brilliant essay on speed and futurism, a perfect statement of "freshness" in both senses (fig. 231). The aura of a bright, lustrous future also carried over to magazine covers, especially those for *Popular Science*. One especially evocative work came from William John Heaslip (who later become well-known for his paintings of space travel): a flying rocket ship that appeared on the cover of *American Boy* magazine (fig. 232). More prosaic, though no less lovely, is a luggage label from Transcontinental & Western Air (TWA) featuring one of its new Stratoliners (the same model that would become the B-17 in the war) making its way across country (fig. 233).

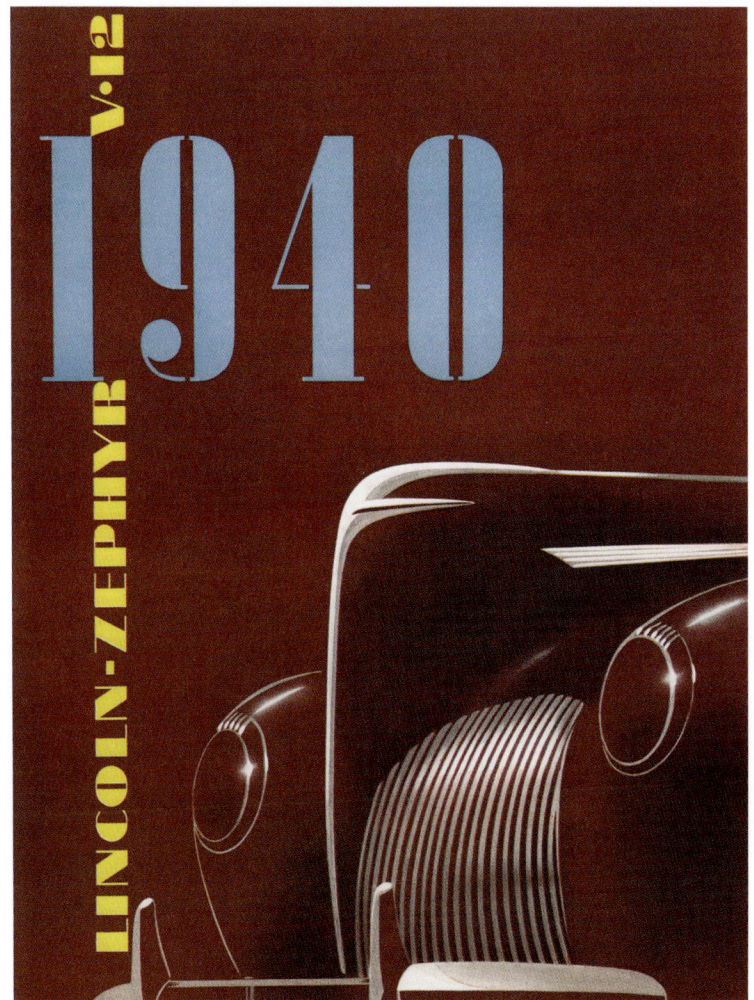

231 | *Streamline Selected California Pears*, ca. 1937. Label, printed for Day & Young, Santa Clara, CA. Lithograph on paper, 19.1 × 27.2 cm. CL.

232 | William John Heaslip, cover of *American Boy*, November 1937. Half-tone print on paper, 33 × 24.4 cm. CL.

233 | *Route of the Stratoliners Shortest Fastest Coast-To-Coast*, ca. 1940. Luggage label, printed for Transcontinental & Western Air, Kansas City, MO. Offset print on paper, diameter: 9.8 cm. CL.

234 | *Lincoln Zephyr V-12*, 1936. Brochure, printed for the Lincoln Motor Company, Detroit, MI. Offset print on paper, 21.2 × 27.3 cm. CL.

235 | *The New Lincoln–Zephyr V-12 for 1938*, 1937. Brochure, printed for Lincoln Motor Company, Detroit, MI. Offset lithograph on paper, 23.5 × 31.3 cm. CL.

236 | *1940 Lincoln-Zephyr V-12*, 1939. Brochure, printed for Lincoln Motor Company, Detroit, MI. Halftone print on paper, 27.8 × 21.6 cm. CL.

237 | *Modes and Motors*, 1938. Booklet, printed for General Motors Corporation, Detroit, MI. Offset print on paper, 21 × 13.3 cm. CL.

In 1935, the Lincoln Motor Company released its own streamlined model, the Lincoln Zephyr, its competitor to the Chrysler Airflow. Lincoln's new car was not only more upscale, but the sales materials the company prepared (all by an unnamed designer or designers, as was standard for the big Detroit automobile manufacturers) are among the signal works of the era. An especially "resonant" design is a brochure for the 1936 Zephyr V-12 model (fig. 234). Borrowing from the motion studies then being conducted in the aircraft industry, it depicts "flow lines" sweeping around a wing-shaped logo—a visual confirmation of how the car's form was supposed to enhance its aerodynamic performance. More customary for Lincoln's ads and handouts, however, were pictures of the cars—or some detail. But they were always set out in such a manner that the sleek, sinuous contours of each model were emphasized (figs. 235, 236).

General Motors Corporation, equally keen to show the inherent modernity of their cars, distributed brochures (at the 1939 New York World's Fair and at various

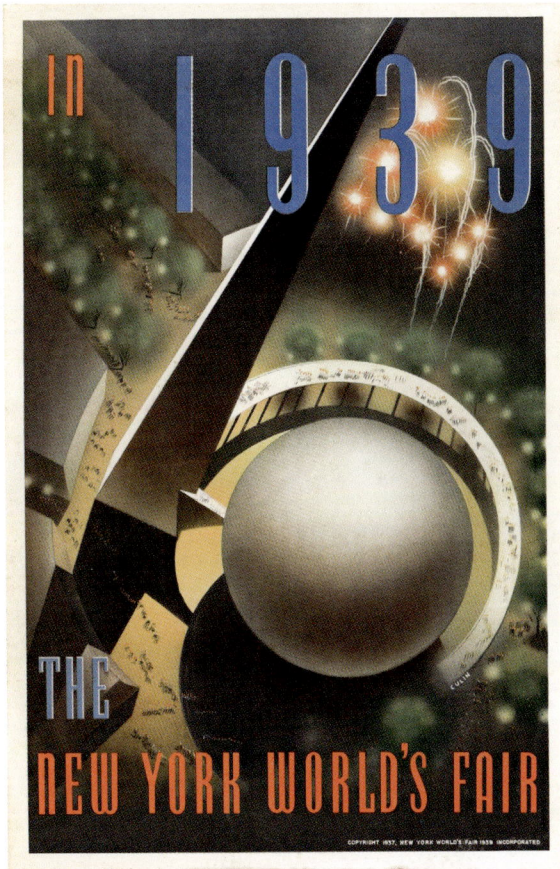

238| Nembhard N. Culin, *In 1939 the New York World's Fair*, 1937. Poster, printed for the New York World's Fair Corporation, New York, NY. Photolithograph on paper, 99.7 × 70.2 cm. The Resnick Collection.

239| Joseph Binder, *New World's Fair The World of Tomorrow*, 1939. Poster. Offset print on paper, 50.7 × 34.1 cm. Private collection.

trade shows) stressing their technological advances and styling—with covers that were at times surprisingly freed of text or overt advertising (fig. 237).

It was the 1939 New York World's Fair that marked the apotheosis of the streamlining era. Depictions of the fair, especially the Trylon and Perisphere, the two monumental modernistic structures (designed by architects Wallace Harrison and J. André Fouilhoux) that formed what was known as the "Theme Center," were everywhere to be seen. Nearly all the posters and other advertising for the fair feature these iconic forms, including designs by Nembhard N. Culin and Joseph Binder (figs. 238, 239).

These posters offer a summary of American design at the end of the decade and its two dominant directions: in Culin's work, the quasirealistic, closely attached to the long tradition of illustration; and, for Binder, the trend toward restraint and diminishment, which was becoming increasingly mainstream. Binder's poster, even more than Culin's, points in the direction of a luminous futurism, a vivid imagining of what might come.

The true adept of this futuristic form-language was Arthur Radebaugh. Born in Coldwater, Michigan, in 1906, Radebaugh began his career as a sign painter; a few years later, in 1925, he entered the School of the Art Institute of Chicago. He worked mainly in advertising, producing art for Bendix, Coca-Cola, Chrysler, Dodge, National Motor Bearing, and Studebaker. He also illustrated the train menu for the Burlington Zephyr and covers for *Fortune*, *Motor*, *The Saturday Evening Post*, and other magazines.[4] His ads of the late 1930s and 1940s for the Bohn Aluminum Company are showpieces of his distinctive airbrush technique, sleek and theatrical images of a future world (fig. 240).[5]

Streamlining, the evocation of speed and progress, bore witness to American dreams and ambitions in the Depression years—and well after. It was a deeply romanticized gesture, a testament of faith in the machine and its potential for transformation when the country was still mired in economic uncertainty. For a time, it *was* American modernism, an aesthetic born from a belief in the power of technology and a yearning for better times. But it remained for a new generation, then just emerging, to formulate an even more incisive vision of the modern.

240| Arthur Radebaugh, *Bohn Trucks to Come*, 1943. Magazine advertisement for Bohn Aluminum and Brass Corporation, Detroit, MI. Halftone print on paper, 32.9 × 26.2 cm (trimmed). CL.

BOHN

The engineers of the Bohn organization have made extensive studies in light alloys which will be of great importance in the development of tomorrow's new designs. Among other things, new types of highly efficient motor trucks will come forth. Bohn is the only organization in the world specializing in large volume, in three of the most essential alloys—aluminum, magnesium and brass. Thus this company is in a position to give unbiased advice. Consult us freely for the correct use of the correct light alloys.

TRUCKS TO COME

BOHN ALUMINUM AND BRASS CORPORATION, DETROIT, MICHIGAN
GENERAL OFFICES—LAFAYETTE BUILDING
Designers and Fabricators—ALUMINUM • MAGNESIUM • BRASS • AIRCRAFT-TYPE BEARINGS

BUY WAR BONDS

8 American

Modernness

In the spring of 1930, Earnest Elmo Calkins spoke at the annual convention of the American Federation of Arts in Washington, D.C. (fig. 241). Calkins had turned sixty-two a few months before, and, though he was still robust—he would live well into his late nineties—he sensed that time was passing him by. The advent of radio and, with it, radio advertising, a field in which he believed he had nothing to contribute because of his deafness, compelled him to question whether he still had any part to play in advancing his profession. And he felt a deep sense of loss. Ralph Holden, his longtime partner and loyal confidante, had died a few years before of a blood clot following an operation.[1] Holden had been Calkins's "voice," translating Calkins's ideas and setting them into action. Now, Calkins was on his own, and he was struggling.

Calkins was also acutely aware of another great shift, a seismic reordering that was transforming the world of advertising: the rise of modernism. His talk that day, in a special session titled "Art and Commerce," was an effort to come to terms with the changes he saw taking place around him. In a shrill, slightly flat tone, the sound of someone whose hearing had long been severely impaired, he laid out what he and others had achieved in ushering in a new art—the art of the two-dimensional advertising page—and what he thought the future held.

In his hour-long speech, Calkins showed a surprising awareness of the new graphic design. "Advertising art," he said,

being flexible and assimilative, was quick to appreciate the possibilities of modernism. Realistic art had reached a dead level of excellence. It was no longer possible to make an advertisement striking, conspicuous and attractive by still pictures and realistic groups, however competently painted. Modernism offered the possibility of expressing the inexpressible, of suggesting not so much a motor car as speed, not so much a gown as a style, not so much a compact as beauty. Commonplace objects were shown in new patterns, or from new angles, and gained a fresh interest thereby. The field for inventiveness was widened; text and pictures were woven together, and the advertising pages achieved a liveliness and interest they had not hitherto revealed.[2]

Calkins went on to speak about how modernism was being adopted by industry, how new colors, patterns, and features were showing up in industrially made goods. He was now keenly aware that modern advertising art constituted a separate category, that it could not rightfully be compared with "fine art." "There can be no argument," he told the audience, "as to whether a shortening advertisement by René Clarke is a better work of art than a Madonna by Botticelli or a motor car by Jay Hambridge is greater than a Hermes by Praxiteles, or a book illustration by Rockwell Kent is more precious than a print by Albrecht Dürer."[3] Calkins nonetheless continued his old refrain, asserting that the value in modern advertising art lay in its capacity to elevate the taste of the masses—that its essential modernity resided in its broad appeal. And he was certain, he said, that any real beauty in modern advertising would "grow out of our modern industrial civilization."[4]

Calkins was still firm in his belief that the annual Art Directors exhibitions—the ninth one was held that spring—had the potential to separate the "grain from the chaff."[5] But modernism, at least in the world of the Art Directors, was slow to arrive. American advertising of the 1920s had, to a large degree, reflected the cultural conservatism of the era. To anyone now looking back at that time, it is clear that much of the art in these shows was stolid and conventional. Change, however, was coming. Calkins retired later in 1931; within a few years, American graphic design would undergo an epochal reorientation.

It is one of the ironies of this story of the new advertising and design that the onset of the Great Depression, while crippling the nation and threatening the progress of capitalism as never before, also helped to spur the rise of modernism. Even more remarkably, the shift to the new design came partly as a result of government fiat.

In 1935, President Franklin D. Roosevelt launched the Works Progress Administration (WPA) to restart the economy and boost public morale. Included within the WPA was a much smaller agency, the Federal Art Project (FAP), which was meant to support out-of-work artists and performers. Thousands of visual artists, writers, and theater people were hired to present cultural events, plays, and art exhibitions. One subgroup of the Federal Art Project, the Poster Division, was charged with raising awareness of these many cultural programs.

Over the course of its eight-year existence—until it was discontinued in 1943—the Poster Division printed some two million posters, from thirty-five thousand designs.[6] The basis for this mass outpouring of public art had already been laid two

241 | Earnest Elmo Calkins, ca. 1924. From Earnest Elmo Calkins, *"Louder Please!" The Autobiography of a Deaf Man* (Boston: Atlantic Monthly Press, 1924), frontispiece.

years before. In 1933, Charles T. Coiner, art director of the N. W. Ayer advertising agency in Philadelphia, was tasked with creating a logo for one of the first of the Roosevelt administration's programs, the short-lived National Recovery Administration (fig. 242). Widely displayed in shop windows and government offices across the country, it was a forthright, propagandistic exercise, as many of the WPA posters would be. The symbolism was unambiguous: an American eagle clutching in its twin talons a gear of industry and the lightning bolts of energy. The slogan, "We Do Our Part," was no less straightforward. The near irreducibility of the lettering and the eagle itself, was surprising—at least in the American context of the time. Not since the propaganda posters of World War I had the United States government engaged in such ambitious messaging.

Yet little about Coiner's design was truly new in graphic terms. Greatly more radical is a less well-known design from that time, Clarence P. Hornung's logo for the Civilian Conservation Corps (fig. 243). Not only is its typeface for the triple Cs even more "diminished," but the three figures, carrying their tools, are almost fully abstracted. Hornung's design is more clever than it might first appear. By detaching the heads and legs from the torsos of the three figures, he gave them a notable vitality and dynamism.

The early master of this new language of considered reductivism was Dorothy Waugh. Over the course of a little less than two years, Waugh designed seventeen posters for the National Parks Service that were truly and momentously ground-breaking.

Waugh was born in 1896, in Burlington, Vermont. In 1902, her family moved to Amherst, Massachusetts, after her father became the director of the department of horticulture at Massachusetts State College. Waugh excelled as a writer and artist. Her parents sent her to George School, a Friends' boarding institution in Bucks County, Pennsylvania. After graduating, she studied at a string of art schools, including the Massachusetts School of Art, the Museum School of the Cleveland Museum of Art, and the John Herron Art Institute in Indianapolis. Waugh also studied landscape architecture at Massachusetts State College. For a time, she worked for landscape architects in Boston, Cleveland, New Orleans, and Charlotte, before completing her art studies at the School of the Art Institute of Chicago. She then spent a few years in a Chicago art studio before moving to New York City to seek a career in the publishing industry.[7]

With the deepening Depression, Waugh was forced to look elsewhere for work. Through her father's connections and her very evident abilities, she landed a position at the National Park Service. Waugh was first assigned to develop an illustrated manual for the Civilian Conservation Corps, but by 1934, she was tasked with making posters promoting the park system.[8]

One of her early efforts was *The Adventures of Today are the Memories of Tomorrow* (fig. 244). Probably made in August of that year, it shows a figure fishing in a mountain lake. It is a luminous image, made more so by the stark yellow background and the bold black frames on either side. The full scene—the blue highlights, the moun-

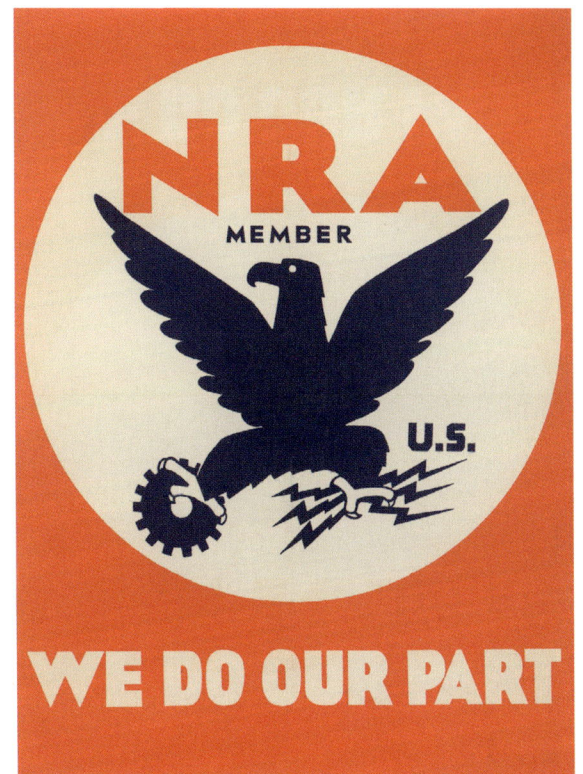

242 | Charles T. Coiner, *NRA We Do Our Part*, 1934. Poster, printed for the National Recovery Administration, Washington, D.C. Lithograph on paper, 70.5 × 52.7 cm. The Resnick Collection.

243 | Clarence Hornung, logo for the Civilian Conservation Corps, 1934. Published in *Advertising Arts*, May 1934, 18. CL.

ADVENTURES of TODAY are the
MEMORIES of TOMORROW

NATIONAL PARKS

DOROTHY WAUGH

tains, a lone bird in flight, the ripple of the lake where the man is fishing—is both serene and sophisticated. And yet, for all that, the poster is activated: by setting the black bars on either side at different heights, she creates a visual tension that stands in sharp contrast with the quiet majesty of the setting.

Waugh's understanding of the power of two-dimensional space is announced in another of her 1934 posters, *Mystery Veils the Desert* (fig. 245). We again see a solitary figure, a man, in profile, seated on horseback. He is framed by two impressive cacti. The rest of the scene is taken up with a resplendent night sky. Some stars are mere points of light; others are twinkling crosses. It is the sheer contrast of light and dark (for the entire poster is only in black and white) that is so affective. There is again a studied quietude—except for the two different fonts, both in the manner of the "modernistic."

244| Dorothy Waugh, *The Adventures of Today are the Memories of Tomorrow National Parks*, 1934. Poster, printed by the U.S. Government Printing Office, Washington, D.C., for the National Parks Service, Washington, D.C. Lithograph on paper, 101 × 69.5 cm. Prints and Photographs Division, Library of Congress, Washington, D.C.

245| Dorothy Waugh, *Mystery Veils the Desert National Parks*, 1934. Poster, printed by the U.S. Government Printing Office, Washington, D.C., for the National Parks Service. Lithograph on paper, 101 × 69 cm. Prints and Photographs Division, Library of Congress, Washington, D.C.

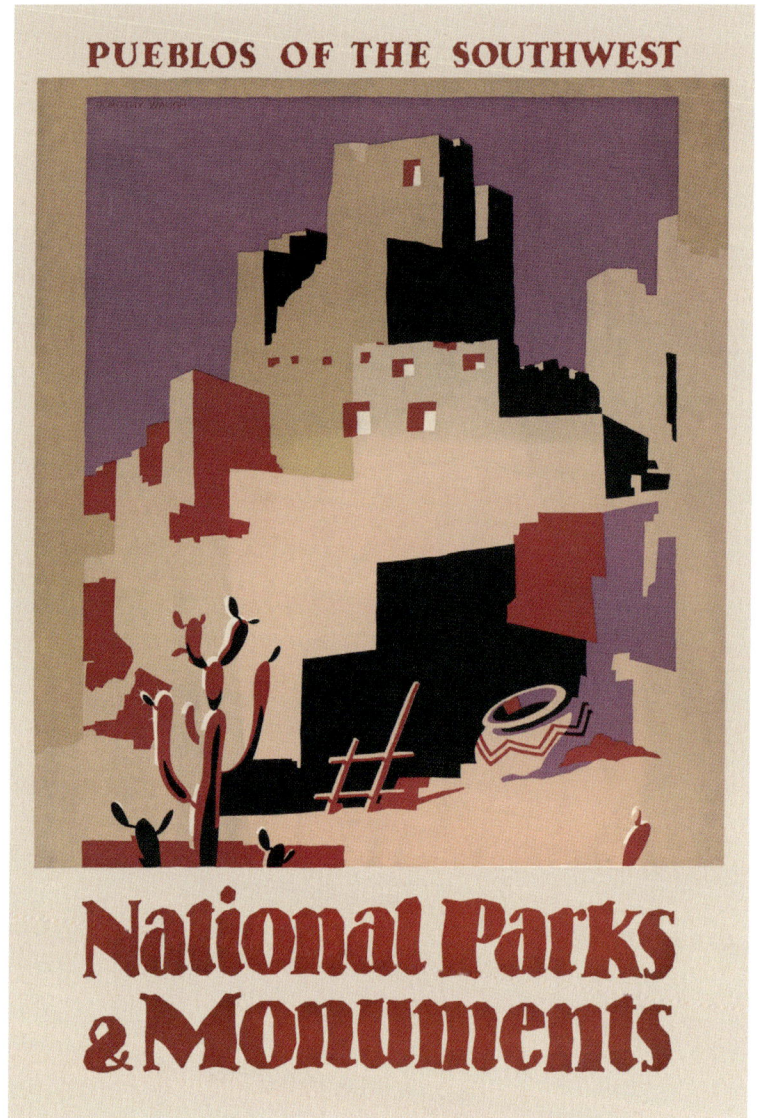

246 | Dorothy Waugh, *The Lure of the National Parks*, 1934. Poster, printed by the U.S. Government Printing Office, Washington, D.C., for the National Parks Service, Washington, D.C. Lithograph on paper. Prints and Photographs Division, Library of Congress, Washington, D.C.

247 | Dorothy Waugh, *National Parks and Monuments, Pueblos of the Southwest*, 1935. Poster, printed by the U.S. Government Printing Office, Washington, D.C., for the National Parks Service, Washington, D.C. Lithograph on paper, 101.6 × 69 cm. Prints and Photographs Division, Library of Congress, Washington, D.C.

———————

248 | Dorothy Waugh, *National and State Parks*, 1936. Poster, printed by the U.S. Government Printing Office, Washington, D.C., for the National Parks Service, Washington, D.C. Lithograph on paper, 101.6 × 70.2 cm. The Resnick Collection.

Another of Waugh's posters, *The Lure of the National Parks*, reads like a fresh-air *pièce de théâtre* (fig. 246). We see five figures on horseback, riding single file through a stream at the edge of a forest. It is all recognizable, yet nothing seems quite real. The trees are jagged shapes forming a continuous backdrop; the horses appear to hover oddly above the water. Much of the surface is taken up by a blue field of color, with decidedly "Deco" lettering presenting the message. Waugh treads between conventional portrayal and modernist restraint: we can read the scene as if it were realism, though it already belongs to a very different domain of art.

One of Waugh's 1935 posters, *National Parks and Monuments, Pueblos of the Southwest*, is about a very different form of projection (fig. 247). It is also a landscape, if a mostly manmade one. Waugh carries out two operations, a decided flattening—everything in the scene is reduced into sharply delimited blocks of color—and a remaking of the color scheme into shades of red and blue. The resulting scene is still "objective" (or realistic), but if one focuses on a specific area of the image, it reads almost as an exercise in abstraction.

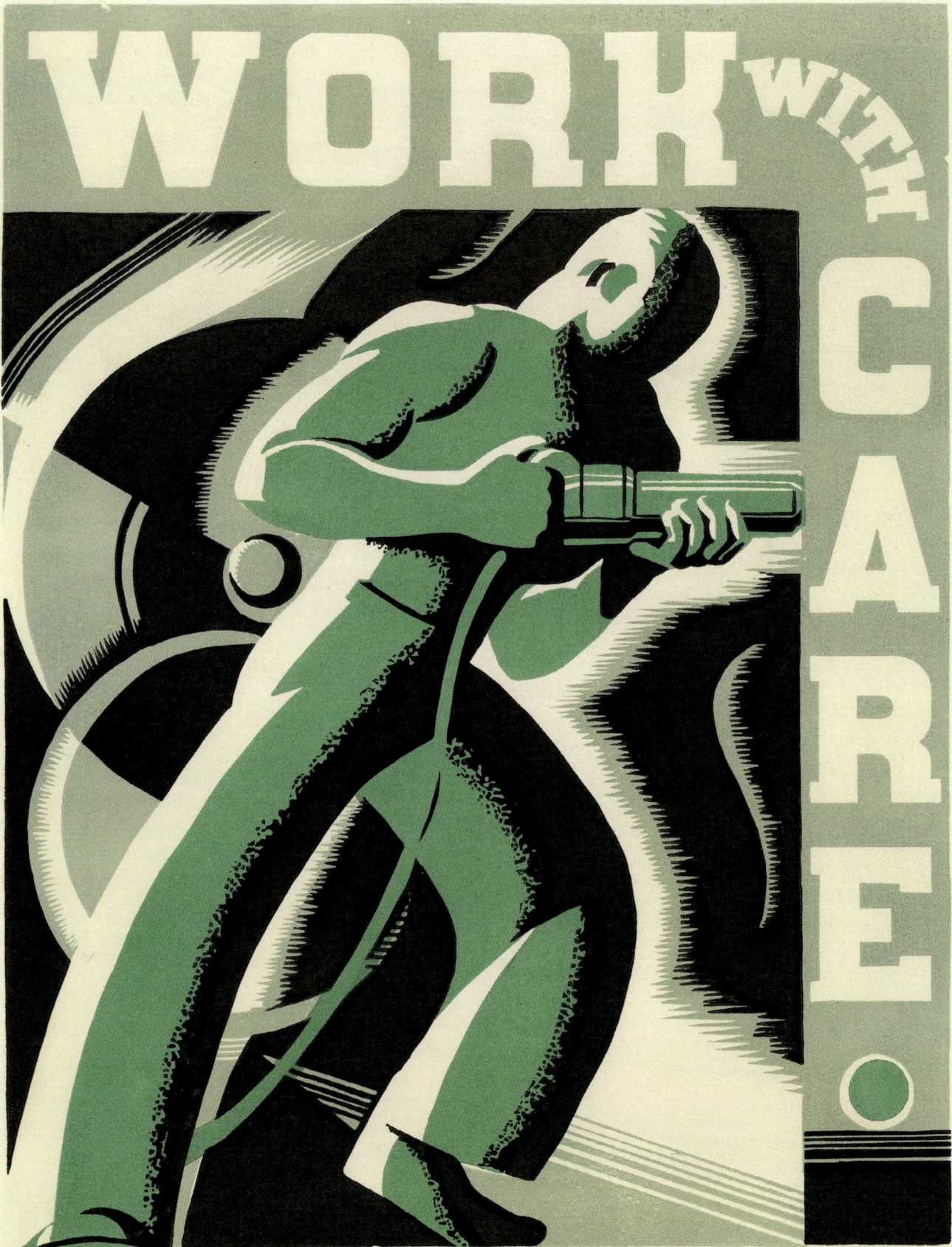

WORK WITH CARE

W P A FEDERAL ART PROJECT PENNSYLVANIA

Waugh's masterwork came a year later, in 1936. *National and State Parks* was intended to promote winter sports—skiing, skating, sliding, and sleighing (fig. 248). At its center is a figure holding a pair of skis, and across the middle, in two parallel black bands, "National and State Parks" is written out. The "skier" is reduced to mere lines and shapes—in places, such as the face, it is almost fully geometricized—so much so that the figure could be interpreted as either human or machine. The vivid color scheme—red, yellow, black, and white—only enhances the artificiality of the image. It is stridently modern and transfixing.

The inventiveness of Waugh's posters was only occasionally matched by the artists of the WPA poster division. It is sometimes claimed that Waugh was part of the Federal Art Project. She was not. She was employed throughout the mid-1930s by the Park Service, and she resigned in 1937 to take a position as the head of the children's book department at Alfred A. Knopf, in New York City.[9] Some very good artists were part of the Federal Art Project, among them Will Barnet, Stuart Davis, Lee Krasner, Louise Nevelson, Alice Neel, Jackson Pollock, and Willem de Kooning.[10] But most of the posters were the work of lesser talents, and a large percentage of their designs suffered from a tendency to put too much on the surface—too many words, images, or colors—and, not infrequently, all three. They often worked far better as instruments of public messaging—of propaganda for the government's efforts—than they did as art.

The very best of the WPA posters, however, contributed to the rise of a distinctly American graphic style. Robert Muchley's *Work With Care*, of 1937, borrows from the look shaped by the artists of the political left. A beefy worker is operating a riveting machine, with enormous, spinning machinery set behind him (fig. 249). The man is fully engaged; every sinew of his body and his full concentration are given over to the task—precisely what the poster was intended to convey. Muchley's skill for drama is evident: it is literally a riveting image, and he no doubt might have gone on to find real fame had he not died shortly later, in France.[11]

Muchley's poster was relief printed, a printmaking technique in which the surface of the plate or block is cut away so that the image alone appears raised on the surface. Relief printing, which includes woodcut, linoleum cut, and letterpress, was an old technique; by the 1930s, newer methods—especially rubber stamping—were coming into standard use. Some of the WPA posters were also lithographs. But by far the largest number were made employing screen printing.

Screen printing, too, was not exactly new; it had originated in China during the Song dynasty, a thousand years before. Screen printing in Europe and the United States, however, dates only to the beginning of the last century. An Englishman, Samuel Simon, patented the modern form of screen printing in 1907 that involved using squeegees to push the ink through a screen mesh. Others, including Roy Beck, Charles Peter, and Edward Owens, revolutionized the commercial screen-printing industry with photo-imaged stencils. The screen printing of artistic images was developed mid 1910s, mostly in California.[12] But the introduction of screen printing to the WPA program—and its elevation to a fine art form—

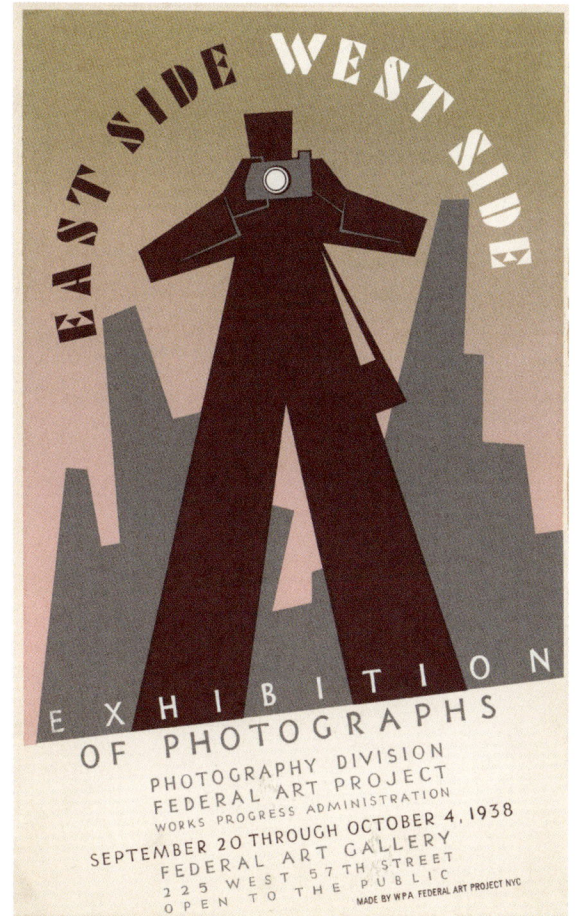

249| Robert Muchley, *Work with Care*, 1937. Poster, printed by the Graphic Arts Workshop, WPA Federal Art Project, Philadelphia, PA. Relief print on paper, 63.2 × 47.3 cm. The Resnick Collection.

250| Anthony Velonis, *East Side West Side Exhibition of Photographs*, 1938. Poster, for the Works Progress Administration, Washington, D.C. Screenprint on board, 56 × 35.6 cm. Prints and Photographs Division, Library of Congress, Washington, D.C.

THE **ONLY** SAFE WEAPONS
AGAINST CANCER ARE

 ← SURGERY

 ← X-RAYS

 ← RADIUM

DO NOT TRUST YOUR LIFE TO OTHER METHODS

U.S. PUBLIC HEALTH SERVICE IN COOPERATION WITH THE AMERICAN SOCIETY FOR THE CONTROL OF CANCER

MADE BY WORKS PROGRESS ADMINISTRATION · FEDERAL ART PROJECT NYC

POSTER
EXHIBIT

POSTER
EXHIBIT
MAY 1 · MAY 31
ILLINOIS ART PROJECT GALLERY
211 NORTH MICHIGAN AVENUE

MADE BY ILLINOIS WPA·ART PROJECT CHICAGO

was very largely the achievement of one artist employed in the New York office, Anthony Velonis.

Born to poor Greek immigrants in New York City, Velonis began to experiment with the silkscreen process around 1932. Working with another artist, Fritz Brosius, in Velonis's brother's sign shop, he gradually developed a mastery of the process.[13] In 1934, he was hired by the New York City Mayor's Poster Project, instituted by Mayor Fiorello La Guardia, to publicize city projects. The following year, the Mayor's Poster Project became the New York Poster Division of the Federal Art Project.

With several others, including Louis Lozowick, Velonis began researching new methods for screen printing. He produced a short pamphlet on the subject providing explicit how-to instructions for others in the program to make their own prints.[14] It was distributed to the WPA art centers around the country, and soon, screen printing, also called silk screening, became the preferred method for the program's artists. Velonis coined his own term for the result: serigraph, or "silk drawing."

Velonis's own works, both those at the Poster Division and the Graphic Arts Division, were highly advanced stylistically (figs. 250, 251). And that was true of many of the posters that he and others produced in the New York office, which was headed up by Richard Floethe. The German-born Floethe had attended the Bauhaus before moving to the United States; he was already a renowned designer and book illustrator before he assumed the leadership of the group, and his influence—especially a tendency toward restraint and the use of bold pictorial imagery—is apparent in many of the works of the New York artists.[15]

Floethe strongly supported Velonis's effort to spread screen printing to others in the New York division. Rapidly, other FAP groups across the nation also picked up the technique, including the Illinois branch in Chicago. One of the best designs to come out of that office, the work of an unknown artist for a local poster exhibit, is a splendid bit of modernist compression and abstraction (fig. 252).[16]

Still, most of the best silkscreen designs were issued from the New York office. The 1936 poster *Eliminate Crime in the Slums Through Housing*, now attributed to Herman Kessler, relies not only on the new reductivism coming from Europe, but it also suggests the influence of the Hollywood movies—the bold chiaroscuro effect that lighting technicians were then achieving (fig. 253) Another of the New York artists, Jack Rivolta, made two of the strongest (and now most frequently reproduced) WPA posters, *United States' First Foreign Trade Zone* and *Up Where Winter Calls to Play* (figs. 254, 255). Rivolta's works are essays on simplification, bold color blocking, and repetition. Most remarkable, though, are the contrasts he engenders, between large, essentially inert forms and scenes that are alive with movement and action. His portrayal of a four-man bobsled hurtling down the run at Lake Placid, all diagonals, splotches, and sinuous forms, is fully vitalized, even while the means he deploys are surprisingly basic.

Another poster, *See America Welcome to Montana*, made by Jerome Henry Rothstein, is a related design, but it is also an advance on what Rivolta was doing (fig. 256). Rothstein, then still in his teens (he was the youngest of all the program's artists), contrived a complete montage—of mountains, a lake, a forest, and Native American tipis

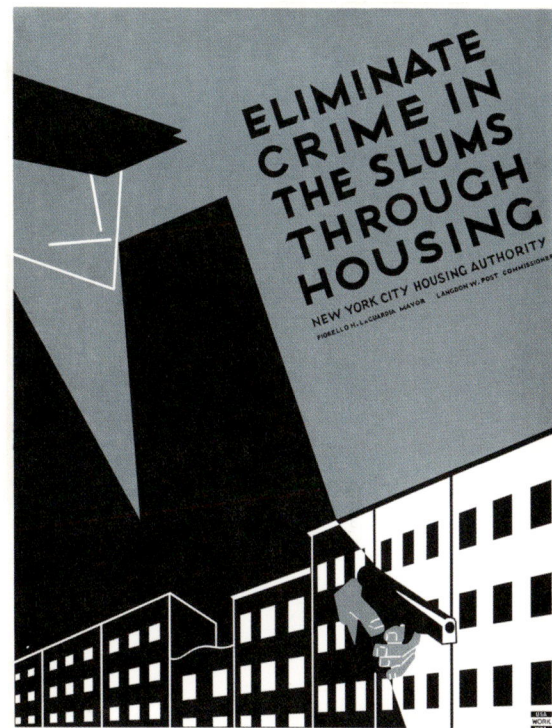

251 | Anthony Velonis, *The only safe weapons against cancer are surgery, x-rays [and] radium Do not trust your life to other methods*, 1938. Poster, for the Works Progress Administration, Washington, D.C. Screenprint on board. Prints and Photographs Division, Library of Congress, Washington, D.C.

252 | *Poster Exhibit*, ca. 1937. Poster, printed by the Illinois WPA Art Project, Chicago, IL, for the WPA Federal Art Project Illinois. Screenprint on paper, 55.9 × 35.6 cm. The Resnick Collection.

———

253 | Herman Kessler [attrib.], *Eliminate Crime in the Slums Through Housing*, 1936. Screenprint on paper, 71.1 × 55.9 cm. Prints and Photographs Division, Library of Congress, Washington, D.C.

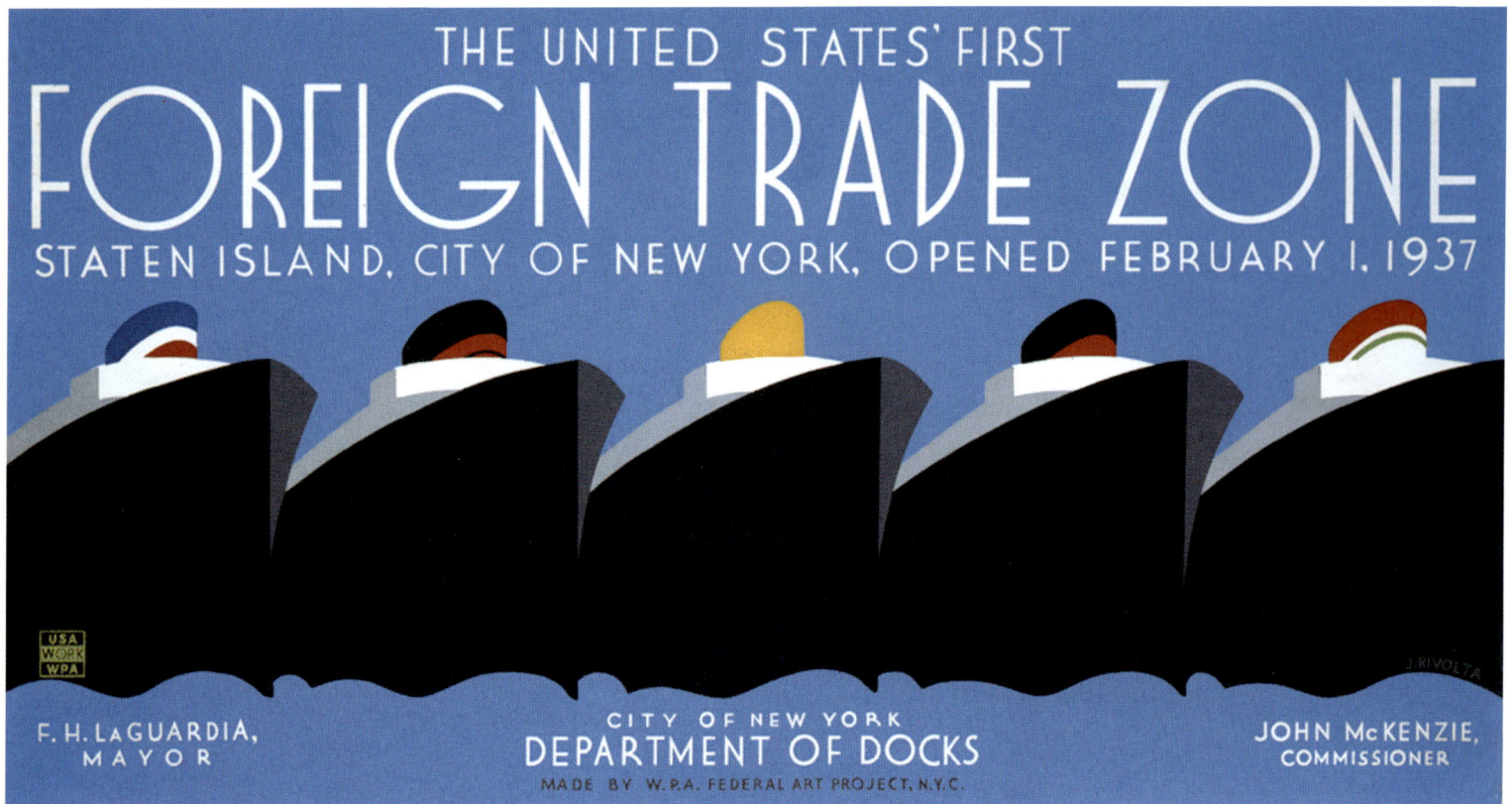

THE UNITED STATES' FIRST
FOREIGN TRADE ZONE
STATEN ISLAND, CITY OF NEW YORK, OPENED FEBRUARY 1, 1937

USA WORK WPA

F. H. LaGUARDIA,
MAYOR

CITY OF NEW YORK
DEPARTMENT OF DOCKS
MADE BY W.P.A. FEDERAL ART PROJECT, N.Y.C.

JOHN McKENZIE,
COMMISSIONER

254 | Jack Rivolta, *United States' First Foreign Trade Zone*, 1937. Poster, printed by WPA Federal Art Project, for City of New York, Department of Docks. Screenprint on board, 27.9 × 54 cm. Prints and Photographs Division, Library of Congress, Washington, D.C.

---

255 | Jack Rivolta, *Up Where Winter Calls to Play Olympic Bobsled Run Lake Placid*, ca. 1937. Poster, printed by WPA Federal Art Project, for the New York State Conservation Department. Screenprint on board, 63.5 × 41.9 cm. Prints and Photographs Division, Library of Congress, Washington, D.C.

and symbols—to represent the state and express why one should visit it. (The United States Travel Bureau commissioned the poster.) The motion here, though, is not in the scene; rather it comes through in the way the eye is made to travel across the surface, "visiting" each feature or place. The individual elements are pulled apart; it's only when we recombine them in our minds that the poster becomes "whole."

A contrast between movement and stasis is also what underlies the effectiveness of another very good WPA poster, for a marionette performance of the Karel Čapek play *Rossum's Universal Robots* or *R.U.R.* (fig. 257). The robot, looking fittingly the part of a machine-age monster, is both fixed and activated, his helmet firing off light beams like a weapon. The oppositions of bold color and jagged and curving forms only further enhance these effects.

Not every accomplished design was so "doubled"—i.e., part statis, part movement. Perhaps the most arresting of all the WPA posters, *Keep Your Teeth Clean*, is effective precisely because it is so very fixed and rudimentary (fig. 258). The unsigned poster is now known to be the work of Erik Hans Krause, who was one of the supervisors of the Rochester unit of the New York State Art Project.[7] Everything in the image—the human figure, the teeth, the toothbrush, the toothpaste—is presented so matter-of-factly that it almost comes off as a child-made still life—until one registers how supremely well the scene is condensed and presented.

A similar expression of considered restraint also underlies another WPA poster of note, *Know for sure—get a blood test for Syphilis* (fig. 259). Its maker, Leonard Karsakov, used an airbrush, which allowed him to contrive the impression of an "every-

UP WHERE WINTER
≈ CALLS TO PLAY ≈

OLYMPIC
BOBSLED RUN
OPERATED BY N.Y. STATE CONSERVATION DEPT.
LAKE PLACID

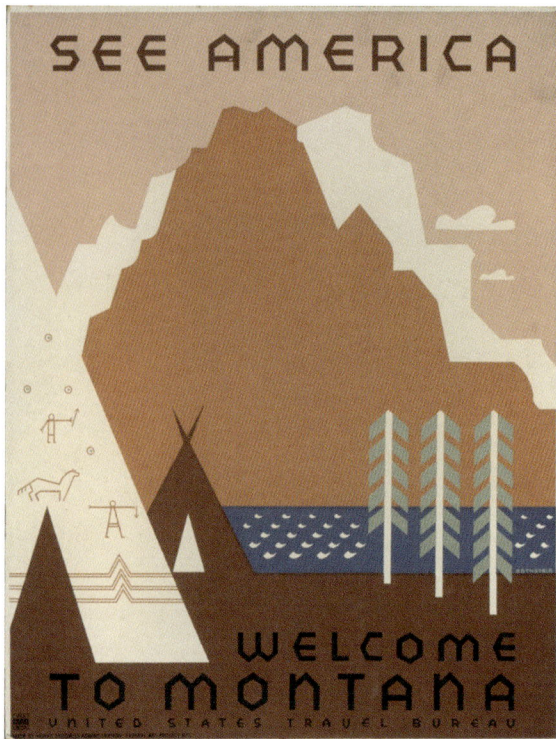

256 | Jerome Henry Rothstein, *See America Welcome to Montana*, ca. 1937. Poster, printed for the United States Travel Bureau. Screenprint on board, 71.1 × 55.9 cm. Prints and Photographs Division, Library of Congress, Washington, D.C.

257 | Charles Verschuuren, *R.U.R.*, ca. 1939. Poster, printed for the Federal Theater Project, Marionette Theater. Screenprint on board, 55.9 × 35.6 cm. Prints and Photographs Division, Library of Congress, Washington, D.C.

258 | Erik Hans Krause, *Keep Your Teeth Clean*, ca. 1938. Poster. Screenprint on board, 55.8 × 35.3 cm. Prints and Photographs Division, Library of Congress, Washington, D.C.

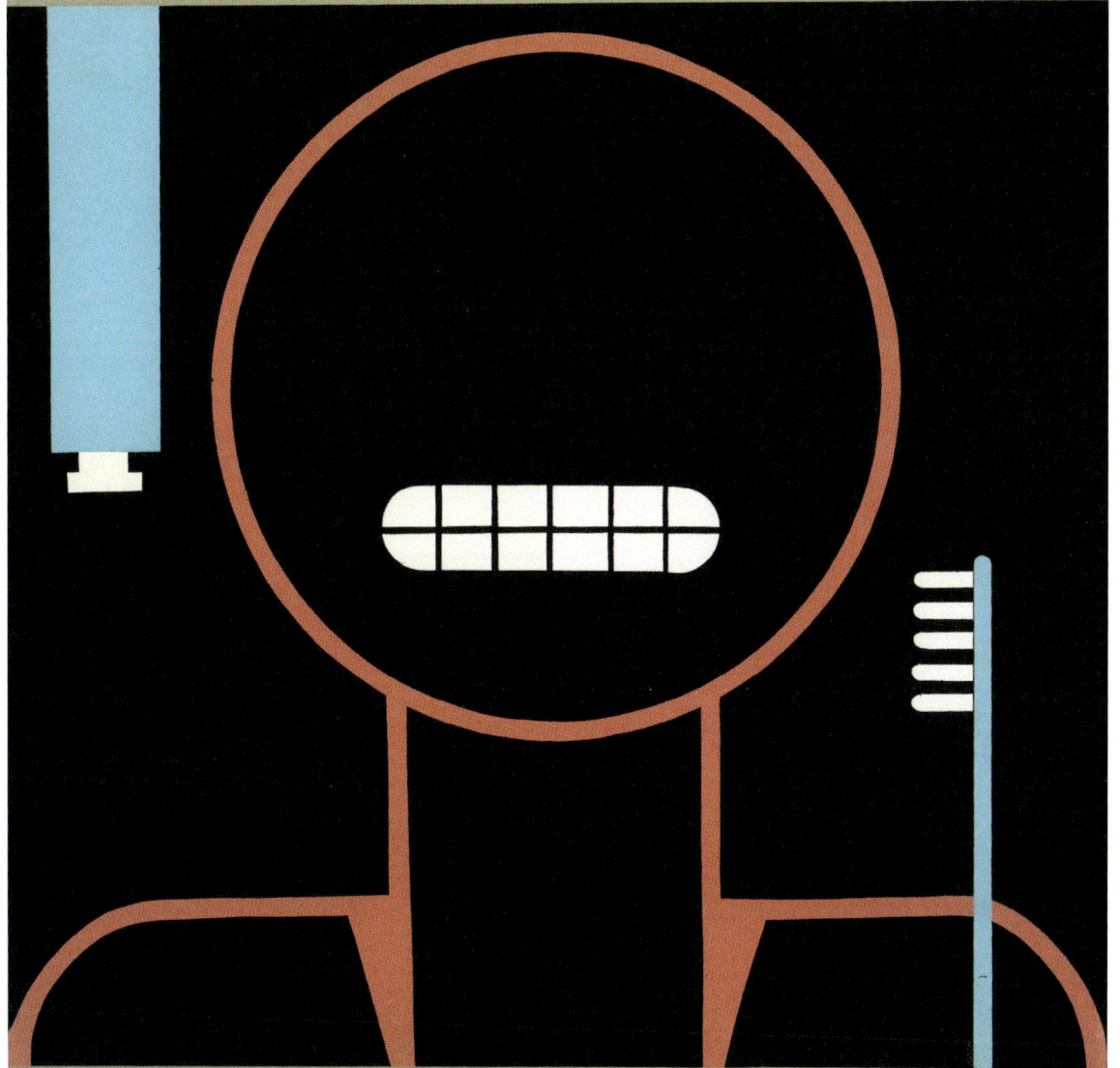

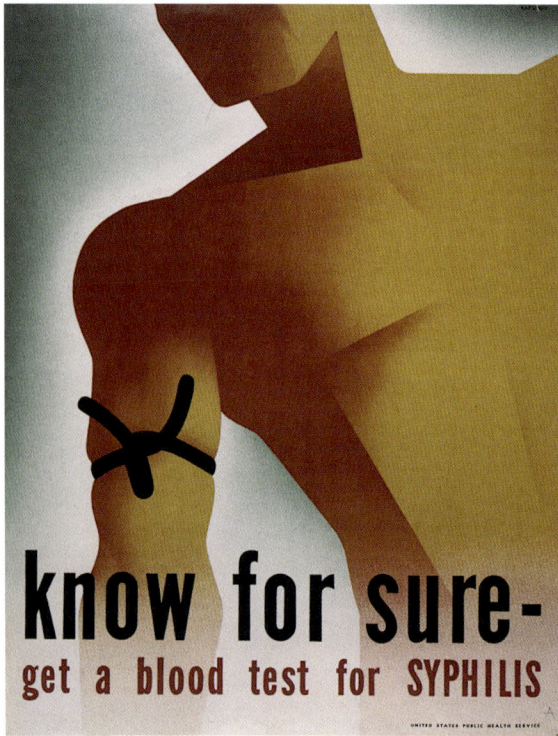

259 | Leonard Karsakov, *Know for sure—get a blood test for Syphilis*, 1941. Poster, printed for the U.S. Public Health Service. Lithograph on paper, 71.1 × 55.8 cm. Prints and Photographs Division, Library of Congress, Washington, D.C.

260 | John Atherton, cover of *Advertising Arts*, May 1934. CL.

one"—the perfect vehicle for suggesting that syphilis did not discriminate. But the design is even more deft than that, for what we see above all is the tourniquet on the arm, a visual stand-in for the blood draw itself. Everything is expressly modern: the imagery and its presentation, the mode of messaging, and the typography.

Karsakov's poster, printed in 1941, marked an end, however. A short time later, with the United States' entry into World War II, the Federal Art Project was transferred to the Department of Defense and renamed the Graphics Section of the War Service Division. The move effectively spelled the program's end.[18]

What had begun as a work-relief program became over time something else, a concerted attempt to change the nature of visual communication. The best of the posters did precisely that. Still, the foremost accomplishment of the program was less the creation of new examples of modern design than their dissemination, for a broad swath of the American public was exposed to advanced modern design, many for the first time.

Even before the Federal Art Project was established, the transformation of the graphic arts in America was already taking place, and much of this activity was in venues most Americans didn't see. The full liberation of the page and poster—its separation from traditional modes of representation—was evident as early as 1934.

That year, Earnest Calkins, now retired from Calkins & Holden but, as always, irrepressible, wrote an op-ed for *Advertising Arts*, the leading organ for the print advertising and package "styling" industries. At that moment, at the very depth of the Depression, Calkins complained about the "pressure of the need to sell, more insistent now than in the gilded age." The result, he noted, was "advertising design that was pleasant to contemplate, but also much that was merely extravagant, bizarre." It was, in his pointed phrase, "a false modernism that was bound to be ephemeral."[19]

Calkins was reacting to the modernistic—the Art Deco and its offshoots. Prescient as ever, he detected the appearance of its replacement, a new realism, which he ascribed to the advent of documentary photography.[20] He wasn't entirely correct, however, because, as it would turn out, he was missing a vital part of the new synthesis.

It was fully on display on the cover of another issue of *Advertising Arts* from just four months later (fig. 260). The image was the work of John Atherton, a Scottish-born artist who had arrived in New York from California in 1929. Atherton would go on to make advertisements for General Motors, Shell Oil, Container Corporation of America, and Dole, as well as covers for *The Saturday Evening Post*. At that time, though, he was still establishing himself.

The cover he designed for *Advertising Arts* is about visual fracturing. It is—very directly—a metaphor of the graphic artist. We see a man, his drafting triangle, his hands, his brush. Atherton also places a megaphone in the artist's mouth, a symbol of his role as a broadcaster of messages. Yet the image is ruptured, the man's face split apart, the hands are joined to each other but not to the body. Half of the man's face is a photograph, the other half a crude rendering, and the megaphone looks as if it has been cut out and merely affixed to the surface. Surrounding it all are airbrushed blotches and very advanced typography.

The sources Atherton drew upon are all too obvious. We can detect, especially, the spirit of postwar French Cubism and Russian Constructivism. It is Atherton's introduction of realism, in the form of the half-photographed face, however, that makes it all so predictive (fig. 261). Within a very short time, everything he is doing would become a key constituent of the new design.

But Atherton's design was only one of many new approaches. The mid-1930s was a period of extraordinary and varied experimentation in American design. One current was the language of geometry that had evolved out of Art Deco, which was at the center of Robert Foster's twenty-four-sheet billboards for White Flash gasoline (fig. 262). Then there was the bold play of form and type in Alexey Brodovitch's magazine ad for the New Jersey Zinc Company (fig. 263). And more striking still was the

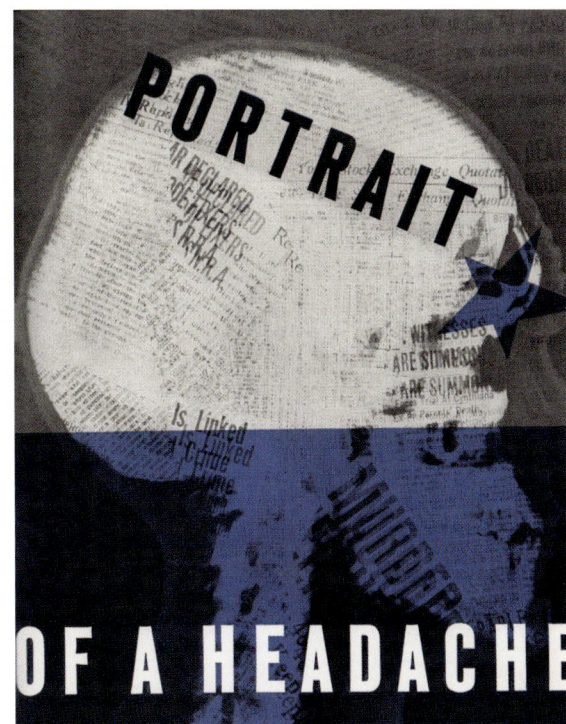

261 | Paul Smith, *Portrait of a Headache*, 1934. Sample advertisement from Art Directors Club, *Thirteenth Annual of Advertising Art* (New York: Book Service Company, 1934), 72. Halftone print on paper, 24.9 × 20.2 cm. CL.

ATLANTIC
White flash
FOSTER
A SUPER FUEL • NO EXTRA COST

ATLANTIC
white flash
A SUPER FUEL
NO EXTRA COST
FOSTER

262 | Robert Foster, 24-sheet posters for White Flash gas, 1934. From *Advertising Arts*, March 1934, after page 24. CL.

263 | Alexey Brodovitch, *The New Jersey Zinc Co.*, 1934. Sample advertisement for New Jersey Zinc Co., New York, NY, from *Advertising Arts*, March 1934, after page 41. Offset print on paper, 10.2 × 20.9 cm. CL.

264 | Boris Artzybasheff, *Corn Kernel*, 1937. Magazine advertisement. Halftone print on paper, 35.5 × 28.3 cm. CL.

expressive (and slightly bizarre) anthropomorphism and biologism of Russian-born Boris Artzybasheff. One of his most remarkable designs is a "growing" diagram showing the many uses of corn—set out like roots emanating from a single kernel (fig. 264).

At that moment, American design was careening through a period of very hurried change, much of it owing to the arrival of several leading designers from abroad. Some of these designers had disembarked already in the 1920s and early 1930s. Lucian Bernhard began regularly visiting New York in 1923; he settled in the city permanently a few years later.[21] It would, however, take nearly a decade before Bernhard began to have a significant impact on American design. Eventually, his billboards and ads for Rem Cough Syrup and Amoco Gas would become some of the iconic images of the Depression years. Little of Bernhard's American work was an advancement of the new design, however; he adapted to American modes far more than he fostered new directions.

Greatly more important for the new American graphic language was another German-speaking émigré, Joseph Binder. Binder was Viennese, born in 1898. After serving in the Austro-Hungarian army during World War I, he studied at the Vienna Kunstgewerbeschule (School of Applied Arts) with Bertold Löffler, one of the leading practitioners of *fin-de-siècle* design. In 1924, Binder established his own studio, Wiener Graphik; almost immediately, he acquired a reputation for his clean, modern designs, employing direct and saturated colors. Responding to the dismal economic and political situation in Austria, he went on a lecture tour of the U. S. in the early 1930s, speaking at the Art Institute of Chicago and the Minneapolis School of Art. Binder also published an influential book in London, *Colour in Advertising*—with the intention, it seems, of laying the groundwork for leaving Austria.[22] He finally did so in 1936, settling in New York, where he opened an office on Central Park South.[23]

Like other European émigrés, Binder found that he had to adjust his style to match American tastes. He moved in the direction of pictorial realism, remaking his forms to be more commercial and familiar. His 1937 cover for *Fortune*, a looming, stair-stepped skyscraper jauntily set back, has come to be regarded as one of the landmarks of the era (fig. 265). More characteristic of his work at this time, though, was an almost impressionistic image of a cotton plant in a magazine advertisement for the Pepperell Manufacturing Company (fig. 266).

Joseph Sinel was another of the foreign-born designers who contributed to the new American modernism in the 1930s. Born in New Zealand in 1889, Sinel arrived in San Francisco in 1918 after serving in France during the war. Harold von Schmidt hired him on at Foster & Kleiser, where he joined a staff that included relative newcomers Charles Stafford Duncan, Judson Starr, and Otis Shepard.[24] A few years afterward, he made his way to New York, laboring there both as an industrial and graphic designer. Sinel's early designs reflected a direct reading of Art Deco. His later graphic work, however, tended toward a considered reticence. A cover he designed for *PM* in 1936 is already gesturing toward minimalism (fig. 267).

The contrast between Sinel's cover and a Winold Reiss design of the late 1930s underscores the growing divide between the older and newer modernisms (fig. 268).

265 | Joseph Binder, cover of *Fortune*, December 1937. Offset print on heavy rag paper, 29.2 × 35.6 cm. CL.

266 | Joseph Binder, *Buy Cottons By Pepperell*, ca. 1939. Magazine advertisement for Pepperell Manufacturing Company, Boston, MA. Halftone print on paper, 3 5.7 × 26.2 cm. CL.

267 | Joseph Sinel, cover of *PM*, 1936. Magazine, printed by Frederick Photogelatine Press, for PM Publishing, New York, NY. Two-color photogelatine on heavy paper, 21.1 × 13.7 cm. CL.

268 | Winold Reiss, cover of *You Can Design* by Winold Reiss and Albert C. Schweizer (London: Whittlesey House; New York: McGraw-Hill), 1939. CL.

Reiss's book cover, as lovely as it is, looks back to earlier graphic and typological ideas; Sinel's almost rough and ready language is something else altogether.

In those years, Reiss was spending much of his time engaging in his passion, painting portraits of Native Americans, which he undertook during annual summer pilgrimages to the West. During the late 1920s and early 1930s, he also made captivating images of some of the culturati of the Harlem Renaissance. His main source of income, however, continued to come from commercial work, which included interiors and graphics for the Longchamps restaurant chain in New York. Throughout the later 1930s, in a series of designs for menus, signs, and advertisements, he honed the Jugendstil and modernistic inflections of his earlier years. The results were some of the most lyrical and elegant designs of the period (fig. 269). Yet Reiss's work was more updated than it was genuinely new, for he was still working within the visual strictures of the previous two decades. His designs, despite their apparent freshness, are based on consistent geometries, with even spacing and a willful regularity.

One of the major changes that came in the mid-1930s was precisely what Calkins had predicted. The use of photography, and, especially, a way of making photographs that no longer relied on the "straight-on view" that had long dominated the medium, now began appearing in numerous advertisements.

In effect, this new approach involved two strategies. One was taking the camera off the tripod. Holding the camera by hand meant that a whole world of angles and new perspectives opened. It became a liberated way of seeing. But, beyond that, was a second set of new techniques. Photography as a medium also allowed for many forms of technical manipulation: images could be cut, spliced, reassembled, silhouetted, reversed, enhanced, highly focused, lightly or fully softened, or placed whole or in bits, like a bricolage.[25]

A photo in an advertisement for *Good Housekeeping* magazine by Gray O'Reilly, one of the ablest practitioners of those years, shows what could be achieved (fig. 270). We see a group of women, but only the bottoms of their skirts, their lower legs, and shoes are visible. The ad is about the "science" of testing stockings—how it was rigorously investigated in the magazine's laboratory. O'Reilly not only crops the image in such a way that the stockings are front and center, but he tilts it, which has the effect of making it appear as if the women are walking or even dancing, thus animating the whole scene. A related magazine ad for Van Raalte gloves (probably by Brodovitch, though it is unsigned) functions in a similar way. This photograph presents a wonderful conundrum: all the gloves are on left hands (fig. 271). We are not seeing two women and their two hands, but one or more women, with overlaid images.

The Van Raalte layout is also inventive in another way. The sidebar on the right gives the name of each glove style; they, in turn, are even more identifiable because they seem to hover in space, above, or in front of, two or three (how many is quite ambiguous) overlapping circles.

Photography in these advertisements performs multiple roles: it is depiction, but it is also enhanced focus. And the images are set in ways that seemingly defy reality. Often, however, the graphic artists of the late 1930s took different cues from what a photograph might do. At times, they become overlays—a photographic

COCKTAIL
TIME

THERE IS NO COMPROMISE WITH QUALITY AT LONGCHAMPS

RESTAURANTS
LONGCHAMPS

269| Winold Reiss, *Cocktail Time*, ca. 1940. Cocktail card for Longchamps restaurants, New York, NY. Offset lithograph on paper, 28.5 × 50.5 cm. Prints and Photographs Division, Library of Congress, Washington, D.C.

Laboratory Legs

STOCKINGS ARE WORN on legs. Worn, washed, worn, washed, until they are worn out.
Average girls, with average shoes, and average garters.
But in a few weeks, they wear out more pairs of stockings than a single woman would use in many years.
Good Housekeeping's scientific methods are strongly tempered by common sense.
Common sense readers know this—trust Good Housekeeping, trust its advertising pages.

Good Housekeeping
{ EVERYWOMAN'S MAGAZINE }

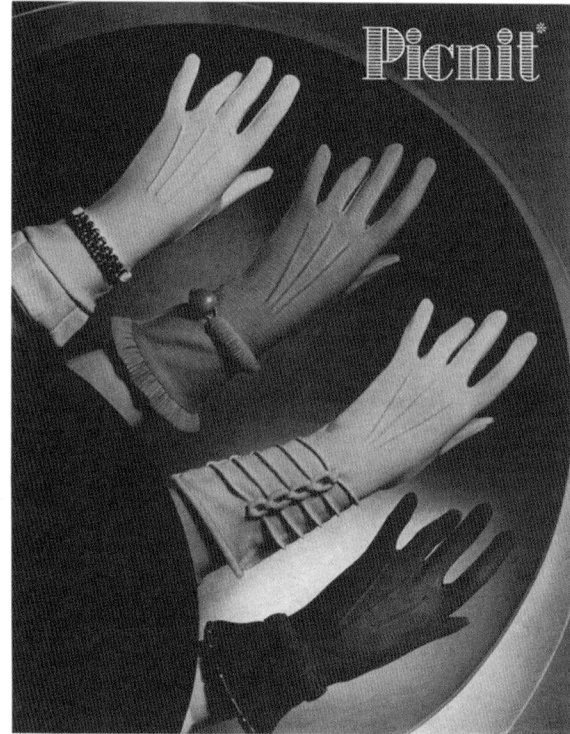

Van Raalte GLOVES

Picnit*

SCOTTISH GUARD

COURTIER

MAYFAIR

CORONET

Van Raalte gives you a royal treat this coronation season—top, the brightly chained "Scottish Guard", $1.50; next, "Courtier", wearing a dainty frill, $1; third, fashionable "Mayfair", gay with tucks, $1; and "Coronet", with crown-shaped cuff, $1.50. Picnits* all—and always the treat of every new season!

"because you love nice things"

Van Raalte
STOCKINGS · UNDERTHINGS · GLOVES
295 FIFTH AVENUE, NEW YORK CITY
*Reg. U.S. Pat. Off.

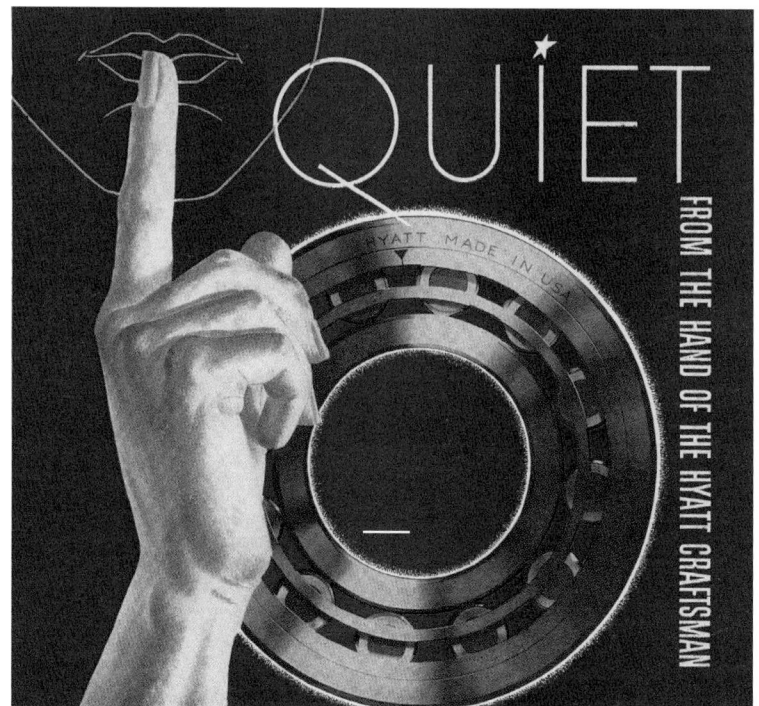

QUIET
FROM THE HAND OF THE HYATT CRAFTSMAN

270| Gray O'Reilly, *Laboratory Legs*, 1936. Advertisement from *Good Housekeeping*, February 1936, 151. Halftone print on paper, 35 × 27.4 cm. CL.

271| Alexey Brodovitch [attrib.], *Picnit Van Raalte Gloves*, 1937. Magazine advertisement for Van Raalte, New York, NY, from *Vogue*, March 1, 1937, 16. Halftone print on paper, 32.4 × 23.3 cm. CL.

272| *Quiet from the Hand of the Hyatt Craftsman*, 1937. Magazine advertisement for Hyatt Roller Bearings Division, General Motors Corporation, Newark, NJ. Offset print on paper, 16.5 × 17.9 cm (detail). CL.

273| Otis Shepard, *Catalina*, 1938. Poster, printed for the Wrigley Company, Chicago, IL. Lithograph on paper, 99 × 129.5 cm. The Resnick Collection.

CATALINA Now see Santa Catalina the Scenic Riviera of the U.S.A. . . . .yet only a short delightful voyage from Los Angeles

image set on a scene that is drawn or assembled from nonphotographic elements (fig. 272). And there are also hints—even in nonphotographic designs—of the coming idea of photorealism.

Some commercial artists also experimented with a new direction, blending realism and an idealized way of projecting form. Otis Shepard, who by this time was working steadily for the Wrigley family (the Chicago chewing gum moguls), made a lovely poster advertising Catalina Island, off the coast of Southern California, which the Wrigleys owned (fig. 273). It is not quite pure verisimilitude, nor was it intended to be. Shepard instead combines the "semi-realistic" view of the island with a form of studied exoticism. He not only projected that image; he had also created it. He and Dorothy spent four years on the island, remaking the town of Avalon into a Spanish Colonial dreamscape.

By 1938, when Shepard was at work on his Catalina poster, American design—at least at its leading edge—was already showing the new approaches being introduced

274 | A. M. (Adolphe Mouron) Cassandre, *Dole Pineapple Juice*, 1938. Magazine advertisement for Dole Company, San Francisco, CA. Halftone print on paper, 31 × 23.9 cm. CL.

---

275 | A. M. (Adolphe Mouron) Cassandre, *Concentration*, 1937. Magazine advertisement for Container Corporation of America, Chicago, IL. Halftone print on paper, 30 × 24.5 cm (trimmed). CL.

by the European émigrés.[26] In his role as art director for *Harper's Bazaar*, Brodovitch commissioned art and photographs from many of the Europeans, including some who had remained in Europe, among them, Henri Cartier-Bresson and Salvador Dalí. A skilled photographer in his own right, Brodovitch also taught American photographers and designers how to employ photography to achieve new effects.[27]

But it was Charles Coiner, still the art director at N. W. Ayer, who would have an even greater impact than Brodovitch, for it was he who engaged A. M. Cassandre to work on a series of projects.

Cassandre, born Adolphe Jean-Marie Mouron, to French parents in Kharkiv, Ukraine, was already famed at the time for his luminous and arresting posters, especially his gracile *Normandie* ship poster. These interwar poster designs and especially a small number of works from his time in New York in the later 1930s would greatly influence the next generation of American designers.

Several ads Cassandre made for the Dole Company and its pineapple products revealed how the fracturing and recombination of objects and scenes coming out of late Cubism could be recast so that they could function as commercial advertising (fig. 274). More far reaching in their influence, though, were the posters Cassandre produced for another company, the Container Corporation of America (CCA).

The director of the CCA, Walter Paepcke, was a true visionary. He not only foresaw how corrugated-fiber containers—cardboard—could replace traditional wood shipping boxes, but he also pursued the idea that his product might be marketed in an entirely new way. Encouraged by his brilliant and cultured wife, Elizabeth, who found the company's advertising (and even its stationery) thoroughly tasteless, Paepcke bought into the notion—as Calkins had been proclaiming for years—that art could be put in service to industry.

With no knowledge of how to introduce good design into the company, Paepcke asked Elizabeth to set up an art department. She wisely declined, suggesting instead that he hire a professional art director. After making inquiries at J. Walter Thompson and N. W. Ayer, Paepcke hired Egbert Jacobson, then known as an expert in color theory and typography. Jacobson planned with Coiner to hire some of the leading graphic designers of the time—both American and European—to create a series of revolutionary ads. They would feature not only striking images but dispense with copy almost entirely.[28]

Coiner discovered that Cassandre was then aboard ship, on his way to New York; he met him at the pier with a contract to design for CCA in his pocket.[29] He got Cassandre to sign on the spot, agreeing to make twelve black-and-white drawings for $500.[30]

One of these, a masterpiece, is *Concentration* (fig. 275). It has three figures, shown in partial profile, staring at a box (a cardboard box, the CCA's logo, which Jacobson had devised) at its center. The text below reads: "Research, experience, and talent focused on advanced paperboard packaging." It appeared, as did the other CCA ads (all published between 1937 and 1939) in *Fortune*, pointedly targeting the upper echelon of the business community, who made up much of the magazine's readership.

CONCENTRATION

RESEARCH, EXPERIENCE AND TALENT FOCUSSED ON ADVANCED PAPERBOARD PACKAGING

CONTAINER CORPORATION OF AMERICA

A.M.CASSANDRE

· 111 ·

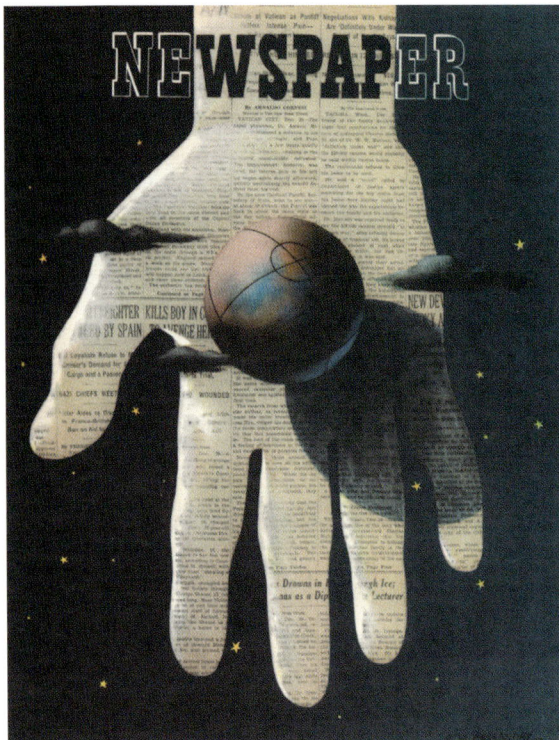

The lessons of Cassandre's revolutionary design were not lost on the art directors and artists in New York and elsewhere: art, even cutting-edge art, it stated, could be adapted to sell products. Modernism, far more than Madison Avenue or its designers had imagined, had the potential to bring about real change, not only in terms of how messages might be communicated, but also how new imagery could function to entice consumers.

Calkins had foreseen this possibility and even advocated for it. "Artists," he wrote in 1934, "are being selected more and more for the specific styles of work, because they are what they are" and because the art directors were "reaching farther and farther into the world of art for its most novel, striking and arresting creations."[31] By 1937, the truth of this had fully hit home.

What Calkins couldn't predict was the impact a veritable flood of European émigré designers would have on American advertising art. By 1938, it was not only Cassandre who was reshaping American modes. A large coterie of Germans, Austrians, Czechs, and others—most fleeing Hitler and the Nazis—would quickly bear upon American advertising, changing it radically and forever. Cassandre's "trial poster" for the newspapers was just one of many new and experimental designs reaching the American public (fig. 276). Even more advanced designs for the CCA campaign were coming from others, including Austrian-born Herbert Bayer.

Bayer had been central to the outpouring of new graphic ideas from the Bauhaus; he, too, was already very well known when he arrived in New York. Bayer's 1939 CCA ad, *Strength Out of Straw*, is a particularly notable example of the new design, though less for what it says than what it does with so few means (fig. 277). It consists of little more than a single, small swatch of cardboard, a box, and a few bits of straw. The text, explaining that the new packaging was made from straw, was almost incidental; the images, spare as they were, made the point.

The important narrative of this period, though, is not about the impact of the Europeans or European modernism—or only tangentially so. It is about how the Americans responded. The most astounding aspect of this story is how rapidly—and broadly—the new impulses were felt and how very quickly the Americans translated them into everyday life. One can witness this in, of all places, fruit crate labels. They were ubiquitous at the time, one of the lowliest forms of commercial art. Most of these labels were made by large printing firms in Los Angeles and San Francisco—companies like Crocker-Union, Lehmann, and Western Litho. These firms employed staff artists—many of them old-timers, to be sure, but also young aspirants, just out of the art or trade schools. The great share of this work was hackneyed at best, but some of the artists—they were almost always anonymous—took the time and care to make something better.

Some of the more ambitious had no doubt recently been exposed to the newest currents in art. In those years, when the Depression still made a job, any job, worth holding on to, these younger artists worked—probably almost subversively—to translate novel ideas into labels for the most prosaic of food items: apples, oranges, lemons, and all sorts of vegetables. Thus, an unnamed artist, around 1938, made an extraordinary label for *Hi Yu Brand Apples*, a brand of the Northern Fruit Co. in Wenatchee, Washington (fig. 278).

276 | A. M. (Adolphe Mouron) Cassandre, *Project for a Newspaper Poster*, 1937. Magazine advertisement. Halftone print on paper, image: 32.8 × 25.7 cm (trimmed). CL.

277 | Herbert Bayer, *Strength Out of Straw*, 1939. Magazine advertisement for Container Corporation of America, Chicago, IL. Halftone print on paper, 35.5 × 28.1 cm. CL.

278| *Hi Yu Brand Apples*, ca. 1938. Label, printed by Crocker-Union Lithographers, San Francisco, CA, for Northern Fruit Co., Inc., Wenatchee, WA. Lithograph on paper, 22.4 × 26.4 cm. CL.

At first, it reads like a naïve setting of a Native American chief. We see the chief in profile, wearing a multihued war bonnet. An arrow, its flight indicated by a diagonal line, is hitting a target placed between the words "Hi" and "Yu." In the lower-right corner is a pattern from a Navajo weaving. It is all forthright, matter of fact—even cliched. Whoever made it knew something more, however. It is a translation, a rather splendid and radiant one, of Cassandre's 1925 poster *L'Intransigeant*, transformed into a decidedly American picture. The features are close—so close in fact, that it almost appears as if the image might have been traced.

This sort of direct appropriation, it should be said, wasn't typical; but a few more of the modernist fruit labels drew from European ideas in spirit (such as one for Green Circle oranges; fig. 279), or they fused elements of European design with American streamlining, like a rather marvelous one for Whiz Brand lemons (fig. 280). Occasionally, though, one can find examples that are even more drastically reduced, more radical even than the most cutting-edge European designs. The maker of the *Crescent California Extra Choice Sliced Evaporated Apples* label produced a masterwork of what the Germans called *Sachlichkeit*, a blunt, no-nonsense purism (fig. 281). And, just on the eve of the war, another unnamed designer, presumably working somewhere in the Midwest, made a label for a coffee can in a related language that is wonderfully purist, if, with its steaming cup of coffee, slightly more exuberant (fig. 282).

One can find other such examples from the late 1930s and early 1940s. They are modern. In their own ways, they are even original. Yet they do not fundamentally

279 | *Green Circle*, 1939. Label, printed by Western Litho. Co., Los Angeles, for McDermont Fruit Company, Riverside, CA. Lithograph on paper, 25.1 × 27.7 cm. CL.

---

280 | *Whiz Brand*, ca. 1940. Label, printed by Crocker-Union Lithographers, Los Angeles, CA, for Culbertson Lemon Association, Saticoy, CA. Halftone print on paper, 22.3 × 31.8 cm. CL.

281 | *Crescent California Extra Choice Sliced Evaporated Apples*, ca. 1939. Label, printed by Lehmann, San Francisco, CA, for Rosenberg Bros. & Co., San Francisco, CA. Offset print on paper, 16.2 × 24.2 cm. CL.

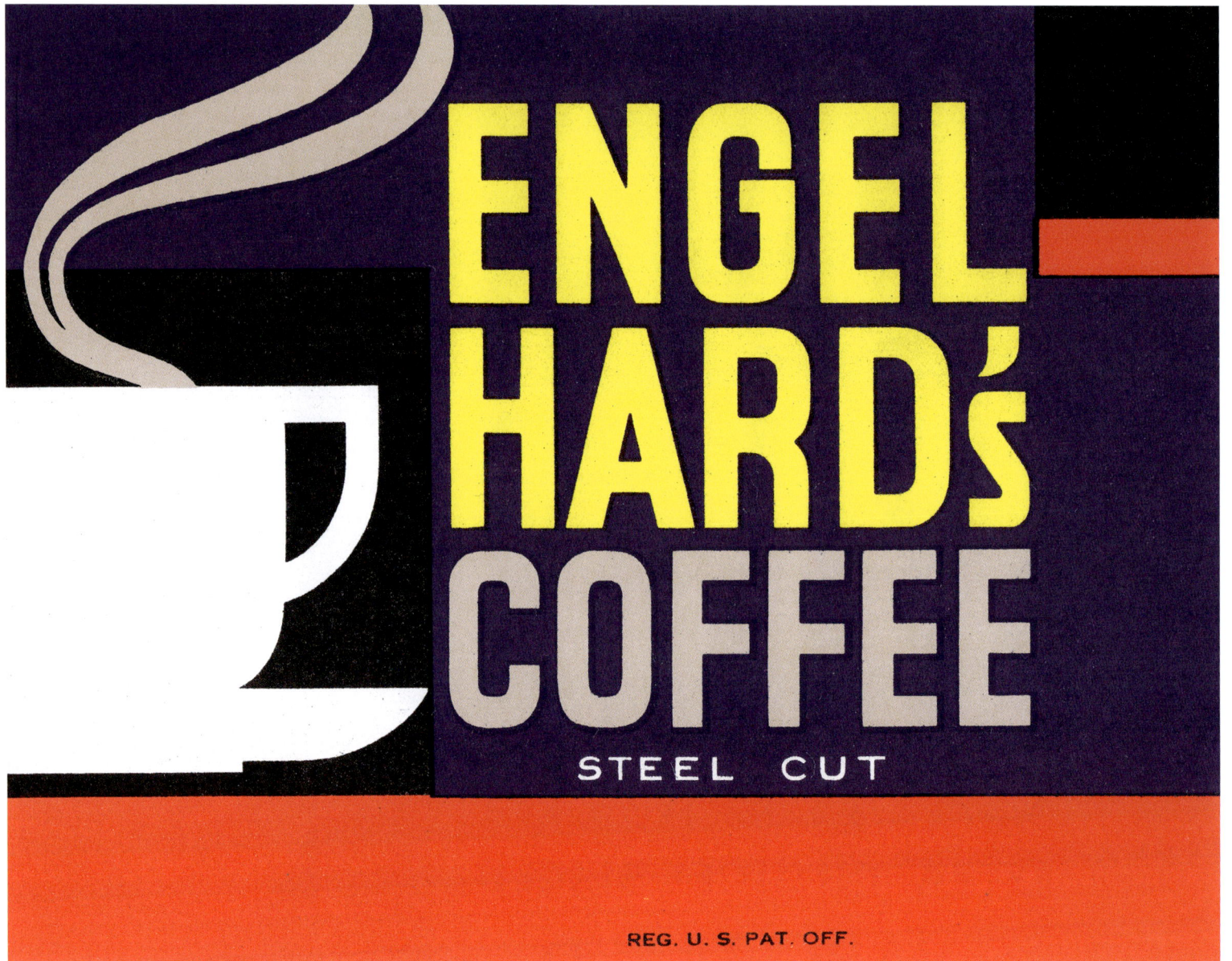

282| *Engelhard's Coffee Steel Cut*, ca. 1940. Label, printed for A. Engelhard & Sons, Co., Louisville, KY. Offset print on paper, 13.8 × 17.6 cm (detail). CL.

alter the codes of how a graphic design language might function. The architect of that revolution was Lester Beall.

Beall was born in Kansas City, Missouri, in 1903 to middle-class parents. His father, Walter Beall, worked for a printing company; his mother, Effie, was an amateur artist. While he was still a child, the family moved first to St. Louis, then to Chicago. There Beall attended a local technical school, and, after graduation, he entered the University of Chicago as a physics major. He switched to art history in his junior year, completed his bachelor's degree in 1926, and began a career as a freelance graphic designer. (Beall turned down an offer of a fellowship to pursue a master's degree in art history, preferring to pursue a more hands-on path.[32])

There was nothing about Beall then that would have predicted his emergence. His background was ordinary middle class, and, as a young man at least, he was neither especially affecting as a personality nor obviously brilliant. He had a solid education, though little practical knowledge of the field he was about to enter, and, while he was culturally aware (he was especially fond of jazz, which he often listened to as he worked), his knowledge of art and design were limited.

Until the end of the 1920s, Beall's illustrations were skilled but conventional. With the onset of the Depression, he was finding less and less work; soon, he was barely eking out a living. He used the opportunity to take drawing classes at the School of the Art Institute of Chicago. During breaks, Beall scoured the bookstores and the Ryerson Library at the Art Institute, looking at examples of current European art and design. He found inspiration and a mounting sense of the possibilities of modernism in all its guises.[33]

Beall discovered an ally in Fred Hauck, the art director at the advertising firm of Batten, Barton, Durstine & Osborn. Hauck had studied with Hans Hofmann in Munich and visited the Bauhaus; he and Beall spent hours looking at, and conversing about, the newest currents in design. Beall would later recall how much he owed to Hauck, stating that his friend had "influenced" him "more than any other person."[34]

In 1933, he and Hauck opened an office on Michigan Avenue. They worked together seamlessly, but it was Beall who began to draw attention—even well beyond Chicago. By 1934, four of his designs were included in the Art Directors Club *Thirteenth Annual of Advertising Art*, and one, *"Around! Around! Around!" Dance Drink Dine*, won an honorable mention from the group (fig. 283). His rising success (and the lure of bigger and better clients) prompted him to make the move to New York.

He quickly found his way in the city's design scene, meeting Brodovitch, Binder, M. F. Agha, and others. And he became ever more intent on devising new ways to express the essential modernity he saw all around him. He later wrote of his impatience with any form of traditionalism—especially in the face of the enormous changes that were taking place in American life: "My objection is to men thinking, during certain parts of the day, of streamlining trains, sub-stratosphere planes, and super-charged autos and then, during other parts of the day, mentally returning, misty-eyed and reverent, to the aesthetics of yesterday."[35]

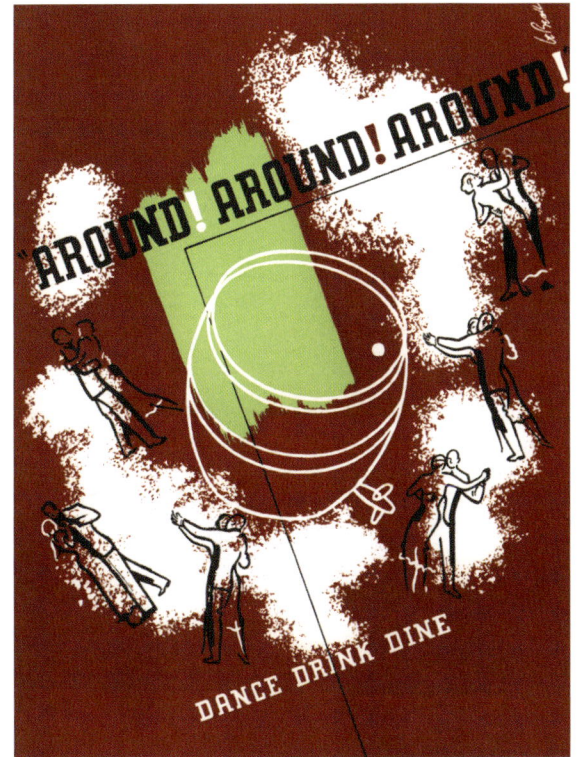

283 | Lester Beall, *"Around! Around! Around!" Dance Drink Dine*, 1934. Advertisement for Mills Novelty Company, Chicago, IL, from Art Directors Club, *Thirteenth Annual of Advertising Art* (New York: Book Service Company, 1934), 63. CL.

Three paintings by Vassily Kandinsky, the Russian painter whose work played an important part in the development of abstract tendencies in art. Influenced by the poetry of Maeterlinck and the music of Debussy, Scriabine and others.

(Top) Blue Area (Blauer Kreis), 1922. A composition with geometrical and architectural qualities derived from Russian Constructivism. (Center) Black Lines, 1913. An "Improvisation."

(Bottom) Above and Left, 1925. Illustrating the progression of abstract painting toward a plastic treatment of geometrical forms realizable in typographic design.

Herbert Bayer, Berlin

81

284 | Herbert Bayer, collage in Werner Gräff, *Es kommt der neue Fotograf!* (Berlin: H. Reckendorf), 1929, 81. CL.

285 | Lester Beall, design for an article about Bauhaus typography, 1938. From *PM*, June-July 1938, 2. CL.

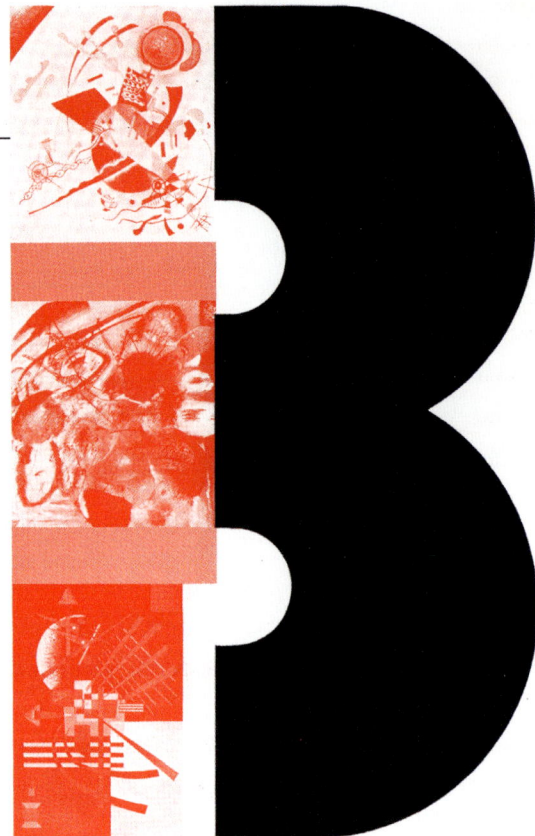

Beall, though, was still working out the rudiments of his own personal modernism. He continued to browse the bookstores, and he read the latest European journals. One of the books he came across, a German photography book, *Es kommt der neue Fotograf!* (Here comes the new photographer), by Werner Gräff, would prove pivotal for him.[36]

Gräff had studied at the Bauhaus in the early 1920s. He was especially influenced by Theo van Doesburg, and in 1922, the same year Van Doesburg lectured at the school in Weimar, Gräff joined the De Stijl artists group. Later, in Berlin, Gräff became friendly with Ludwig Mies van der Rohe and filmmaker Hans Richter. Together, they founded the magazine G (for *Gestaltung*, or design), one of the key avant-garde publications of the era, which would have an outsized influence on architecture and object design. Gräff, though, also became interested in new forms of photography, publishing his landmark 1929 book and, subsequently, several others.

According to Beall's biographer, R. Roger Remington, Beall may have encountered *Es kommt der neue Fotograf!* even before he left Chicago.[37] Regardless of whether he saw the book before or after his move to New York, he took away a sense that images—photographic and otherwise—could project reality in new ways. It was not only, as Beall was to write after the war, that Gräff's work "took the camera off the tripod and introduced to us odd angles and bird's eye views and so forth."[38] Beall began to see how all forms of visual communication—drawing, lettering, photographs, symbols, arrows, lines, geometric forms, even blocks of color—could be chopped apart, edited, recast, and recombined. In the process, new forms of meaning could be established, often through a stratagem that was tantamount to shorthand or abbreviation. One of the plates in Gräff's book, by Herbert Bayer, is a veritable route map for this type of visual reframing (fig. 284).

By 1937, Beall was not only fully aware of Bauhaus graphic ideas (he illustrated an article for *PM* the next year specifically employing them; fig. 285), but he was also working out precise ways to express his new language. He soon added one other crucial ingredient: the possibility of repetition as a form of visual rhythm—a jazz for the eye.

Beall's stunning cover for the 1938 Art Directors annual was not wholly unprecedented (fig. 286). Frederick Kiesler's cover for *Contemporary Art Applied to the Store and Its Display*, from 1930, for instance, was based on a related idea.[39] But Beall went one better: Kiesler presents "clusters" of repetitions; Beall—unabashedly—repeats the title over and over, like a mantra.

That the design of the 1938 annual was given over to Beall is testimony to his swift rise. The most progressive of the Art Directors—Agha, Brodovitch, Coiner, Walter Geoghagen (who served as president of the group that year), and William Kittredge—knew very well that Beall was one of the handful of younger designers who were overturning everything that had long been doctrine in the field. Beall also had eight works illustrated in the book—another indication of his growing import.

Yet it wasn't merely that Beall was becoming highly adept at manipulating images: his real virtuosity was not how he deployed a wide array of pictures, symbols, and forms, but also how he did so with extraordinary clarity. The true mark of his perspicacity came in 1937, in what at first appeared to be a less than promising commission.

The U.S. Department of Agriculture, under the Roosevelt administration, launched an ambitious campaign to electrify the rural areas of the country. To publicize the effort, they hired Beall to make a series of six posters. Beall might have tossed them off quickly, focusing instead on his work for commercial clients. But he took the opportunity to rethink how messages might be sent using almost entirely pictorial means, with only a few words to complete the narrative. The six posters have the simplest possible themes—farm work, light, radio, temperature control, running water, and laundry—and how electricity could enhance each (figs. 287–292). In the posters, Beall inserts one object or "object string" (essentially, a brief narrative of forms) to make the point. *Farm Work* has an industrial fan connected to a power pole; *Heat Cold* similarly shows the outline of a thermometer placed over (or in between) power lines. The other four posters, however, have larger groups or "strings" to indicate activization—a linkage between electrical power and its wonders. *Light* is an oversize lightbulb set before a home, which is glowing in the night. Connecting them are four lines of "power." *Radio* functions in a similar way, except that Beall has chosen not to use an image of a radio but radio waves in the form of three arrows

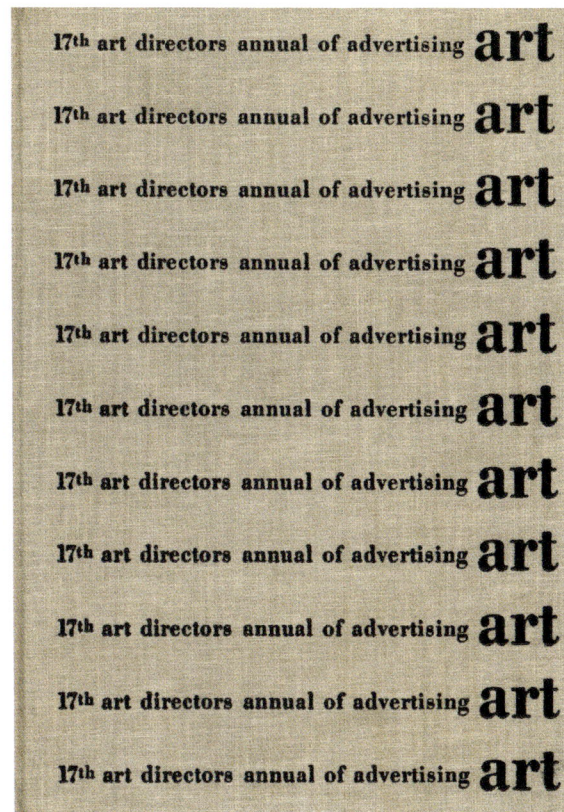

286| Lester Beall, cover of the *17th Art Directors Annual of Advertising Art* (New York: Longman Green & Company), 1938. CL.

287 | Lester Beall, *Farm Work*, 1937. Poster, printed for
the Rural Electrification Administration, U.S. Department of
Agriculture, Washington, D.C. Screenprint on paper,
101.6 × 76.2 cm. Courtesy Poster House, New York.

288| Lester Beall, *Light*, 1937. Poster, printed for the Rural Electrification Administration, U.S. Department of Agriculture, Washington, D.C. Screenprint on paper, 101.6 × 76.2 cm. Courtesy Poster House, New York.

289| Lester Beall, *Radio*, 1937. Poster, printed for the Rural Electrification Administration, U.S. Department of Agriculture, Washington, D.C. Screenprint on paper, 101.6 × 76.2 cm. Courtesy Poster House, New York.

290| Lester Beall, *Heat Cold*, 1937. Poster, printed for
the Rural Electrification Administration, U.S. Department of
Agriculture, Washington, D.C. Screenprint on paper,
101.6 × 76.2 cm. Courtesy Poster House, New York.

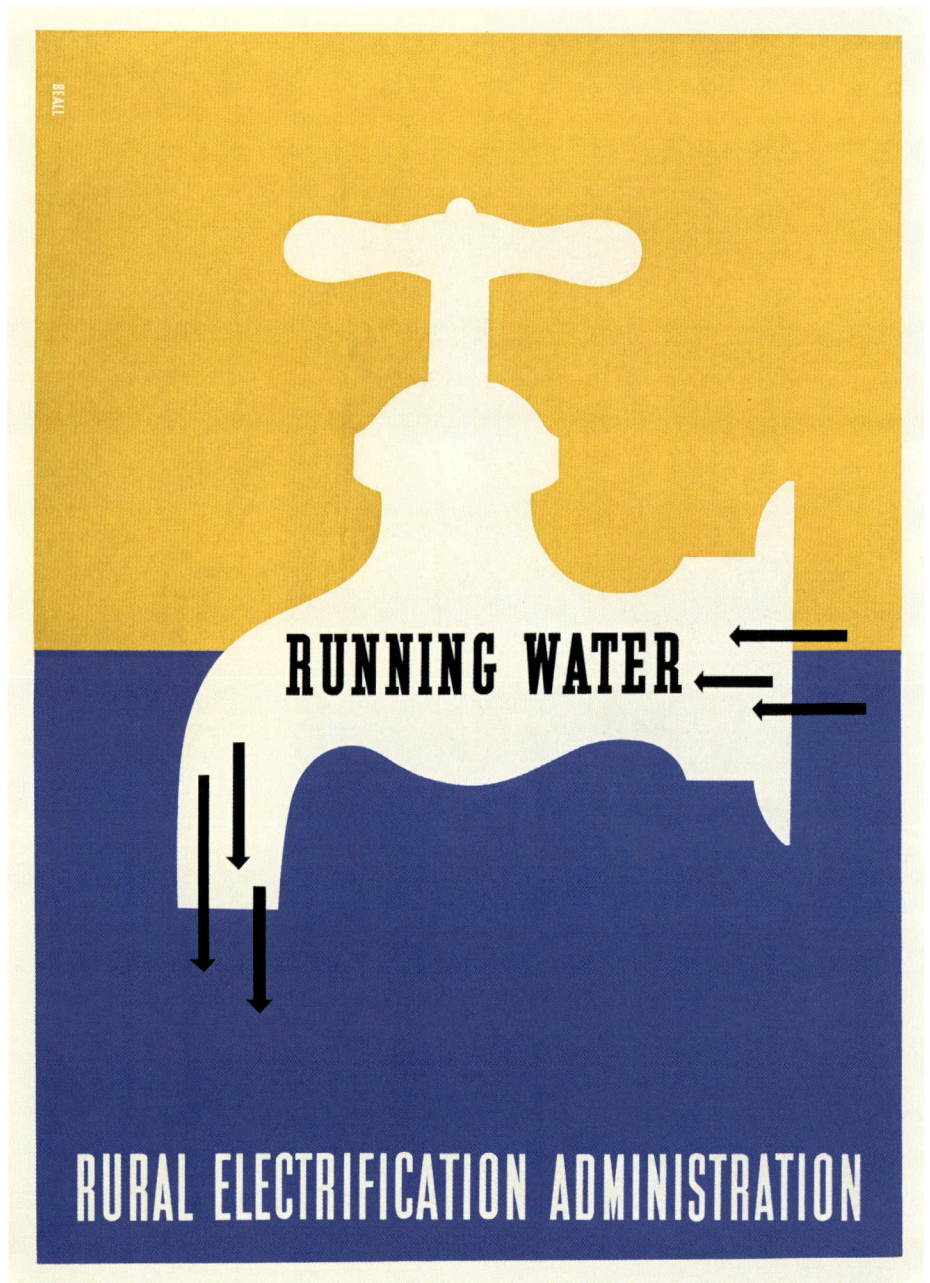

291 | Lester Beall, *Running Water*, 1937. Poster, printed for the Rural Electrification Administration, U.S. Department of Agriculture, Washington, D.C. Screenprint on paper, 101.6 × 76.2 cm. Courtesy Poster House, New York.

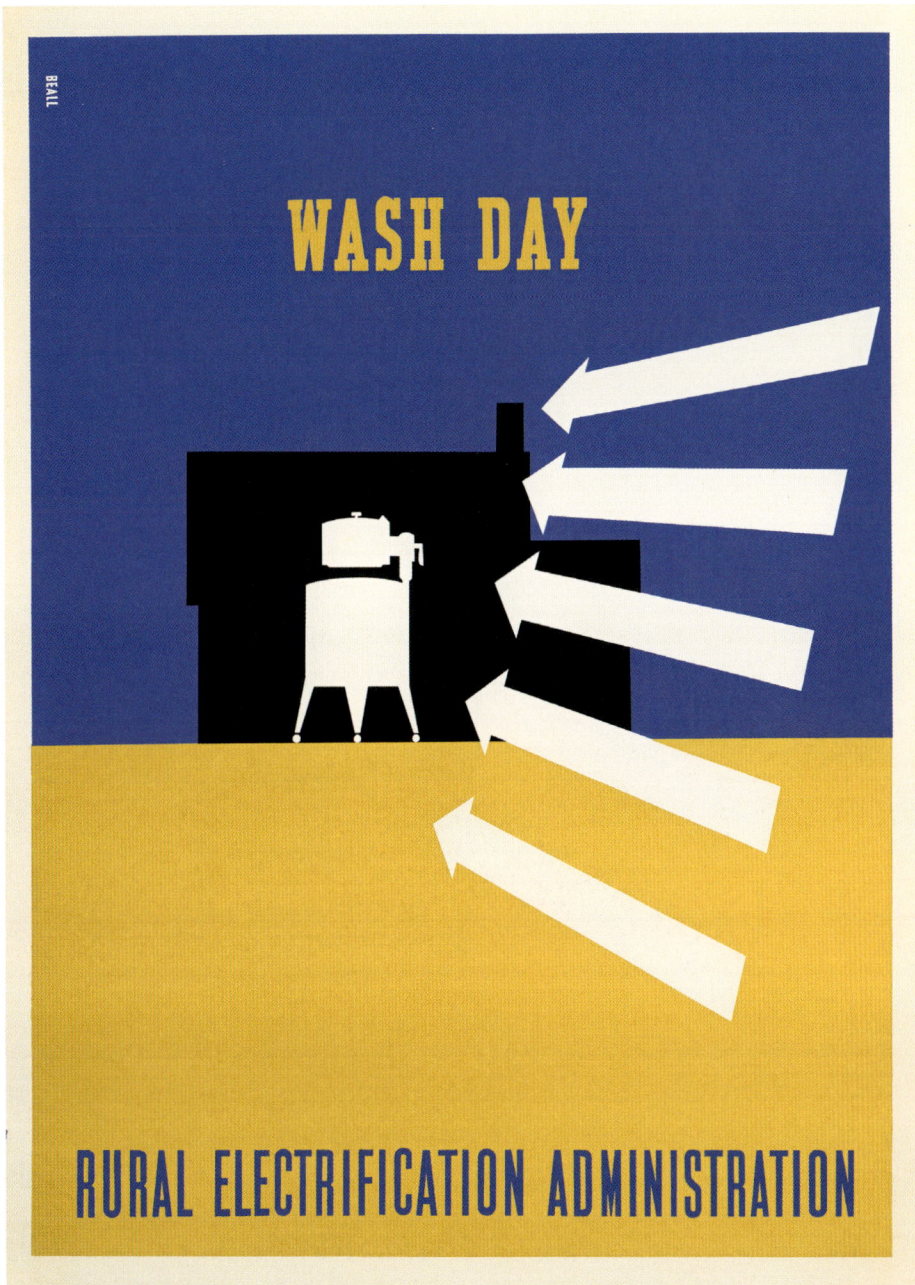

292 | Lester Beall, *Wash Day*, 1937. Poster, printed for the Rural Electrification Administration, U.S. Department of Agriculture, Washington, D.C. Screenprint on paper, 101.6 × 76.2 cm. Courtesy Poster House, New York.

pointing insistently at the home. *Wash Day* rests between these two forms of messaging: we see the washing machine at the center, and powering it are four arrows of electricity. *Running Water*, on the other hand, dispenses with the source of power, presenting only the spigot with arrows of water flowing through it.

Despite these slightly varied devices, Beall's 1937 Rural Electrification Administration posters share important commonalities: all sport the same simple serif and sans-serif typefaces, and they rely on large blocks of bold colors. Red, blue, black, white, and yellow appear in the series, though each poster has a different combination, so that when they are seen together (certainly something Beall must have thought about) they appear both as individual designs and as a unified group.

What Beall had achieved was not lost on the professionals in the field, and the six posters were front and center in Beall's solo exhibition at the Museum of Modern Art that year.[40] Beall, however, was not finished: a second group of six posters for the Rural Electrification Administration, which appeared in 1939, were graphically more radical still (figs. 293–298). The obvious change is that he now applied photomontage, using cutouts of ordinary country folk going about their daily lives. We see a woman contentedly sewing, a man holding his plow horse, two children leaning over a wooden fence, a young lineman installing the new power lines, a man in a rocking chair tuning his radio, and an elderly woman pouring milk into an electric churn. The similarities with the WPA documentary photography of Dorothea Lange and others is obvious, but the profound shift has less to do with these snippets of realism than it does with how Beall places them in suspension, divorcing them from their normal surroundings. They are instead set into decidedly modernist backgrounds, among pure color wedges and masses. The main legends become banners (except for the one with the two children on the fence, which has no "description"), "glued" on or beside each photographic vignette. It is all both normative and exceptional, seemingly traditional but isolated and enhanced. We understand each scene inherently, building around the photographic image what else we might require to make meaning out of it. Beall forces us both into engagement and imagination; the bold colors and their geometries enliven the scenes, even as they cause us to focus on what is taking place. Everything that was about to come in the new graphic design is already present here. Beall's revolution was total, and nothing would be the same after that.

It would be tempting to say that Beall merely repurposed what the Europeans were already doing. He unquestionably took over some of their strategies and ideas. Yet there is nothing in the end that looks "imported" in Beall's designs. They are the outcome of all that had preceded them in American design, fused with his own distinctive modes of messaging. They are pure expressions of Americanness.

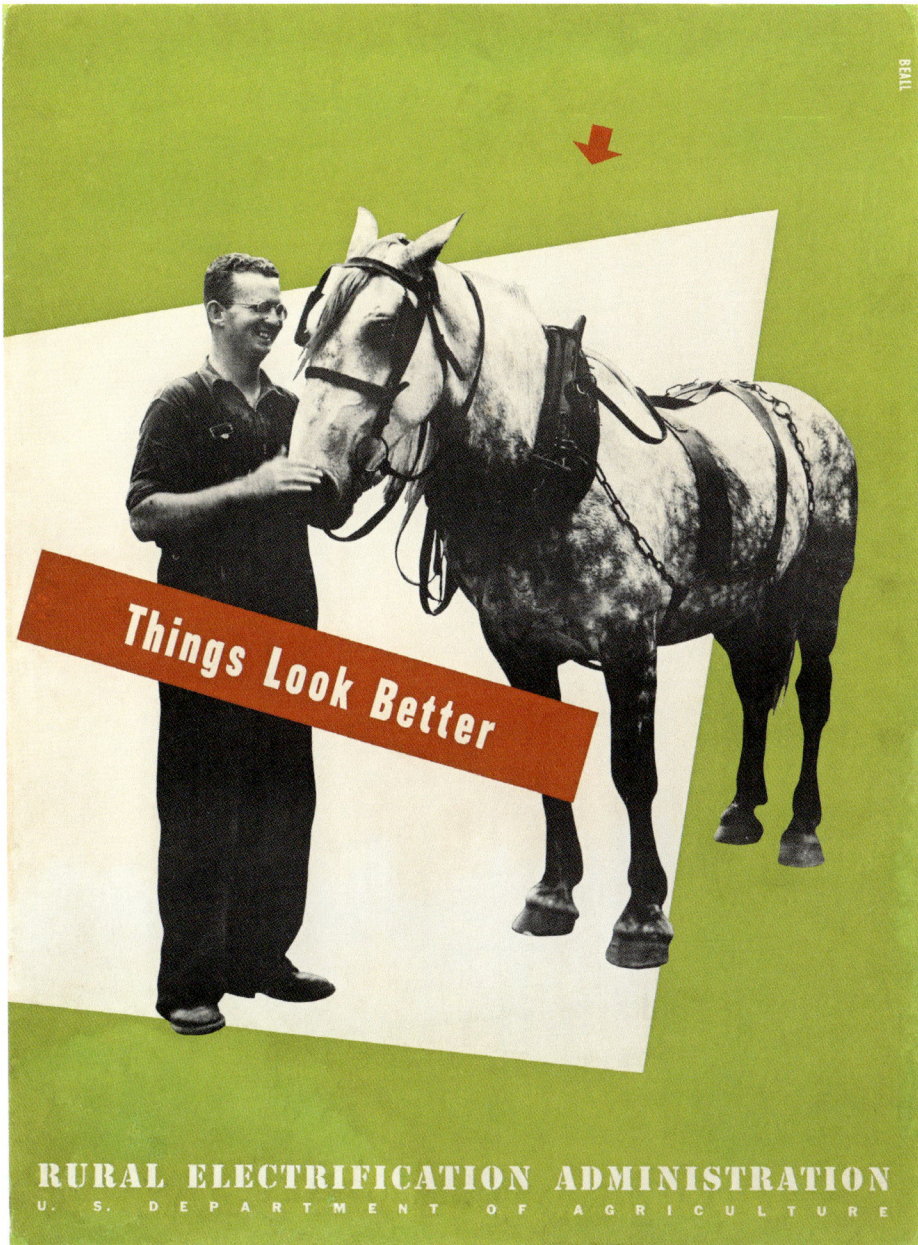

293 | Lester Beall, *Things Look Better*, 1939. Poster, printed for the Rural Electrification Administration, U.S. Department of Agriculture, Washington, D.C. Screenprint on paper, 101.6 × 76.2 cm. Courtesy Poster House, New York.

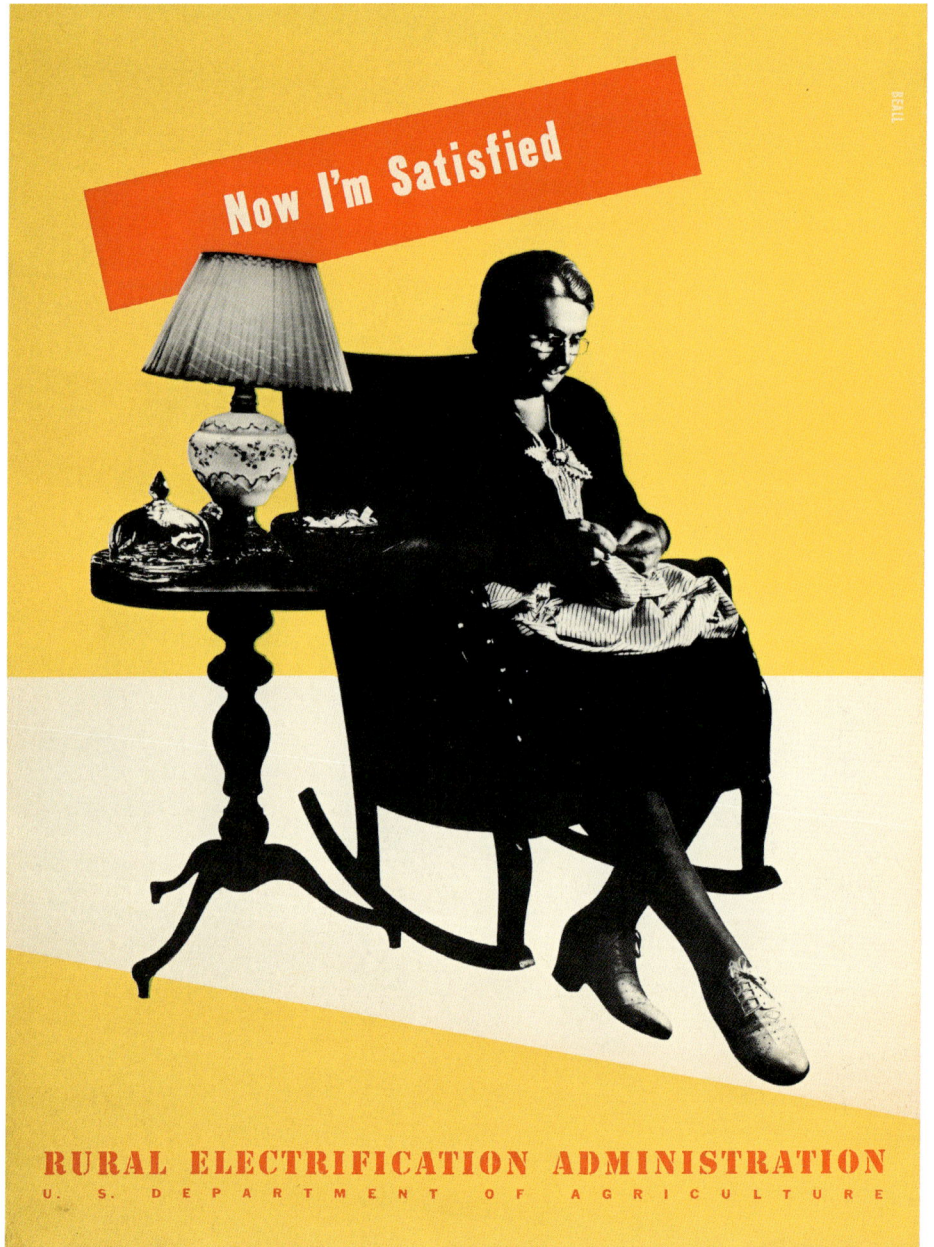

294| Lester Beall, *Now I'm Satisfied*, 1939. Poster, printed
for the Rural Electrification Administration, U.S. Department
of Agriculture, Washington, D.C. Screenprint on paper,
101.6 × 76.2 cm. Courtesy Poster House, New York.

295| Lester Beall, *Rural Electrification Administration*, 1939. Poster, printed for the Rural Electrification Administration, U.S. Department of Agriculture, Washington, D.C. Screenprint in paper, 101.6 × 76.2 cm. Courtesy Poster House, New York.

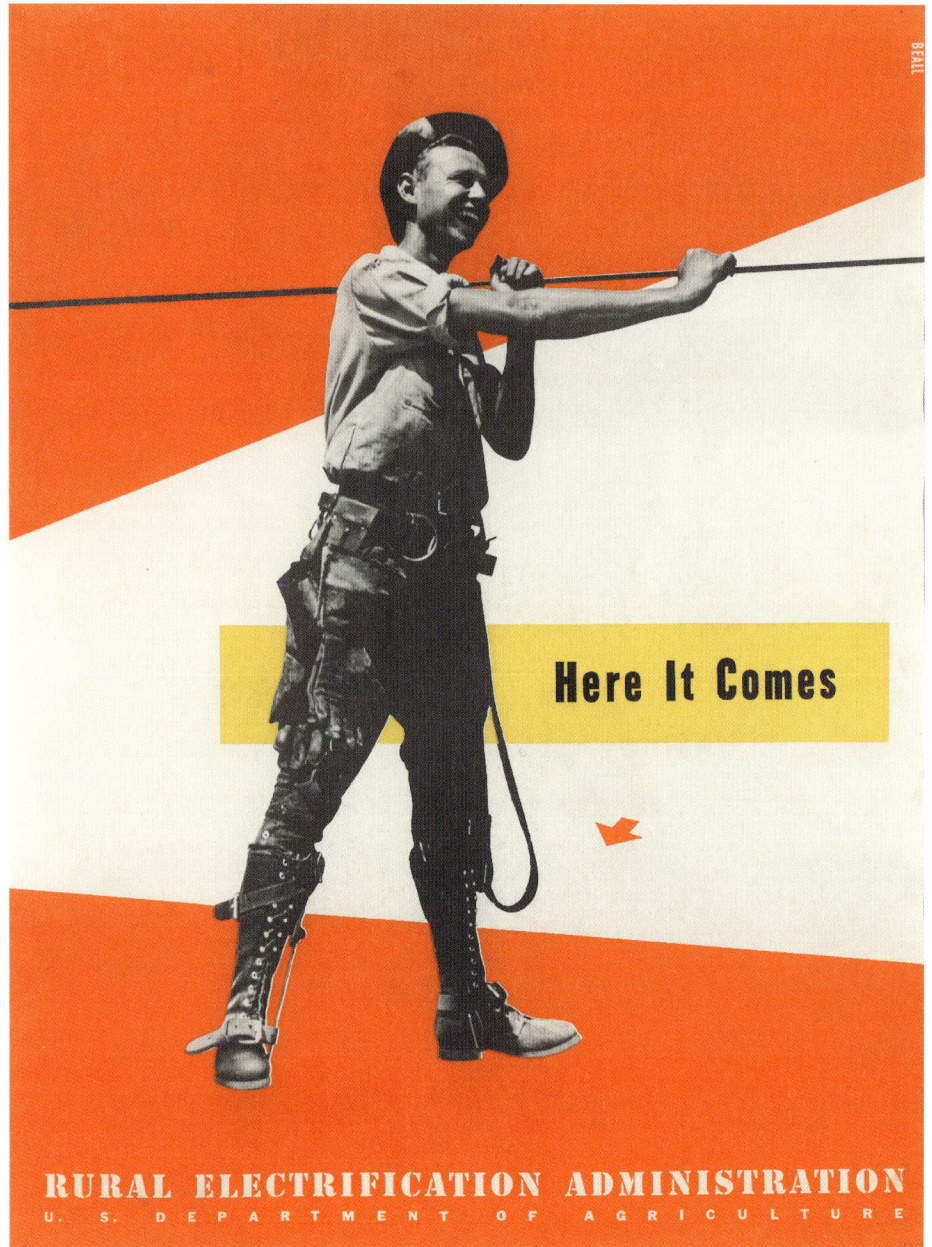

296| Lester Beall, *Here It Comes*, 1939. Poster, printed for the Rural Electrification Administration, U.S. Department of Agriculture, Washington, D.C. Screenprint on paper, 101.6 x 76.2 cm. Courtesy Poster House, New York.

297 | Lester Beall, *When I Think Back*, 1939. Poster, printed for the Rural Electrification Administration, U.S. Department of Agriculture, Washington, D.C. Screenprint on paper, 101.6 × 76.2 cm. Courtesy Poster House, New York.

298 | Lester Beall, *It's Fine For US*, 1939. Poster, printed for the Rural Electrification Administration, U.S. Department of Agriculture, Washington, D.C. Screenprint on paper, 101.6 × 76.2 cm. Courtesy Poster House, New York.

Epilogue: The Exigencies

of Two-Dimensional Space

In 1947, Paul Rand, then already emerging as one of America's greatest graphic designers, published a short book (fig. 299). Rand was never a confident writer, and the book, *Thoughts on Design*, mostly contains images of his work. Sprinkled here and there, though, are brief passages of text explicating his ideas. Despite their brevity, these lines contain extraordinary insights into the nature of graphic design, its meanings, and how it might be practiced in the future.[1]

Rand was thirty-three years old when *Thoughts on Design* appeared. In his teens, he had attended night school at the Pratt Institute; afterward, he enrolled at the Art Students League and Yale University. He drew from the works of Cassandre, Gustav Jensen, László Moholy-Nagy, and other moderns. But he acquired his graphic sensibilities mostly on his own. Before the war, he had been one of the first Americans to see the value in the new, European-inspired graphic language; by the time it ended, he was blazing a wholly original—and decidedly personal—design direction.

Several of Rand's prewar works, including a poster design he made for *Direction* magazine and a page for *PM*, had been groundbreaking. The *Direction* piece represented nothing less than the suspension of conventional ordering, taking it to its logical extreme (fig. 300). He disassembled the body of the dancer, putting it onto the page in a way that was seemingly indiscriminate. In the *PM* layout, he went even further. He undermined the standard syntax of arranging text, running the lines in such a way that they were broken into random bits. He then added a symbol set—a triangle, a plus sign, and a circle—that was so condensed and so detached that the whole page essentially became a presentation of pure form (fig. 301).

Rand argues in *Thoughts on Design* that good graphic work, in his perfect and concise formulation, brings together "the beautiful and the useful." The message of each page or poster, he writes, should be conveyed succinctly, logically, and clearly. At the outset of Rand's book is a prose poem that sets this out in a splendidly lyrical way:

Graphic design —
which fulfills esthetic needs,
complies with the laws of form
and the exigencies of two-dimensional space;
which speaks in semiotics, sans-serifs,
and geometries;
which abstracts, transforms, translates,
rotates, dilates, repeats, mirrors,
groups, and regroups —
is not good design
if it is irrelevant.

299 | Paul Rand, cover of his book *Thoughts on Design* (New York: Wittenborn), 1947. Halftone print on paper, 27.3 × 21.6 cm. Private collection.

300 | Paul Rand, design for the cover of *Direction* magazine, March 1939. Silkscreen on paper, 27.3 × 21 cm. Prints and Photographs Division, Library of Congress, Washington, D.C.

Graphic design –
which evokes the symmetria of Vitruvius,
the dynamic symmetry of Hambidge,
the asymmetry of Mondrian;
which is a good gestalt;
which is generated by intuition or by computer,
by invention or by a system of co-ordinates —
is not good design
if it does not co-operate
as an instrument
in the service of communication.[2]

Rand's phrase, the "exigencies of two-dimensional space," is his moment of brilliance. It encapsulates the central truth of graphic design: that it is about designing on the page, on a flat surface, freely—though only if it is "in the service of communication." The greatness of Rand's work is that he stayed true to this idea.

301 | Paul Rand, insert to *A Student's Guide to the New York World's Fair*, 1939. From *PM* (August–September 1939), 21.1 × 13.2 cm. Private collection.

302 | E. McKnight Kauffer, *Organic Design in Home Furnishings*. 1941. Poster, printed for the Museum of Modern Art, New York, NY. Screenprint on paper, 25.4 × 17.8 cm. The Resnick Collection.

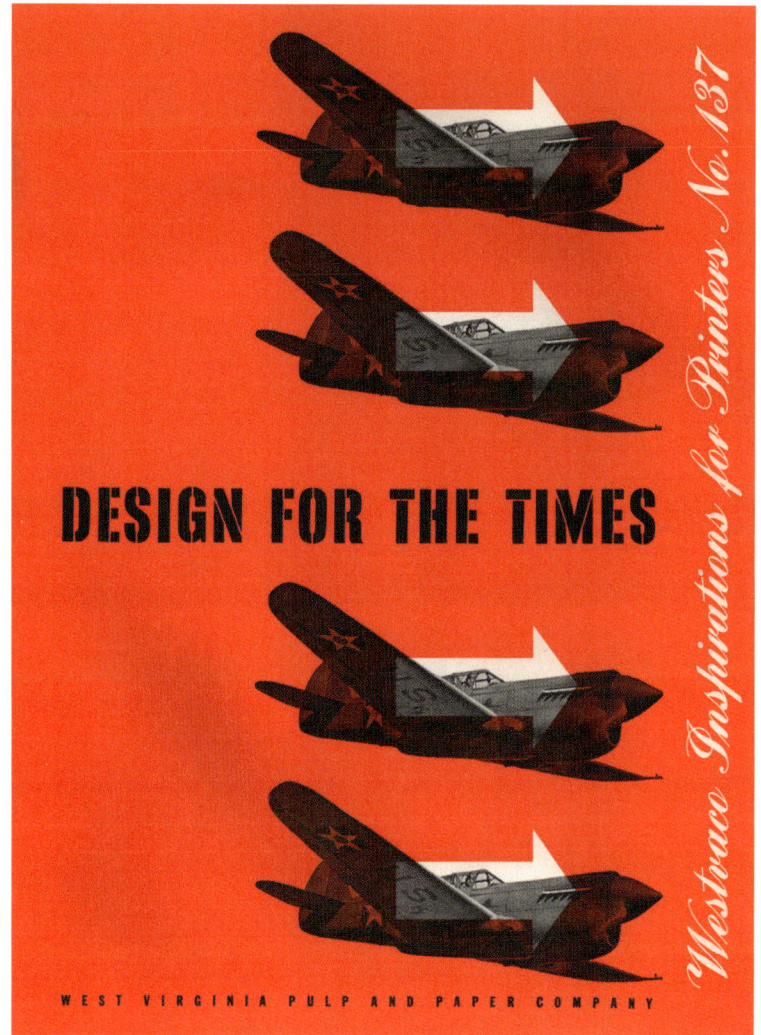

303 | Otis Shepard, *Wrigley's Spearmint Chewing Gum*, ca. 1942. Advertising card for the Wrigley Company, Chicago, IL. Lithograph on card stock, 27.8 × 35.4 cm. CL.

304 | Lester Beall, *Design for the Times*, 1942. Poster concept for *Westvaco: Inspiration for Printers* 137, West Virginia Pulp and Paper Company, 1942, plate 2723. Halftone print on paper, 30.8 × 23.5 cm. CL.

During the war years, the revolution that Rand and Beall—and a few others, including E. McKnight Kauffer and the young Alvin Lustig—put into motion would become the prevailing modus for all later modern graphic art (fig. 302). One could then still see conventional "illustrator's art" in magazines and wartime propaganda posters. And the old forms were still popular with the public. J. Howard Miller's *We Can Do It* poster (featuring the Rosie the Riveter character) was one of the great works of the era. But such images were beginning to look quaint. Even Otis Shepard's advertising card for Wrigley's Chewing Gum, with its serially repeated Liberty ships and gum packages, seems almost ingenuous when compared with Beall's ad for Westvaco papers, with its stacked fighter planes (figs. 303, 304). Both, it should be said, are inherently modern in their imagery and in their sensibilities. Yet what Beall was making by then was already something apart, freer in its compositional logic, less beholden to past forms.

Beall and Rand had learned much from scrutinizing European design. Yet their work was still American—despite their borrowings. The same was true, albeit in the reverse way, for the recently arrived émigré designers, Herbert Bayer and Ladislav Sutnar among them (figs. 305, 306). They had brought with them the newest trends

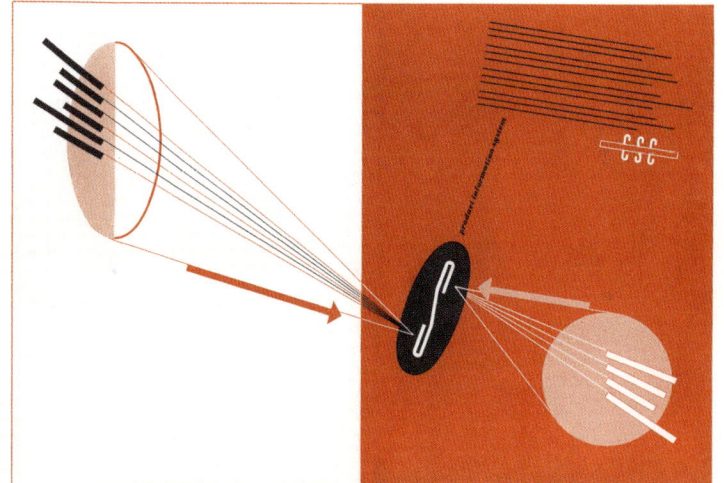

in European art. But like Joseph Binder a few years before, they quickly adopted American motifs and practices. Their works at first were an amalgam, of before and after, of European and American. By the middle years of the war (if not before), however, their transition was nearly complete. And the work they produced in the later 1940s and beyond was an integral part of the story of American, not European, design.

Other Americans also soon found their way to modernism. William H. Campbell, who studied at the University of Pennsylvania and graduated from the Philadelphia College of Art in 1937, was quick to take up the new style. A magazine advertisement he made for the Container Corporation of America—a collage of disparate pictorial parts—was cutting-edge in 1943; within a few years, such ads would be everywhere (fig. 307). Egbert Jacobson's *Safe delivery in paper all over the world*, from 1944, represents the apotheosis of this new design (fig. 308).

All this begs the important question, the one with which I began this book. What defined Americanness in early American graphic design? Erwin Panofsky's ready def-

305 | Herbert Bayer, *Fire Steals*, 1942. Magazine advertisement for Container Corporation of America, Chicago, IL. Offset print on paper, sheet: 29.4 × 20.5 cm. CL.

306 | Ladislav Sutnar, two pages from *Design and Paper 13* (New York: Marquardt & Company), 1943. Offset print on paper, each page: 19.7 × 12.3 cm. CL.

more of these

these

these

these

Campbell

CONTAINER CORPORATION OF AMERICA

inition of Englishness was that it was the romantic fused with the rational, the Arcadian blended with the classical. I have long thought he was being flippant, engaging in a little game of harmlessly poking the British for their sensibilities. But whether he was being serious or not isn't a useful question for us here. And Panofsky's suggestion that disparate formal directions were at the heart of British design doesn't seem to apply to the American context. We must search elsewhere for answers.

One response to the Americanness question is easy—too easy. Americanness could be said to be about specific symbols—the star-spangled banner, Uncle Sam, red-white-and-blue crests, and bald eagles. Or that could be expanded to the American lifestyle—hard work and leisure, the suburban dream, the suburban landscape. These things—these glimpses at American life or American mores—do indeed show up in many American designs of the fifty years before World War II, and more so afterward. Yet that answer, too, seems shallow. The presence—especially, the branding—of quintessential American products, from Coca-Cola and Wrigley's Chewing Gum to the big cars made by General Motors, Ford, and Chrysler, gets us a little closer to an answer. They, too, are intrinsically American, though they do not define the course of American graphic modernism, at least not entirely.

When I wrote that Americanness crept into the designs of the European émigrés of the late 1930s and early 1940s, I was stating something observable and real. Very quickly, they learned to sell products, American products, in a way that appealed to American consumers. They had to, for their very economic survival depended on it. I have come to wonder if that's not the answer: that it is the relentless selling, not the products, that defines Americanness, and that the selling, in turn, was what drove the development of American graphic identity.

To state my point differently—and more directly—I now see that the rise of modern American graphic design was only occasionally about pure artistic experimentation. The selling nearly always came first, the language through which the items were sold was mostly secondary. That was certainly true for the big advertising agencies. Design in these houses was not entirely an afterthought, but it was rarely the primary driving force. That is why the copywriter remained king for so long in American advertising. Even with Calkins's persistent urgings for a new advertising art, his firm, just like all the others, was bound to the idea that the visuals mattered, just not quite as much as the necessity of relaying the message.

Modern American graphic design in its first blush—at least a very great part of it—grew out of the exigencies of advertising, not the other way around—as was the case in Europe where aesthetics prevailed—at least a little more often. There were, to be correct, brief periods when "art" reigned in American design: during the decade of the poster craze, around the beginning of World War I, in the political and cultural ferment of the early 1920s avant-garde, and in the time of the Harlem Renaissance. Also, in the world of the fashion magazines, style did sometimes eclipse popularity. Yet for most graphic artists, even ambitious and farseeing ones like Beall and Rand, their daily labors were filled with compromise—how far they could go and still *sell*. Beall became the early virtuoso of this double life, always pushing ahead, but never so far ahead that he lost his audience (or his commercial clients). Rand was slower

307| William H. Campbell, *More of These*, 1943. Design for a magazine advertisement for the Container Corporation of America, Chicago, IL. Gouache and paper on paperboard, sheet: 48.5 × 40.3 cm. Smithsonian American Art Museum, Gift of Container Corporation of America.

to figure out where the boundary line between art and selling lay, but he, too, would become highly adept at discerning its precise position.

Still, selling isn't the full answer. At the risk of falling into the snare of a *reductio ad finem*, I am tempted to say that American Modernness was always about two other things (beyond the necessity of selling): it was a statement of the conditions of modernity—new lifestyles, new products, new ways of finding meaning in the world— and it was a visual spectacle of how these things played out in American reality. I am not referring to the clichés of the American experience, but the truths of day-to-day living: a set of codes and practices that were distinctive to the United States in the era of late industrialization. I recognize that this all may be far too nebulous, too pat, but for anyone who cares to look closely, that's a reasonably good description of American visual culture in the half decade before World War II.

There is a second point to be gleaned from this story. American modernism had its own trajectory, its own distinctive development. The many accounts that state either that nothing (or almost nothing) important was happening in the United States in terms of modern graphic art before the mid-1930s are simply wrong. And those that suggest that when there was something happening it was solely because of European influences are equally as mistaken. It is correct that American designers at times were keen to borrow from the new art coming out of Europe. And it is unquestionably true that some of the significant shifts in American design came from European émigrés. But American design had a lane of its own. And what the best American designers made was sui generis. Will H. Bradley was a unique phenomenon. So was Dorothy Waugh. And that was also the case for Lester Beall, even with his large library of European publications. Many of the foremost American designers— Parrish, Penfield, Dixon, Cooper, Phillips, Heinrich, Baker, Flagg, Purcell, Clarke, Walts, Douglas, Teague, Vassos, Radebaugh, Coiner, Velonis, Rivolta, Rothstein, to name only some—created individual and affecting works, while having little or no interaction with their European peers. Their achievements—and the achievements of many I didn't name or whose designs were and remain anonymous—constitute a full and rich history of its own.

308| Egbert Jacobson, *Safe delivery in paper all over the world*, 1944. Magazine advertisement for Container Corporation of America, Chicago, IL. Offset print on paper, 32.7 × 25 cm. CL.

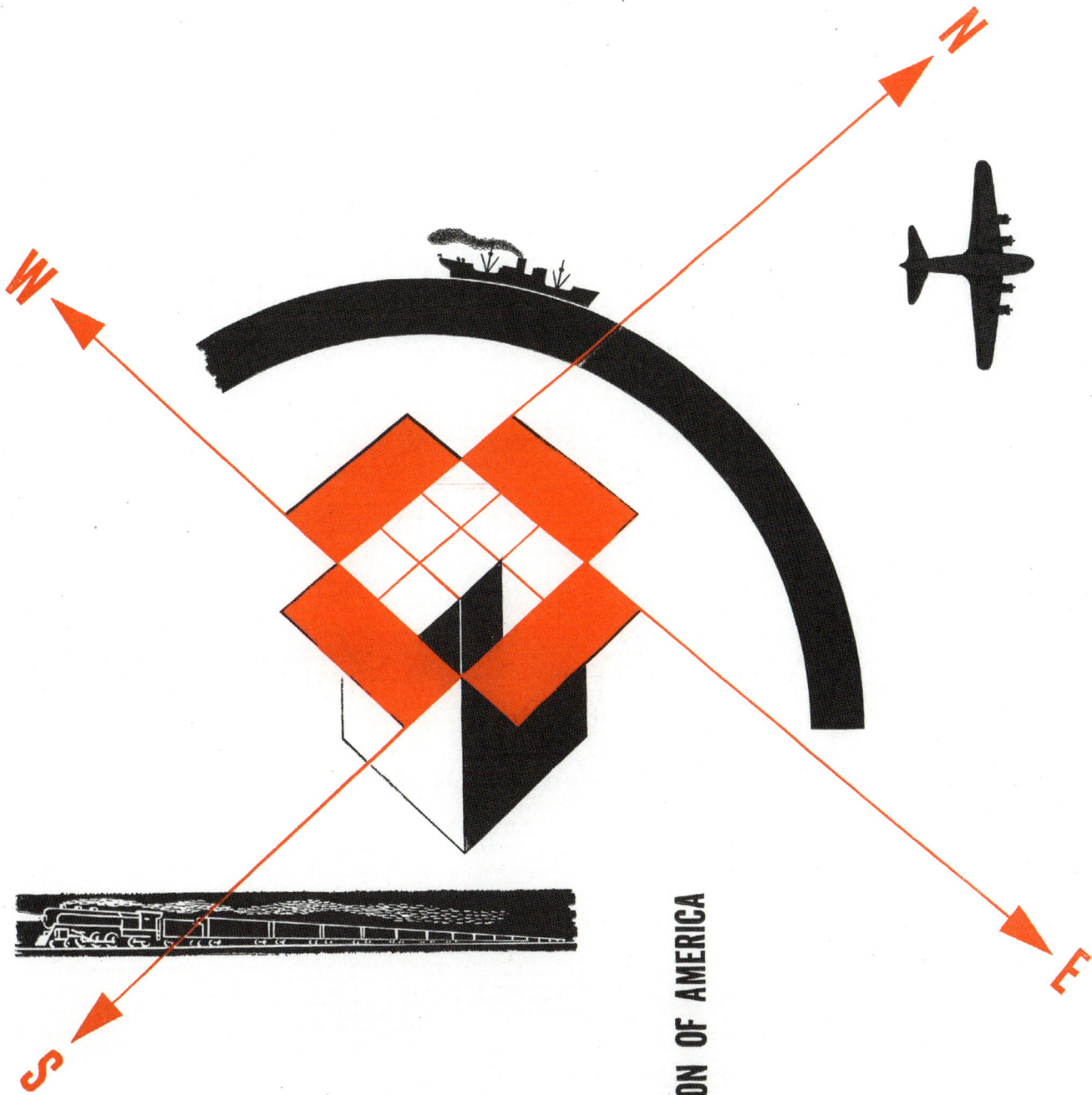

N

W

S

E

CONTAINER CORPORATION OF AMERICA

Safe delivery in paper   all over the world

EGBERT JACOBSON

Notes

Preface

1| Erwin Panofsky, "The Ideological Antecedents of the Rolls-Royce Radiator," *Proceedings of the American Philosophical Society* 107, no. 4 (August 15, 1963): 273–88.

2| Irving Lavin, "Panofsky's Humor," typescript, Institute for Advanced Study, Princeton, N.J., January 1993, https://publications.ias.edu/sites/default/files/Lavin_PanHumor_Eng_1993.pdf,

accessed February 11, 2024, 4.

1 Earnest Elmo Calkins and the Birth of Modern Advertising Art

1| Earnest Elmo Calkins, *"And Hearing Not"—Annals of an Adman* (New York: Charles Scribner's Sons, 1946), 168. For a brief, insightful survey of Calkins's career and impact, see Stephen Heller, "Commercial Modern: American Design Style, 1925–1963," *Print Magazine* 49 (September–October 1995): 58–68, and "Father of Modern Advertising," *Print*, August 28, 2011, https://www.printmag.com/daily-heller/father-of-modern-advertising/, accessed March 30, 2022. Knox College, where Calkins graduated in 1891, has a collection of biographical and other materials related to his life and career. Ernest Elmo Calkins Papers, Special Collections and Archives, Knox College, Galesburg, Illinois.

2| Calkins, *"And Hearing Not,"* 168.

3| Ibid., 169.

4| Ibid., 9.

5| Ibid.

6| Earnest Elmo Calkins, *"Louder Please!" The Autobiography of a Deaf Man* (Boston: Atlantic Monthly Press, 1924), 14.

6| Ibid., 61.

6| Calkins, *"And Hearing Not,"* 50.

6| See David Jury, *Graphic Design Before Graphic Designers: The Printer as Designer and Craftsman: 1700–1914* (New York: Thames & Hudson, 2012).

10| Ibid., 120.

11| Ibid., 115.

12| Ibid, 133–34.

13| Calkins, *"Louder Please!,"* 116.

14| Ibid., 116–17.

15| Ibid. 117–19.

16| Calkins, *"And Hearing Not,"* 151–58.

17| Rob Schorman, "Claude Hopkins, Earnest Calkins, Bissell Carpet Sweepers and the Birth of Modern Advertising," *The Journal of the Gilded Age and Progressive Era* 7, no. 2 (April 2008), 181.

18| Ibid., 211.

19| Calkins, *"And Hearing Not,"* 169.

20| See Michele H. Bogart, *Artists, Advertising, and the Borders of Art* (Chicago and London: University of Chicago Press, 1995), esp. 15–72.

21| Calkins, *"And Hearing Not,"* 169.

22| Ibid.

23| Etheridge was born in New York in 1867. He studied art in Europe in the early 1890s. He had returned to the New York from Germany in February 1893, not long before Bates hired him. *Passenger Lists of Vessels Arriving at New York, New York, 1820–1897*. Microfilm Publication M237, 1893; arrival: *New York, New York, line 34,* 13. Records of the U.S. Customs Service, Record Group 36. National Archives at Washington, D.C.

24| Calkins, *"And Hearing Not,",* 170.

25| Ibid.

26| Ibid.

27| Carl Richard Greer, *Advertising and Its Mechanical Production* (New York: Thomas Y. Crowell, 1931), 5–13.

28| Ibid., 13–14.

29| Ibid., 234–35.

30| In France, photogravure is known as héliogravure, while the term photogravure refers to any photo-based printing technique.

31| Calkins, *"And Hearing Not,"* 161.

32| Schorman, "Birth of Modern Advertising," 214–15.

33| Quoted in ibid., 215.

34| Ibid.

35| Charles Austin Bates, "First Person Singular, Chapter 8," *Advertising and Selling* 13 (June 26, 1929): 62, 64–65.

36| Calkins, *"And Hearing Not,"* 179–80. Calkins later expounded on his role in early photography in advertising and his work with live models. See the Calkins and Holden advertisement in *Profitable Advertising* 12 (December 1902): 492–93; and Earnest Elmo Calkins, "The Camera as an Ad.-Writer," *Profitable Advertising* 12 (April 1903): 1040–45.

2 The Poster Craze

1| The Grolier Club was the perfect venue for such an exhibition. Founded in 1884 as a private society of bibliophiles, it was named for Jean Grolier, the Renaissance collector renowned for sharing his library with friends. Its stated mission was to foster "the study, collecting, and appreciation of books and works on paper." "A Brief History of the Grolier Club," Grolier Club, https://www.grolierclub.org/Default.aspx?p=dynamicmodule&pageid=384895&ssid=322516&vnf=1, accessed February 22, 2022.

2| Phillip Dennis Cate, "The French Poster, 1868–1900," in David W. Kiehl, *American Art Posters of the 1890s* (New York: Metropolitan Museum of Art, 1987), 57, exhib. cat. For a contemporary account of the "poster craze," see Brander Matthews, "The Pictorial Poster," *Century* 44, January 1, 1892, 748–56.

3 | Grolier Club, *Catalogue of an Exhibition of Illustrated Bill-Posters* (New York: The Grolier Club, 1890).

4 | Alois Senefelder, *Vollständiges Lehrbuch der Steindruckerey enthaltend eine richtige und deutliche Anweisung zu den verschiedenen Manipulations-Arten derselben in allen ihren Zweigen und Manieren, belegt mit den nöthigen Musterblättern, nebst einer vorangehenden ausführlichen Geschichte dieser Kunst von ihrem Entstehen bis auf gegenwärtige Zeit* (Munich: Thienemann, 1818).

5 | Alois Senefelder, *A Complete Course in Lithography: Containing Clear and Explicit Instructions in all the Different Branches and Manners of that Art* (London: R. Ackermann, 1819).

6 | Victor Margolin, *American Poster Renaissance: The Great Age of Poster Design, 1890–1900* (New York: Watson-Guptill, 1975), 13

7 | Michele H. Bogart, *Artists, Advertising, and the Borders of Art* (Chicago and London: University of Chicago Press, 1995), 81.

8 | David W. Kiehl, "American Art Posters of the 1890s," in Kiehl, *American Art Posters*, 11.

9 | Martin S. Lindsay, "Edward Penfield: A Biography," Edward Penfield (website), https://edwardpenfield.com/biography/, accessed February 22, 2022.

10 | Margolin, *American Poster Renaissance*, 29.

11 | Quoted in Margolin, *American Poster Renaissance*, 29.

12 | Of Bird's early career, see Winifred Porter Truesdell, *E. B. Bird: His Bookplates* (Boston: Troutsdale Press, 1904).

13 | Bird's inclusion of the textile was perhaps an homage to Morris, who died the same year.

14 | Walter Dorwin Teague, foreword to Paul A. Bennett, ed., *Will Bradley, His Chap Book* (New York: Typophiles, 1955), iv–v.

15 | Bennett, *Will Bradley, His Chap Book*, 3–14.

16 | Ibid., 30–35.

17 | Melinda Knight, "Little Magazines and the Emergence of Modernism in the *Fin de Siècle*," *American Periodicals* 6 (1996): 29–45; William H. Bradley, "The Twins," Art Institute, Chicago, www.artic.edu/artworks/55158/the-twins, accessed March 6, 2020; and Julie L. Mellby, "Will H. Bradley," Princeton University (website), October 3, 2011, www.princeton.edu/~graphicarts/2011/10/post_14.html, accessed March 6, 2020.

18 | Bradley, *Will Bradley, His Chap Book*, 38.

19 | "The Ault & Wiborg Poster Album: The American Art Nouveau Ad," Codex 99, January 17, 2017, http://www.codex99.com/design/ault-and-wiborg-poster-album.html, accessed March 19, 2022.

20 | Ault & Wiborg later featured Bradley's designs in a book of their artist advertisements. See Ault & Wiborg Co., *Poster Album* (Cincinnati: The Ault & Wiborg Co., 1902).

21 | Bradley, *Will Bradley, His Chap Book*, 38.

22 | "One day in 1895," Bradley writes in his autobiography, "while busy with the establishment of the Wayside Press, I was inspired by some quickening of interest to visit Boston and visit the Public Library. There I was graciously permitted access to the Boston collection of books printed in New England in the Colonial period; and, thrilled beyond words, I gained some knowledge of Caslon's noble ancestry . . . . Such gorgeous title pages! I gloated over dozens of them, making pencil memoranda of type arrangements and pencil sketches of wood-cut head and tail pieces and initials." Bradley, *Will Bradley, His Chap Book*, 41–43.

23 | Ibid., 69–75.

24 | Will H. Bradley, *Will Bradley's Art Service for Advertisers* (New York, c. 1912), n. p.

25 | Ibid.

26 | "The Passing of the Poster Craze," *New York Times*, July 8, 1899, A4.

3 Supremely Satisfying

1 | Schorman, "Birth of Modern Advertising," 212.

2 | Charles Austin Bates, "Department of Criticism," *Printers' Ink* 27 (April 5, 1899), 61.

3 | Ibid., 60–61.

4 | Bogart, *Artists, Advertising, and the Borders of Art*, 49–50.

5 | 1880 United States Federal Census, Philadelphia, Pennsylvania; Roll 1188, 382D, Enumeration District 639. Holden died young, at age 54, after an operation on his mastoid bone. "Ralph Holden Dies at 54: Member of an Advertising Firm Stricken With Blood Poisoning," *New York Times*, January 4, 1926, 4.

6 | Calkins, "*And Hearing Not*," 195–204.

7 | Ibid., 206.

8 | Ibid., 214–17, 20.

9 | Calkins, "*Louder Please!*," 206.

10 | Earnest Elmo Calkins and Ralph Holden, *Modern Advertising* (New York: D. Appleton and Company, 1907), 326–28.

11 | Calkins, "*And Hearing Not*," 217–20.

12 | George French, "Advertising Men of Mark: Calkins, of Calkins and Holden," *Associated Advertising* 5 (May 1914): 33.

13 | Calkins, "*And Hearing Not*," 225.

14 | Calkins and Holden, *Modern Advertising*, 330.

15 | Ibid., 330–32.

16 | Rodney O. Davis, "Earnest Elmo Calkins and Phoebe Snow," *Railroad History* 163 (Autumn 1990): 91.

17 | Earnest Elmo Calkins, "Exhibition of Advertising Art," *International Studio* 34 (May 1908): cix.

18 | Bogart, *Artists, Advertising, and the Borders of Art*, 50; and Michele H. Bogart, "Artistic Ideal and Commercial Practices: The Problem of Status for American Illustrators," *Prospects* 15 (October 1990): 225–81.

19 | Ibid., 51.

20 | On the history of the company's advertising efforts, see Anne H. Hoy,

Coca-Cola: The First Hundred Years (Atlanta: Coca-Cola Company, 1986).

21 | In 1915, to distinguish its signature drink from copycat competitors, the Coca-Cola Company announced a design competition, offering $500 for "a bottle so distinct that you would recognize it by feel in the dark or lying broken on the ground." See Anne Quito, "The Coke Bottle's Iconic Design Happened by Sheer Chance," *Quartz*, November 17, 2015, https://qz.com/551682/the-coke-bottles-iconic-design-happened-by-sheer-chance/, accessed April 4, 2022.

22 | Michael Reineck, "Atlanta Ad Club's Founder, St. Elmo Massengale, Was Atlanta's First Man of Advertising," Atlanta Ad Club, https://atlantaadclub.org/history/, accessed April 13, 2022.

23 | Ibid.

24 | "Dodds, Samuel Candler," *Who's Who in Advertising* (Detroit: Business Service Corporation, 1916), 21.

25 | Michael Reineck, "Atlanta Ad Club's Founder."

26 | "Dodds, Samuel Candler;" 21; W. C. D'Arcy, "The Why of the Coca-Cola Arrow," *The Poster* 1 (February 1911), 165.

27 | Ben Kesling, "Tootsie's Secret Empire," *Wall Street Journal*, August 22, 2012, B1–2.

28 | Bogart, *Artists, Advertising, and the Borders of Art*, 50–55.

29 | Ibid., 320, n. 104.

30 | Wyeth also made drawings for Lucky Strike and Coca-Cola, and paintings of famous musicians for Steinway & Sons.

31 | Brandywine River Museum, *An American Vision: Three Generations of Wyeth Art* (Boston: Little Brown and Company, 1987), 18.

32 | See Rob Schorman, "'The Astounding Car for $1500': The Year Automobile Advertising Came of Age," *Enterprise & Society* 11 (September 2010): 468–523.

33 | Earnest Elmo Calkins, "Advertising and Design," *American Printer* (November 1900), 42.

34 | Before the rise of Virginia tobacco during and after World War I, Turkish-grown tobacco, sold mostly by Greek companies in the Ottoman Empire, held a sizeable segment of the American market, especially for "luxury" brands. See, for example, Relli Shechter, "Selling Luxury: The Rise of the Egyptian Cigarette and the Transformation of the Egyptian Tobacco Market, 1850-1914," *International Journal of Middle East Studies* 35 (February 2003): 51–75.

35 | Claude C. Hopkins, *My Life in Advertising* (New York: Harper and Brothers, 1927), 183. See also Bogart, *Artists, Advertising, and the Borders of Art*, 209–10.

36 | Calkins expressed these ideas most poignantly in an essay he wrote years later for *The American Magazine of Art*. See Earnest Elmo Calkins, "Advertising, Builder of Taste," *The American Magazine of Art* 21 (September 1930): 497–502.

37 | Bogart, *Artists, Advertising, and the Borders of Art*, 209–12.

38 | Laurence S. Cutler and Judy Goffman Cutler, *J. C. Leyendecker: American Imagist* (New York: Abrams / The National Museum of American Il-

lustration, 2008), 19–22, exhib. cat.

39 | Quoted in ibid., 22.

40 | Ibid., 22–23.

41 | Ibid., 23.

42 | J. C. Leyendecker, illustrator, *An Illuminated Life of Christ, including the Principal Events: The Royal Scroll: A Complete Panorama of the Sacred Story*, by Levi Walter Yaggy (Chicago: Powers, Fowler & Lewis, 1896).

43 | Cutler and Cutler, *J. C. Leyendecker: American Imagist*, 23.

44 | Ibid.

45 | Ibid., 25–35.

46 | Blake Gopnik, "J. C. Leyendecker: The 'Arrow Collar Man' Who Hid a Radical Idea," *New York Times*, June 29, 2023.

47 | Ibid., 55–71.

48 | Bogart, *Artists, Advertising, and the Borders of Art*, 209–11.

49 | Cutler and Cutler, *J. C. Leyendecker: American Imagist*, 73–75.

4 Stopping the Rushing Eye

1 | Calkins, "*And Hearing Not*," 254–56.

2 | Ibid., 257.

3 | Ibid., 242.

4 | Ibid.

5 | On Iannelli's life and work, see David Johnson, *Alfonso Iannelli: Modern by Design* (Oak Park, IL: Top Five Books, 2013).

6 | Interview with Mark Resnick by the author, August, 13, 2024.

7 | George W. Kleiser, *Seventy-Seven Years: The Autobiography of Geo. W. Kleiser, Chairman and Co-founder of Foster and Kleiser Company, Outdoor Advertising* (San Francisco, 1951); and Foster and Kleiser Company, *Forty Years of Advertising, 1901–1941* (San Francisco, 1941).

8 | John Tyronne Kelly, Poster Artists Wins $1,000 Prize," *The Poster* 7 (September 1916): 33–34.

9 | Margaret Frances Robinson's activity as a graphic designer was short lived. She was born in Hull, Massachusetts, in 1904, and died in Boulder, Colorado, in 1993. She enrolled in the California School of Fine Arts and started working for Foster & Kleiser around the time she produced her award-winning poster design. Later, she lived in New Orleans, where she made numerous paintings of the French Quarter, for which she is now best known, and San Francisco.

10 | Otto Spengler, ed., "Arthur Wiener," in *Das deutsche Element der Stadt New York: Biographisches Jahrbuch der Deutsch-Amerikaner New Yorks und Umgebung* (New York: Otto Spengler, 1913), 278; and Rudolph Rosenthal and Helena L. Ratzka *The Story of Modern Applied Art* (New York: Harper & Brothers, 1948), 165.

11 | Arthur F. Wiener, "What a Good Poster Is, and How to Get It," *Advertising & Selling* 22 (June 1912): 33; and "Sales Possibilities in Modernly Designed Posters," *Advertising & Selling* 23 (July 1913): 28. On

Lucian Bernhard and the origins of the *Sachplakat*, see Christopher Long, *Lucian Bernhard* (Prague: Kant, 2023), esp. chapter 1.

12| See, for example, Amos Stote, "Some Gum—Also Some Advertising," *Printing Art* 24 (February 1915): 483–88.

13| *Real Estate Record and Builders' Guide* (New York) 90 (July–December 1912), 1007.

14| In a short article he penned for *The Poster* in 1913—intended to drum up business—Wiener enumerated Sesser's abilities: "Educated in all applied arts, he has laid out plans for private residences and their interior decorations; he has designed and with his own hands put together, furniture of all kinds; he has devised combinations of silks with which by means of laying one on top of the other then cutting out the designs of broad treatment, he has created color schemes of unusual beauty." Arthur F. Wiener, "Willy Sesser," *The Poster* 4 (November 1913): 22.

15| Ibid., 22–23.

16| Arthur F. Wiener, "Bernhard," *The Poster* 4 (October 1913): 27–29, 61.

17| *German Applied Arts: Touring Exhibition of the Deutsches Museum für Kunst in Handel und Gewerbe Hagen I.W. with the co-operation of the Oesterreichisches Museum für Kunst und Industrie in Wien: Newark, Chicago, Indianapolis, Pittsburgh, Cincinnati, St. Louis, 1912–1913* (Newark, N.J.: Newark Museum Association, 1912), exhib. cat.; *Österreichisches Museum für Angewandte Kunst, Vienna; and Deutsches Museum für Kunst in Handel und Gewerbe, Hagen*, exhib. cat. (Dortmund, 1912); and "German Arts on View," *Brooklyn Daily Eagle*, March 11, 1913, 8. See also Barry Shifman, "Design for Industry: The 'German Applied Arts' Exhibition in the United States, 1912–13," *Journal of the Decorative Arts Society* 22 (1998): 19–31; and Christopher Long, "The Viennese *Secessionsstil* and Modern American Design," *Studies in the Decorative Arts* 14 (Spring–Summer 2007): 6–44.

18| Newark Museum Association, *German Advertising Art, January 2–31, 1914*, exhib. cat. (Newark, 1914).

19| The phrase appears in a caption for an image published in *Printing Art* in 1916. See "A Booklet Cover that Stops the Rushing Eye," *Printing Art* 27, no. 2 (April 1916): 124. It is possible that Wiener wrote the caption himself. It was common practice for firms to send "press releases" that periodicals like *Printing Art* would print verbatim.

20| On Reiss and his circle, see Jewel Stern and Christopher Long, *The Vanguard: Central European Émigrés and Modern American Design, 1910–1940* (New Haven: Yale University Press, 2024), esp. chapter 1.

21| "Foreword," *Modern Art Collector* 1 (September 1915): n.p.

22| Winold Reiss, "About the Modern German Artist," *Modern Art Collector* 1 (September 1915): n.p.

23| "New Incorporations," *New York Times*, July 16, 1915, 14.

24| *Plakat und Plagiat: Beilagen zum Plakat* (July 1915); and *Plakat und Plagiat: Beilagen zum Plakat, Zweite Folge* (March 1917).

5 Over Here!

1| See J. L. Frazier, "Specimens," *The Inland Printer* 62 (November 1918): 181–86.

2| Obituary of Harry Arnold Weissberger," *Sea Cliff (New York) News*, February 23, 1929.

3| On Weissberger's draft registration card, dated November 4, 1918, he described himself as the secretary-treasurer of Advertising Artists, Inc., listing the address of the new firm as the Aeolian Building on West Forty-Second Street. U.S. Draft Registration Cards, 1917–1918, National Archives and Records Administration, Washington, D.C. I owe a large debt of thanks to Jewel Stern for her assistance in helping me to sort out the history of the two firms.

4| Ross J. Wilson, *New York and the First World War: Shaping an American City* (Farnham: Ashgate, 2014), 74.

5| Only two weeks later, apparently cleared, Wiener testified as a government witness at the highly publicized trial. "Says He Gave O'Leary $5,000 For Dr. Albert," *New York Herald*, January 25, 1919, 8; and "Says O'Leary Got $5,000 From Albert," *New York Times*, February 5, 1919, 24.

6| The *Inland Printer*, in its November 1918 issue, gives us what is perhaps the clearest picture of the changeover of the IAS to it new incarnation: "Announcement has been received to the effect that the International Art Service, 33 West 42nd Street, New York, has been completely reorganized and will hereafter do business under the name Advertising Artists, Incorporated at the same address. Arthur F. Wiener has sold his interest in the company and has completely severed his connections with it. The business will hereafter be conducted by the American members of the firm, the officers being Le-Roy Latham, president, W. G. Sesser, vice-president; Harry A. Weissberger, secretary and treasurer. Mr. Weissberger will also be general manager." "International Art Service Now Advertising Artists, Inc.," *The Inland Printer* 62 (November 1918), 218.

7| Herbert E. Martini, *Applied Art: A Collection of Designs Showing the Tendencies of American Industrial Art* (New York: F. K. Ferenz, 1919). The portfolio's publication was announced in "Notes on Current Art," *New York Times*, October 5, 1919, 108.

8| See, for example, "Martini Tempera Colors" advertisement, *Modern Art Collector*, no. 7 (1916): n.p.

9| Ferenz and Martini originally planned to print annual editions of the portfolio and sell them for nine dollars a copy. F. K. Ferenz to Karl Struss, March 20, 1919, 2, Box 1, Folder 3, Stephen White Collection of Karl Struss Papers, Amon Carter Museum of American Art, Fort Worth, Texas. Only the first edition ever appeared. The project likely failed not only because of its hefty cost, but also because tastes had already begun to change in the wake of the war.

10| See the article by Leroy Fairman, who was also part of the Advertising Artists, Inc., management team: "What a Poster Is and How to Make It."

Advertising & Selling 29 (July 26, 1919): 1–3.

11| Advertising Artists, Inc., *Solving Advertising Art Problems*, 2nd ed. (New York: Advertising Artists, Inc., 1920), 3.

12| Ibid.

13| Ibid., 4.

6 A Renewed Vision

1| Earnest Elmo Calkins, "On Limitations," Art Directors Club of New York, *Fifth Annual of Advertising Art* (New York: The Book Service Company, 1926), [142].

2| "Exhibition of Original Paintings and Drawings," display advertisement, *New York Times*, March 18, 1921, 22.

3| Earnest Elmo Calkins, "The Art Directors' Exhibition." *Printers' Ink Monthly* 2 (April 1921), 16.

4| William Addison Dwiggins, "New Kind of Printing Calls for New Design," Graphic Arts Section 3, *Boston Evening Transcript*, August 29, 1922, 6. See also Ellen Mazur Thomson, *The Origins of Graphic Design in America, 1870–1920* (New Haven: Yale University Press, 1997): 35. Thomson reproduces Dwiggins's full article in her book's appendix.

5| Thomson, *Origins of Graphic Design*, 35.

6| Dwiggins, "New Kind of Printing Calls for New Design," repr. in Thomson, *Origins of Graphic Design*, 187–88.

7| Henry Adams and Lawrence Waldman, *Out of the Kokoon* (Cleveland: Cleveland Public Library and Cleveland Artists Foundation, 2011).

8| Campbell Speelman, the son of Abraham Anderson, one of the Campbell Soup Company's founders, designed the iconic can label around 1898. The cans figured prominently in the company's ads almost from outset. See Patricia J. Condell, *Campbell Soup Can Design, Campbell Soup Company* (Newton, NJ: Historic Conservation and Interpretation, Inc., 1991).

9| My thanks to Maddie and David Sadofski of TFTM, Los Angeles, who pointed me to Held and his designs.

10| On Villa's life and work, see Hernando G. Villa Collection, Autry Museum of the American West, Los Angeles.

11| See Stern and Long, *Vanguard*, esp. chapter 26.

12| Quoted in Steven Heller, "When Adverts Were Earnest," *Print*, August 13, 2015, https://www.printmag.com/daily-heller/when-adverts-were-calkins/, accessed May 3, 2024.

13| Ibid.

14| M. F. Agha, "The Genealogy of Modern Art," *Vanity Fair* (1932), quoted in R. Roger Remington, *American Modernism: Graphic Design, 1920 to 1960* (New Haven: Yale University Press, 2003), 56.

15| On Brodovitch's career and impact, see Kerry William Purcell, *Alexey Brodovitch* (London: Phaidon, 2002).

16| Wendy Greenhouse, "Joseph Birren," M. Christine Schwartz Collection (website), https://schwartzcollection.com/artist/joseph-birren/, accessed May 18, 2024.

7 The Dynamic Image

1| See Brendan Cormier and Elizabeth Bisley, "Streamlined Design: Speed Becomes Style," Victoria & Albert Museum, London, 2019, https://www.vam.ac.uk/articles/streamlined-design-speed-becomes-style, accessed May 21, 2024.

2| See, for example, Arthur J. Pulos, *American Design Ethic: A History of Industrial Design* (Cambridge, MA: MIT Press, 1983) and Jeffrey L. Meikle, *Twentieth Century Limited: Industrial Design in America, 1925–1939* (Philadelphia: Temple University Press, 1979).

3| Alfred H. Barr Jr., Henry-Russell Hitchcock, and Philip Johnson, *Machine Art: March 6 to April 30, 1934* (New York: Museum of Modern Art, 1934), exhib. cat.

4| Matt Novak, "Before the Jetsons, Arthur Radebaugh Illustrated the Future," *Smithsonian Magazine*, April 2012, https://www.smithsonianmag.com/science-nature/before-the-jetsons-arthur-radebaugh-illustrated-the-future-122729342/, accessed May 18, 2024.

5| Later, from 1958 to 1963, Radebaugh published a cartoon series titled *Closer Than We Think* depicting futuristic devices and lifestyle. It appeared in more than two hundred newspapers and helped shape Americans' views of what the future might hold. See David Alayón, "Closer Than We Think, the Futuristic View of Arthur Radebaugh," Medium, September 11, 2018, https://medium.com/future-today/closer-than-we-think-the-futuristic-vision-of-arthur-radebaugh-c7362f8a11a7, accessed June 12, 2004.

8 American Modernness

1| Calkins, *"And Hearing Not,"* 284.

2| Earnest Elmo Calkins, "Advertising, Builder of Taste," *The American Magazine of Art* 21 (September 1930): 497.

3| Ibid., 500–501.

4| Ibid., 500.

5| Ibid., 498.

6| Christopher DeNoon, *Posters of the WPA* (Los Angeles: Wheatley, 1987), 13. On the WPA posters, see also Ennis Carter, *Posters for the People: Art of the WPA* (Philadelphia: Quirk Books, 2008).

7| "The Waugh Factor," https://www.nps.gov/articles/000/50-nifty-finds-7-the-waugh-factor.htm, accessed May 3, 2024. To a very large degree, I rely here on Mark Resnick's research on Dorothy Waugh. Resnick has corrected and clarified many aspects of Waugh's story and work. He has also played an important role in resurrecting a figure who is among the most important early modernist designers.

8| Ibid.

9| Ibid.

10| DeNoon, *Posters of the WPA*, 14–15.

11| See Illinois, U.S. Federal Naturalization Records, 1856–1991, for Robert Muchley, Department of Labor, Naturalization Service, Petitions for Naturalization, V. 1070, No. 265951-266350, ca. 1942–1943.

12| See Guido Lengwiler, *A History of Screen Printing: How an Art Evolved into an Industry* (Cincinnati: ST Media Group International, 2013).

13| Anthony Velonis, interview, October 13, 1965. Archives of American Art, Smithsonian Institution, Washington, D.C.; and Anthony Velonis, WPA Posters, interview, May 26, 2015, Library of Congress, Washington, D.C.

14| Anthony Verlonis, *Technical Problems of the Artist: Technique of the Silk Screen Process* (New York: Federal Art Project, Works Progress Administration, n.d.).

15| Richard Floethe, born in 1901 in Essen, Germany, studied art in Dortmund and Munich. At the Bauhaus, he studied color theory with Wassily Kandinsky and painting and drawing with Paul Klee. He first worked in advertising in Munich and Dortmund before moving the United States, where he became the art director for the Harold Advertising Agency in New York. Later, Floethe worked mostly as a freelance book illustrator. Mary Adair Dockery, "About Artist," Richard Floethe (website), https://richardfloethe.com/about-artist.html, accessed May 5, 2023.

16| This design bears a strong resemblance to the prospectus that Lester Beall made for the Society of Typographic Artists in 1934; his work was likely a source for it. See R. Roger Remington, *Lester Beall: Trailblazer of American Graphic Design* (New York: W. W. Norton, 1996), 33.

17| Erik Hans Krause Papers, Archives of American Art, Smithsonian Institution, Washington, D.C.

18| DeNoon, *Posters of the WPA*, 31.

19| Earnest Elmo Calkins, "1934," *Advertising Arts*, January 1934, 9.

20| Ibid., 10–11.

21| See Christopher Long, *Lucian Bernhard* (Prague: Kant, 2023), especially chapter 5.

22| Joseph Binder, *Colour in Advertising* (London: The Studio, 1934).

23| On Binder's early life and later years in New York, see Peter Noever, *Joseph Binder Wien–New York* (Vienna: Österreichisches Museum für angewandte Kunst, 2001), exhib. cat.; and Anita Kern, *Joseph Binder: Art Director in the USA* (Vienna: Designaustria, 2016). See also Joseph Binder, *Joseph Binder: An Artist and a Lifestyle: From the Joseph Binder Collection of Posters, Graphic and Fine Arts, and Records* (Vienna: Anton Schroll & Co. 1976).

24| Percy Seitlin, "Joseph Sinel–Artist to Industry," *PM* 2, no. 10. (June 1936): 3–14.

25| For a contemporary view, see Gordon Stapley and Leonard Sharpe, *Photography in the Modern Advertisement* (Pelham, NY: Bridgman Publishers, 1937).

26| See Lorraine Wild, "Europeans in America," in Mildred Friedman, ed., *Graphic Design in America: A Visual Language History* (Minneapolis: Walker Art Center / New York: Harry N. Abrams, Inc., 1989), exhib. cat., 152–69.

27| Brodovitch taught photography in various schools in New York over many years. He influenced a wide array of designers, art directors, and photographers, among them Richard Avedon, Steve Frankfurt, Bob Gage, Helmut Krone, Irving Penn, and Henry Wolf. See Allen Hurlburt, "Alexey Brodovitch: The Revolution in Magazine Design," *Print* 23, January–February 1969, 55–59.

28| James Sloan Allen, *The Romance of Commerce and Culture: Capitalism, Modernism, and the Chicago-Aspen Crusade for Cultural Reform* (Chicago: University of Chicago Press, 1983), 24–29.

29| Cassandre arrived aboard the *Ile De France* on 5 October 1937. Ellis Island Records, National Archives and Records Administration, Washington, D.C. He remained in the U.S. until 1939.

30| Ibid., 29.

31| Calkins, "1934," 12.

32| Remington, *Lester Beall*, 15–22; R. Roger Remington and Barbara J. Hodik, *Nine Pioneers in American Graphic Design* (Cambridge, MA: MIT Press, 1989), 87–88.

33| Remington, *Lester Beall*, 22–23.

34| Quoted in Remington, *Lester Beall*, 23.

35| Lester Beall, "Foundations for Design," *Production Yearbook* (1954): 1, quoted in Remington, *Lester Beall*, 41.

36| Werner Gräff, *Es kommt der neue Fotograf!* (Berlin: H. Reckendorf, 1929).

37| Remington, *Lester Beall*, 41.

38| Lester Beall, "The Expanding Art of Advertising," *Western Arts Association Convention* (April 1947): 15; quoted in Remington, *Lester Beall*, 41.

39| Frederick Kiesler, *Contemporary Art Applied to the Store and Its Display* (New York, Brentano's, 1930).

40| Remington, *Lester Beall*, 74.

Epilogue

1| Paul Rand, *Thoughts on Design* (New York: Wittenborn Schultz, 1947).

2| Ibid., 9.

Bibliography

| Archival Sources

Archives of American Art, Smithsonian Institution, Washington, D.C.

Ernest Elmo Calkins Papers, Special Collections and Archives, Knox College, Galesburg, Illinois

Hernando G. Villa Collection, Autry Museum of the American West, Los Angeles

Special Collections, Wallace Library, Rochester Institute of Technology

Stephen White Collection of Karl Struss Papers, Amon Carter Museum of American Art, Fort Worth, Texas

| Periodicals

Advertising Agency Magazine
Advertising Arts
Art Directors Club Annual of Advertising (later *Art Directors Annual*)
Design and Paper
Gebrauchsgraphik
The Graphic Arts
The Inland Printer
PM (*Production Manager*; later *AD, Advertising Director*)
The Poster
Profitable Advertising (later *Advertising and Selling*)
Printers' Ink
Printers' Ink Monthly
The Printing Art

| Primary Sources

A

"A Booklet Cover that Stops the Rushing Eye," *Printing Art* 27 (April 1916): 124.

Advertising Artists, Inc. *Solving Advertising Art Problems.* 2nd ed. New York: Advertising Arts, Inc., 1920.

Alexandre, Arsène, H. C. Bunner, M. H. Spielmann, and August Jaccaci. *The Modern Poster.* New York: Scribner's Sons, 1895.

Ault & Wilborg Co. *Poster Album.* Cincinnati: Ault & Wilborg Co., 1902.

B

Barr Jr., Alfred H., Henry-Russell Hitchcock, and Philip Johnson.

Machine Art: March 6 to April 30, 1934. New York: Museum of Modern Art, 1934. Exhibition catalogue.

Bates, Charles Austin. "Department of Criticism." *Printers' Ink* 27 (April 5, 1899): 60–62.

———. "First Person Singular, Chapter 8." *Advertising and Selling* 13 (June 26, 1929): 62, 64–65.

Binder, Joseph. *Colour in Advertising.* London: The Studio, 1934.

———. *Joseph Binder: An Artist and A Lifestyle: From the Joseph Binder Collection of Posters, Graphic and Fine Arts, and Records.* Vienna: Anton Schroll, 1976.

Bolton, Charles Knowles. *The Reign of the Poster.* Boston: Winthrop B. Jones, 1895.

Bradley, Will H. *Will Bradley, His Chap Book.* New York: The Typophiles, 1955.

———. *Will Bradley's Art Service for Advertisers.* New York, n.d. [ca. 1912].

C

Calkins, Earnest Elmo. "1934." *Advertising Arts* (January 1934): 9–12.

———. "Advertising and Design." *American Printer* (November 1900), 42.

———. "Advertising Art in the United States." *Modern Publicity* 7 (1930): 150–71.

———. "Advertising, Builder of Taste." *The American Magazine of Art* 21 (September 1930): 497–502.

———. *And Hearing Not: Annals of an Adman.* New York: Charles Scribner's Sons, 1946.

———. "Art as a Means to an End." *Advertising Arts* (January 8, 1930): 17–23.

———. "The Art Directors' Exhibition." *Printers' Ink Monthly* 2 (April 1921): 15–17, 75.

———. "Beauty: The New Business Tool." *Atlantic Monthly* 140 (August 1, 1927): 145–56.

———. The Business of Advertising. New York: D. Appleton & Company, 1915.

———. "The Camera as an Ad.-Writer." *Profitable Advertising* 12 (April 1903): 1040–45.

———. "Exhibition of Advertising Art," *International Studio* 34 (May 1908): cix.

———. "Louder Please!" *The Autobiography of a Deaf Man.* Boston: Atlantic Monthly Press, 1924.

———. "Psychology of the Poster" *International Studio* 45 (December 1911): 49–50.

———, and Ralph Holden. *Modern Advertising.* New York: D. Appleton and Company 1916.

Catalogue d'affiches Illustrees Anciennes et Modernes. Paris: Librairie Ed. Sagot, 1891.

The Century and Echo Poster Show: Catalogue of Artistic Posters. Chicago: The Echo, 1895. Exhibition catalogue.

Chambers, Robert W. "The Poster: In Three Articles." *New York Times*, February 16, 1896, 32 (part I); February 23, 1896, 32 (part II); March 1, 1896, 32 (part III).

———. "The Poster Craze." *New York Times*, November 21, 1896, A4.

Charlton, D. E. A. *The Art of Packaging*. New York: The Studio, 1937.

Cheney, Sheldon and Martha Cheney. *Art and the Machine*. New York: Whittlesey House, McGraw-Hill, 1936.

Cherington, Paul Terry. *Advertising as a Business Force: A Compilation of Experience Records*. New York: Doubleday, Page & Company, 1913.

Cleland, T. M. *Harsh Words*. New York: The American Institute of Graphic Arts, 1940.

Committee of 100. *The Newark Posters Catalogue*. Newark, NJ: Essex Press, 1915. Exhibition catalogue.

D

D'Arcy, W. C. "The Why of the Coca-Cola Arrow." *The Poster* 1 (February 1911): 165.

Deutsches Museum für Kunst in Handel und Gewerbe. *Lucian Bernhard*. Dortmund: Fr. Wilh. Ruhfus, 1913.

"Dodds, Samuel Candler." *Who's Who in Advertising*. Detroit: Business Service Corporation, 1916, 21.

Duce, Herbert Cecil. *Poster Advertising*. Chicago: Blakeley Printing Company, 1912.

Dwiggins, William A. *Layout in Advertising*. New York and London: Harper & Brothers, 1928.

———. "New Kind of Printing Calls for New Design." Graphic Arts Section, *Boston Evening Transcript*, August 29, 1922, 3:6.

E

Ehrlich, Frederic. *The New Typography and Modern Layouts*. New York: Stokes, 1934.

Ettinger, Paul. "Will H. Bradley." *Das Plakat* 4 (July 1913): 149–64.

"Exhibition of Original Paintings and Drawings." Display advertisement. *New York Times*, March 18, 1921, 22.

F

Fairman, Leroy. "The Booklet Cover as a Selling Force: Your Paper Salesman's Overcoat Merits Attention and Taste." *Advertising & Selling* 29 (March 20, 1920): 19–20, 22.

———. "Planning Effective Window Displays and Hangers: A Message of Importance to Everyone Selling Through Dealers." *Advertising & Selling* 29, (September 13, 1920): 4–7.

———. "Streetcar Cards That Sell Goods." *Advertising & Selling* 29, (August 23, 1919): 3–5.

———. "What a Poster Is and How to Make It." *Advertising & Selling* 29 (July 26, 1919): 1–3.

F

Franken, Richard B., and Carroll B. Larabee. *Packages That Sell*. New York: Harper & Brothers, 1928.

Frankl, Paul T. *Form and Re-Form*. New York: Harper & Brothers, 1930.

Frazier, J. L. "Specimens." *The Inland Printer* 62 (November 1918): 181–86.

French, George. "Advertising Men of Mark: Calkins, of Calkins and Holden." *Associated Advertising* 5 (May 1914): 33, 35.

Friend, Leon, and Joseph Hefter. *Graphic Design: A Library of Old and New Masters in the Graphic Arts*. New York: McGraw-Hill, 1936.

G

Geddes, Norman Bel. *Horizons*. Boston: Little, Brown and Company, 1932.

"German Arts on View." *Brooklyn Daily Eagle*, March 11, 1913, 8.

Giedion, Siegfried. *Mechanization Takes Command*. New York: Oxford, 1948.

Goode, Kenneth M. *Modern Advertising*. New York: Halcyon House, 1937.

Gräff, Werner. *Es kommt der neue Fotograf!* Berlin: H. Reckendorf, 1929.

Greer, Carl Richard. *Advertising and Its Mechanical Production*. New York: Thomas Y. Crowell, 1931.

Gress, Edmund G. *Fashions in Typography 1780–1930*. New York: Harper Brothers, 1931.

Grolier Club. *Catalogue of an Exhibition of Illustrated Bill-Posters*. New York: The Grolier Club, 1890. Exhibition catalogue.

Goudy, Frederic W. *A Half-Century of Type Design and Typography, 1895–1945*. 2 vols. New York: The Typophiles, 1946.

H

Hamill, Alfred E. *The Decorative Work of T. M. Cleland: A Record and Review*. New York: Pynson Printers, 1929.

"Harry Arnold Weissberger." Obituary, *Sea Cliff (New York) News*, February 23, 1929.

Hiatt, Charles. "On Some Recent Designs by Will H. Bradley of Chicago." *The Studio* 4 (Fall 1894): 166–68.

Hölscher, E. "Lester Beall, New York." *Gebrauchsgraphik: International Advertising Art* 16 (April 1939): 17–24.

Hopkins, Claude C. *My Life in Advertising*. New York: Harper and Brothers, 1927.

I

"International Art Service Now Advertising Artists, Inc." *The Inland Printer* 62 (November 1918): 218.

K

Kelly, John Tyronne. "Poster Artists Wins $1,000 Prize." *The Poster* 7 (September 1916): 33–34.

Kepes, Gyorgy. *Language of Vision.* Chicago: Paul Theobald, 1944.

Kimball, Abbott. "Beauty and the Balance Sheet." *Advertising Arts,* May 1931, 28–32.

L

Larned, W. Livingston. *Illustration in Advertising.* New York: McGraw-Hill, 1925.

Lemos, Pedro J. *Applied Art: Drawing, Painting, Design, and Handicraft.* Mountain View, CA: Pacific Press Publishing Organization, 1920.

———. *Applied Art: Drawing, Painting, Design, and Handicraft Arranged for Self-Instruction of Teachers, Parents, and Students.* Mountain View, CA: Pacific Press Publishing Organization, 1933.

Leyendecker, J.C., illustrator. *An Illuminated Life of Christ, including the Principal Events: The Royal Scroll: A Complete Panorama of the Sacred Story.* By Levi Walter Yaggy. Chicago: Powers, Fowler & Lewis, 1896.

Loewy, Raymond. *Never Leave Well Enough Alone.* New York: Simon and Schuster, 1951.

Lustig, Alvin. *The Collected Writings of Alvin Lustig.* New Haven: Holland R. Melton, 1958.

M

Maindron, Ernest. *Les Affiches Illustrees (1886–1895).* Paris: G. Boudet & Ch. Tallandier, 1896.

Martini, Herbert E. *Applied Art: A Collection of Designs Showing the Tendencies of American Industrial Art.* New York: F. K. Ferenz, 1919.

———. *Color: When and How to Use It.* Pelhman, NY: Bridgman, 1928.

Matthews, Brander. "The Pictorial Poster." *Century* 44 (January 1, 1892): 748–56.

McMurtrie, Douglas C. *Modern Typography and Layout.* Chicago: Eyncourt Press, 1929.

Moholy-Nagy, László. *Vision in Motion.* Chicago: Paul Theobald, 1947.

Morris, William. *The Ideal Book: Essays and Lectures on the Arts of the Book.* Edited by William S. Peterson. Berkeley: University of California Press, 1982.

N

"The New Art of Advertising–Or the Redemption of the Billboard." *Current Opinion* 54 (May 1913): 406–8.

Newark Museum Association. *German Advertising Art, January 2–31, 1914.* Newark, NJ: Newark Museum Association, 1914. Exhibition catalogue.

Newark Museum Association. *German Applied Arts: Touring Exhibition of the Deutsches Museum für Kunst in Handel und Gewerbe Hagen I.W. with the co-operation of the Oesterreichisches Museum für Kunst und Industrie in Wien: Newark, Chicago, Indianapolis, Pittsburgh, Cincinnati, St. Louis, 1912–1913.* Newark, NJ: Newark Museum Association, 1912. Exhibition catalogue.

"Notes on Current Art." *New York Times,* October 5, 1919, 108.

O

Österreichisches Museum für Angewandte Kunst, Vienna and Deutsches Museum für Kunst in Handel und Gewerbe, Hagen. *German Applied Arts.* Dortmund, 1912. Exhibition catalogue.

P

"The Passing of the Poster Craze." *New York Times,* July 8, 1899, A4.

Presbrey, Frank. *The History and Development of Advertising.* Garden City, NY: Doubleday, 1928.

Price, Charles Matlack. "The Essentials of the Poster: The Appeal of Informal Art." *Arts & Decoration* 3 (1913): 374–76.

———. "The Opportunity of the Poster: 'Inspiration' versus 'influence.'" *Arts & Decoration* 6 (1916): 466–69.

———. *Poster Design: A Critical Study of the Development of the Poster in Continental Europe, England and America.* New York: George W. Bricka, 1922.

R

"Ralph Holden Dies: Member of an Advertising Firm Stricken With Blood Poisoning." *New York Times,* January 4, 1926, 4.

Rand, Paul. *Thoughts on Design.* New York: Wittenborn Schultz, 1947.

Reece, Thomas. "Color Contrast Catch the Eye." *The Poster* 5 (August 1914): 30–32.

Reiss, Winold, and Frank B. Linderman. *Blackfeet Indians.* St. Paul: Great Northern Railway / Brown & Bigelow, 1935.

Reiss, Winold, and Albert Charles Schweitzer. *You Can Design.* New York: Whittlesey House, 1939.

Rhead, Louis John. "The Moral Aspect of the Artistic Poster." *The Bookman* 1 (June 1895): 312–14.

Rosenthal, Rudolph, and Helena L. Ratzka. *The Story of Modern Applied Art.* New York: Harper & Brothers, 1948.

S

"Says He Gave O'Leary $5,000 For Dr. Albert." *New York Herald*, January 25, 1919, 8.

"Says O'Leary Got $5,000 From Albert." *New York Times*, February 5, 1919, 24.

Seitlin, Percey. "Joseph Sinel–Artist to Industry" *PM* 2, no. 10. (June 1936): 3–14.

Senefelder, Alois. *A Complete Course in Lithography: Containing Clear and Explicit Instructions in all the Different Branches and Manners of that Art*. London: R. Ackermann, 1819.

———. *Vollständiges Lehrbuch der Steindruckerey enthaltend eine richtige und deutliche Anweisung zu den verschiedenen Manipulations-Arten derselben in allen ihren Zweigen und Manieren, belegt mit den nöthigen Musterblättern, nebst einer vorangehenden ausführlichen Geschichte dieser Kunst von ihrem Entstehen bis auf gegenwärtige Zeit*. Munich: Thienemann, 1818.

Sponsel, Jean Louis. *Das Moderne Plakat*. Dresden: Gerhard Kühtmann, 1897.

Stapley, Gordon, and Leonard Shape. *Photography in the Modern Advertisement*. Pelham, NY: Bridgeman Publishing, 1937.

Stote, Amos. "Some Gum—Also Some Advertising." *Printing Art* 24 (February 1915): 483–88.

Strong, Charles Jay, and Lawrence Stewart Strong. *Strong's Book of Designs: A Masterpiece of Modern Ornamental Art*. Chicago: Frederick J. Drake & Company, 1917.

T

Truesdell, Winifred Porter. *A Booklet Devoted to the Book Plates of Elisha Brown Bird. Being a Collection Printed in Photogravure*. New York: Village Press, 1907.

———. *E. B. Bird and His Bookplates*. Boston: Troutsdale Press, 1904.

Turner, Frederick Jackson. *The Frontier in American History*. New York: Henry Holt, 1920.

V

Vassos, John, and Ruth Vassos. *Contempo: The American Tempo*. New York: E. P. Dutton & Company, 1929.

Velonis, Anthony. Interview by Harlan Phillips, October 13, 1965, Hackensack, NJ. Archives of American Art, Smithsonian Institution, Washington, D.C.

———. "WPA Posters." Interview at the symposium "Amassing 'American Stuff': The New Deal Arts Collections of the Library of Congress, December 1994. Library of Congress, Washington, D.C. https://www.loc.gov/pictures/collection/wpapos/interview.html.

———. *Technical Problems of the Artist: Technique of the Silk Screen Process*. New York: Federal Art Project, Works Progress Administration, n.d. [ca. 1938].

W

Wedmore, Frederick. "Art in the Poster." *The Art Journal* 45 (1895): 43–47.

Wiener, Arthur F. "Bernhard," *The Poster* 4 (October 1913): 27–29, 61.

———. "Sales Possibilities in Modernly Designed Posters." *Advertising & Selling* 23 (July 1913): 28.

———. "What a Good Poster Is, and How to Get It." *Advertising & Selling* 22 (June 1912): 33.

———. "Willy Sesser." *The Poster* 4 (November 1913): 21–27.

Y

Young, Frank H. *Advertising Layout*. Chicago: Pascal Covici, 1928.

———. *Modern Advertising Art*. New York: Covici, Friede, 1930.

———. *Technique of Advertising Layout*. New York: Covici, Friede, 1930.

| Secondary Literature

A

Adams, Henry, and Lawrence Waldman. *Out of the Kokoon*. Cleveland: Cleveland Public Library and Cleveland Artists Foundation, 2011. Exhibition catalogue.

Ades, Dawn. *The 20th-Century Poster: Design of the Avant-Garde*. New York: Abbeville Press, 1984.

Alayón, David. "Closer Than We Think, the Futuristic View of Arthur Radebaugh." Future Today, Medium, September 11, 2018. https://medium.com/future-today/closer-than-we-think-the-futuristic-vision-of-arthur-radebaugh-c7362f8a11a7. Accessed June 12, 2004.

Allen, James Sloan. *The Romance of Commerce and Culture: Capitalism, Modernism, and the Chicago-Aspen Crusade for Cultural Reform*. Chicago and London: University of Chicago Press, 1983.

Aysley, Jeremy. *A Century of Graphic Design: 20th Century*. Hauppauge, NY: B. E. S. Publishing, 2001.

B

Best, James J. *American Popular Illustration: A Reference Guide*. Westport, CT: Greenwood Press, 1984.

Bogart, Michele H. "Artistic Ideal and Commercial Practices: The Problem of the Status of American Illustrators." *Prospects* 15 (October 1990): 225–81.

———. *Artists, Advertising, and the Borders of Art, 1880–1960*.

Chicago and London: University of Chicago Press, 1995.

Bolton, Theodore. *American Book Illustrators: Bibliographic Check Lists of 123 Artists*. New York: Bowker, 1938.

Brandywine River Museum. *An American Vision: Three Generations of Wyeth Art*. Boston: Little Brown and Company, 1987. Exhibition catalogue.

Breitenbach, Edgar. "The Poster Craze." *American Heritage* (February 1962): 26–31.

C

Carter, Ennis. *Posters for the People: Art of the WPA*. Philadelphia: Quirk Books, 2008.

Carter, Sebastian. *Twentieth Century Type Designers*. London: Trefoil, 1987.

Castagno, John. *Artists as Illustrators: An International Directory with Signatures and Monograms, 1800 to the Present*. Metuchen, NJ: Scarecrow Press, 1989.

Chantry, Art. *Art Chantry Speaks: A Heretic's History of 20th Century Graphic Design*. Edited by Monica René Rochester. Port Townsend, WA: Feral House, 2015.

Chapman, Kathleen G. *Expressionism and Poster Design in Germany, 1905–1922: Between Spirit and Commerce*. Brill Studies on Art, Art History, and Intellectual History, vol. 288/32. Leiden: Brill, 2019.

Cogdell, Christina. *Streamlining America in the 1930s*. Philadelphia: University of Pennsylvania Press, 2010.

Cohen, Arthur A. *Herbert Bayer: The Complete Work*. Cambridge, MA: MIT Press, 1984.

Condell, Patricia J. *Campbell Soup Can Design, Campbell Soup Company* Newton, NJ: Historic Conservation and Interpretation, Inc., 1991.

Cormier, Brendan, and Elizabeth Bisley. "Streamlined Design: Speed Becomes Style." Victoria & Albert Museum, London (website). https://www.vam.ac.uk/articles/streamlined-design-speed-becomes-style. Accessed May 21, 2024.

Cutler, Laurence S., and Judy Goffman Cutler. *J. C. Leyendecker: American Imagist*. New York: Abrams / The National Museum of American Illustration, 2008. Exhibition catalogue.

D

Davis, Rodney O. "Earnest Elmo Calkins and Phoebe Snow," *Railroad History* 163 (Autumn 1990): 88–92.

DeNoon, Christopher. *Posters of the WPA*. Los Angeles: Wheatley, 1987.

Drew, Ned, and Paul Sternberger. *Purity of Aim: The Book Jacket Designs of Alvin Lustig*. Rochester, NY: RIT Cary Graphic Design Archives, 2010.

F

Friedman, Mildred S., et al. *Graphic Design in America: A Visual Language Story*. Minneapolis: Walker Art Center / New York: Harry N. Abrams, Inc., 1989. Exhibition catalogue.

G

Garfield, Simon. *Just My Type: A Book About Fonts*. New York: Avery, 2012.

Gopnik, Blake. "J. C. Leyendecker: The 'Arrow Collar Man' Who Hid a Radical Idea." *New York Times*, June 29, 2023.

Greenhouse, Wendy. "Birren, Joseph." M. Christine Schwartz Collection (website). https://schwartzcollection.com/artist/joseph-birren.

H

Harris, Neil. *Art, Design, and the Modern Corporation: The Collection of Container Corporation of America, A Gift to the National Museum of American Art*. Washington, D.C.: Smithsonian Institution Press, 1985. Exhibition catalogue.

Hathway, Norman, and Dan Nadel. *Dorothy and Otis: Designing the American Dream*. New York: Harper, 2014.

Helfand, Jessica. *Paul Rand: American Modernist*. New York: William Drenttel, 1998.

Heller, Steven. "Commercial Modern: American Design Style, 1925–1963." *Print Magazine* 49 (September–October 1995): 58–68

———. *Design Literacy: Understanding Graphic Design*, 2nd ed. New York: Allworth Press, 2004.

———. *Paul Rand*. London: Phaidon, 1999.

———, ed. *Teaching Graphic Design History*. New York: Allworth, 2019.

———. "When Adverts Were Earnest," *Print*, August 15, 2013. https://www.printmag.com/daily-heller/when-adverts-were-calkins/.

———, and Georgette Balance, eds. *Graphic Design History*. New York: Allworth Press, 2001.

Heller, Steven, and Seymour Chwast. *Graphic Style from Victorian to Post-Modern*. New York: Harry N. Abrams, 1988.

Heller, Steven, and Greg D'Onofrio. *The Moderns: Midcentury American Graphic Design*. New York: Abrams, 2017.

Heller, Steven, and Louise Fili. *Typology: Type Design from the Victorian Era to the Digital Age*. San Francisco: Chronicle Books, 1999.

Hollis, Richard. *Graphic Design in the Twentieth Century: A Concise History*. London: Thames & Hudson, 2021.

Hornung, Clarence P., and Fridolf Johnson. *200 Years of American Graphic Art: A Retrospective Survey of the Printing Arts and Advertising Since the Colonial Period*. New York: George Braziller, 1976.

Houck, John W. *Outdoor Advertising: History and Regulation.* South Bend, IN: Norte Dame University Press, 1969.

Hoy, Anne H. *Coca-Cola: The First Hundred Years.* Atlanta: Coca-Cola Company, 1986.

Hughes, Robert. "The Decline of the City of Mahagonny." *The New Republic,* June 25, 1990, 27–33.

Hurlburt, Allen. "Alexey Brodovitch: The Revolution in Magazine Design." *Print* 23 (January–February 1969): 55–59.

I

Inglis, Thomas. *Mid-Century Modern Graphic Design.* London: Batsford, 2019.

J

Johnson, David. *Alfonso Iannelli: Modern by Design.* Oak Park, IL: Top Five Books, 2013.

Johnson, J. Stewart. *The Modern American Poster: From the Graphic Design Collection of The Museum of Modern Art, New York.* Kyoto: National Museum of Modern Art / New York: Museum of Modern Art, 1983. Exhibition catalogue.

Jury, David. *Graphic Design Before Graphic Designers: The Printer as Designer and Craftsman: 1700–1914.* New York: Thames & Hudson, 1912.

Jussim, Estelle. *Visual Communication and the Graphic Arts: Photographic Technologies in the Nineteenth Century.* New York: R. R. Bowker, 1974.

K

Keay, Carolyn. *American Posters of the Turn of the Century.* New York: St. Martin's Press, 1975.

Kern, Anita. *Joseph Binder: Art Director in USA.* Vienna: DesignAustria, 2016.

Kesling, Ben. "Tootsie's Secret Empire." *Wall Street Journal,* August 22, 1912, B1–2.

Kiehl, David W., Phillip Dennis Cate, and Nancy Finlay. *American Art Posters of the 1890s.* New York: Harry N. Abrams / Metropolitan Museum of Art, 1987. Exhibition catalogue.

Knight, Melinda. "Little Magazines and the Emergence of Modernism in the Fin de Siècle." *American Periodicals* 6 (1996): 29–45.

Kushner, Marilyn Satin. *The World of Winold Reiss: An Immigrant Modernist.* New York: New York Historical Society / Lewes, UK: D Giles, 2021. Exhibition catalogue.

L

Lavin, Irving. "Panofsky's Humor," typescript. Institute for Advanced Study, Princeton, NJ, January 1993. https://publications.ias.edu/sites/default/files/Lavin_PanHumor_Eng_1993.pdf.

Lears, Jackson. *Fables of Abundance: A Cultural History of Advertising in America.* New York: Basic Books, 1995.

Lengwiler, Guido. *A History of Screen Printing: How an Art Evolved into an Industry.* Cincinnati: ST Media Group International, 2013.

Logemann, Jan L. *Engineered to Sell: European Émigrés and the Making of Consumer Capitalism.* Chicago and London: University of Chicago Press, 2019.

Lönberg-Holm, Knud, and Ladislav Sutnar. *Catalog Design.* New York: Sweet's Catalog Service, 1944.

Long, Christopher. *Lucian Bernhard.* Prague: Kant, 2023.

———. "The Viennese Secessionsstil and Modern American Design." *Studies in the Decorative Arts* 14 (Spring–Summer 2007): 6-44.

M

Marchand, Roland. *Advertising the American Dream: Making Way for Modernity, 1920–1940.* Berkeley and Los Angeles: University of California, Press, 1985.

Margolin, Victor. *American Poster Renaissance.* New York: Watson–Guptill, 1975.

McCoy, Katherine, Lorraine Ferguson, Douglas Scott, and Matthew Carter. "The Evolution of American Typography." Special issue, *Design Quarterly* 148 (1990).

McNeil, Paul. *The Visual History of Type.* London: Laurence King Publishing, 2017.

Meggs, Philip B. *A History of Graphic Design.* 2nd ed. New York: Van Nostrand Reinhold, 1992.

Meikle, Jeffrey L. *Twentieth Century Limited: Industrial Design in America, 1925-1939.* Philadelphia: Temple University Press, 1979.

Meyer, Susan E. *America's Great Illustrators.* New York: Harry N. Abrams, 1978.

Morrison, Mark S. *The Public Face of Modernism: Little Magazines, Audiences, and Reception, 1905–1920.* Madison, WI: University of Wisconsin Press, 2001.

Müller, Jens. *The History of Graphic Design, Vol. 1, 1890–1959.* Edited by Julius Wiedemann. Cologne: Taschen, 2018.

N

National Park Service. "The Waugh Factor." https://www.nps.gov/articles/000/50-nifty-finds-7-the-waugh-factor.htm.

Neumann, Eckhard. *Functional Graphic Design in the 20's.* New York: Reinhold, 1967.

Noever, Peter. *Joseph Binder Wien – New York.* Vienna: Österreichisches Museum für angewandte Kunst, 2001. Exhibition catalogue.

P

Panofsky, Erwin. "The Ideological Antecedents of the Rolls-Royce Radiator." *Proceedings of the American Philosophical Society* 107 (August 15, 1963): 273–88.

Pepper, Jen. "Dorothy and Otis Shepard." *Communication Design: Design Pioneers* 8 (2020). https://research.library.kutztown.edu/cgi/viewcontent.cgi?article=1008&context=designpioneers.

Pope, Daniel. *The Making of Modern Advertising*. New York: Basic Books, 1983.

Pulos, Arthur J. *American Design Ethic: A History of Industrial Design*. Cambridge, MA: MIT Press, 1983.

Purcell, Kerry William, *Alexey Brodovitch*. London: Phaidon, 2002.

Purvis, Alston W. *Graphic Design 20th Century*. New York: Princeton Architectural Press, 2003.

Q

Quito, Anne. "The Coke Bottle's Iconic Design Happened by Sheer Chance." *Quartz*, November 17, 2015. https://qz.com/551682/the-coke-bottles-iconic-design-happe-ned-by-sheer-chance/.

R

Raizman, David. *Reading Graphic Design History: Image, Text, and Context*. London: Bloomsbury, 2021.

Reineck, Michael. "Atlanta Ad Club's Founder, St. Elmo Massengale, Was Atlanta's First Man of Advertising." Atlanta Ad Club, https://atlantaadclub.org/history/.

Remington, R. Roger. *Lester Beall: Trailblazer of American Graphic Design*. New York: W. W. Norton & Company, 1996.

———. *American Modernism: Graphic Art, 1920 to 1960*. With Lisa Bodenstedt. New Haven and London: Yale University Press, 2003.

———, and Barbara J. Hodik. *Nine Pioneers in American Graphic Design*. Cambridge, MA: MIT Press, 1989.

Resnick, Mark. *The American Image: U. S. Posters from the 19th to the 21st Century*. Rochester, NY: RIT Cary Graphic Arts Press, 2006.

Rhodes, Anthony. *Propaganda. The Art of Persuasion: World War II*. New York: Chelsea House, 1976.

Roberts, Caroline. *Graphic Design Visionaries*. London: Laurence King Publishing, 2015.

Rössler, Patrick. *Herbert Bayer, Graphic Designer: From the Bauhaus to Berlin, 1921–1938*. London: Bloomsbury, 2023.

S

Schorman, Rob. "'The Astounding Car for $1500': The Year Automobile Advertising Came of Age." *Enterprise & Society* 11 (September 2010): 468–523.

———. "Claude Hopkins, Earnest Calkins, Bissell Carpet Sweepers and the Birth of Modern Advertising." *The Journal of the Gilded Age and Progressive Era* 7 (April 2008): 181–219.

Shechter, Relli. "Selling Luxury: The Rise of the Egyptian Cigarette and the Transformation of the Egyptian Tobacco Market, 1850-1914." *International Journal of Middle East Studies* 35 (February 2003): 51–75.

Shifman, Barry. "Design for Industry: The 'German Applied Arts' Exhibition in the United States, 1912-13." *Journal of the Decorative Arts Society* 22 (1988): 19–31.

Stern, Jewel, and Christopher Long. *The Vanguard: Central European Émigrés and Modern American Design, 1910–1940*. New Haven: Yale University Press, 2025.

T

Thomson, Ellen Mazur. *American Graphic Design: A Guide to the Literature*. Westport, CT: Greenwood, 1992.

———. *The Origins of Graphic Design in America, 1870–1920*. New Haven and London: Yale University Press, 1997.

W

Wallis, L. W. *A Concise Chronology of Typesetting 1886–1986*. London: Lund Humphries, 1988.

Wardle, Marian, ed. *American Women Modernists: The Legacy of Robert Henri, 1910–1945*. New Brunswick, NJ: Rutgers University Press, 2005.

Weill, Alain. *Graphic Design: A History*. New York: Harry N. Abrams, 2004.

Wilson, Richard Guy, Dianne H. Pilgrim, and Dickran Tashjian. *The Machine Age in America, 1918–1941*. New York: Brooklyn Museum / Harry N. Abrams, 1986. Exhibition catalogue.

Wilson, Ross J. *New York and the First World War: Shaping an American City*. Farnham, UK: Ashgate, 2014.

Wong, Roberta Waddell. *Bradley: American Artist and Craftsman*. New York: Metropolitan Museum of Art, 1972. Exhibition catalogue.

Wrede, Stuart. *The Modern Poster*. New York: Museum of Modern Art, 1988. Exhibition catalogue.

Christopher Long | MODERN AMERICANNESS

The New Graphic Art in the United States
1890–1940

This book has been published with the support of the Martin S. Kermacy Endowment,
School of Architecture, University of Texas at Austin.

Graphic design:
| Jiří Příhoda
Image Editing and pre-press:
| Karel Kerlický – KANT
Published by:
| Karel Kerlický – KANT 2024, Prague
www.kant-books.com

KANT

Tisk Print by:
| PBtisk, Příbram

ISBN: 978-80-7437-440-1